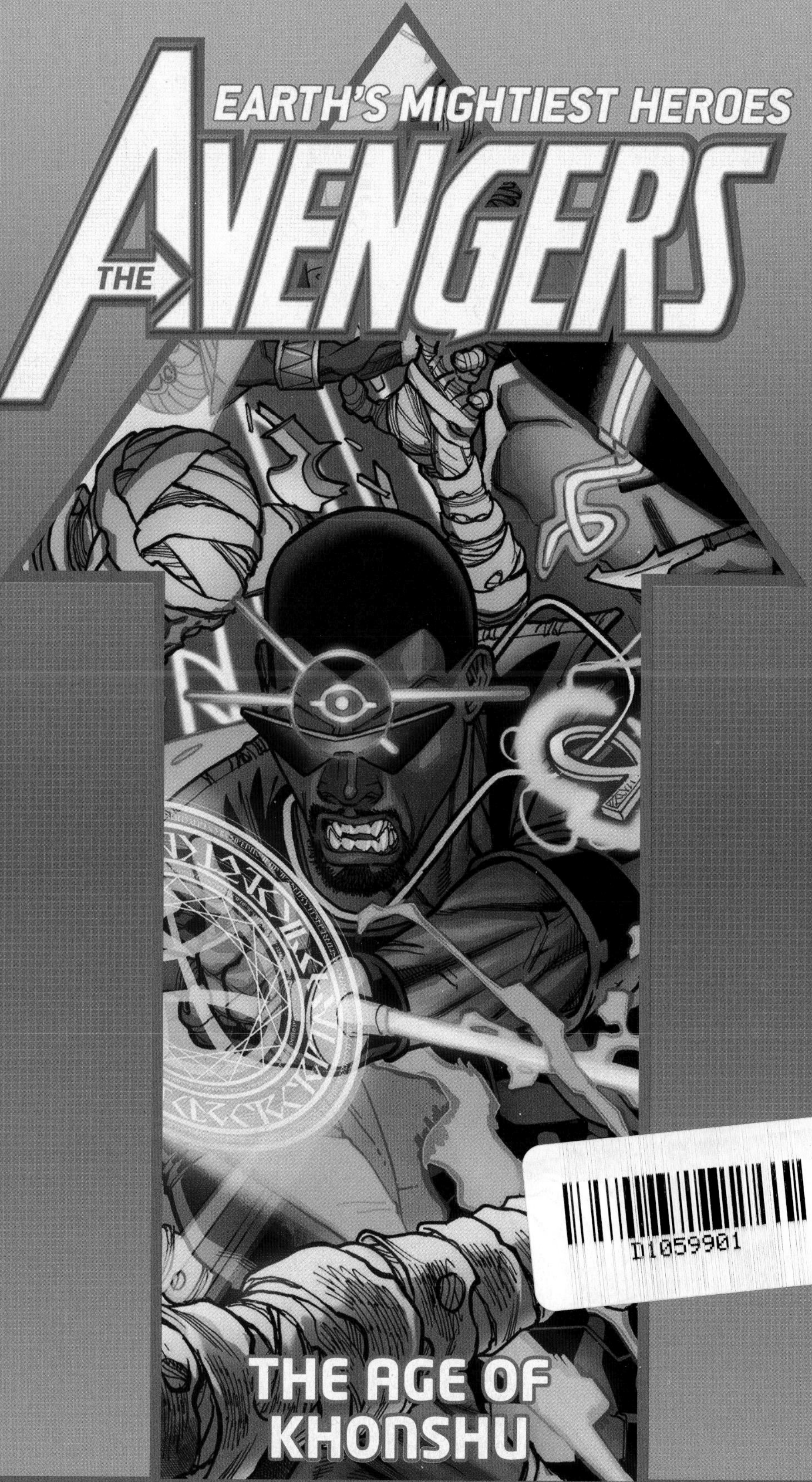

EARTH'S MIGHTIEST HEROES
THE AVENGERS
THE AGE OF KHONSHU

AVENGERS BY JASON AARON VOL. 7: THE AGE OF KHONSHU. Contains material originally published in magazine form as AVENGERS (2018) #31-38. First printing 2020. ISBN 978-1-302-92486-7. Published by MARVEL WORLDWIDE, INC., a subsidiary of MARVEL ENTERTAINMENT, LLC. OFFICE OF PUBLICATION: 1290 Avenue of the Americas, New York, NY 10104. **Printed in the U.S.A.** KEVIN FEIGE, Chief Creative Officer; DAN BUCKLEY, President, Marvel Entertainment; JOE QUESADA, EVP & Creative Director; DAVID BOGART, Associate Publisher & SVP of Talent Affairs; TOM BREVOORT, VP, Executive Editor; NICK LOWE, Executive Editor, VP of Content, Digital Publishing; DAVID GABRIEL, VP of Print & Digital Publishing; JEFF YOUNGQUIST, VP of Production & Special Projects; ALEX MORALES, Director of Publishing Operations; DAN EDINGTON, Managing Editor; RICKEY PURDIN, Director of Talent Relations; JENNIFER GRÜNWALD, Senior Editor, Special Projects; SUSAN CRESPI, Production Manager; STAN LEE, Chairman Emeritus. For information regarding advertising in Marvel Comics or on Marvel.com, please contact Vit DeBellis, Custom Solutions & Integrated Advertising Manager, at vdebellis@marvel.com. For Marvel subscription inquiries, please call 888-511-5480. **Manufactured between 11/13/2020 and 12/14/2020 by FRY COMMUNICATIONS, MECHANICSBURG, PA, USA.**

10 9 8 7 6 5 4 3 2 1

EARTH'S MIGHTIEST HEROES
THE AVENGERS
THE AGE OF KHONSHU

JASON AARON
WRITER

AVENGERS #31
GERARDO ZAFFINO,
GERALDO BORGES,
SZYMON KUDRANSKI,
JAN BAZALDUA, ROBERT GILL
& MATTIA DE IULIS
ARTISTS

RACHELLE ROSENBERG
& MATTIA DE IULIS
COLOR ARTISTS

GERARDO ZAFFINO
COVER ART

AVENGERS #32
ED McGUINNESS &
FRANCESCO MANNA
ARTISTS

JASON KEITH
COLOR ARTIST

ED McGUINNESS,
MARK MORALES
& JASON KEITH
COVER ART

AVENGERS #33-37
JAVIER GARRÓN
ARTIST

JASON KEITH
COLOR ARTIST

MATTEO SCALERA
& RACHELLE ROSENBERG
COVER ART

AVENGERS #38
ED McGUINNESS
ARTIST

MARK MORALES
INKER

JASON KEITH
COLOR ARTIST

ED McGUINNESS
& JASON KEITH
COVER ART

VC'S JOE CARAMAGNA [#31] & **CORY PETIT** [#32-38]
LETTERERS

SHANNON ANDREWS BALLESTEROS & **MARTIN BIRO**
ASSISTANT EDITORS

ALANNA SMITH
ASSOCIATE EDITOR

TOM BREVOORT
EDITOR

AVENGERS CREATED BY **STAN LEE** & **JACK KIRBY**

COLLECTION EDITOR **JENNIFER GRÜNWALD**   BOOK DESIGNERS **SALENA MAHINA** & **ADAM DEL RE**
ASSISTANT MANAGING EDITOR **MAIA LOY**   SVP PRINT, SALES & MARKETING **DAVID GABRIEL**
ASSISTANT MANAGING EDITOR **LISA MONTALBANO**
VP PRODUCTION & SPECIAL PROJECTS **JEFF YOUNGQUIST**   EDITOR IN CHIEF **C.B. CEBULSKI**

31 THE TEMPTATION OF ANTHONY STARK

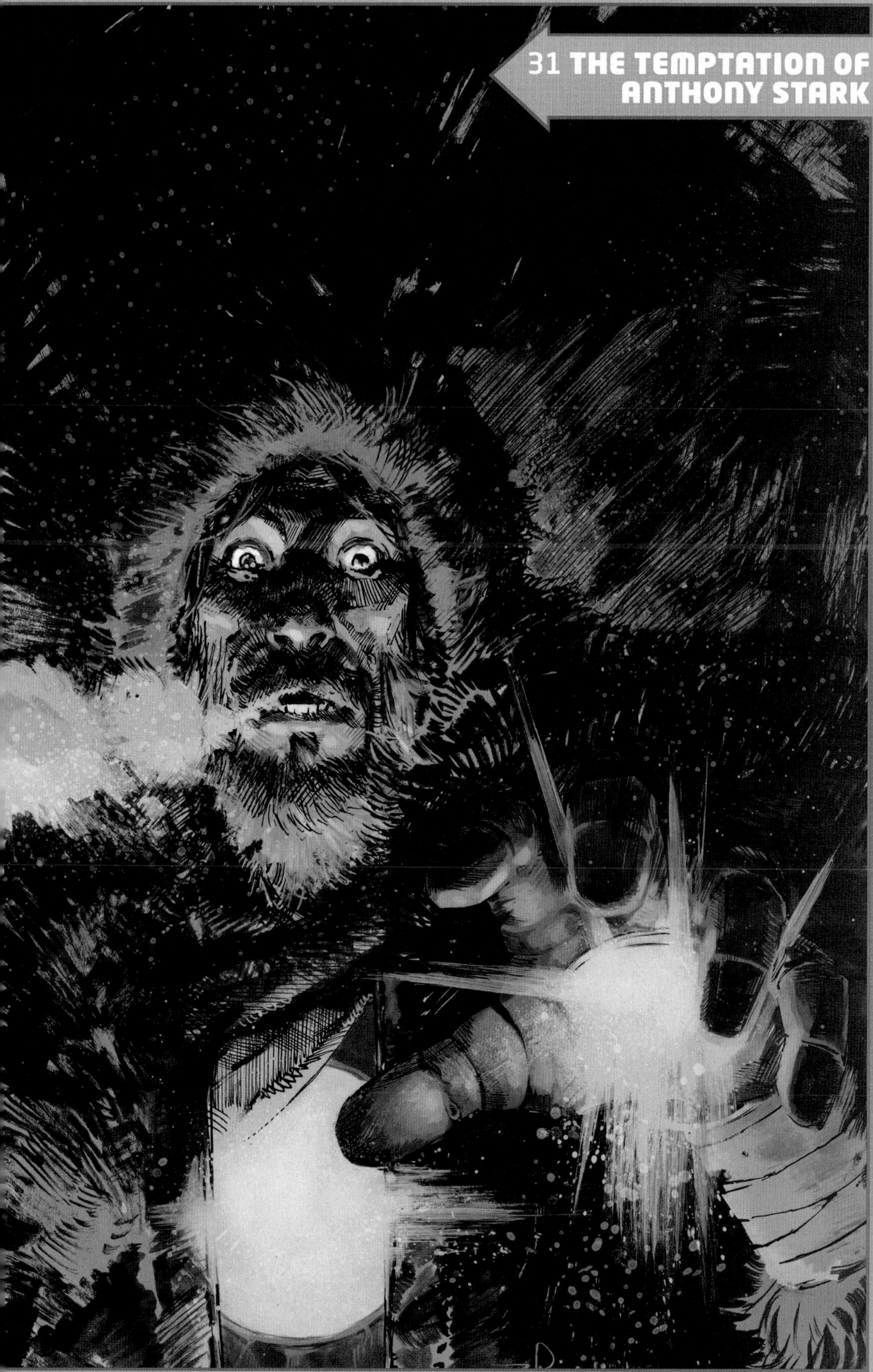

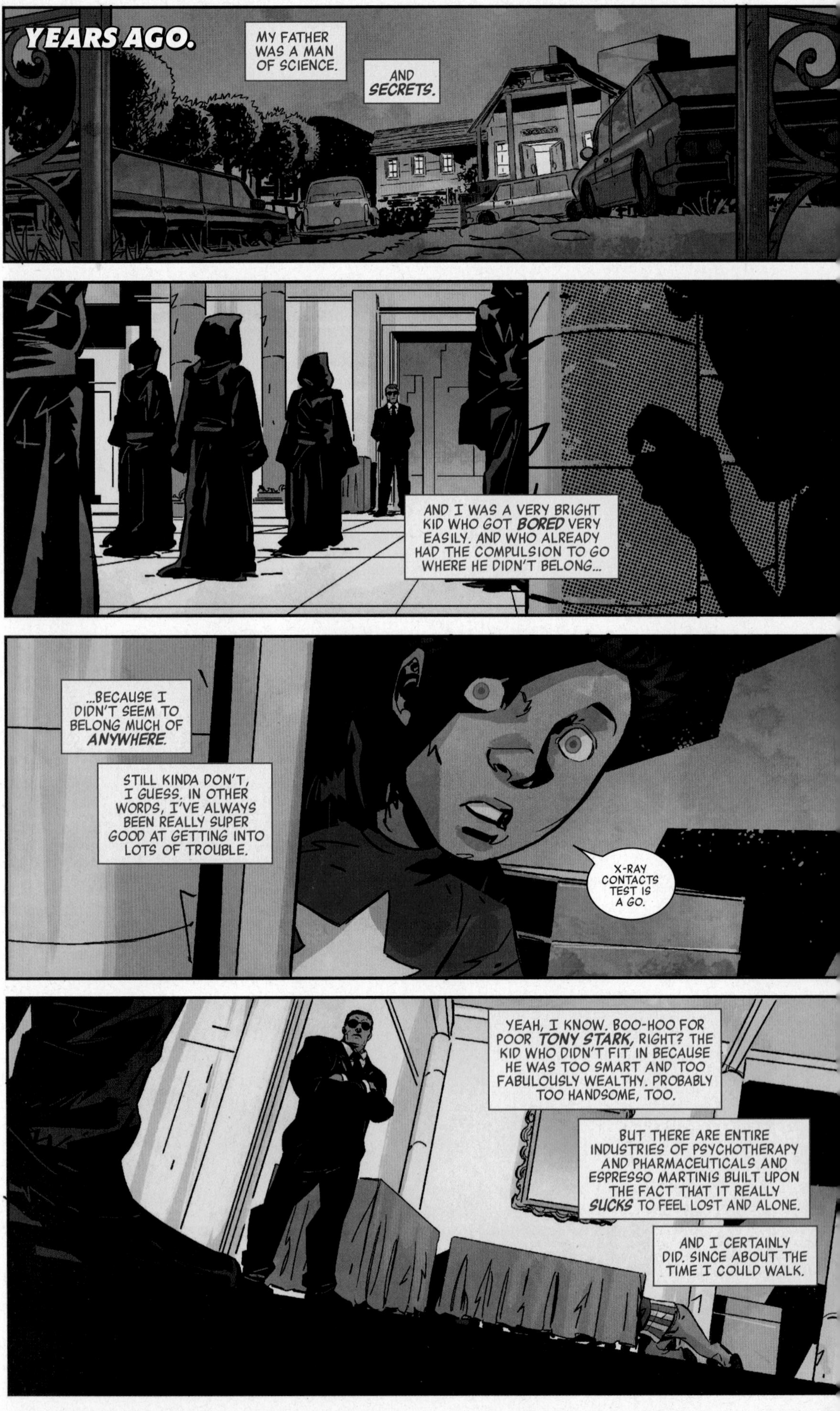

YEARS AGO.
MY FATHER WAS A MAN OF SCIENCE.
AND SECRETS.
AND I WAS A VERY BRIGHT KID WHO GOT BORED VERY EASILY. AND WHO ALREADY HAD THE COMPULSION TO GO WHERE HE DIDN'T BELONG...
...BECAUSE I DIDN'T SEEM TO BELONG MUCH OF ANYWHERE.
STILL KINDA DON'T, I GUESS. IN OTHER WORDS, I'VE ALWAYS BEEN REALLY SUPER GOOD AT GETTING INTO LOTS OF TROUBLE.
X-RAY CONTACTS TEST IS A GO.
YEAH, I KNOW. BOO-HOO FOR POOR TONY STARK, RIGHT? THE KID WHO DIDN'T FIT IN BECAUSE HE WAS TOO SMART AND TOO FABULOUSLY WEALTHY. PROBABLY TOO HANDSOME, TOO.
BUT THERE ARE ENTIRE INDUSTRIES OF PSYCHOTHERAPY AND PHARMACEUTICALS AND ESPRESSO MARTINIS BUILT UPON THE FACT THAT IT REALLY SUCKS TO FEEL LOST AND ALONE.
AND I CERTAINLY DID. SINCE ABOUT THE TIME I COULD WALK.

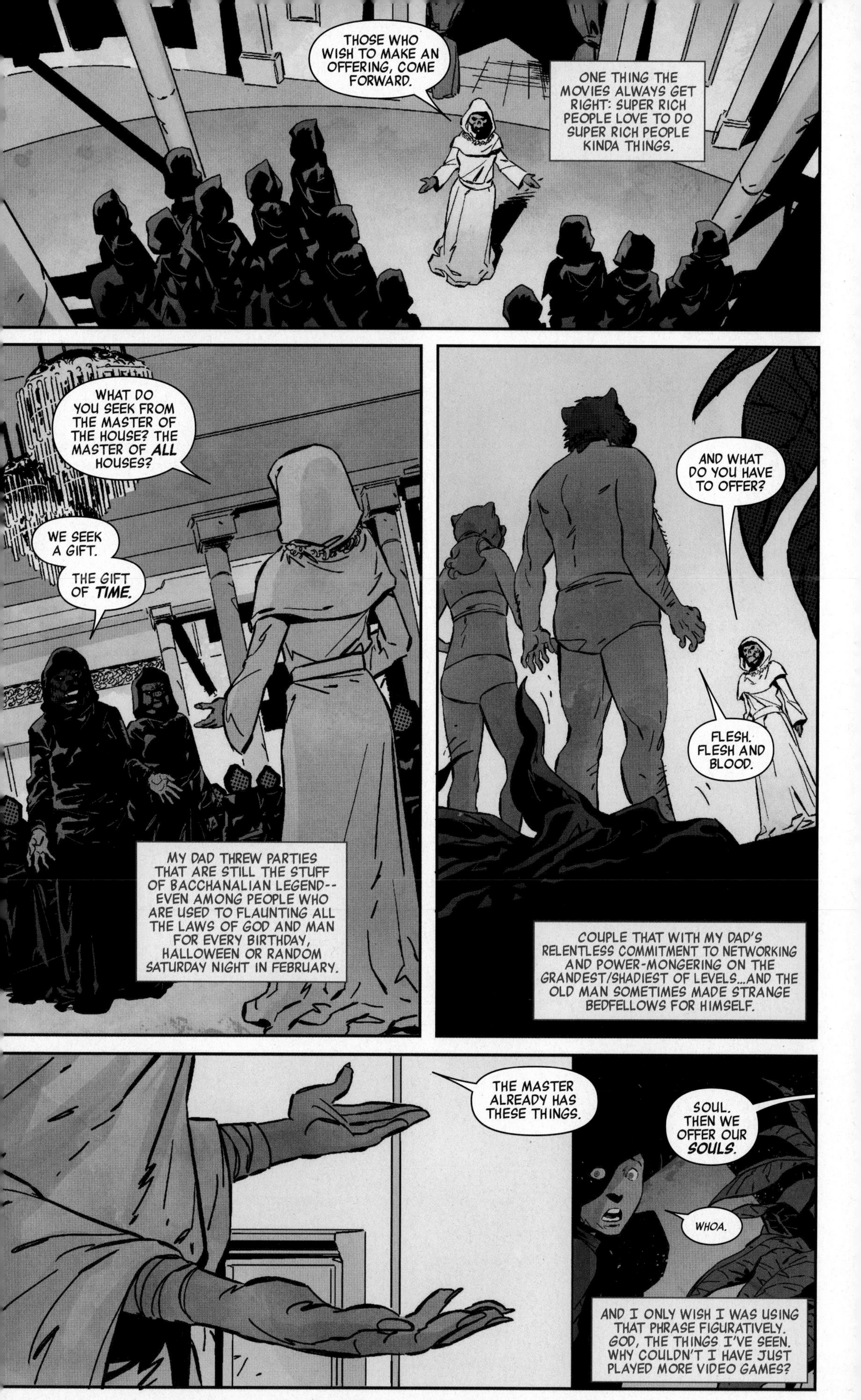
THOSE WHO WISH TO MAKE AN OFFERING, COME FORWARD.
ONE THING THE MOVIES ALWAYS GET RIGHT: SUPER RICH PEOPLE LOVE TO DO SUPER RICH PEOPLE KINDA THINGS.
WHAT DO YOU SEEK FROM THE MASTER OF THE HOUSE? THE MASTER OF ALL HOUSES?
WE SEEK A GIFT.
THE GIFT OF TIME.
MY DAD THREW PARTIES THAT ARE STILL THE STUFF OF BACCHANALIAN LEGEND--EVEN AMONG PEOPLE WHO ARE USED TO FLAUNTING ALL THE LAWS OF GOD AND MAN FOR EVERY BIRTHDAY, HALLOWEEN OR RANDOM SATURDAY NIGHT IN FEBRUARY.
AND WHAT DO YOU HAVE TO OFFER?
FLESH. FLESH AND BLOOD.
COUPLE THAT WITH MY DAD'S RELENTLESS COMMITMENT TO NETWORKING AND POWER-MONGERING ON THE GRANDEST/SHADIEST OF LEVELS...AND THE OLD MAN SOMETIMES MADE STRANGE BEDFELLOWS FOR HIMSELF.
THE MASTER ALREADY HAS THESE THINGS.
SOUL. THEN WE OFFER OUR SOULS.
WHOA.
AND I ONLY WISH I WAS USING THAT PHRASE FIGURATIVELY. GOD, THE THINGS I'VE SEEN. WHY COULDN'T I HAVE JUST PLAYED MORE VIDEO GAMES?

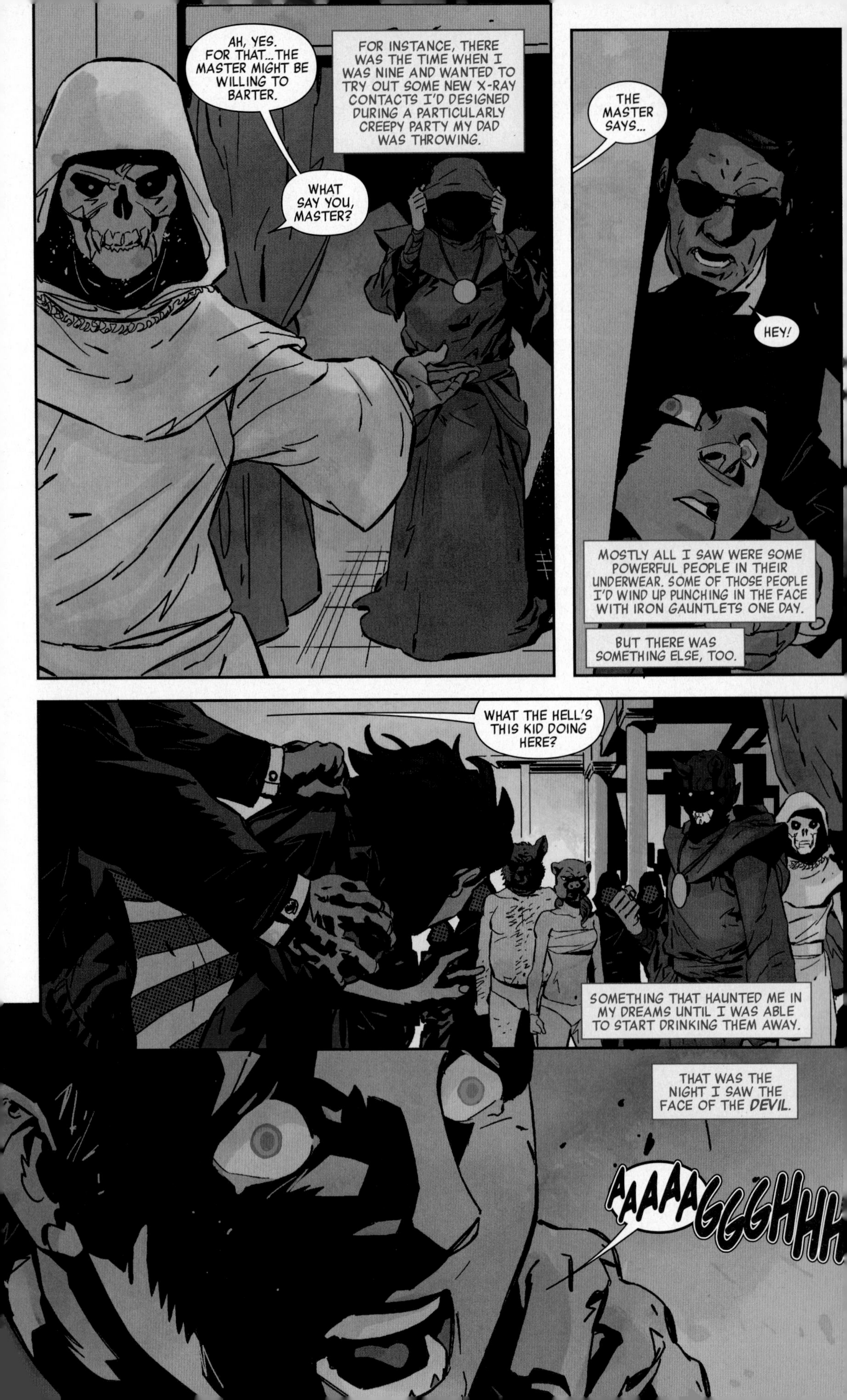
AH, YES. FOR THAT... THE MASTER MIGHT BE WILLING TO BARTER.
FOR INSTANCE, THERE WAS THE TIME WHEN I WAS NINE AND WANTED TO TRY OUT SOME NEW X-RAY CONTACTS I'D DESIGNED DURING A PARTICULARLY CREEPY PARTY MY DAD WAS THROWING.
WHAT SAY YOU, MASTER?
THE MASTER SAYS...
HEY!
MOSTLY ALL I SAW WERE SOME POWERFUL PEOPLE IN THEIR UNDERWEAR. SOME OF THOSE PEOPLE I'D WIND UP PUNCHING IN THE FACE WITH IRON GAUNTLETS ONE DAY.
BUT THERE WAS SOMETHING ELSE, TOO.
WHAT THE HELL'S THIS KID DOING HERE?
SOMETHING THAT HAUNTED ME IN MY DREAMS UNTIL I WAS ABLE TO START DRINKING THEM AWAY.
THAT WAS THE NIGHT I SAW THE FACE OF THE *DEVIL*.
AAAAAGGGHHH

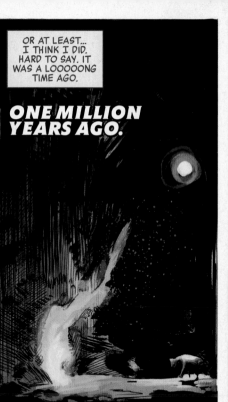

OR AT LEAST... I THINK I DID. HARD TO SAY. IT WAS A LOOOOONG TIME AGO.

ONE MILLION YEARS AGO.

FEELS LONGER THAN EVER THESE DAYS. MAYBE BECAUSE IT *IS*.

REMEMBER WHAT I SAID ABOUT BEING GOOD AT GETTING INTO TROUBLE?

HE SEND YOU? OR ARE YOU JUST HUNGRY?

DOESN'T REALLY MATTER, I GUESS.

YEAH, SOME THINGS NEVER CHANGE.

I'LL ASK HIM MYSELF WHEN HE COMES AROUND.

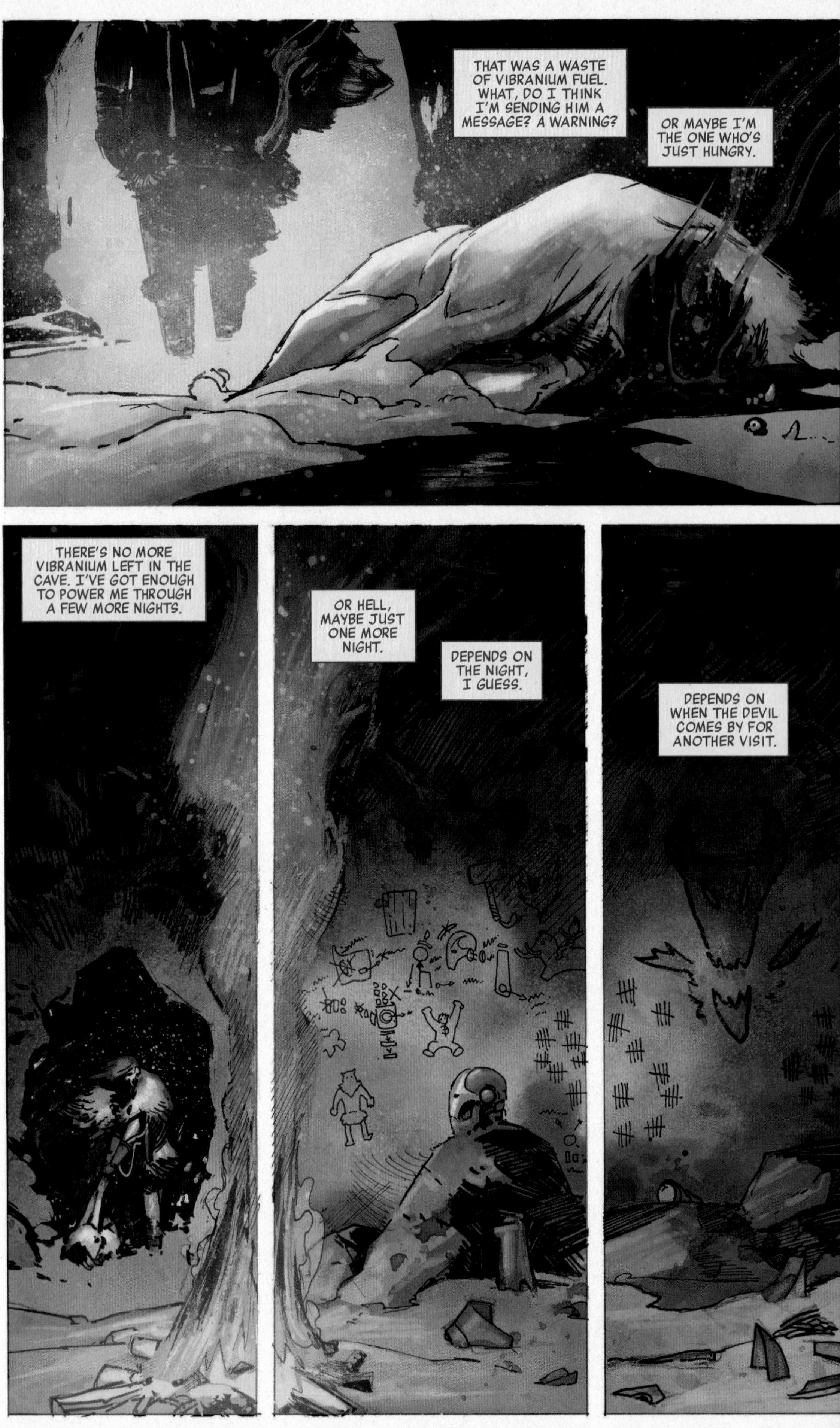
THAT WAS A WASTE OF VIBRANIUM FUEL. WHAT, DO I THINK I'M SENDING HIM A MESSAGE? A WARNING?
OR MAYBE I'M THE ONE WHO'S JUST HUNGRY.
THERE'S NO MORE VIBRANIUM LEFT IN THE CAVE. I'VE GOT ENOUGH TO POWER ME THROUGH A FEW MORE NIGHTS.
OR HELL, MAYBE JUST ONE MORE NIGHT.
DEPENDS ON THE NIGHT, I GUESS.
DEPENDS ON WHEN THE DEVIL COMES BY FOR ANOTHER VISIT.

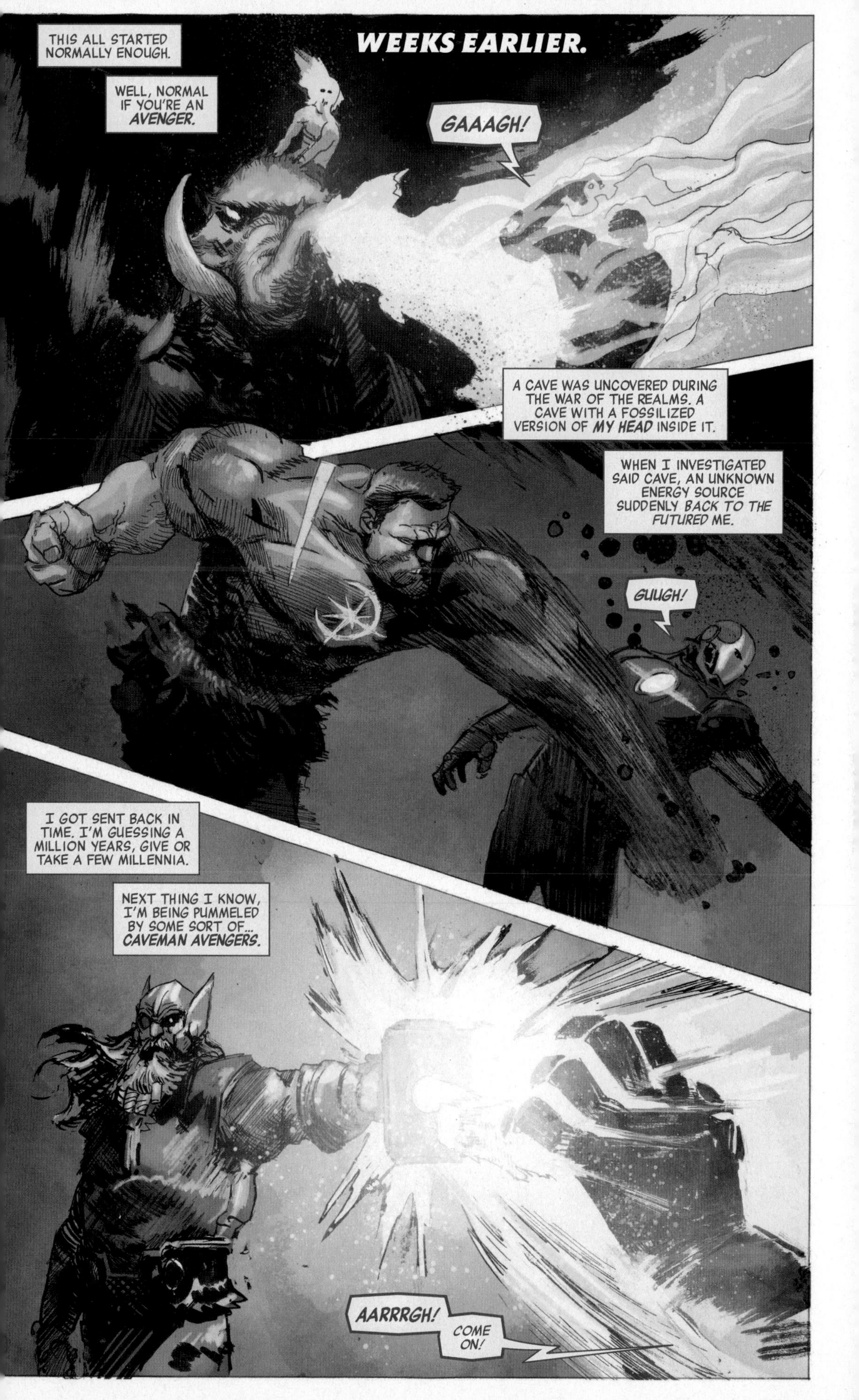

THIS ALL STARTED NORMALLY ENOUGH.
WEEKS EARLIER.
WELL, NORMAL IF YOU'RE AN AVENGER.
GAAAGH!
A CAVE WAS UNCOVERED DURING THE WAR OF THE REALMS. A CAVE WITH A FOSSILIZED VERSION OF MY HEAD INSIDE IT.
WHEN I INVESTIGATED SAID CAVE, AN UNKNOWN ENERGY SOURCE SUDDENLY BACK TO THE FUTURED ME.
GUUGH!
I GOT SENT BACK IN TIME. I'M GUESSING A MILLION YEARS, GIVE OR TAKE A FEW MILLENNIA.
NEXT THING I KNOW, I'M BEING PUMMELED BY SOME SORT OF... CAVEMAN AVENGERS.
AARRRGH!
COME ON!

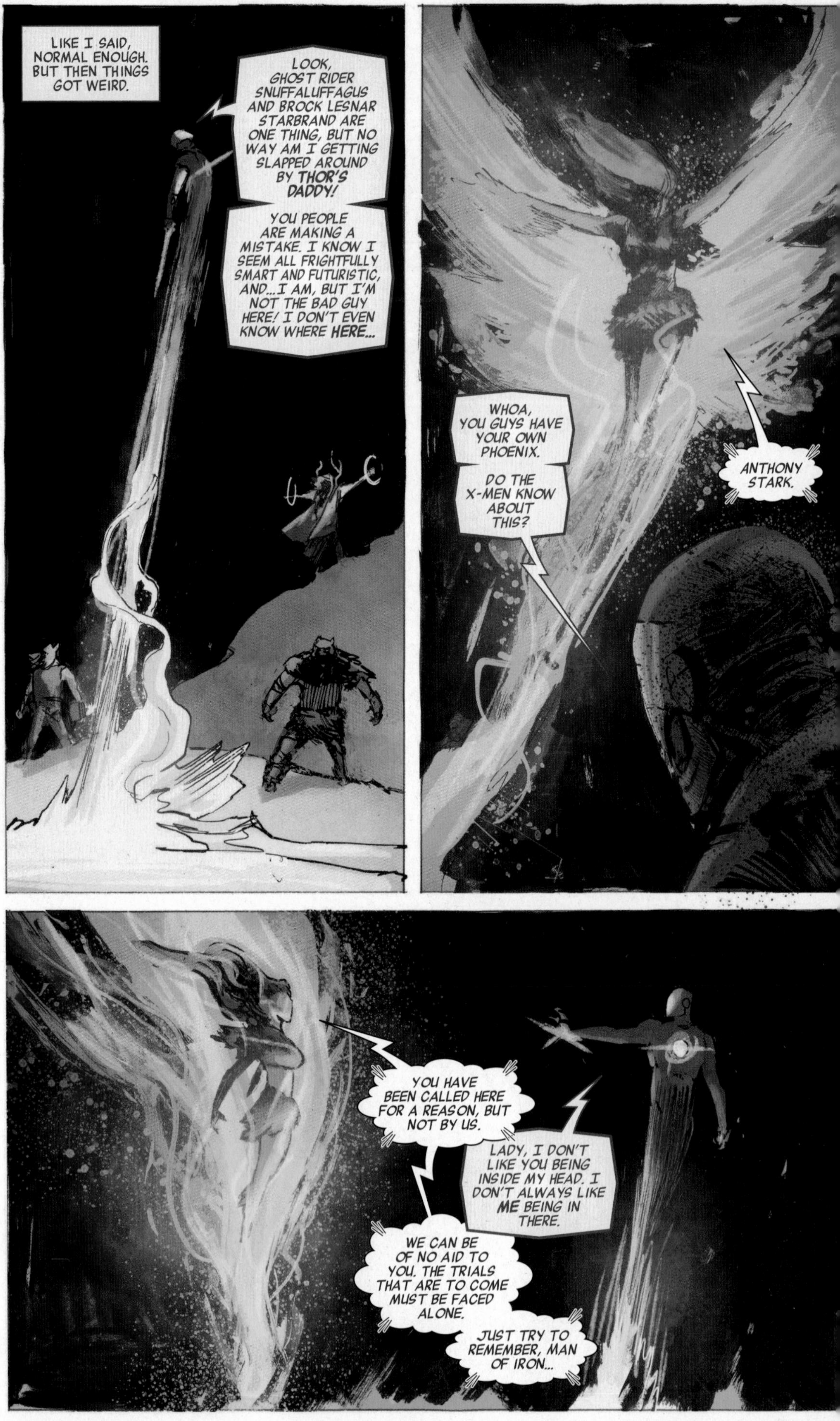
LIKE I SAID, NORMAL ENOUGH. BUT THEN THINGS GOT WEIRD.
LOOK, GHOST RIDER SNUFFALUFFAGUS AND BROCK LESNAR STARBRAND ARE ONE THING, BUT NO WAY AM I GETTING SLAPPED AROUND BY THOR'S DADDY!
YOU PEOPLE ARE MAKING A MISTAKE. I KNOW I SEEM ALL FRIGHTFULLY SMART AND FUTURISTIC, AND...I AM, BUT I'M NOT THE BAD GUY HERE! I DON'T EVEN KNOW WHERE HERE...
ANTHONY STARK.
WHOA, YOU GUYS HAVE YOUR OWN PHOENIX.
DO THE X-MEN KNOW ABOUT THIS?
YOU HAVE BEEN CALLED HERE FOR A REASON, BUT NOT BY US.
LADY, I DON'T LIKE YOU BEING INSIDE MY HEAD. I DON'T ALWAYS LIKE ME BEING IN THERE.
WE CAN BE OF NO AID TO YOU. THE TRIALS THAT ARE TO COME MUST BE FACED ALONE.
JUST TRY TO REMEMBER, MAN OF IRON...

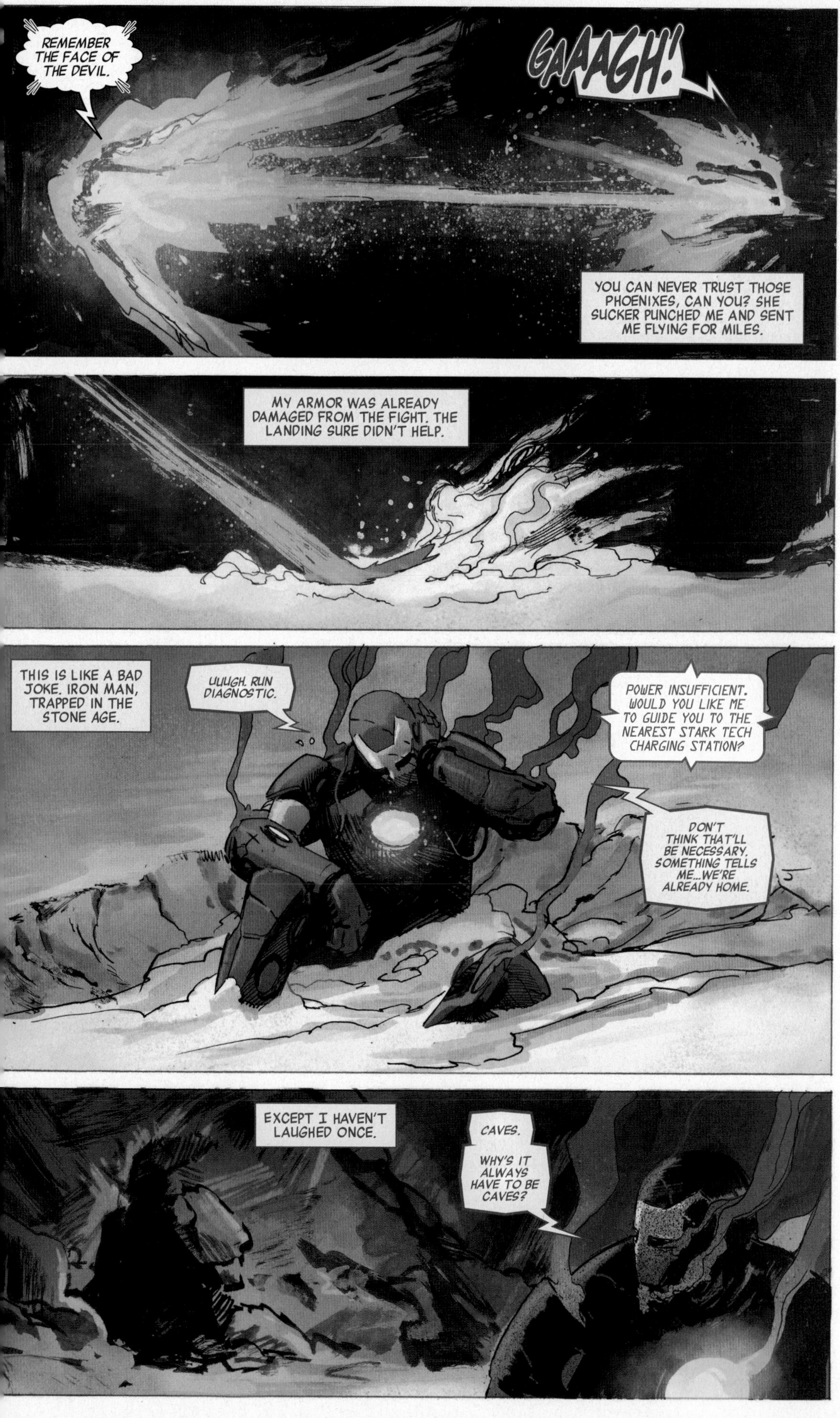
REMEMBER THE FACE OF THE DEVIL.
GAAAGH!
YOU CAN NEVER TRUST THOSE PHOENIXES, CAN YOU? SHE SUCKER PUNCHED ME AND SENT ME FLYING FOR MILES.
MY ARMOR WAS ALREADY DAMAGED FROM THE FIGHT. THE LANDING SURE DIDN'T HELP.
THIS IS LIKE A BAD JOKE. IRON MAN, TRAPPED IN THE STONE AGE.
UUUGH. RUN DIAGNOSTIC.
POWER INSUFFICIENT. WOULD YOU LIKE ME TO GUIDE YOU TO THE NEAREST STARK TECH CHARGING STATION?
DON'T THINK THAT'LL BE NECESSARY. SOMETHING TELLS ME...WE'RE ALREADY HOME.
EXCEPT I HAVEN'T LAUGHED ONCE.
CAVES.
WHY'S IT ALWAYS HAVE TO BE CAVES?

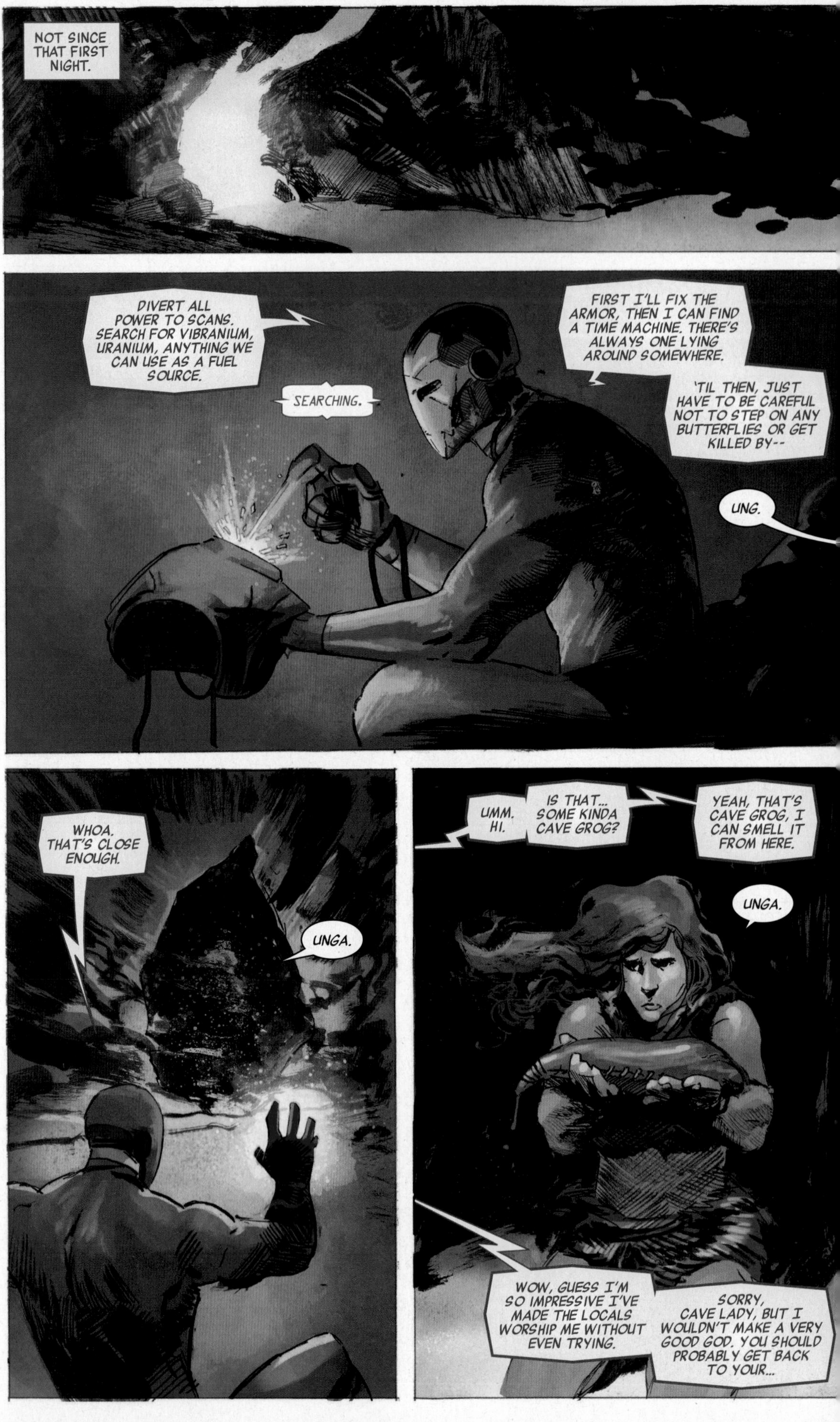
NOT SINCE THAT FIRST NIGHT.
DIVERT ALL POWER TO SCANS. SEARCH FOR VIBRANIUM, URANIUM, ANYTHING WE CAN USE AS A FUEL SOURCE.
SEARCHING.
FIRST I'LL FIX THE ARMOR, THEN I CAN FIND A TIME MACHINE. THERE'S ALWAYS ONE LYING AROUND SOMEWHERE.
'TIL THEN, JUST HAVE TO BE CAREFUL NOT TO STEP ON ANY BUTTERFLIES OR GET KILLED BY--
UNG.
WHOA. THAT'S CLOSE ENOUGH.
UNGA.
UMM. HI.
IS THAT... SOME KINDA CAVE GROG?
YEAH, THAT'S CAVE GROG, I CAN SMELL IT FROM HERE.
UNGA.
WOW, GUESS I'M SO IMPRESSIVE I'VE MADE THE LOCALS WORSHIP ME WITHOUT EVEN TRYING.
SORRY, CAVE LADY, BUT I WOULDN'T MAKE A VERY GOOD GOD. YOU SHOULD PROBABLY GET BACK TO YOUR...

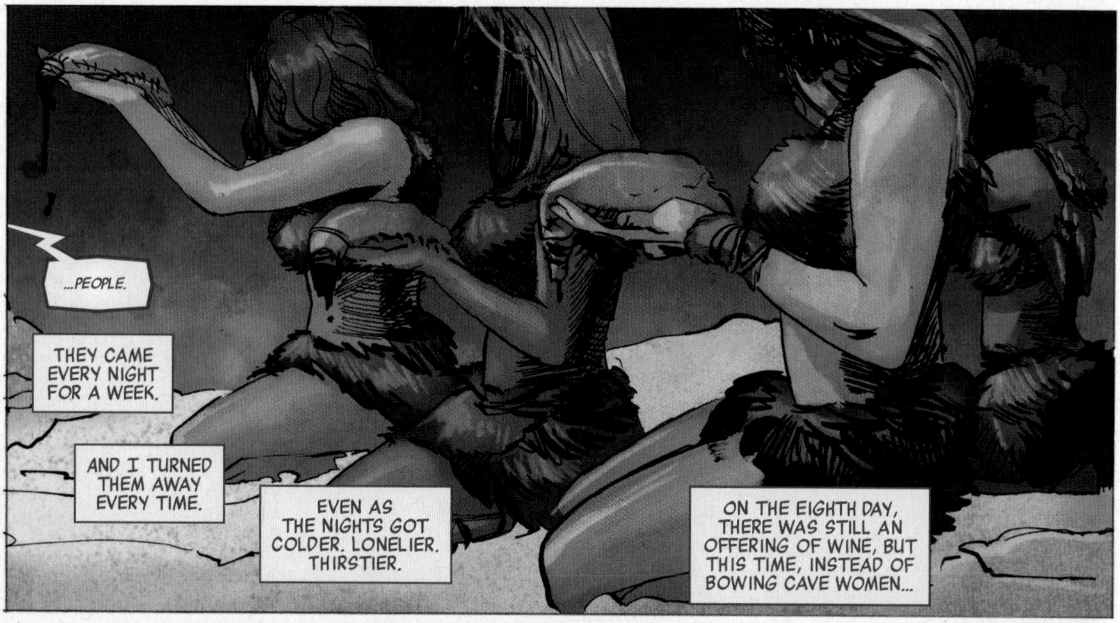
...PEOPLE.
THEY CAME EVERY NIGHT FOR A WEEK.
AND I TURNED THEM AWAY EVERY TIME.
EVEN AS THE NIGHTS GOT COLDER. LONELIER. THIRSTIER.
ON THE EIGHTH DAY, THERE WAS STILL AN OFFERING OF WINE, BUT THIS TIME, INSTEAD OF BOWING CAVE WOMEN...

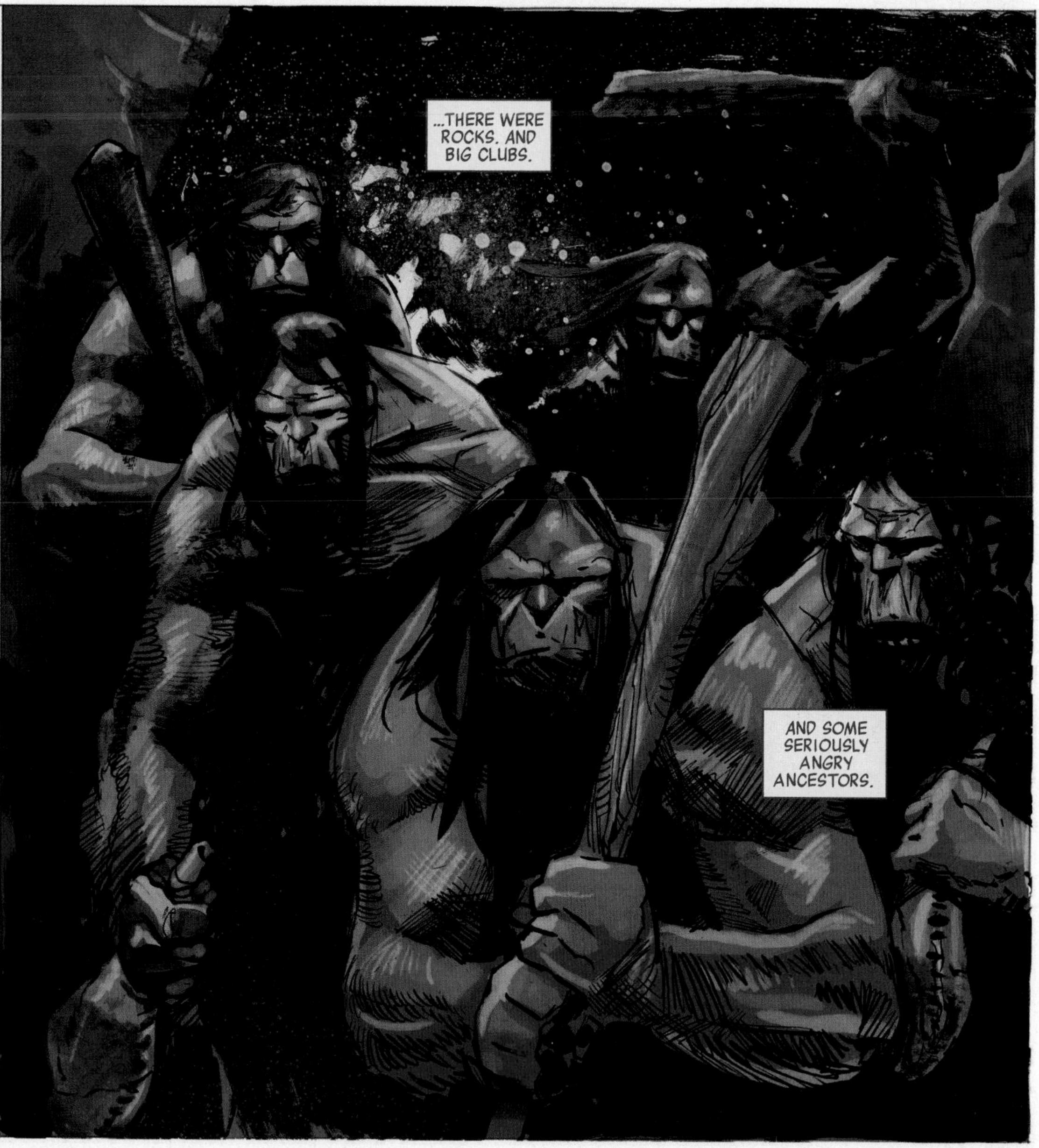
...THERE WERE ROCKS. AND BIG CLUBS.
AND SOME SERIOUSLY ANGRY ANCESTORS.

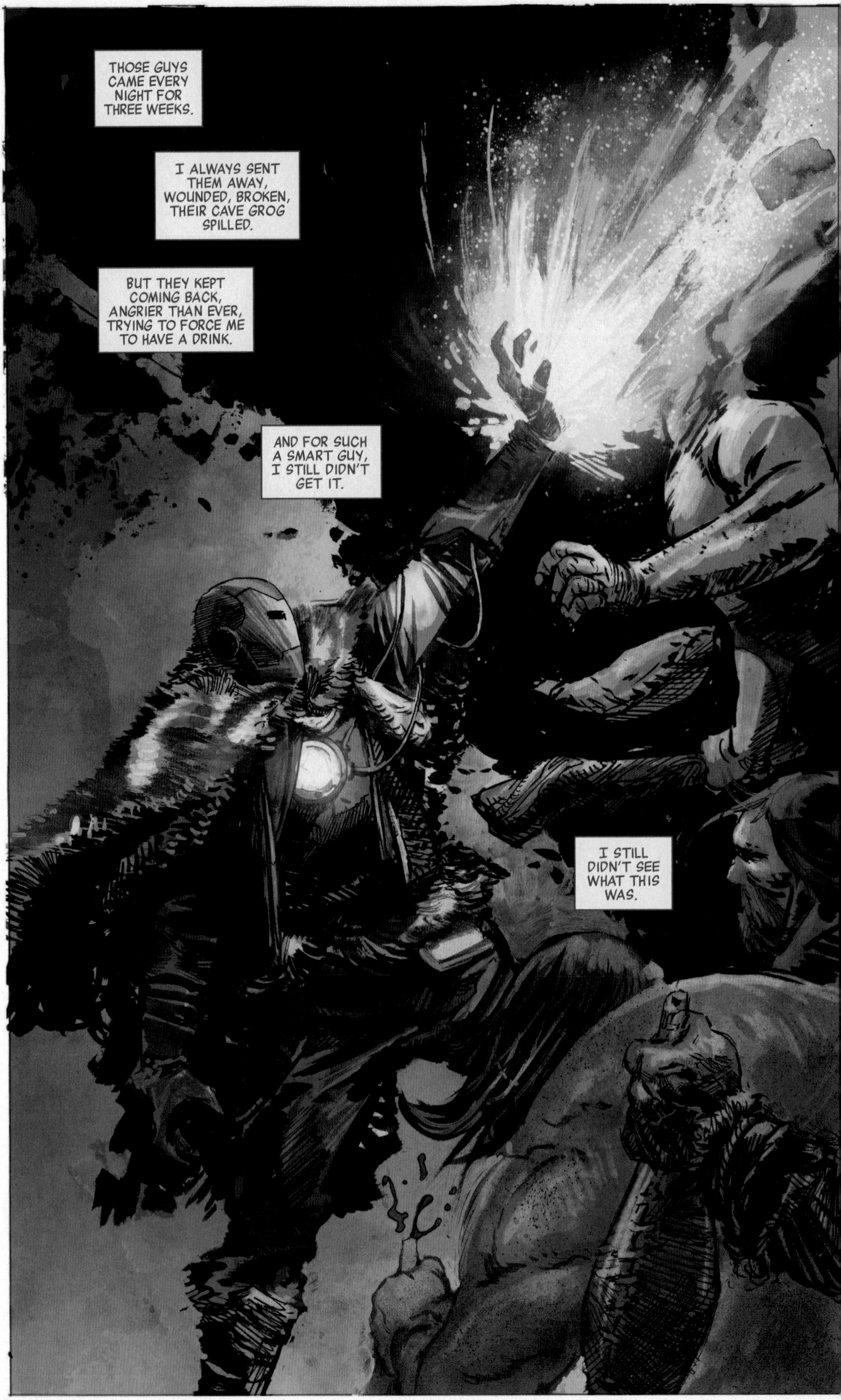
THOSE GUYS CAME EVERY NIGHT FOR THREE WEEKS.
I ALWAYS SENT THEM AWAY, WOUNDED, BROKEN, THEIR CAVE GROG SPILLED.
BUT THEY KEPT COMING BACK, ANGRIER THAN EVER, TRYING TO FORCE ME TO HAVE A DRINK.
AND FOR SUCH A SMART GUY, I STILL DIDN'T GET IT.
I STILL DIDN'T SEE WHAT THIS WAS.

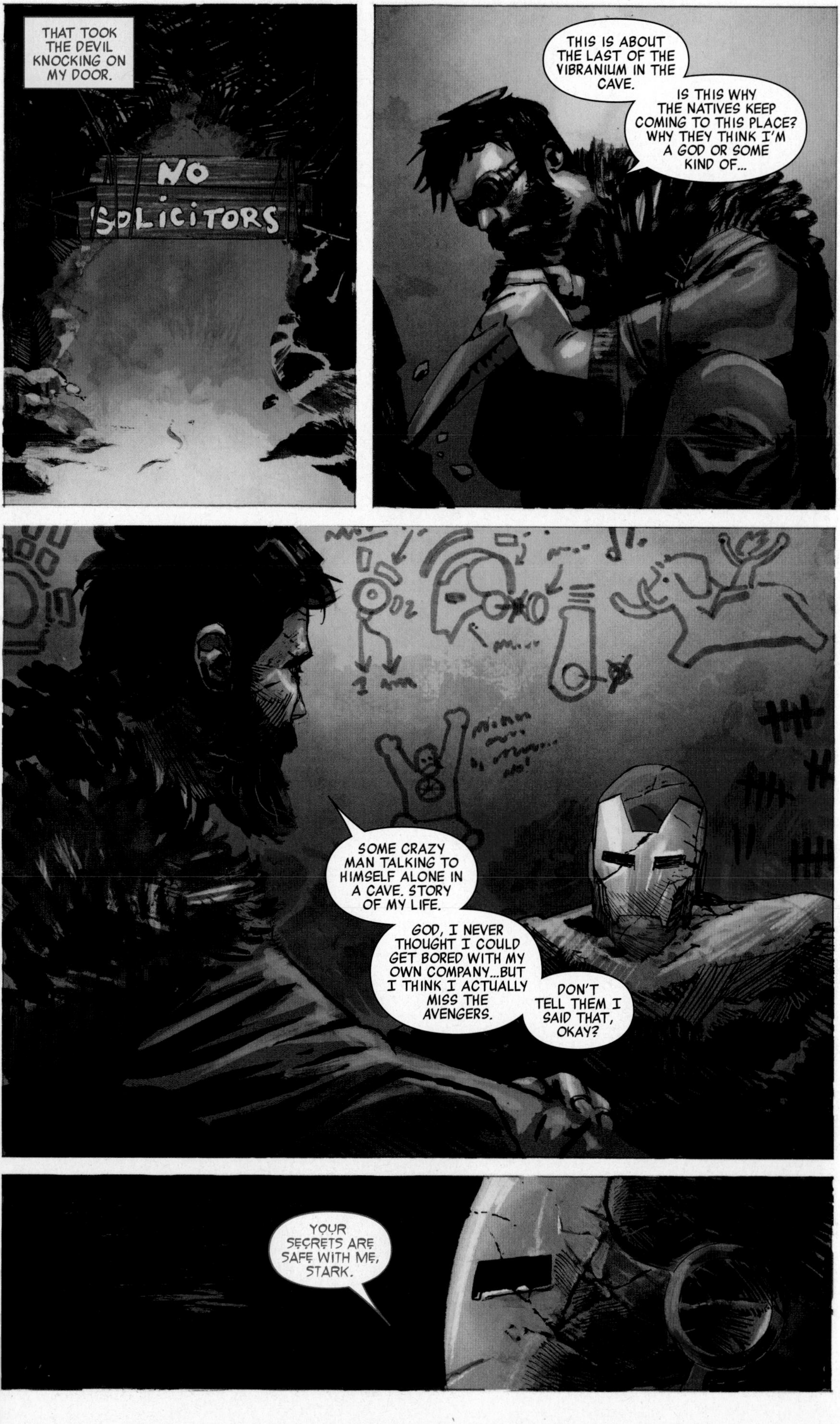
THAT TOOK THE DEVIL KNOCKING ON MY DOOR.
NO SOLICITORS
THIS IS ABOUT THE LAST OF THE VIBRANIUM IN THE CAVE.
IS THIS WHY THE NATIVES KEEP COMING TO THIS PLACE? WHY THEY THINK I'M A GOD OR SOME KIND OF...
SOME CRAZY MAN TALKING TO HIMSELF ALONE IN A CAVE. STORY OF MY LIFE.
GOD, I NEVER THOUGHT I COULD GET BORED WITH MY OWN COMPANY...BUT I THINK I ACTUALLY MISS THE AVENGERS.
DON'T TELL THEM I SAID THAT, OKAY?
YOUR SECRETS ARE SAFE WITH ME, STARK.

THE ONBOARD SYSTEMS DIED YESTERDAY. INCLUDING THE VOICE MODULE.

AND THIS IS A VOICE I CAN FEEL IN MY COCKLES.

I DIDN'T EVEN KNOW I *HAD* COCKLES.

WHO AM I TALKING TO?

A VERY OLD FRIEND.

I DIDN'T REALIZE I HAD ANY OF THOSE HERE.

OH, WE HAVEN'T MET YET. NOT IN THIS AGE. BUT I'M A BIT BEYOND THINGS LIKE TIME.

I TEND TO AGREE MYSELF. EXCEPT WHEN IT'S *MY* TIME. I ASSUME YOU'RE THE ONE WHO'S BEEN SENDING ME THE NIGHTLY GIFTS?

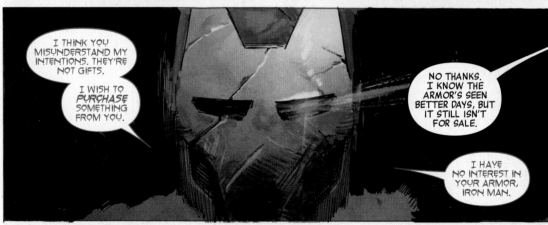

I THINK YOU MISUNDERSTAND MY INTENTIONS. THEY'RE NOT GIFTS.

I WISH TO *PURCHASE* SOMETHING FROM YOU.

NO THANKS. I KNOW THE ARMOR'S SEEN BETTER DAYS, BUT IT STILL ISN'T FOR SALE.

I HAVE NO INTEREST IN YOUR ARMOR, IRON MAN.

NOT THE ONE YOU WEAR ON THE OUTSIDE, AT LEAST.

TELL ME, STARK...WHAT WOULD YOU TAKE FOR YOUR *SOUL?*

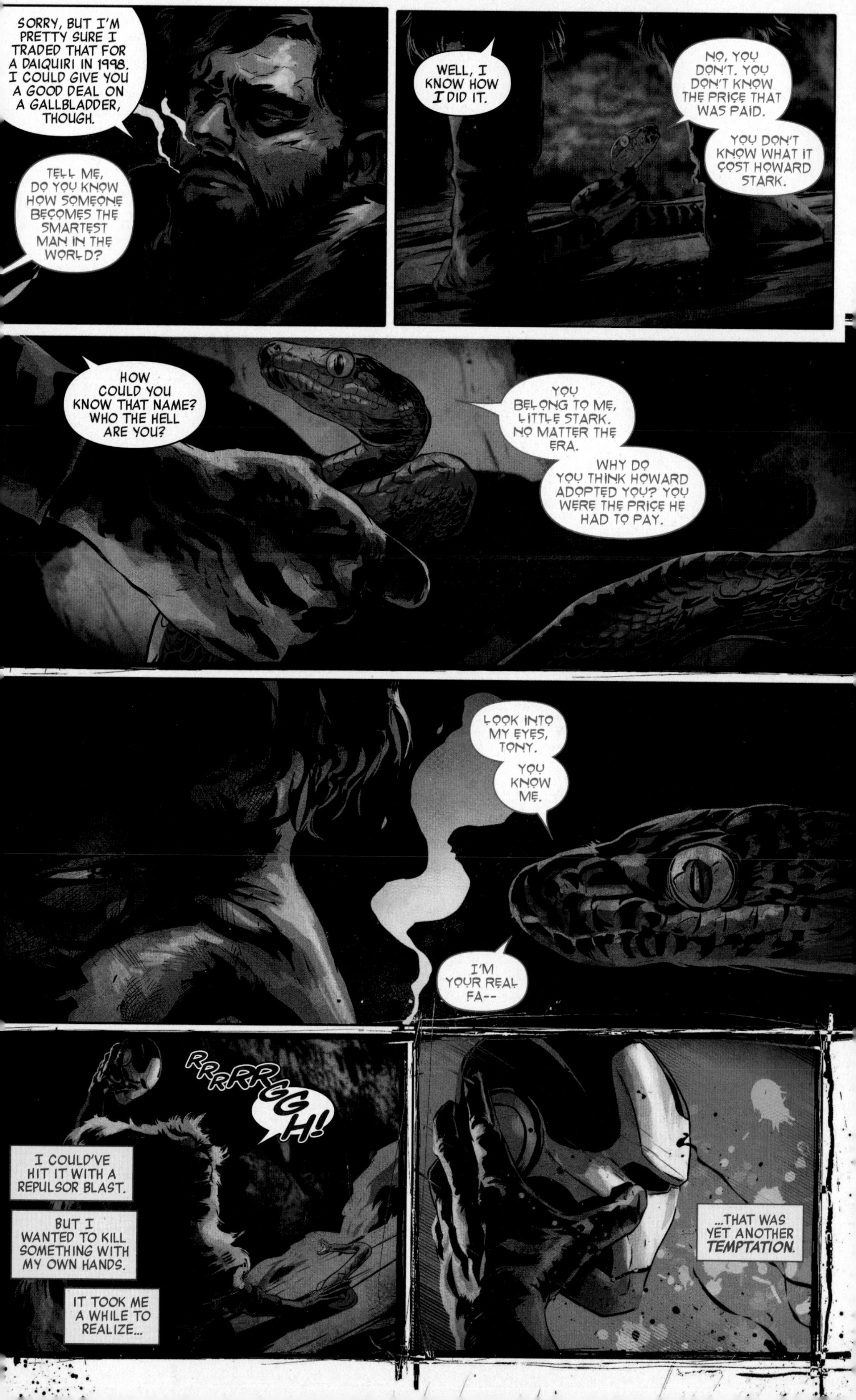
SORRY, BUT I'M PRETTY SURE I TRADED THAT FOR A DAIQUIRI IN 1998. I COULD GIVE YOU A GOOD DEAL ON A GALLBLADDER, THOUGH.
TELL ME, DO YOU KNOW HOW SOMEONE BECOMES THE SMARTEST MAN IN THE WORLD?
WELL, I KNOW HOW I DID IT.
NO, YOU DON'T. YOU DON'T KNOW THE PRICE THAT WAS PAID.
YOU DON'T KNOW WHAT IT COST HOWARD STARK.
HOW COULD YOU KNOW THAT NAME? WHO THE HELL ARE YOU?
YOU BELONG TO ME, LITTLE STARK. NO MATTER THE ERA.
WHY DO YOU THINK HOWARD ADOPTED YOU? YOU WERE THE PRICE HE HAD TO PAY.
LOOK INTO MY EYES, TONY.
YOU KNOW ME.
I'M YOUR REAL FA--
RRRRRGGH!
I COULD'VE HIT IT WITH A REPULSOR BLAST.
BUT I WANTED TO KILL SOMETHING WITH MY OWN HANDS.
IT TOOK ME A WHILE TO REALIZE...
...THAT WAS YET ANOTHER TEMPTATION.

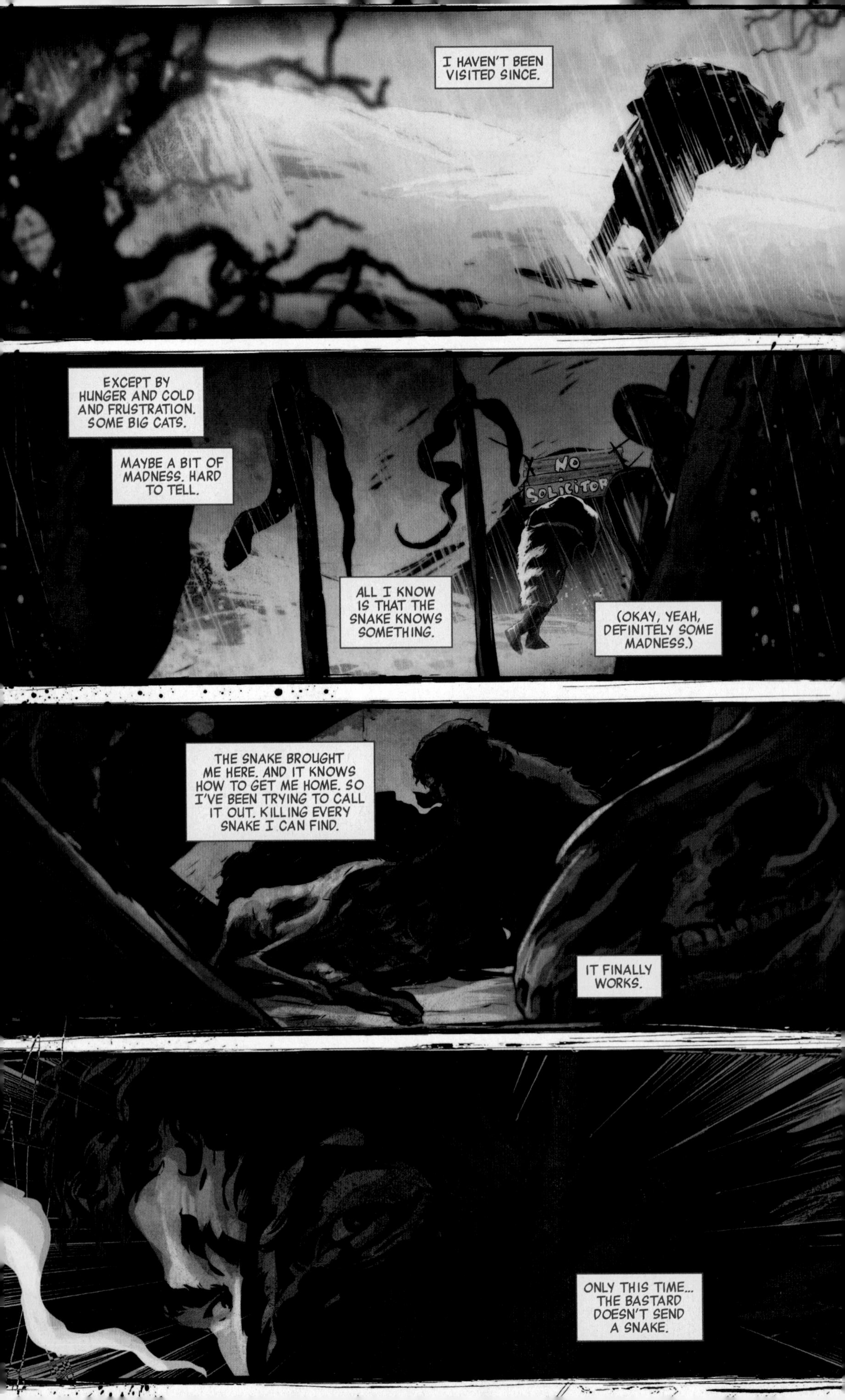
I HAVEN'T BEEN VISITED SINCE.
EXCEPT BY HUNGER AND COLD AND FRUSTRATION. SOME BIG CATS.
MAYBE A BIT OF MADNESS. HARD TO TELL.
NO SOLICITOR
ALL I KNOW IS THAT THE SNAKE KNOWS SOMETHING.
(OKAY, YEAH, DEFINITELY SOME MADNESS.)
THE SNAKE BROUGHT ME HERE. AND IT KNOWS HOW TO GET ME HOME. SO I'VE BEEN TRYING TO CALL IT OUT. KILLING EVERY SNAKE I CAN FIND.
IT FINALLY WORKS.
ONLY THIS TIME... THE BASTARD DOESN'T SEND A SNAKE.

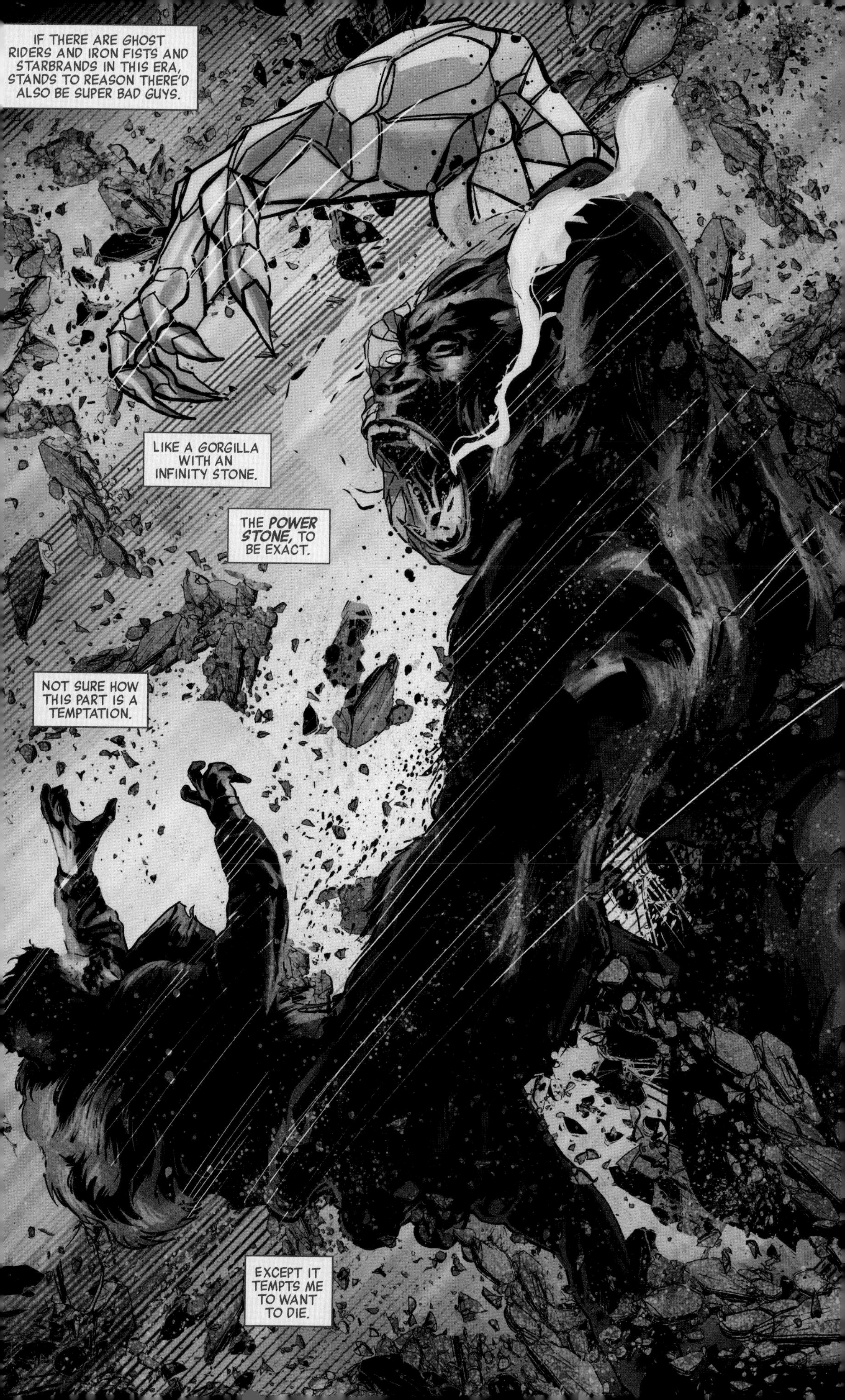
IF THERE ARE GHOST RIDERS AND IRON FISTS AND STARBRANDS IN THIS ERA, STANDS TO REASON THERE'D ALSO BE SUPER BAD GUYS.
LIKE A GORGILLA WITH AN INFINITY STONE.
THE *POWER STONE,* TO BE EXACT.
NOT SURE HOW THIS PART IS A TEMPTATION.
EXCEPT IT TEMPTS ME TO WANT TO DIE.

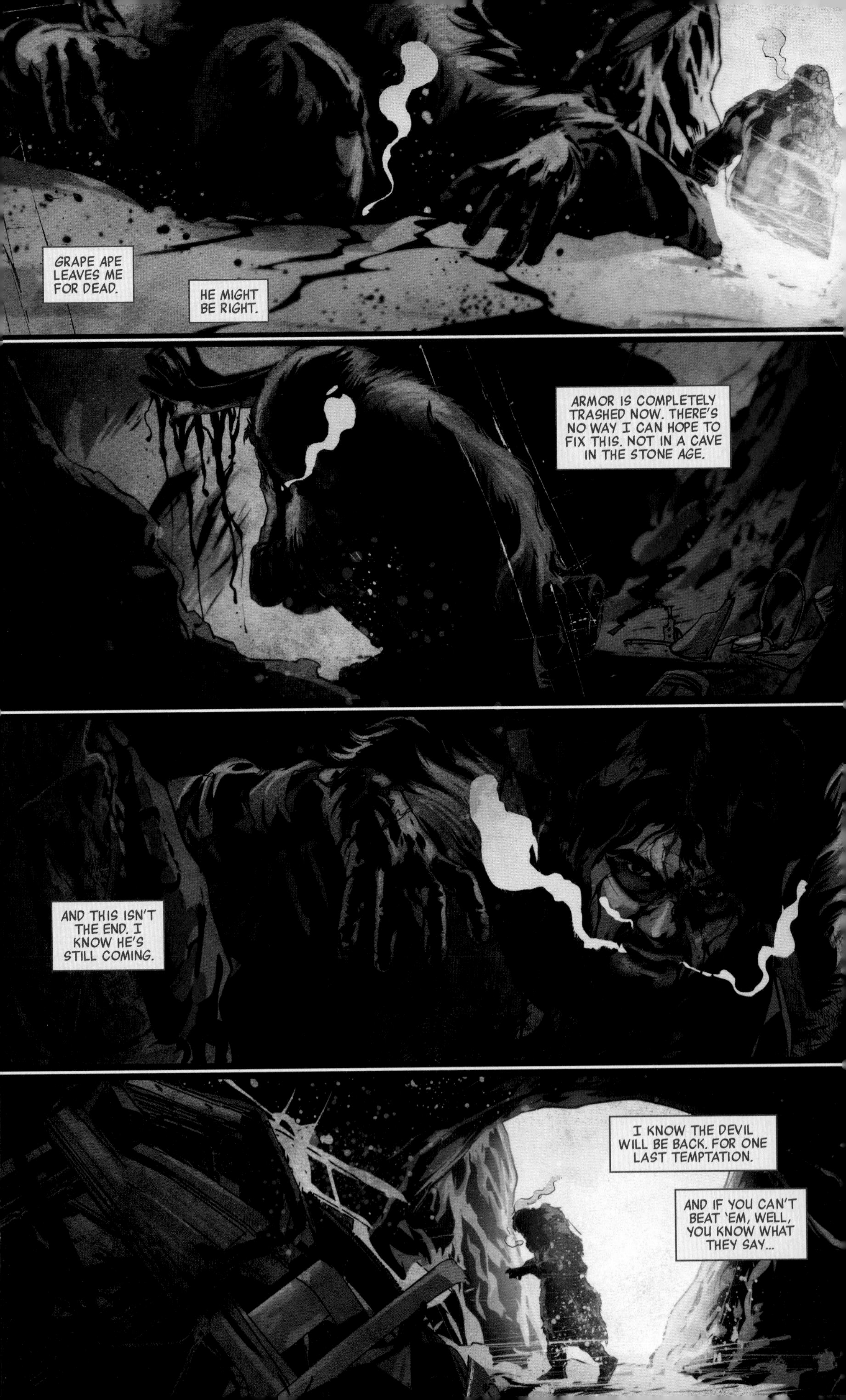
GRAPE APE LEAVES ME FOR DEAD.
HE MIGHT BE RIGHT.
ARMOR IS COMPLETELY TRASHED NOW. THERE'S NO WAY I CAN HOPE TO FIX THIS. NOT IN A CAVE IN THE STONE AGE.
AND THIS ISN'T THE END. I KNOW HE'S STILL COMING.
I KNOW THE DEVIL WILL BE BACK. FOR ONE LAST TEMPTATION.
AND IF YOU CAN'T BEAT 'EM, WELL, YOU KNOW WHAT THEY SAY...

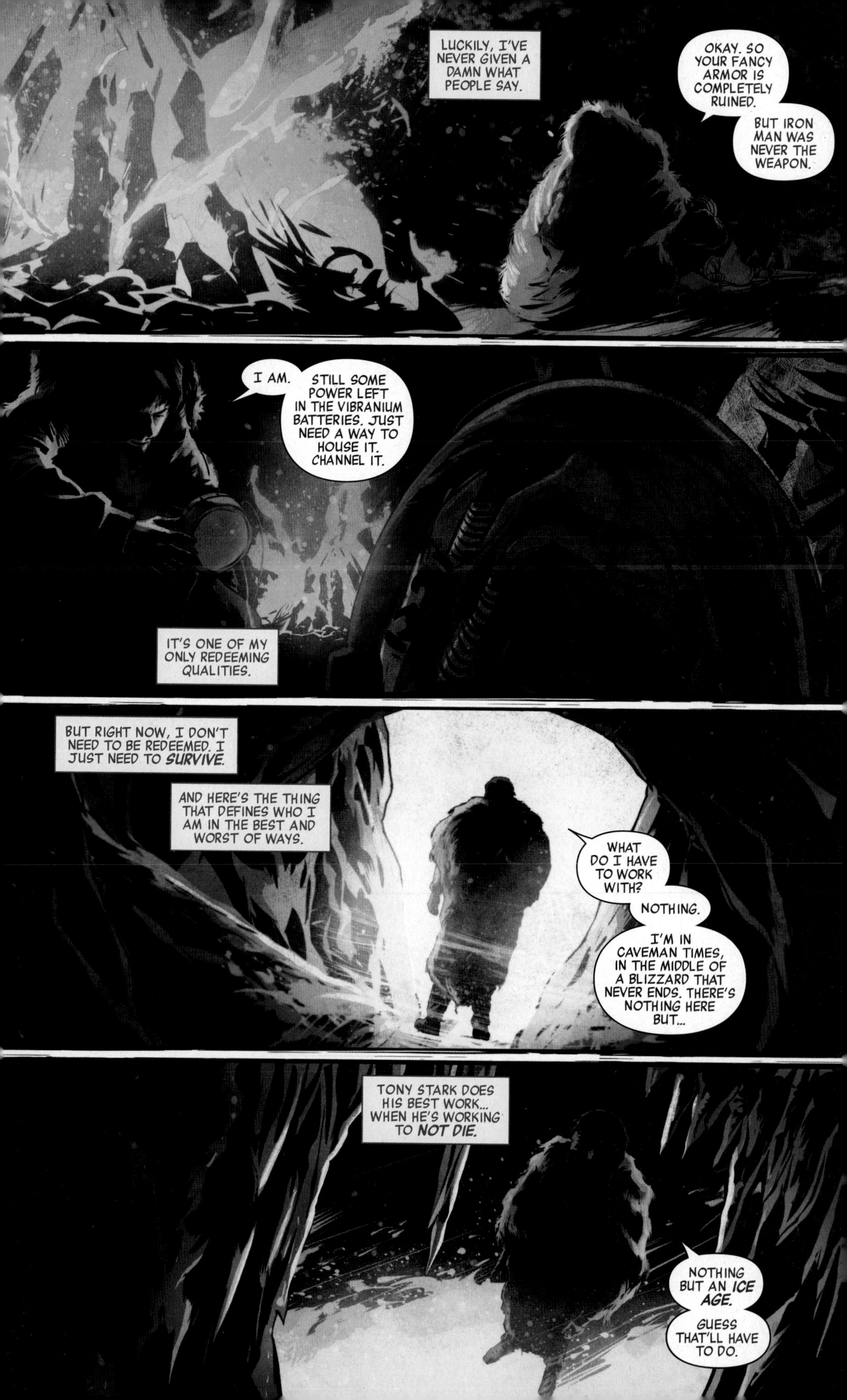
LUCKILY, I'VE NEVER GIVEN A DAMN WHAT PEOPLE SAY.
OKAY. SO YOUR FANCY ARMOR IS COMPLETELY RUINED.
BUT IRON MAN WAS NEVER THE WEAPON.
I AM.
STILL SOME POWER LEFT IN THE VIBRANIUM BATTERIES. JUST NEED A WAY TO HOUSE IT. CHANNEL IT.
IT'S ONE OF MY ONLY REDEEMING QUALITIES.
BUT RIGHT NOW, I DON'T NEED TO BE REDEEMED. I JUST NEED TO *SURVIVE.*
AND HERE'S THE THING THAT DEFINES WHO I AM IN THE BEST AND WORST OF WAYS.
WHAT DO I HAVE TO WORK WITH?
NOTHING.
I'M IN CAVEMAN TIMES, IN THE MIDDLE OF A BLIZZARD THAT NEVER ENDS. THERE'S NOTHING HERE BUT...
TONY STARK DOES HIS BEST WORK... WHEN HE'S WORKING TO ***NOT DIE.***
NOTHING BUT AN ***ICE AGE.***
GUESS THAT'LL HAVE TO DO.

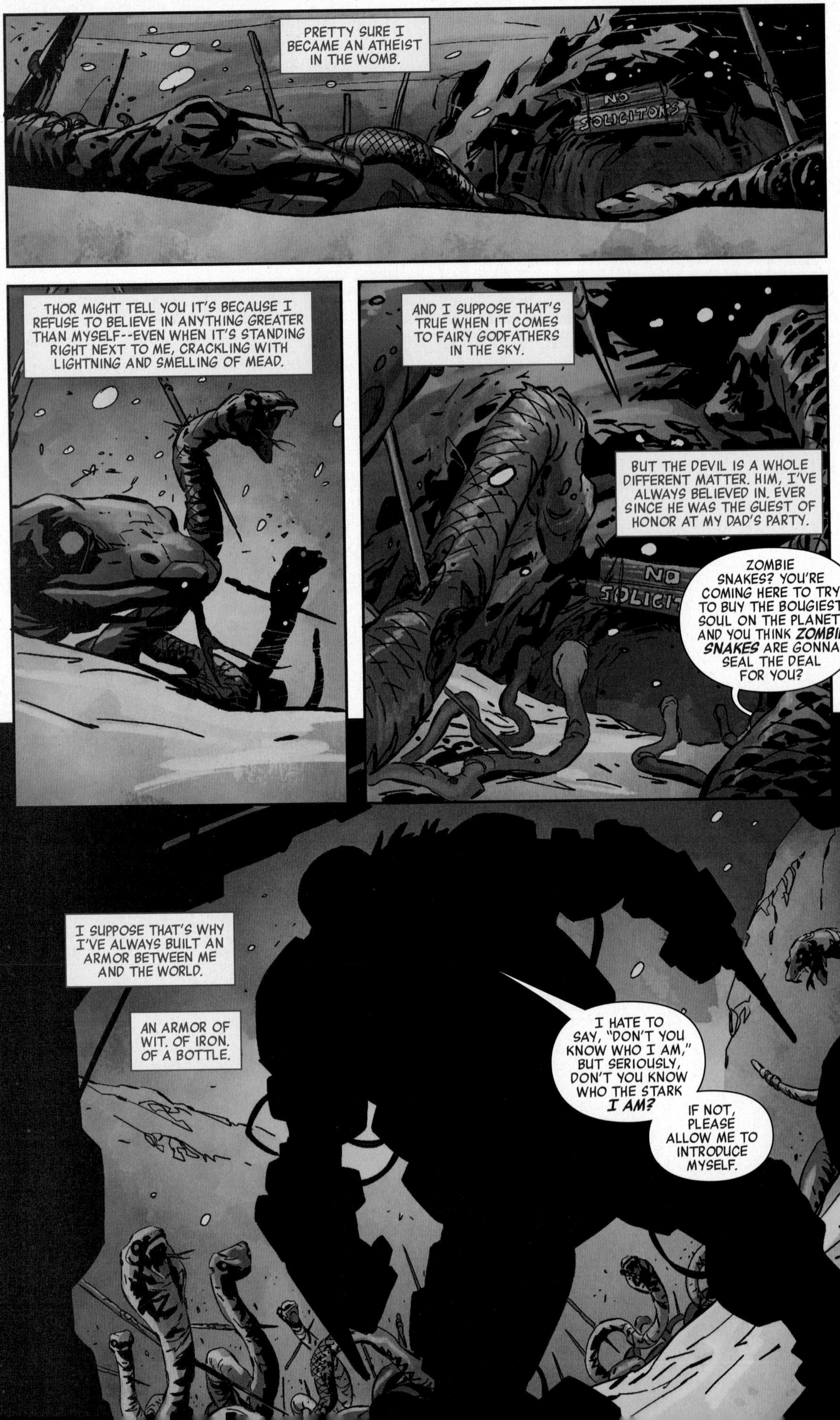
PRETTY SURE I BECAME AN ATHEIST IN THE WOMB.
NO SOLICITORS
THOR MIGHT TELL YOU IT'S BECAUSE I REFUSE TO BELIEVE IN ANYTHING GREATER THAN MYSELF--EVEN WHEN IT'S STANDING RIGHT NEXT TO ME, CRACKLING WITH LIGHTNING AND SMELLING OF MEAD.
AND I SUPPOSE THAT'S TRUE WHEN IT COMES TO FAIRY GODFATHERS IN THE SKY.
BUT THE DEVIL IS A WHOLE DIFFERENT MATTER. HIM, I'VE ALWAYS BELIEVED IN. EVER SINCE HE WAS THE GUEST OF HONOR AT MY DAD'S PARTY.
NO SOLICIT
ZOMBIE SNAKES? YOU'RE COMING HERE TO TRY TO BUY THE BOUGIEST SOUL ON THE PLANET, AND YOU THINK *ZOMBIE SNAKES* ARE GONNA SEAL THE DEAL FOR YOU?
I SUPPOSE THAT'S WHY I'VE ALWAYS BUILT AN ARMOR BETWEEN ME AND THE WORLD.
AN ARMOR OF WIT. OF IRON. OF A BOTTLE.
I HATE TO SAY, "DON'T YOU KNOW WHO I AM," BUT SERIOUSLY, DON'T YOU KNOW WHO THE STARK *I AM?*
IF NOT, PLEASE ALLOW ME TO INTRODUCE MYSELF.

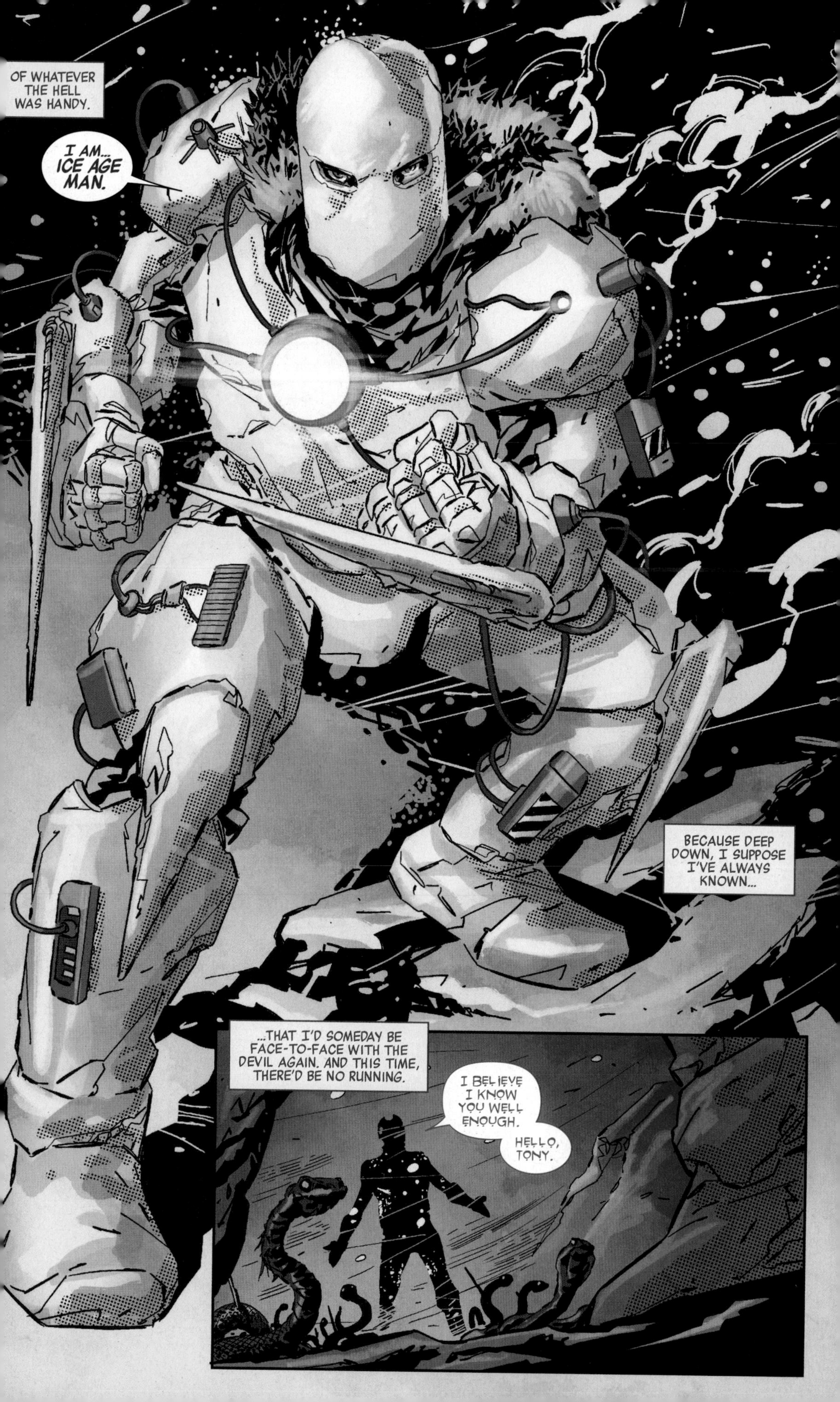
OF WHATEVER THE HELL WAS HANDY.
I AM... ICE AGE MAN.
BECAUSE DEEP DOWN, I SUPPOSE I'VE ALWAYS KNOWN...
...THAT I'D SOMEDAY BE FACE-TO-FACE WITH THE DEVIL AGAIN. AND THIS TIME, THERE'D BE NO RUNNING.
I BELIEVE I KNOW YOU WELL ENOUGH.
HELLO, TONY.

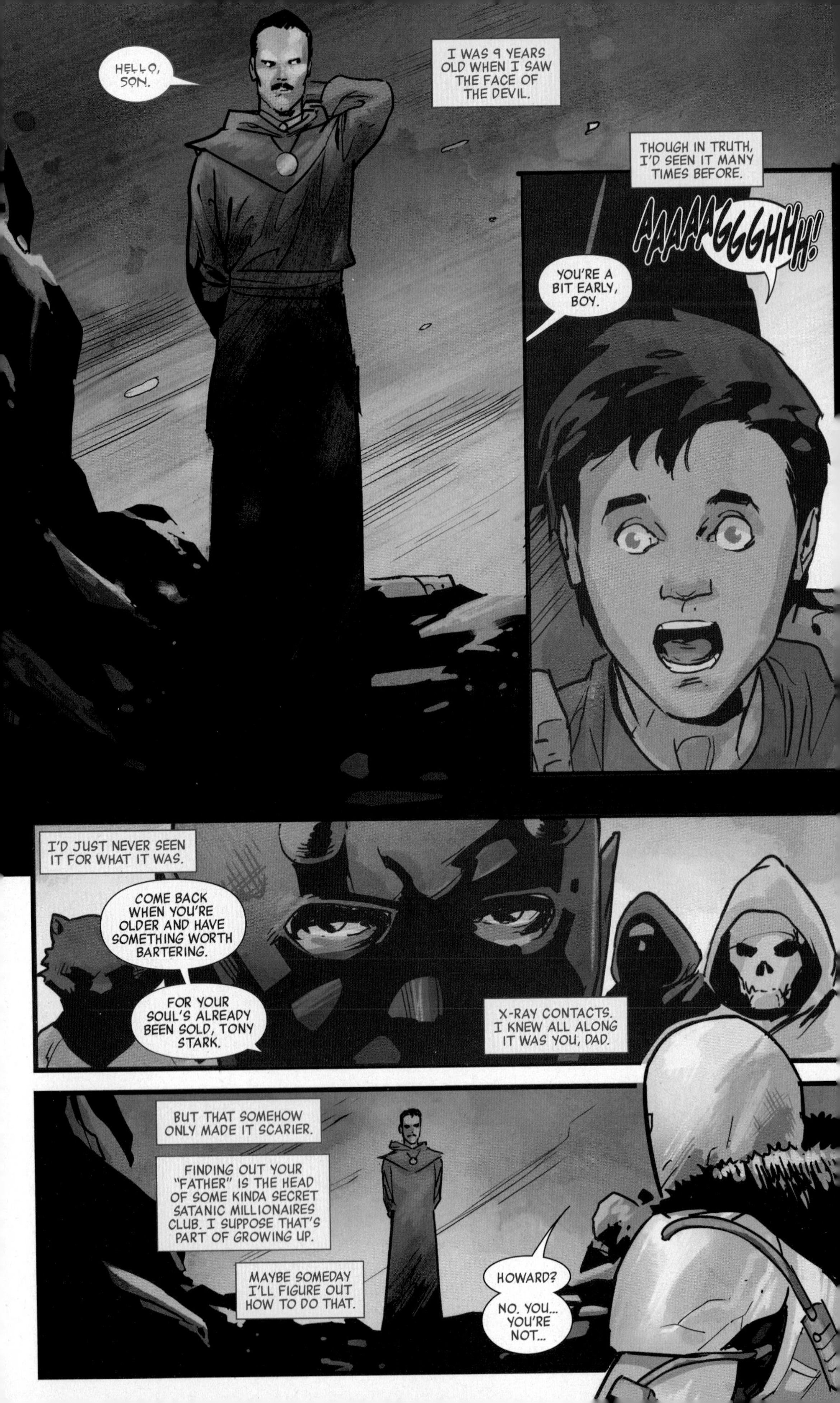
HELLO, SON.
I WAS 9 YEARS OLD WHEN I SAW THE FACE OF THE DEVIL.
THOUGH IN TRUTH, I'D SEEN IT MANY TIMES BEFORE.
AAAAAGGGHHH!
YOU'RE A BIT EARLY, BOY.
I'D JUST NEVER SEEN IT FOR WHAT IT WAS.
COME BACK WHEN YOU'RE OLDER AND HAVE SOMETHING WORTH BARTERING.
FOR YOUR SOUL'S ALREADY BEEN SOLD, TONY STARK.
X-RAY CONTACTS. I KNEW ALL ALONG IT WAS YOU, DAD.
BUT THAT SOMEHOW ONLY MADE IT SCARIER.
FINDING OUT YOUR "FATHER" IS THE HEAD OF SOME KINDA SECRET SATANIC MILLIONAIRES CLUB. I SUPPOSE THAT'S PART OF GROWING UP.
MAYBE SOMEDAY I'LL FIGURE OUT HOW TO DO THAT.
HOWARD?
NO. YOU... YOU'RE NOT...

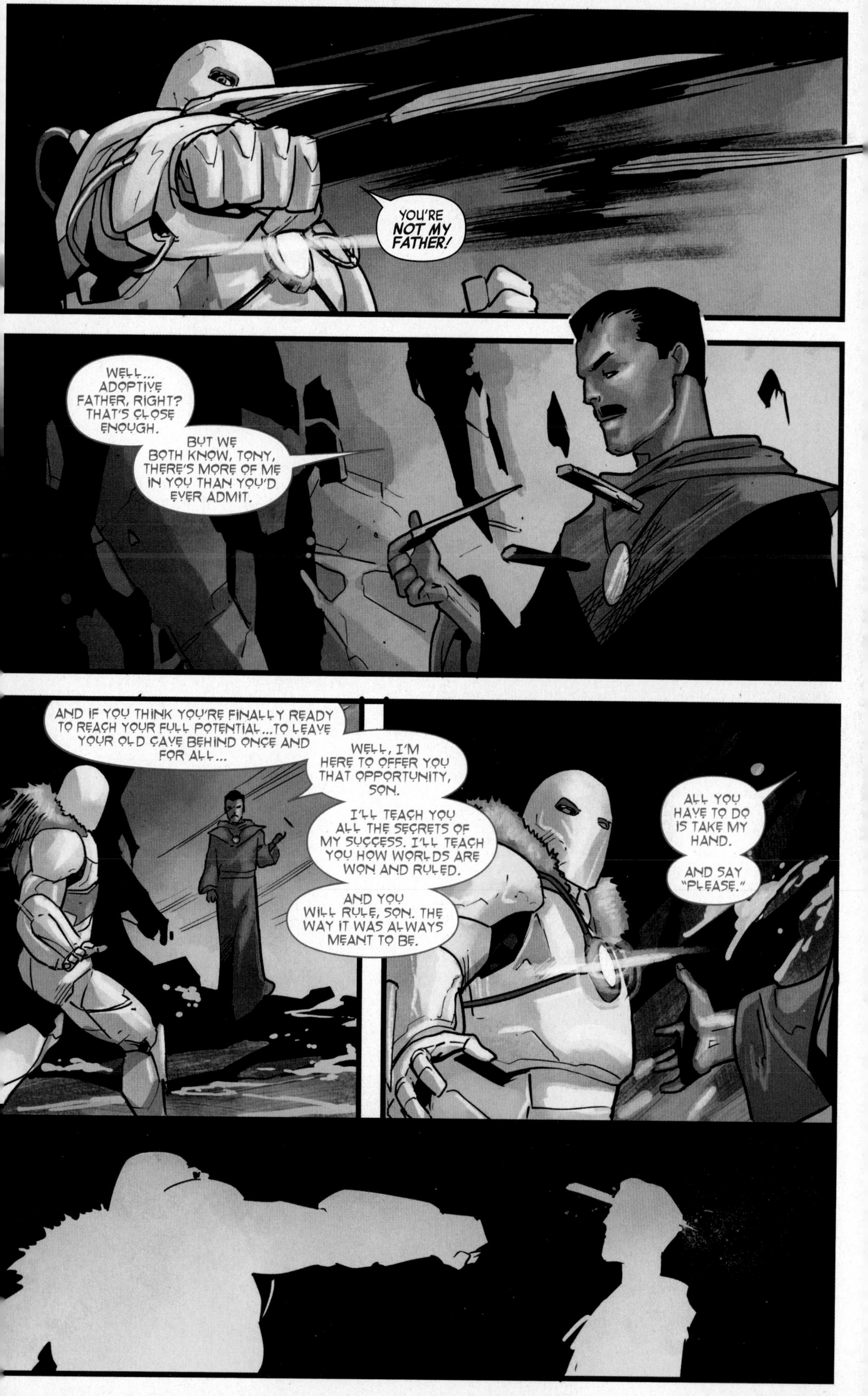
YOU'RE NOT MY FATHER!
WELL... ADOPTIVE FATHER, RIGHT? THAT'S CLOSE ENOUGH.
BUT WE BOTH KNOW, TONY, THERE'S MORE OF ME IN YOU THAN YOU'D EVER ADMIT.
AND IF YOU THINK YOU'RE FINALLY READY TO REACH YOUR FULL POTENTIAL...TO LEAVE YOUR OLD CAVE BEHIND ONCE AND FOR ALL...
WELL, I'M HERE TO OFFER YOU THAT OPPORTUNITY, SON.
I'LL TEACH YOU ALL THE SECRETS OF MY SUCCESS. I'LL TEACH YOU HOW WORLDS ARE WON AND RULED.
AND YOU WILL RULE, SON. THE WAY IT WAS ALWAYS MEANT TO BE.
ALL YOU HAVE TO DO IS TAKE MY HAND.
AND SAY "PLEASE."

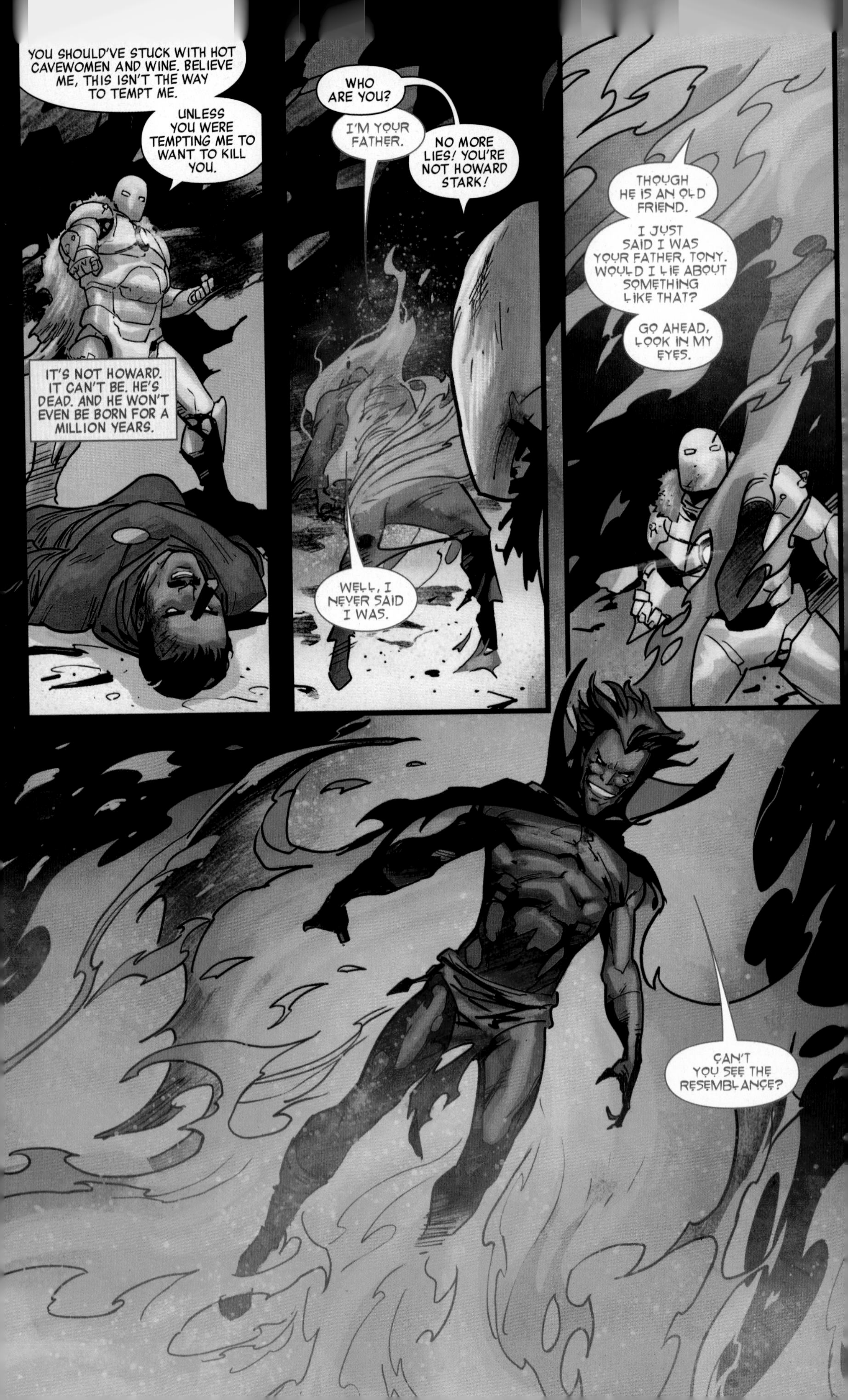
YOU SHOULD'VE STUCK WITH HOT CAVEWOMEN AND WINE. BELIEVE ME, THIS ISN'T THE WAY TO TEMPT ME.
UNLESS YOU WERE TEMPTING ME TO WANT TO KILL YOU.
IT'S NOT HOWARD. IT CAN'T BE. HE'S DEAD. AND HE WON'T EVEN BE BORN FOR A MILLION YEARS.
WHO ARE YOU?
I'M YOUR FATHER.
NO MORE LIES! YOU'RE NOT HOWARD STARK!
WELL, I NEVER SAID I WAS.
THOUGH HE IS AN OLD FRIEND.
I JUST SAID I WAS YOUR FATHER, TONY. WOULD I LIE ABOUT SOMETHING LIKE THAT?
GO AHEAD, LOOK IN MY EYES.
CAN'T YOU SEE THE RESEMBLANCE?

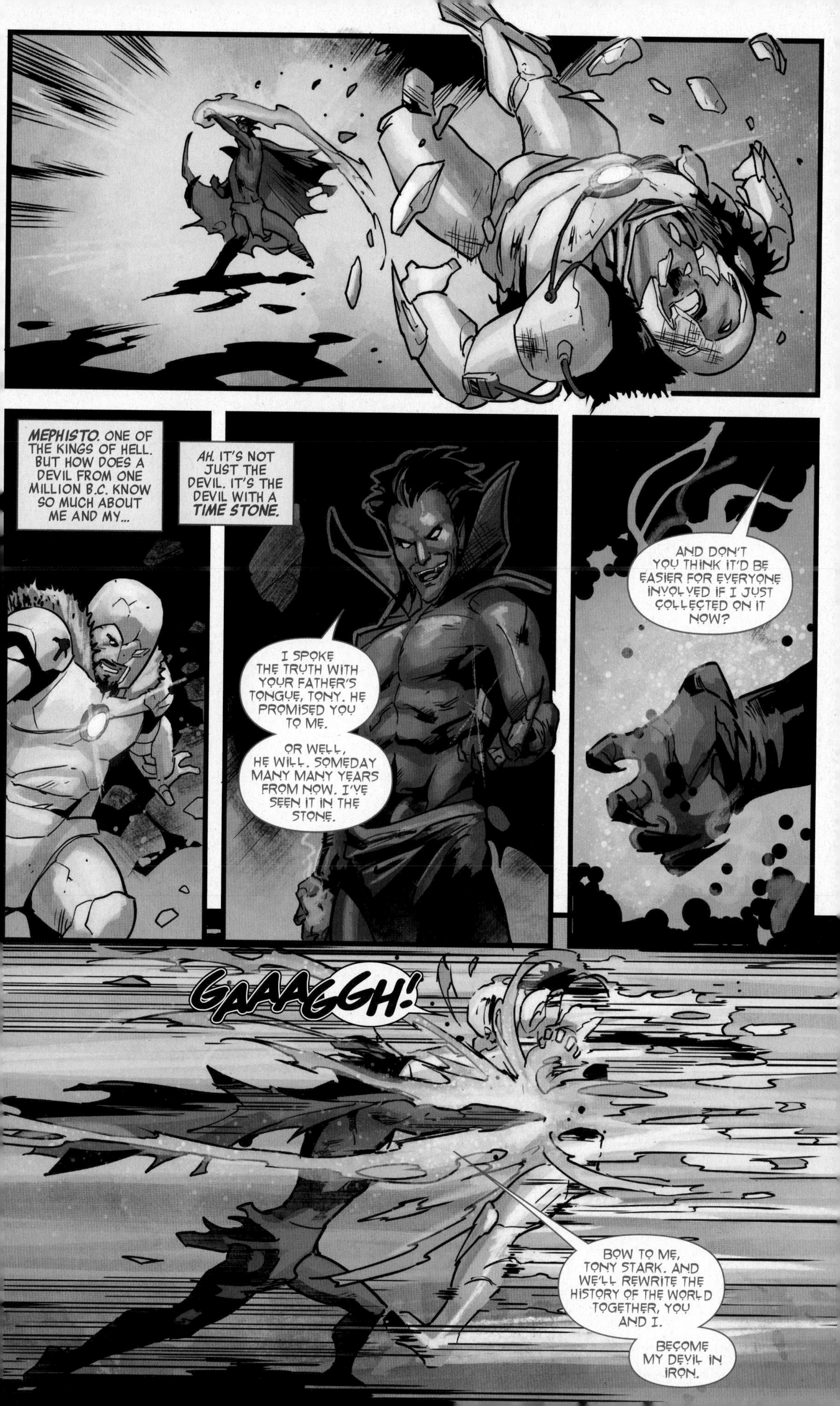
MEPHISTO. ONE OF THE KINGS OF HELL. BUT HOW DOES A DEVIL FROM ONE MILLION B.C. KNOW SO MUCH ABOUT ME AND MY...
AH. IT'S NOT JUST THE DEVIL. IT'S THE DEVIL WITH A TIME STONE.
I SPOKE THE TRUTH WITH YOUR FATHER'S TONGUE, TONY. HE PROMISED YOU TO ME.
OR WELL, HE WILL. SOMEDAY MANY MANY YEARS FROM NOW. I'VE SEEN IT IN THE STONE.
AND DON'T YOU THINK IT'D BE EASIER FOR EVERYONE INVOLVED IF I JUST COLLECTED ON IT NOW?
GAAAGGH!
BOW TO ME, TONY STARK. AND WE'LL REWRITE THE HISTORY OF THE WORLD TOGETHER, YOU AND I.
BECOME MY DEVIL IN IRON.

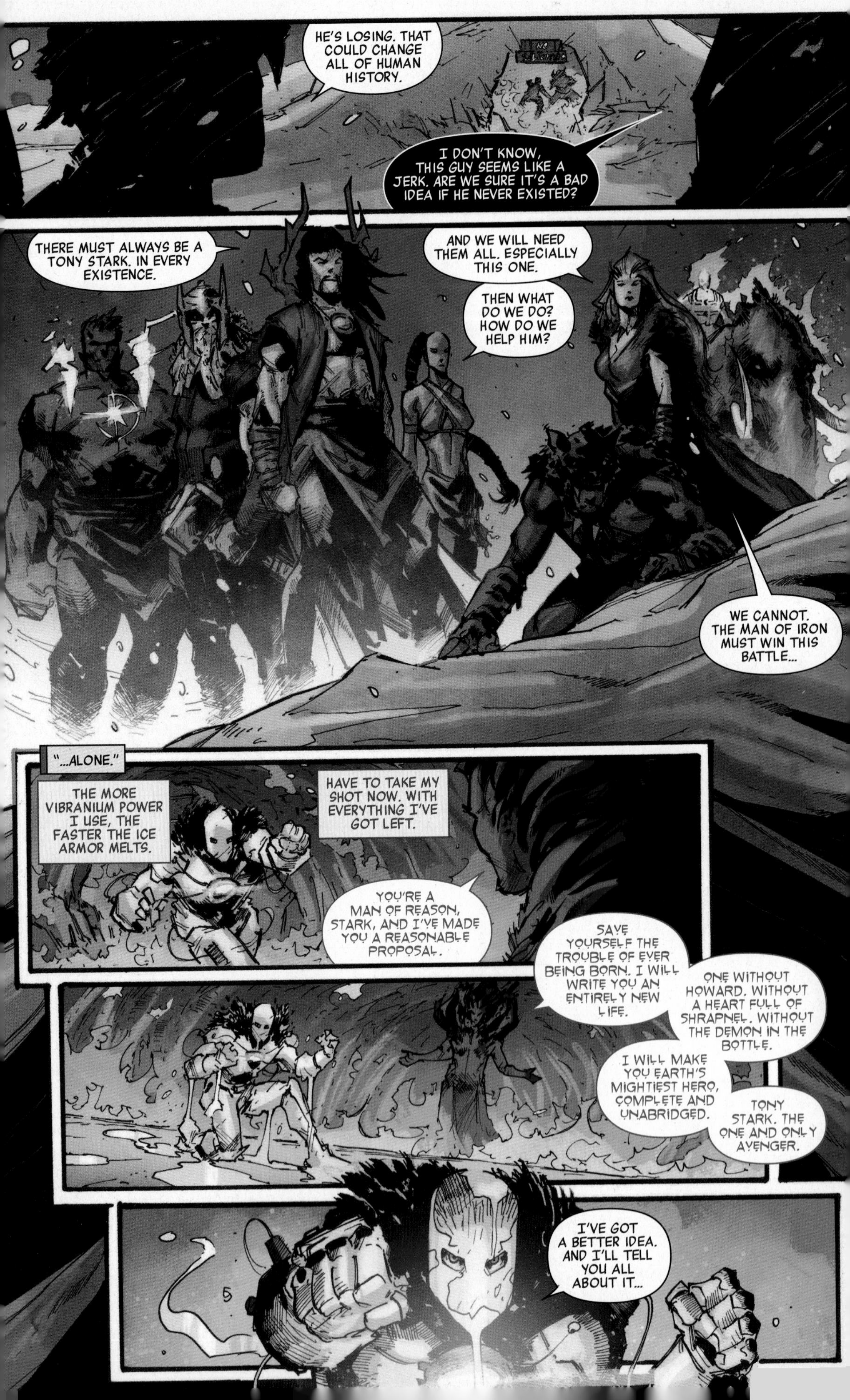
HE'S LOSING. THAT COULD CHANGE ALL OF HUMAN HISTORY.
I DON'T KNOW, THIS GUY SEEMS LIKE A JERK. ARE WE SURE IT'S A BAD IDEA IF HE NEVER EXISTED?
THERE MUST ALWAYS BE A TONY STARK. IN EVERY EXISTENCE.
AND WE WILL NEED THEM ALL. ESPECIALLY THIS ONE.
THEN WHAT DO WE DO? HOW DO WE HELP HIM?
WE CANNOT. THE MAN OF IRON MUST WIN THIS BATTLE...
"...ALONE."
THE MORE VIBRANIUM POWER I USE, THE FASTER THE ICE ARMOR MELTS.
HAVE TO TAKE MY SHOT NOW. WITH EVERYTHING I'VE GOT LEFT.
YOU'RE A MAN OF REASON, STARK, AND I'VE MADE YOU A REASONABLE PROPOSAL.
SAVE YOURSELF THE TROUBLE OF EVER BEING BORN. I WILL WRITE YOU AN ENTIRELY NEW LIFE.
ONE WITHOUT HOWARD. WITHOUT A HEART FULL OF SHRAPNEL. WITHOUT THE DEMON IN THE BOTTLE.
I WILL MAKE YOU EARTH'S MIGHTIEST HERO, COMPLETE AND UNABRIDGED.
TONY STARK. THE ONE AND ONLY AVENGER.
I'VE GOT A BETTER IDEA. AND I'LL TELL YOU ALL ABOUT IT...

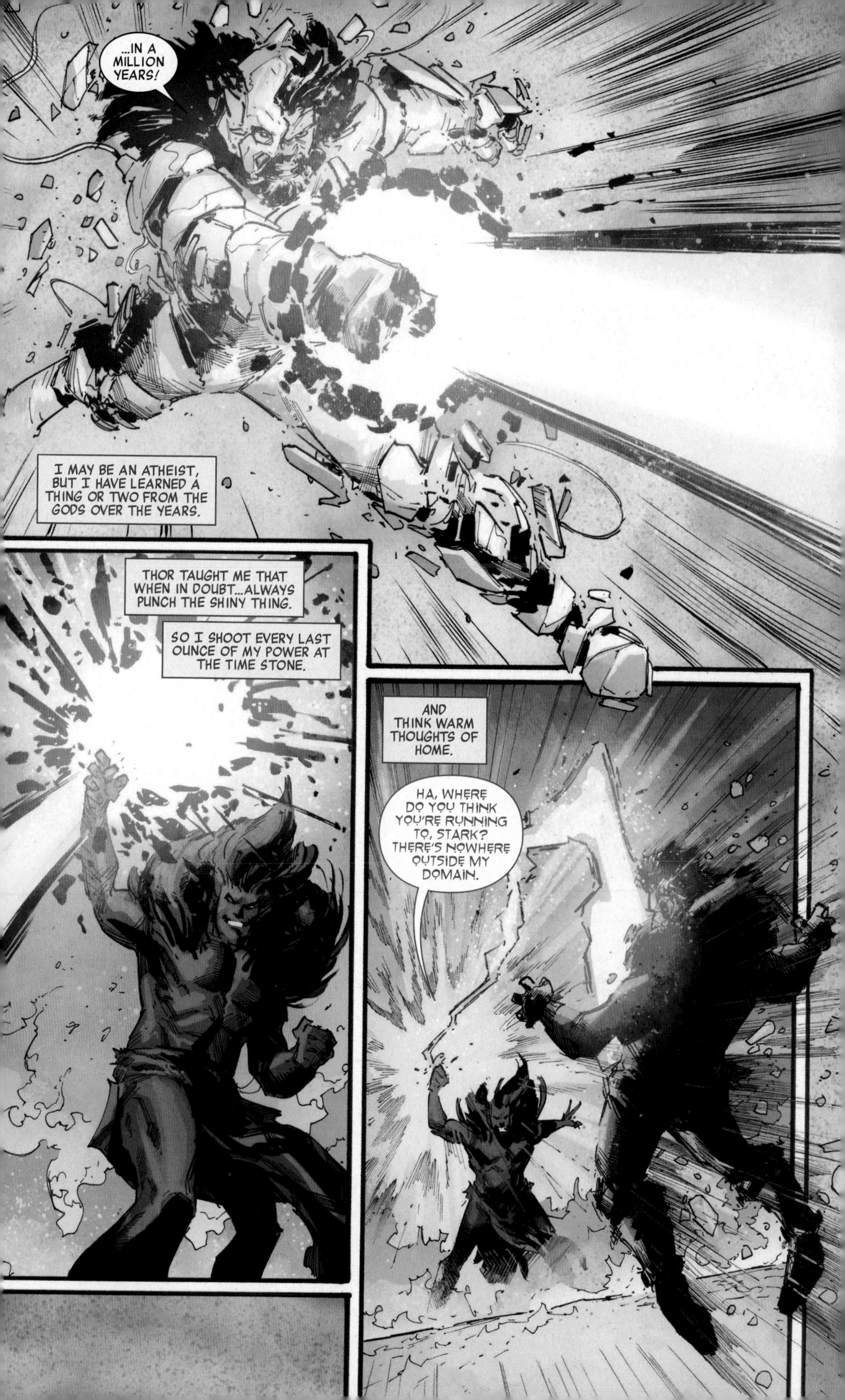

...IN A MILLION YEARS!
I MAY BE AN ATHEIST, BUT I HAVE LEARNED A THING OR TWO FROM THE GODS OVER THE YEARS.
THOR TAUGHT ME THAT WHEN IN DOUBT...ALWAYS PUNCH THE SHINY THING.
SO I SHOOT EVERY LAST OUNCE OF MY POWER AT THE TIME STONE.
AND THINK WARM THOUGHTS OF HOME.
HA, WHERE DO YOU THINK YOU'RE RUNNING TO, STARK? THERE'S NOWHERE OUTSIDE MY DOMAIN.

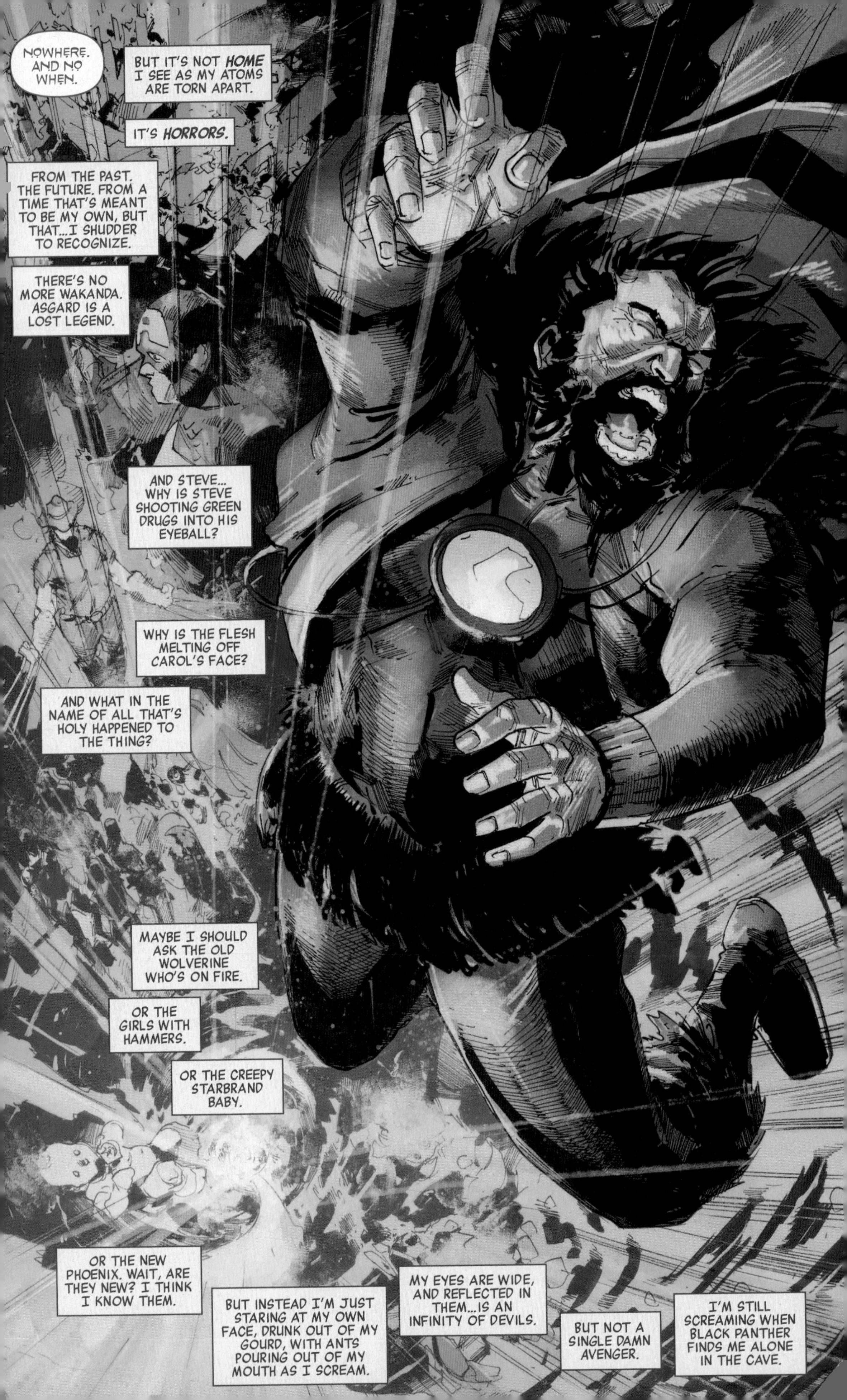

NOWHERE. AND NO WHEN.
BUT IT'S NOT HOME I SEE AS MY ATOMS ARE TORN APART.
IT'S HORRORS.
FROM THE PAST. THE FUTURE. FROM A TIME THAT'S MEANT TO BE MY OWN, BUT THAT...I SHUDDER TO RECOGNIZE.
THERE'S NO MORE WAKANDA. ASGARD IS A LOST LEGEND.
AND STEVE... WHY IS STEVE SHOOTING GREEN DRUGS INTO HIS EYEBALL?
WHY IS THE FLESH MELTING OFF CAROL'S FACE?
AND WHAT IN THE NAME OF ALL THAT'S HOLY HAPPENED TO THE THING?
MAYBE I SHOULD ASK THE OLD WOLVERINE WHO'S ON FIRE.
OR THE GIRLS WITH HAMMERS.
OR THE CREEPY STARBRAND BABY.
OR THE NEW PHOENIX. WAIT, ARE THEY NEW? I THINK I KNOW THEM.
BUT INSTEAD I'M JUST STARING AT MY OWN FACE, DRUNK OUT OF MY GOURD, WITH ANTS POURING OUT OF MY MOUTH AS I SCREAM.
MY EYES ARE WIDE, AND REFLECTED IN THEM...IS AN INFINITY OF DEVILS.
BUT NOT A SINGLE DAMN AVENGER.
I'M STILL SCREAMING WHEN BLACK PANTHER FINDS ME ALONE IN THE CAVE.

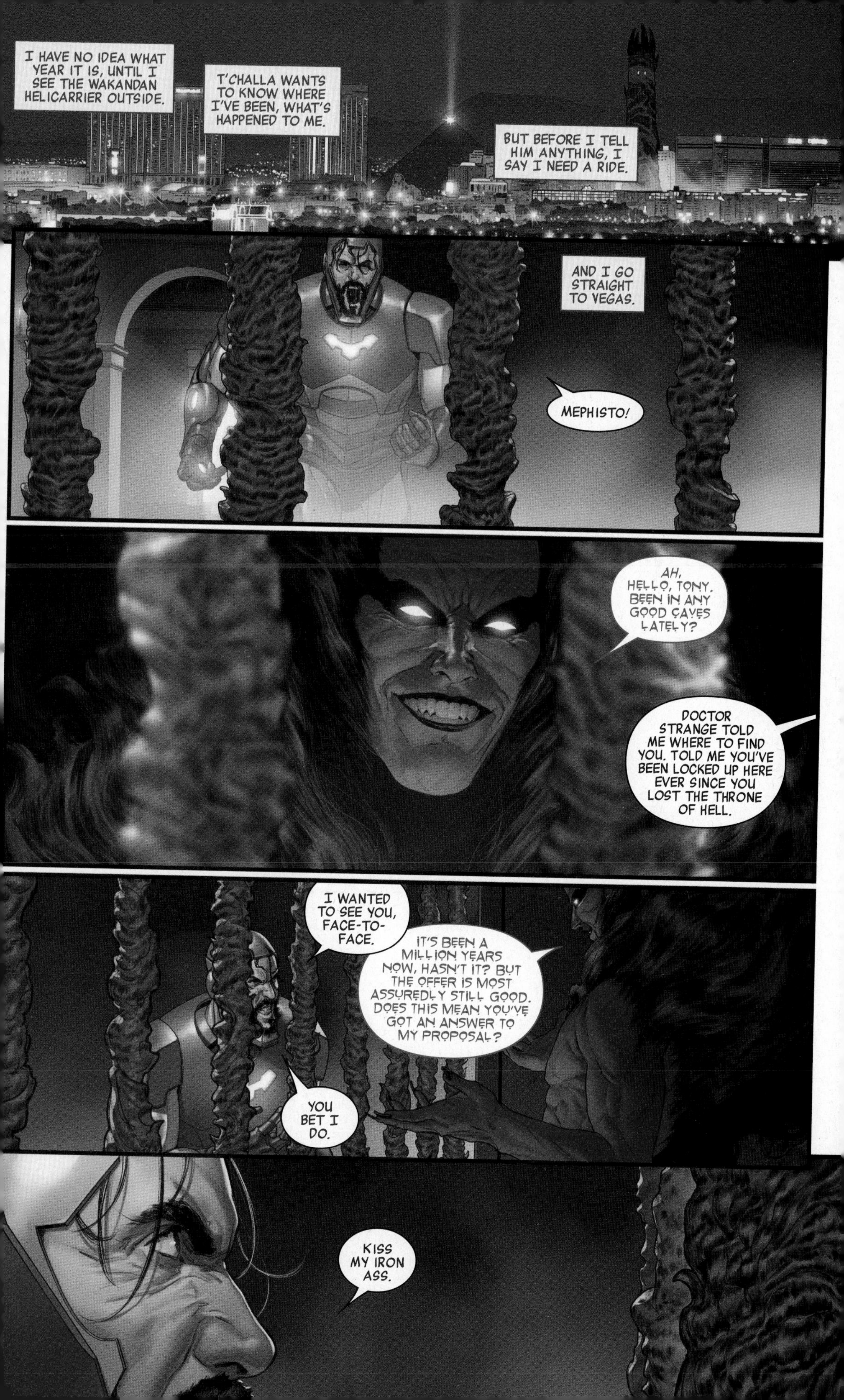
I HAVE NO IDEA WHAT YEAR IT IS, UNTIL I SEE THE WAKANDAN HELICARRIER OUTSIDE.
T'CHALLA WANTS TO KNOW WHERE I'VE BEEN, WHAT'S HAPPENED TO ME.
BUT BEFORE I TELL HIM ANYTHING, I SAY I NEED A RIDE.
AND I GO STRAIGHT TO VEGAS.
MEPHISTO!
AH, HELLO, TONY. BEEN IN ANY GOOD CAVES LATELY?
DOCTOR STRANGE TOLD ME WHERE TO FIND YOU. TOLD ME YOU'VE BEEN LOCKED UP HERE EVER SINCE YOU LOST THE THRONE OF HELL.
I WANTED TO SEE YOU, FACE-TO-FACE.
IT'S BEEN A MILLION YEARS NOW, HASN'T IT? BUT THE OFFER IS MOST ASSUREDLY STILL GOOD. DOES THIS MEAN YOU'VE GOT AN ANSWER TO MY PROPOSAL?
YOU BET I DO.
KISS MY IRON ASS.

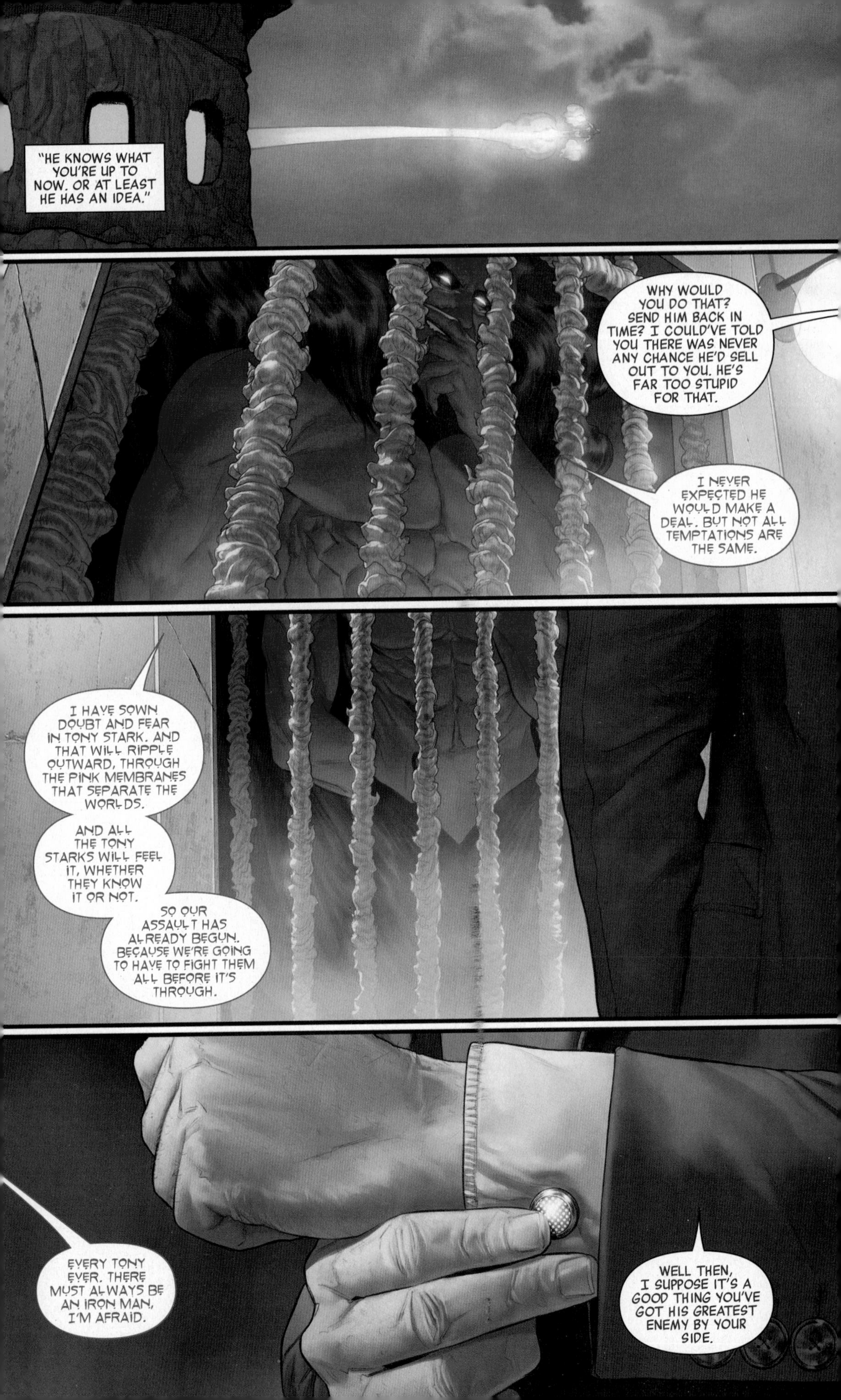
"HE KNOWS WHAT YOU'RE UP TO NOW. OR AT LEAST HE HAS AN IDEA."
WHY WOULD YOU DO THAT? SEND HIM BACK IN TIME? I COULD'VE TOLD YOU THERE WAS NEVER ANY CHANCE HE'D SELL OUT TO YOU. HE'S FAR TOO STUPID FOR THAT.
I NEVER EXPECTED HE WOULD MAKE A DEAL. BUT NOT ALL TEMPTATIONS ARE THE SAME.
I HAVE SOWN DOUBT AND FEAR IN TONY STARK. AND THAT WILL RIPPLE OUTWARD, THROUGH THE PINK MEMBRANES THAT SEPARATE THE WORLDS.
AND ALL THE TONY STARKS WILL FEEL IT, WHETHER THEY KNOW IT OR NOT.
SO OUR ASSAULT HAS ALREADY BEGUN. BECAUSE WE'RE GOING TO HAVE TO FIGHT THEM ALL BEFORE IT'S THROUGH.
EVERY TONY EVER. THERE MUST ALWAYS BE AN IRON MAN, I'M AFRAID.
WELL THEN, I SUPPOSE IT'S A GOOD THING YOU'VE GOT HIS GREATEST ENEMY BY YOUR SIDE.

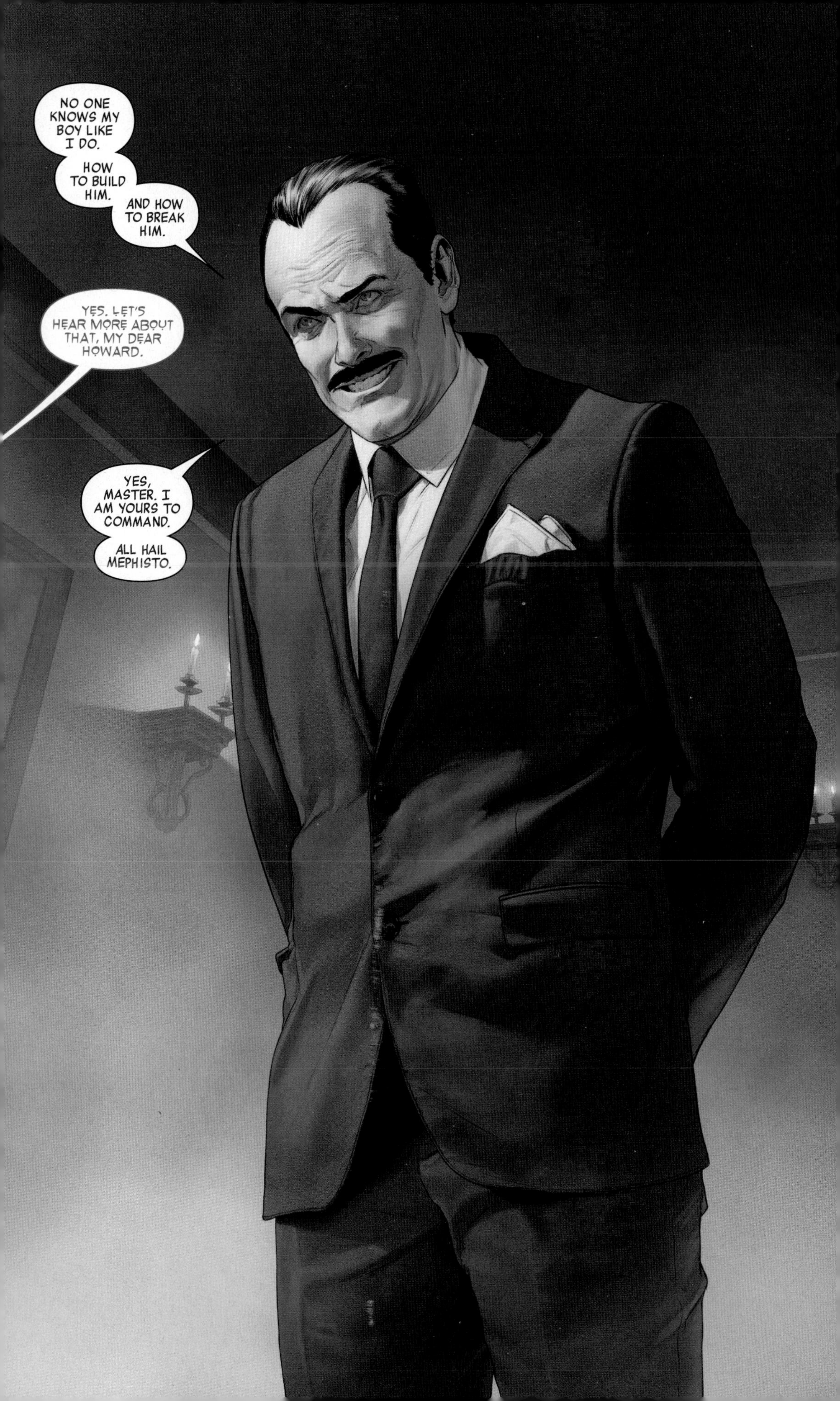
NO ONE KNOWS MY BOY LIKE I DO.
HOW TO BUILD HIM.
AND HOW TO BREAK HIM.
YES. LET'S HEAR MORE ABOUT THAT, MY DEAR HOWARD.
YES, MASTER. I AM YOURS TO COMMAND.
ALL HAIL MEPHISTO.

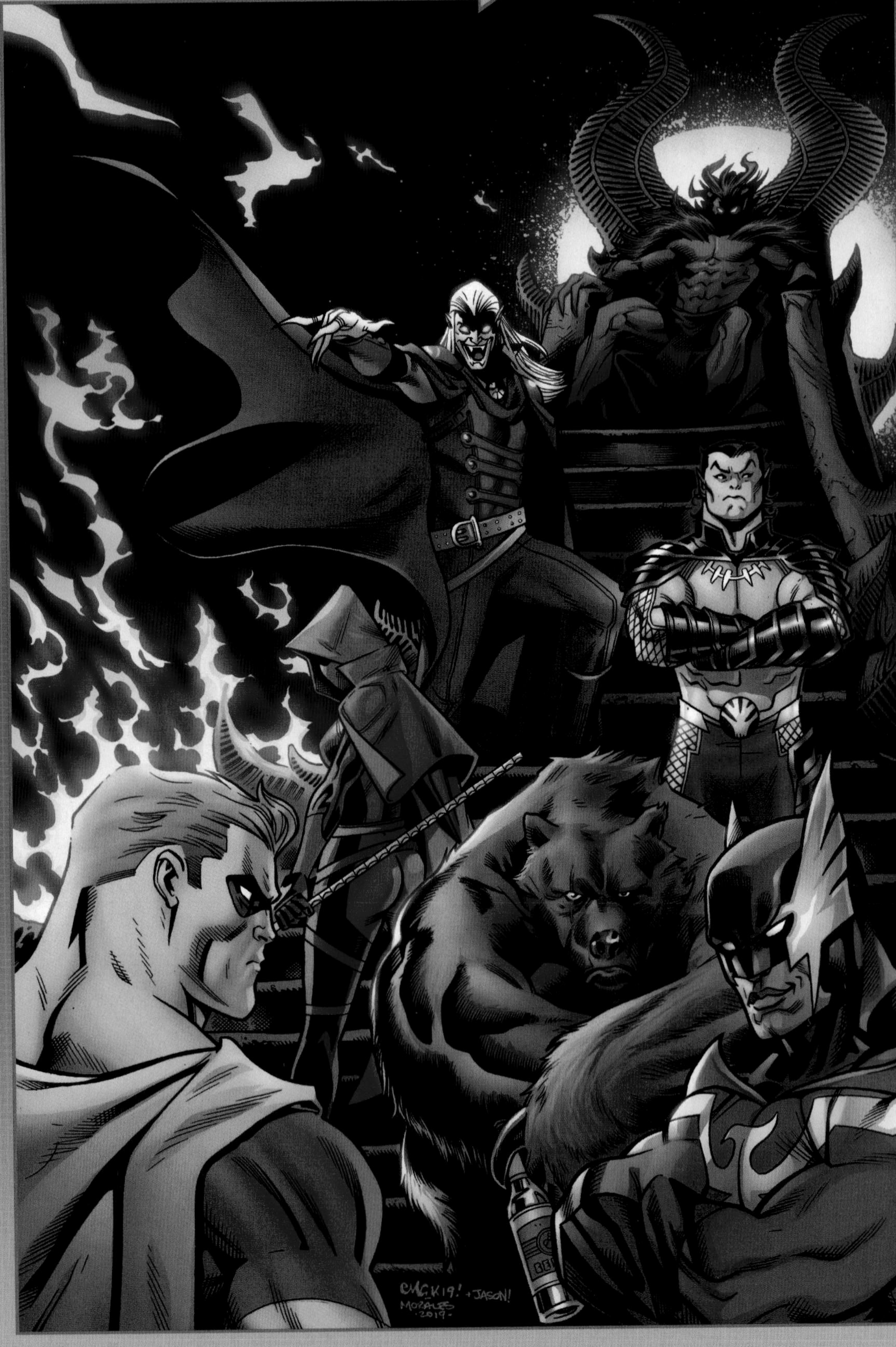

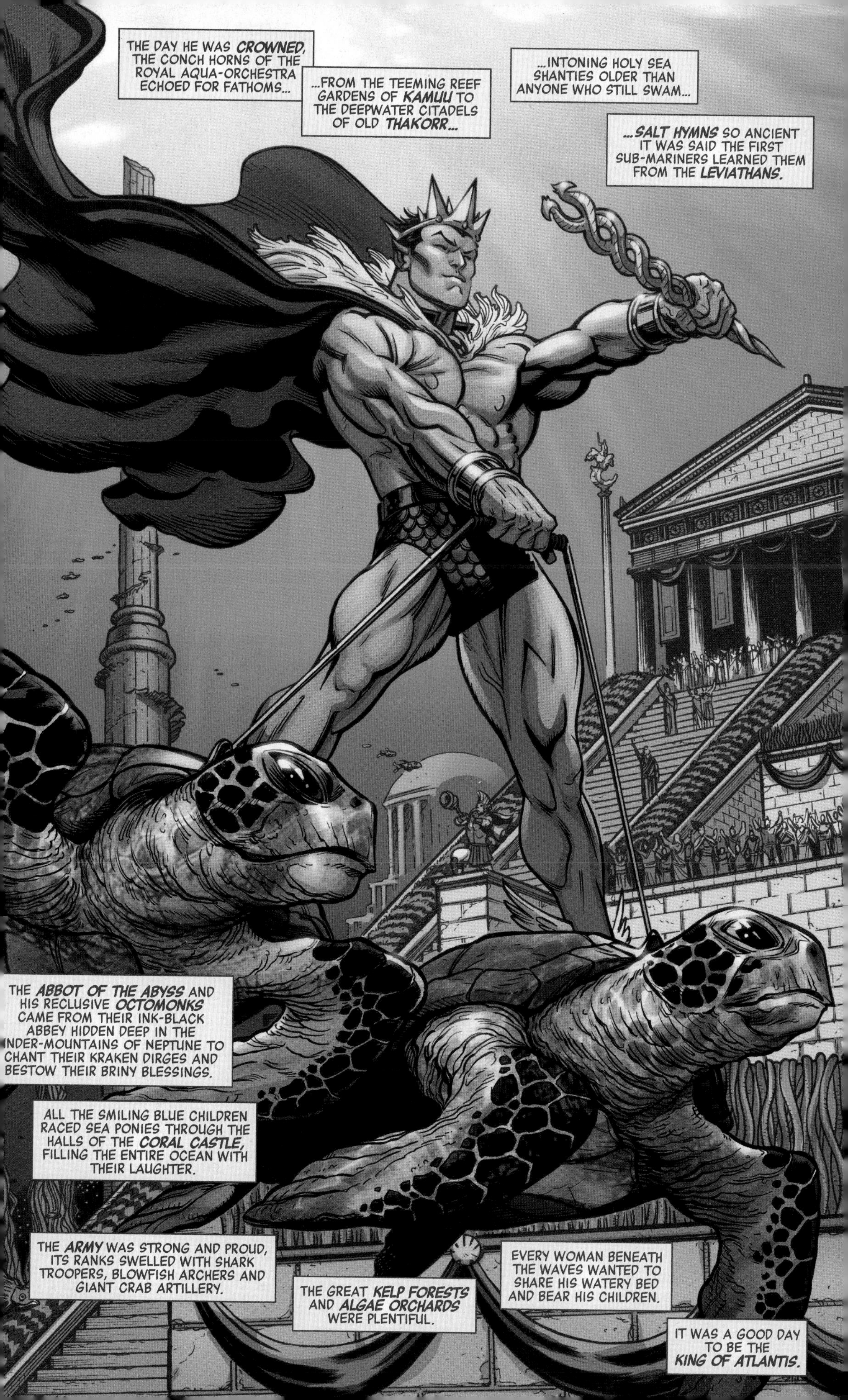
THE DAY HE WAS CROWNED, THE CONCH HORNS OF THE ROYAL AQUA-ORCHESTRA ECHOED FOR FATHOMS...
...FROM THE TEEMING REEF GARDENS OF KAMUU TO THE DEEPWATER CITADELS OF OLD THAKORR...
...INTONING HOLY SEA SHANTIES OLDER THAN ANYONE WHO STILL SWAM...
...SALT HYMNS SO ANCIENT IT WAS SAID THE FIRST SUB-MARINERS LEARNED THEM FROM THE LEVIATHANS.
THE ABBOT OF THE ABYSS AND HIS RECLUSIVE OCTOMONKS CAME FROM THEIR INK-BLACK ABBEY HIDDEN DEEP IN THE NDER-MOUNTAINS OF NEPTUNE TO CHANT THEIR KRAKEN DIRGES AND BESTOW THEIR BRINY BLESSINGS.
ALL THE SMILING BLUE CHILDREN RACED SEA PONIES THROUGH THE HALLS OF THE CORAL CASTLE, FILLING THE ENTIRE OCEAN WITH THEIR LAUGHTER.
THE ARMY WAS STRONG AND PROUD, ITS RANKS SWELLED WITH SHARK TROOPERS, BLOWFISH ARCHERS AND GIANT CRAB ARTILLERY.
THE GREAT KELP FORESTS AND ALGAE ORCHARDS WERE PLENTIFUL.
EVERY WOMAN BENEATH THE WAVES WANTED TO SHARE HIS WATERY BED AND BEAR HIS CHILDREN.
IT WAS A GOOD DAY TO BE THE KING OF ATLANTIS.

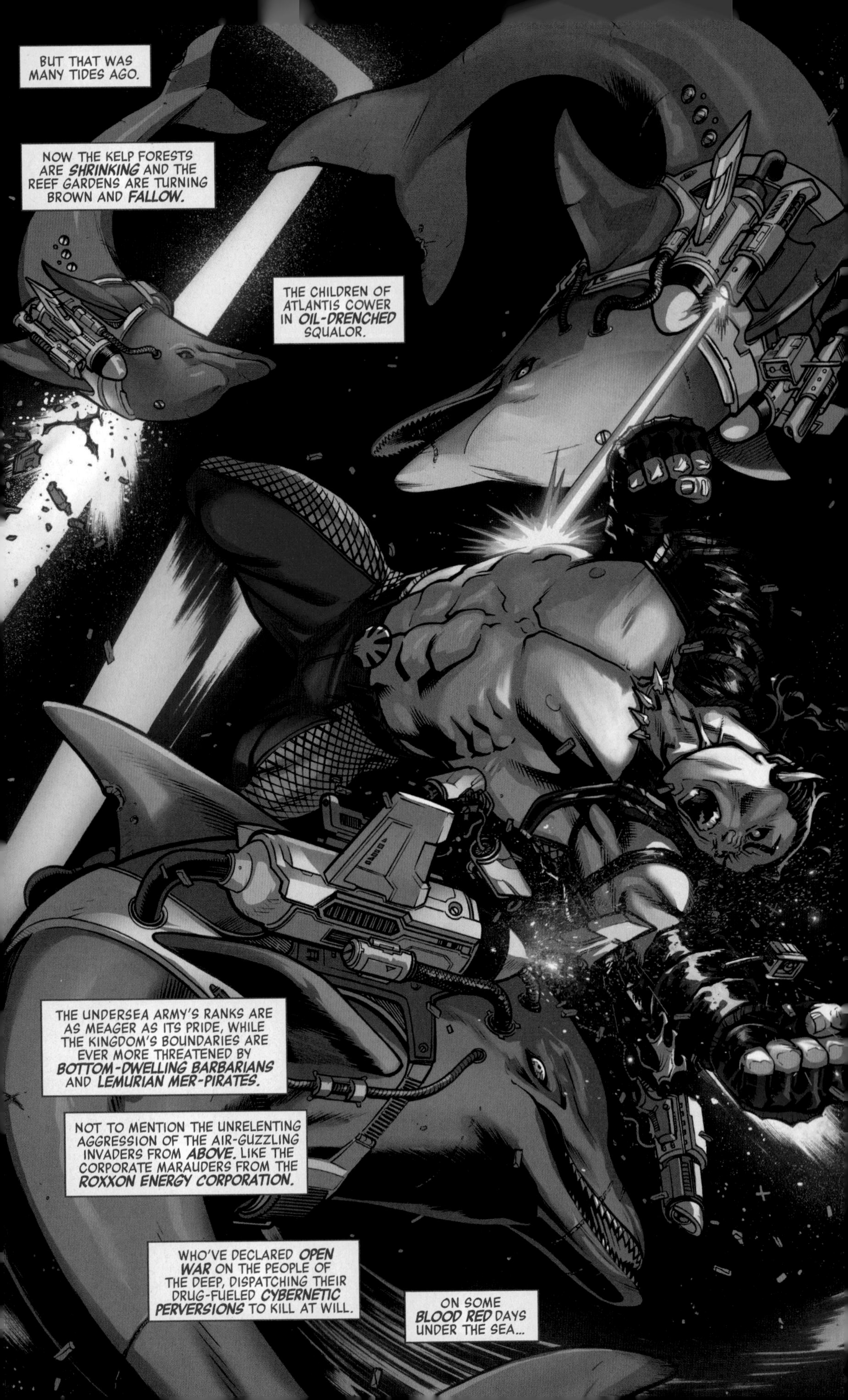
BUT THAT WAS MANY TIDES AGO.
NOW THE KELP FORESTS ARE SHRINKING AND THE REEF GARDENS ARE TURNING BROWN AND FALLOW.
THE CHILDREN OF ATLANTIS COWER IN OIL-DRENCHED SQUALOR.
THE UNDERSEA ARMY'S RANKS ARE AS MEAGER AS ITS PRIDE, WHILE THE KINGDOM'S BOUNDARIES ARE EVER MORE THREATENED BY BOTTOM-DWELLING BARBARIANS AND LEMURIAN MER-PIRATES.
NOT TO MENTION THE UNRELENTING AGGRESSION OF THE AIR-GUZZLING INVADERS FROM ABOVE. LIKE THE CORPORATE MARAUDERS FROM THE ROXXON ENERGY CORPORATION.
WHO'VE DECLARED OPEN WAR ON THE PEOPLE OF THE DEEP, DISPATCHING THEIR DRUG-FUELED CYBERNETIC PERVERSIONS TO KILL AT WILL.
ON SOME BLOOD RED DAYS UNDER THE SEA...

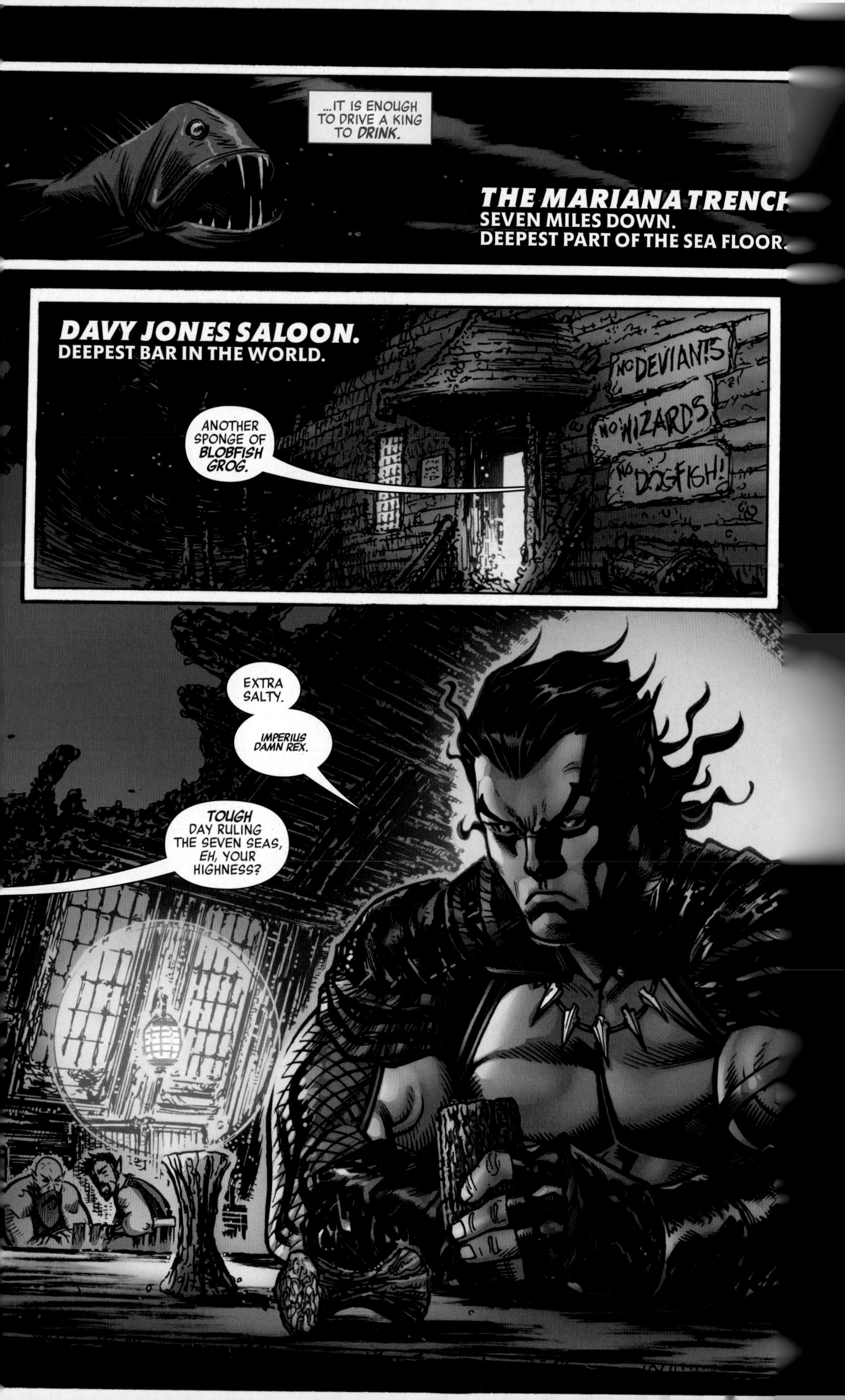
...IT IS ENOUGH TO DRIVE A KING TO DRINK.
THE MARIANA TRENCH
SEVEN MILES DOWN.
DEEPEST PART OF THE SEA FLOOR.
DAVY JONES SALOON.
DEEPEST BAR IN THE WORLD.
ANOTHER SPONGE OF BLOBFISH GROG.
NO DEVIANTS
NO WIZARDS
NO DOGFISH!
EXTRA SALTY.
IMPERIUS DAMN REX.
TOUGH DAY RULING THE SEVEN SEAS, EH, YOUR HIGHNESS?

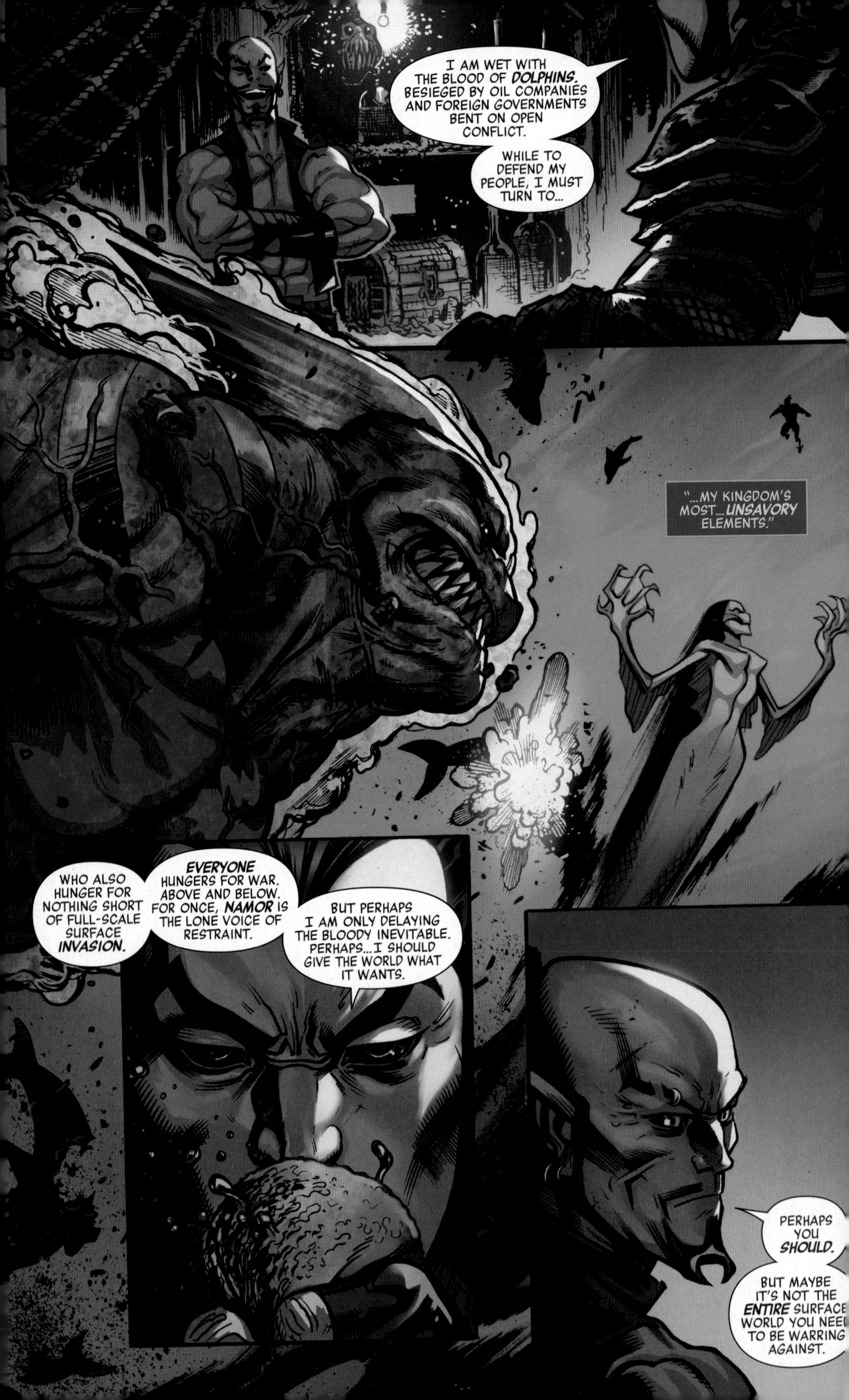

I AM WET WITH THE BLOOD OF DOLPHINS. BESIEGED BY OIL COMPANIES AND FOREIGN GOVERNMENTS BENT ON OPEN CONFLICT.
WHILE TO DEFEND MY PEOPLE, I MUST TURN TO...
"...MY KINGDOM'S MOST...UNSAVORY ELEMENTS."
WHO ALSO HUNGER FOR NOTHING SHORT OF FULL-SCALE SURFACE INVASION.
EVERYONE HUNGERS FOR WAR. ABOVE AND BELOW. FOR ONCE, NAMOR IS THE LONE VOICE OF RESTRAINT.
BUT PERHAPS I AM ONLY DELAYING THE BLOODY INEVITABLE. PERHAPS...I SHOULD GIVE THE WORLD WHAT IT WANTS.
PERHAPS YOU SHOULD.
BUT MAYBE IT'S NOT THE ENTIRE SURFACE WORLD YOU NEED TO BE WARRING AGAINST.

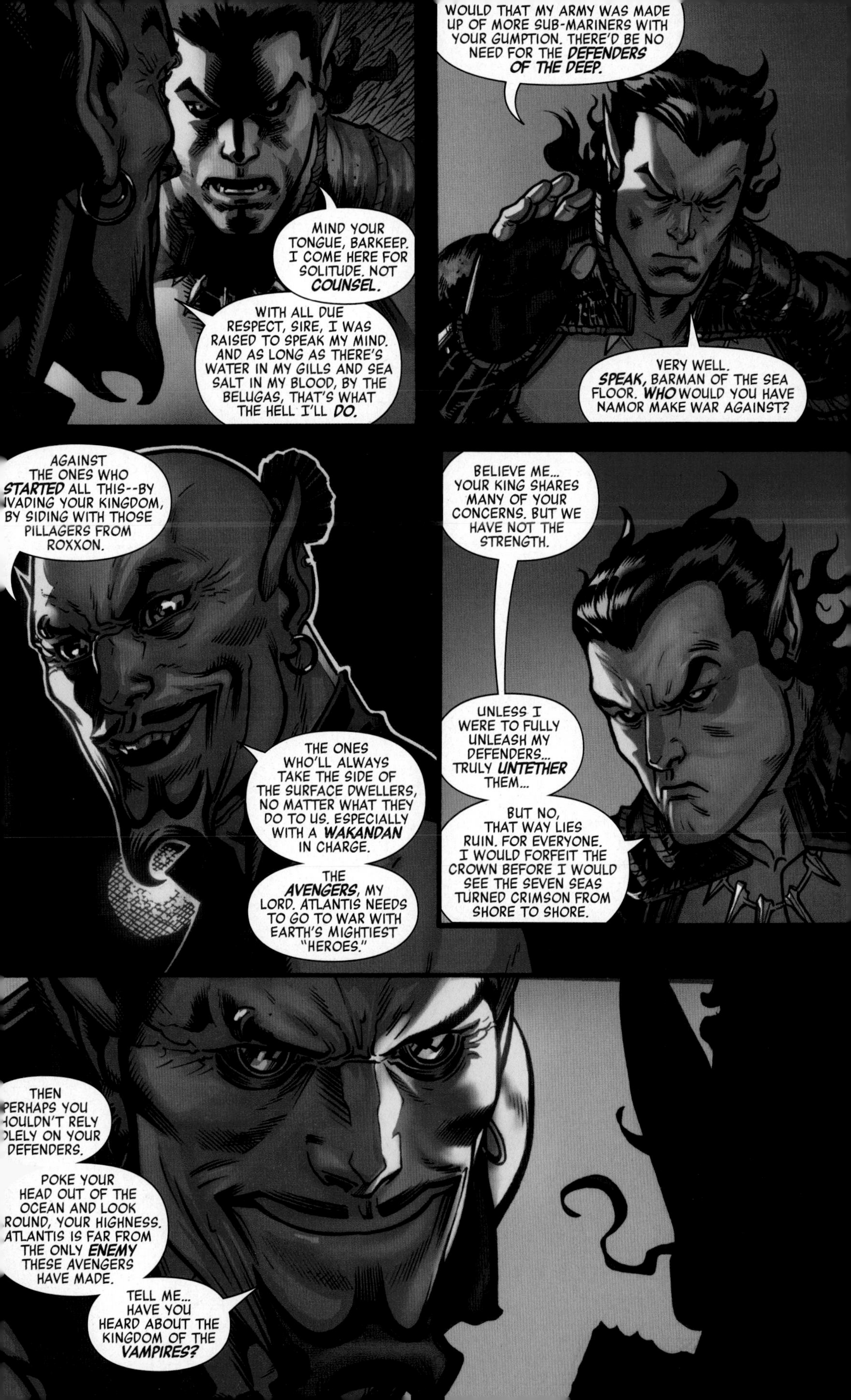
MIND YOUR TONGUE, BARKEEP. I COME HERE FOR SOLITUDE. NOT COUNSEL.
WITH ALL DUE RESPECT, SIRE, I WAS RAISED TO SPEAK MY MIND. AND AS LONG AS THERE'S WATER IN MY GILLS AND SEA SALT IN MY BLOOD, BY THE BELUGAS, THAT'S WHAT THE HELL I'LL DO.
WOULD THAT MY ARMY WAS MADE UP OF MORE SUB-MARINERS WITH YOUR GUMPTION. THERE'D BE NO NEED FOR THE DEFENDERS OF THE DEEP.
VERY WELL. SPEAK, BARMAN OF THE SEA FLOOR. WHO WOULD YOU HAVE NAMOR MAKE WAR AGAINST?
AGAINST THE ONES WHO STARTED ALL THIS--BY IVADING YOUR KINGDOM, BY SIDING WITH THOSE PILLAGERS FROM ROXXON.
THE ONES WHO'LL ALWAYS TAKE THE SIDE OF THE SURFACE DWELLERS, NO MATTER WHAT THEY DO TO US. ESPECIALLY WITH A WAKANDAN IN CHARGE.
THE AVENGERS, MY LORD. ATLANTIS NEEDS TO GO TO WAR WITH EARTH'S MIGHTIEST "HEROES."
BELIEVE ME... YOUR KING SHARES MANY OF YOUR CONCERNS. BUT WE HAVE NOT THE STRENGTH.
UNLESS I WERE TO FULLY UNLEASH MY DEFENDERS... TRULY UNTETHER THEM...
BUT NO, THAT WAY LIES RUIN. FOR EVERYONE. I WOULD FORFEIT THE CROWN BEFORE I WOULD SEE THE SEVEN SEAS TURNED CRIMSON FROM SHORE TO SHORE.
THEN PERHAPS YOU HOULDN'T RELY OLELY ON YOUR DEFENDERS.
POKE YOUR HEAD OUT OF THE OCEAN AND LOOK ROUND, YOUR HIGHNESS. ATLANTIS IS FAR FROM THE ONLY ENEMY THESE AVENGERS HAVE MADE.
TELL ME... HAVE YOU HEARD ABOUT THE KINGDOM OF THE VAMPIRES?

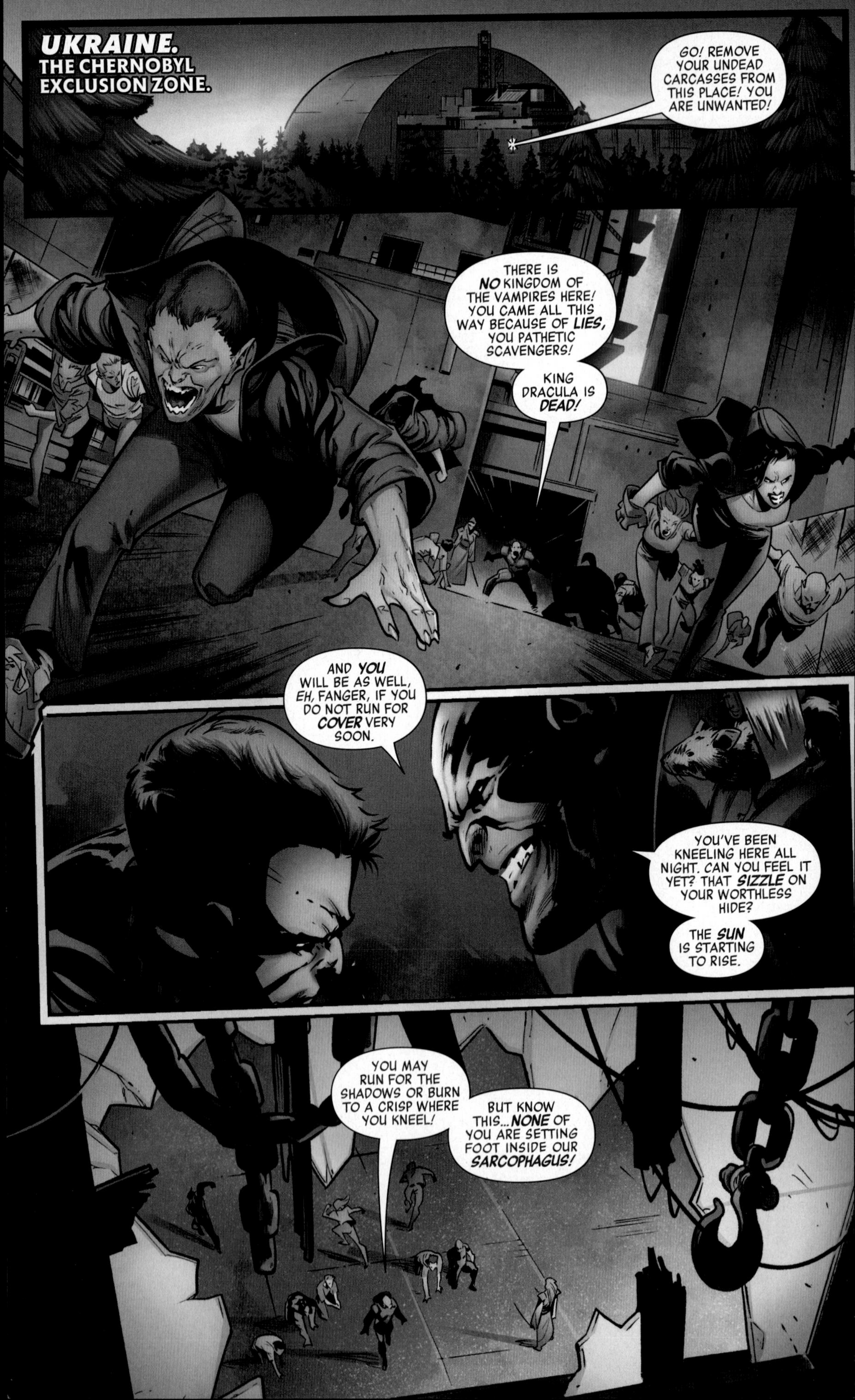
UKRAINE.
THE CHERNOBYL EXCLUSION ZONE.
GO! REMOVE YOUR UNDEAD CARCASSES FROM THIS PLACE! YOU ARE UNWANTED!
THERE IS NO KINGDOM OF THE VAMPIRES HERE! YOU CAME ALL THIS WAY BECAUSE OF LIES, YOU PATHETIC SCAVENGERS!
KING DRACULA IS DEAD!
AND YOU WILL BE AS WELL, EH, FANGER, IF YOU DO NOT RUN FOR COVER VERY SOON.
YOU'VE BEEN KNEELING HERE ALL NIGHT. CAN YOU FEEL IT YET? THAT SIZZLE ON YOUR WORTHLESS HIDE?
THE SUN IS STARTING TO RISE.
YOU MAY RUN FOR THE SHADOWS OR BURN TO A CRISP WHERE YOU KNEEL!
BUT KNOW THIS... NONE OF YOU ARE SETTING FOOT INSIDE OUR SARCOPHAGUS!

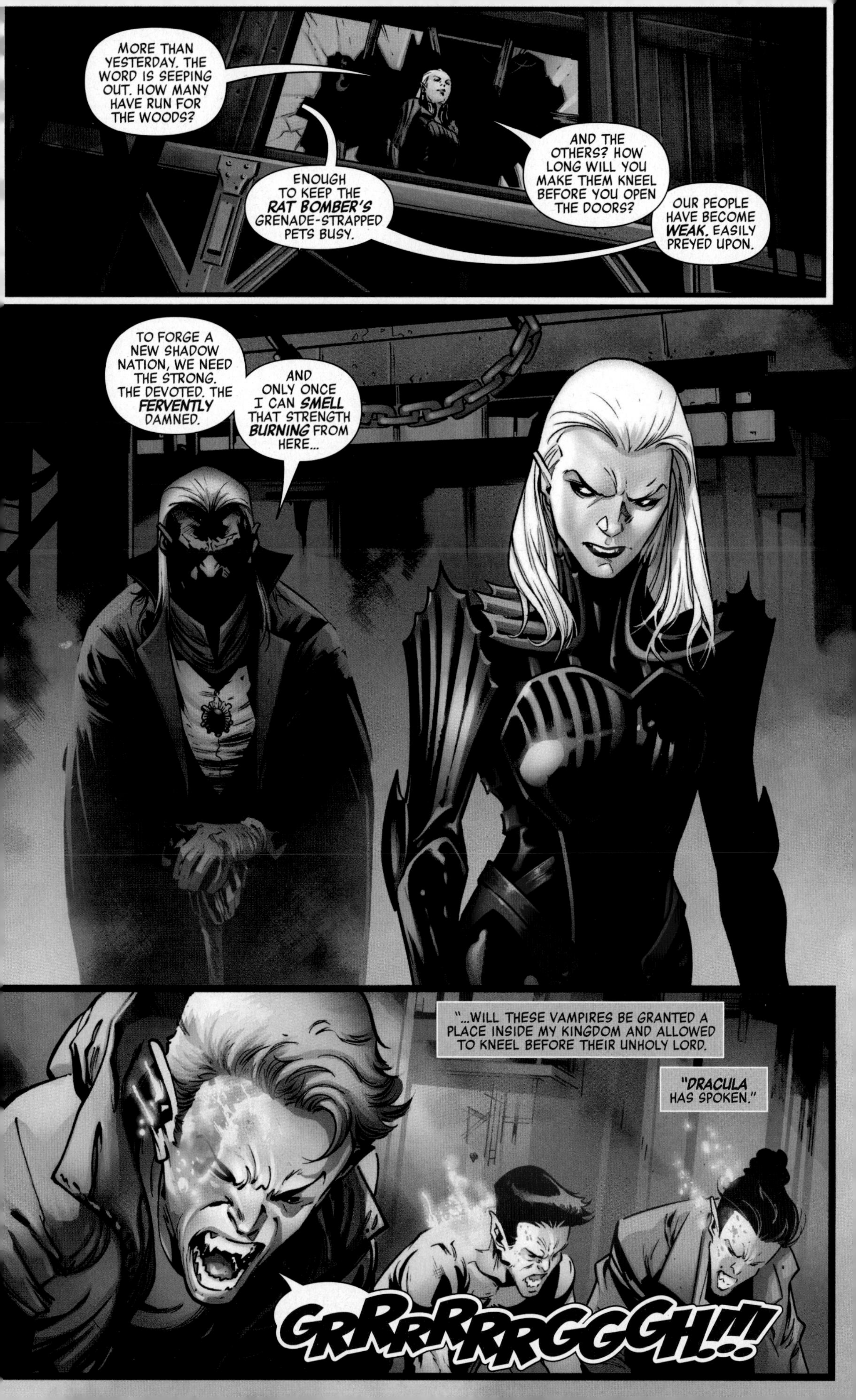
MORE THAN YESTERDAY. THE WORD IS SEEPING OUT. HOW MANY HAVE RUN FOR THE WOODS?
ENOUGH TO KEEP THE RAT BOMBER'S GRENADE-STRAPPED PETS BUSY.
AND THE OTHERS? HOW LONG WILL YOU MAKE THEM KNEEL BEFORE YOU OPEN THE DOORS?
OUR PEOPLE HAVE BECOME WEAK. EASILY PREYED UPON.
TO FORGE A NEW SHADOW NATION, WE NEED THE STRONG. THE DEVOTED. THE FERVENTLY DAMNED.
AND ONLY ONCE I CAN SMELL THAT STRENGTH BURNING FROM HERE...
"...WILL THESE VAMPIRES BE GRANTED A PLACE INSIDE MY KINGDOM AND ALLOWED TO KNEEL BEFORE THEIR UNHOLY LORD.
"DRACULA HAS SPOKEN."
GRRRRRRGGGH!!!

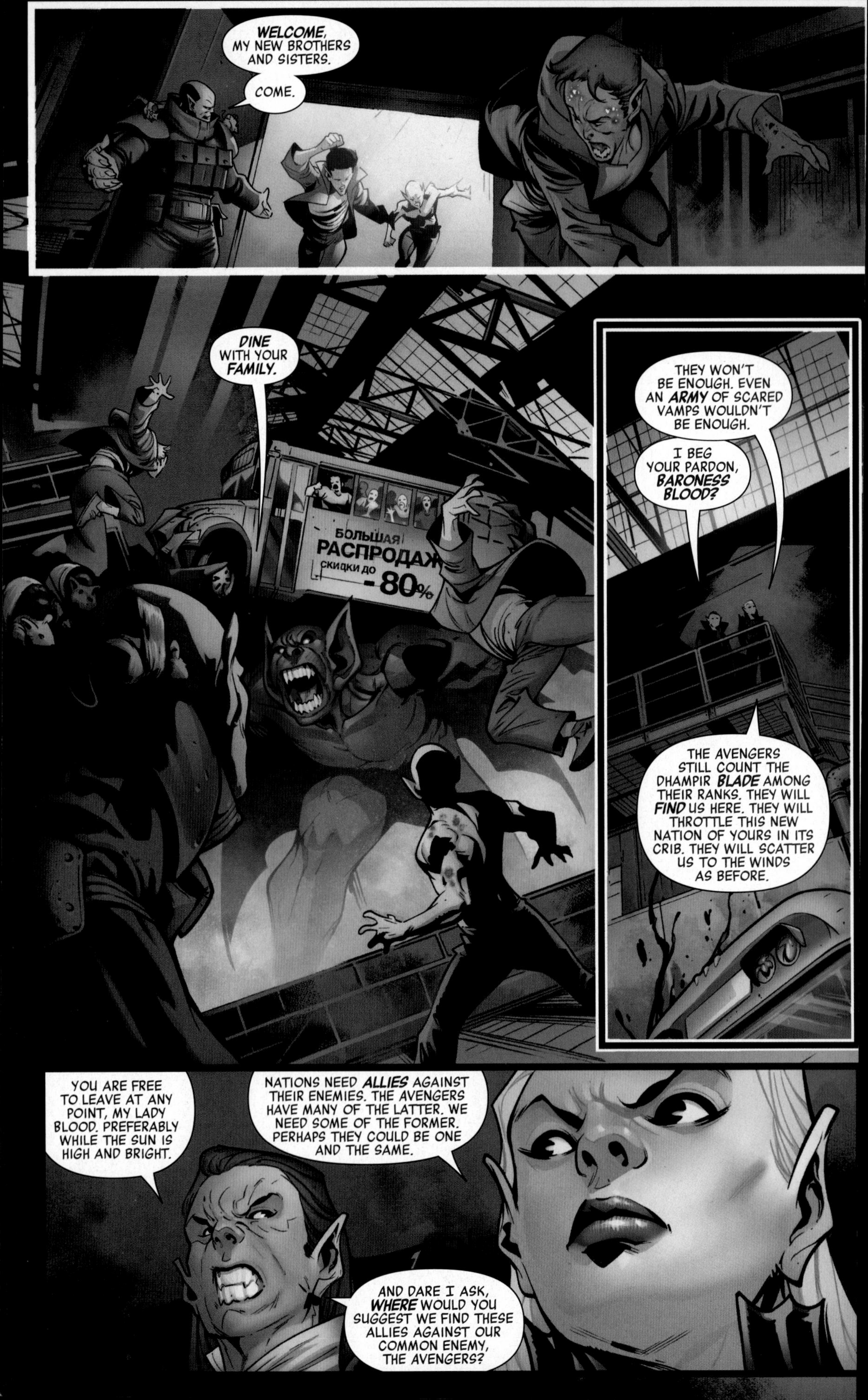

WELCOME, MY NEW BROTHERS AND SISTERS.
COME.
DINE WITH YOUR FAMILY.
БОЛЬШАЯ РАСПРОДАЖ СКИДКИ ДО -80%
THEY WON'T BE ENOUGH. EVEN AN ARMY OF SCARED VAMPS WOULDN'T BE ENOUGH.
I BEG YOUR PARDON, BARONESS BLOOD?
THE AVENGERS STILL COUNT THE DHAMPIR BLADE AMONG THEIR RANKS. THEY WILL FIND US HERE. THEY WILL THROTTLE THIS NEW NATION OF YOURS IN ITS CRIB. THEY WILL SCATTER US TO THE WINDS AS BEFORE.
YOU ARE FREE TO LEAVE AT ANY POINT, MY LADY BLOOD. PREFERABLY WHILE THE SUN IS HIGH AND BRIGHT.
NATIONS NEED ALLIES AGAINST THEIR ENEMIES. THE AVENGERS HAVE MANY OF THE LATTER. WE NEED SOME OF THE FORMER. PERHAPS THEY COULD BE ONE AND THE SAME.
AND DARE I ASK, WHERE WOULD YOU SUGGEST WE FIND THESE ALLIES AGAINST OUR COMMON ENEMY, THE AVENGERS?

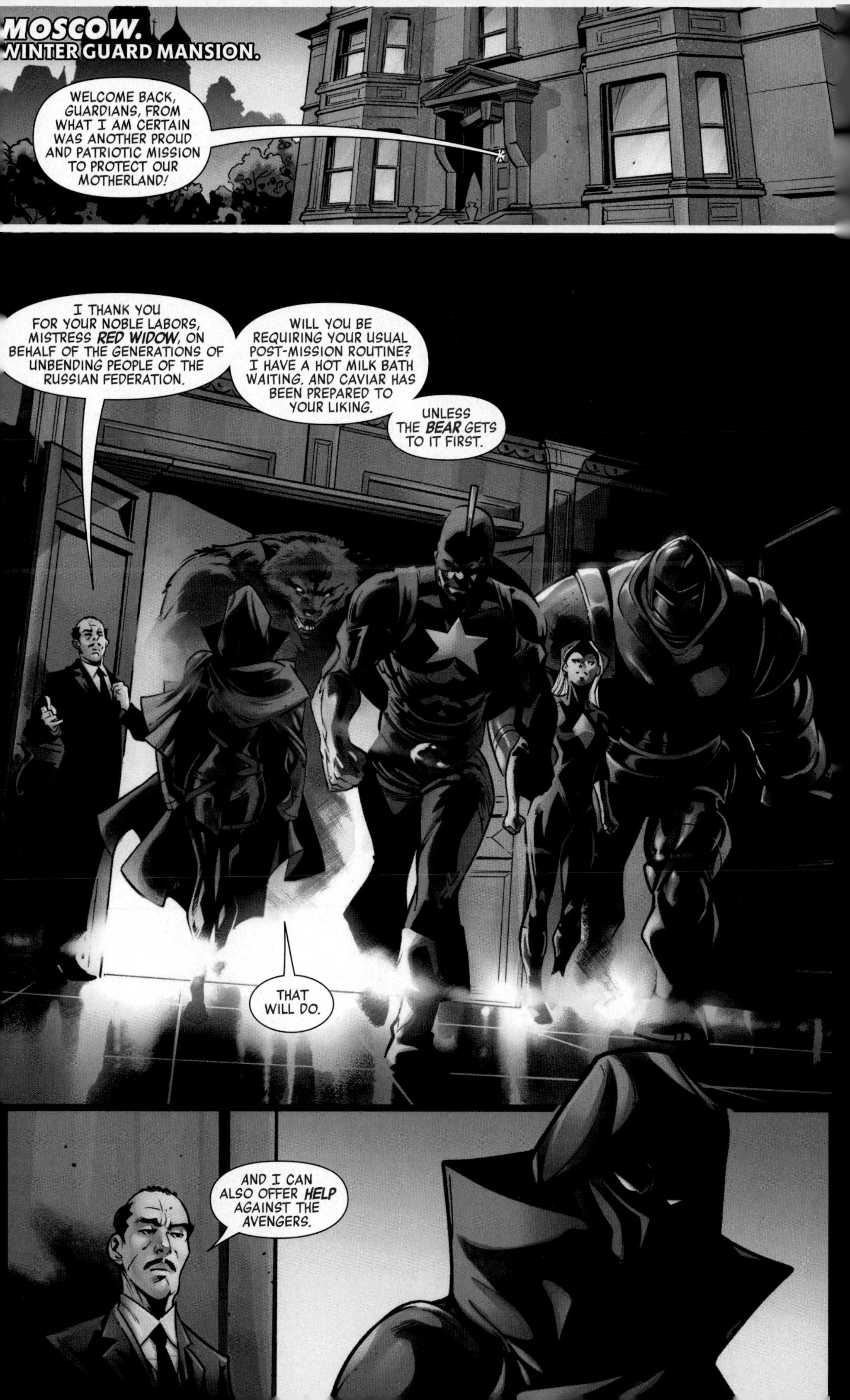
MOSCOW.
WINTER GUARD MANSION.
WELCOME BACK, GUARDIANS, FROM WHAT I AM CERTAIN WAS ANOTHER PROUD AND PATRIOTIC MISSION TO PROTECT OUR MOTHERLAND!
I THANK YOU FOR YOUR NOBLE LABORS, MISTRESS RED WIDOW, ON BEHALF OF THE GENERATIONS OF UNBENDING PEOPLE OF THE RUSSIAN FEDERATION.
WILL YOU BE REQUIRING YOUR USUAL POST-MISSION ROUTINE? I HAVE A HOT MILK BATH WAITING. AND CAVIAR HAS BEEN PREPARED TO YOUR LIKING.
UNLESS THE BEAR GETS TO IT FIRST.
THAT WILL DO.
AND I CAN ALSO OFFER HELP AGAINST THE AVENGERS.

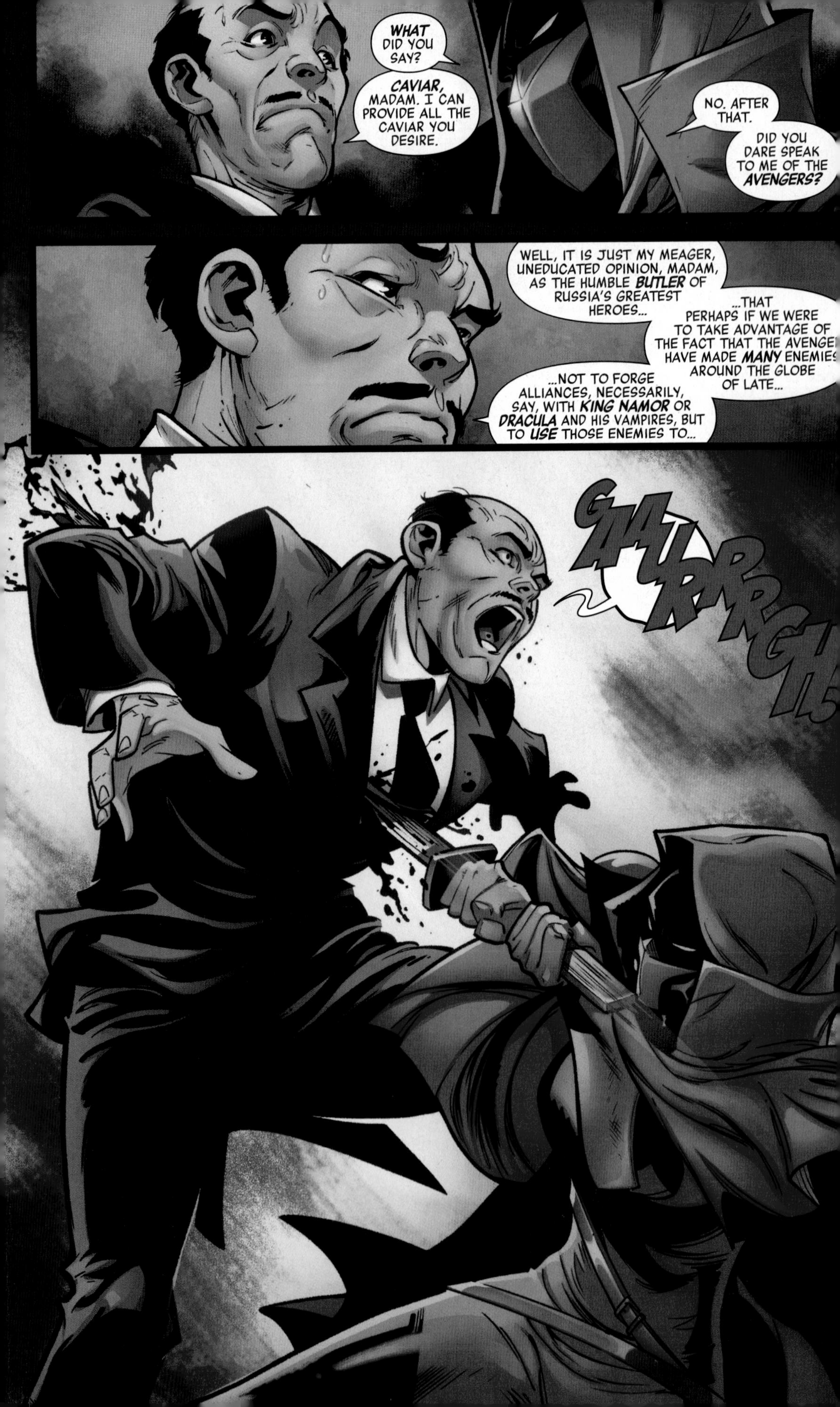

WHAT DID YOU SAY?
CAVIAR, MADAM. I CAN PROVIDE ALL THE CAVIAR YOU DESIRE.
NO. AFTER THAT.
DID YOU DARE SPEAK TO ME OF THE AVENGERS?
WELL, IT IS JUST MY MEAGER, UNEDUCATED OPINION, MADAM, AS THE HUMBLE BUTLER OF RUSSIA'S GREATEST HEROES...
...THAT PERHAPS IF WE WERE TO TAKE ADVANTAGE OF THE FACT THAT THE AVENGE HAVE MADE MANY ENEMIES AROUND THE GLOBE OF LATE...
...NOT TO FORGE ALLIANCES, NECESSARILY, SAY, WITH KING NAMOR OR DRACULA AND HIS VAMPIRES, BUT TO USE THOSE ENEMIES TO...
GHAURRRRGH

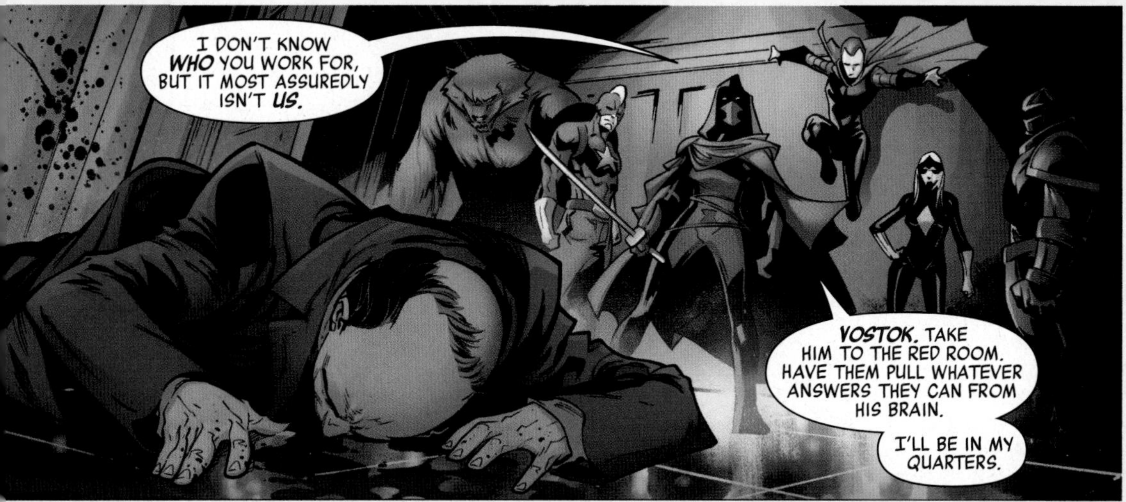
I DON'T KNOW WHO YOU WORK FOR, BUT IT MOST ASSUREDLY ISN'T US.
VOSTOK. TAKE HIM TO THE RED ROOM. HAVE THEM PULL WHATEVER ANSWERS THEY CAN FROM HIS BRAIN.
I'LL BE IN MY QUARTERS.

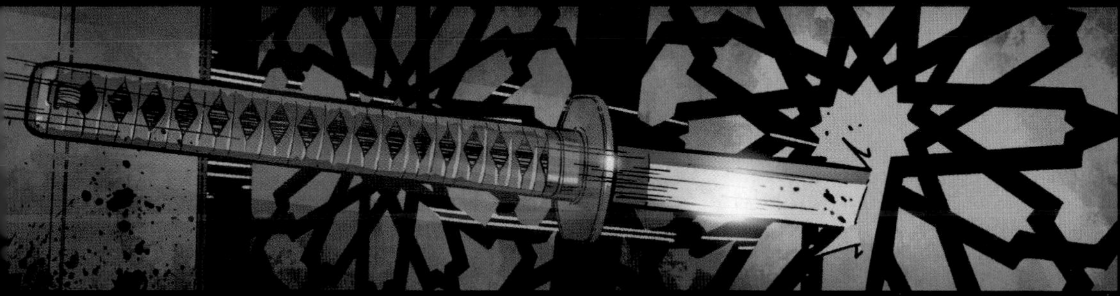

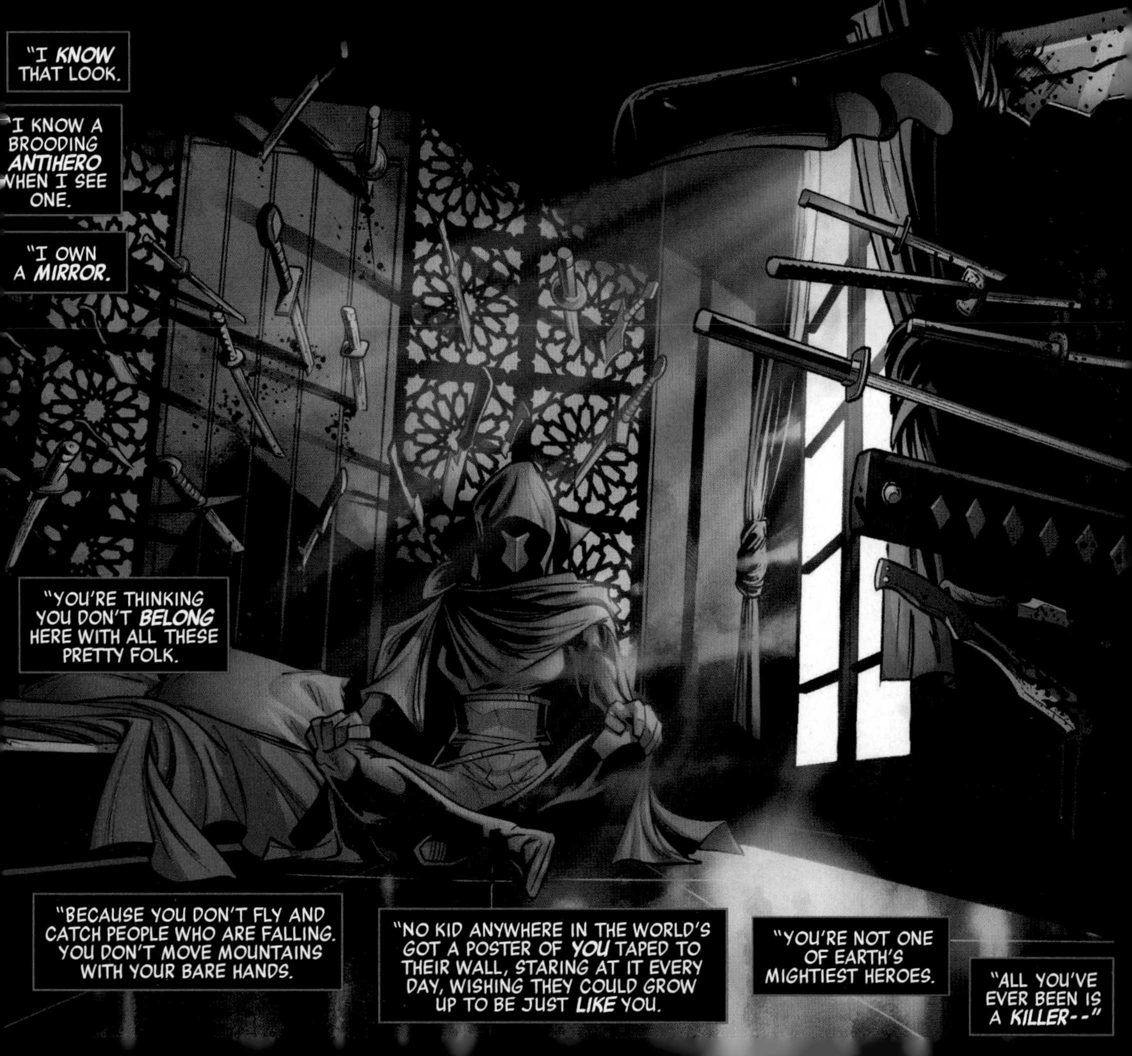
"I KNOW THAT LOOK.
"I KNOW A BROODING ANTIHERO WHEN I SEE ONE.
"I OWN A MIRROR.
"YOU'RE THINKING YOU DON'T BELONG HERE WITH ALL THESE PRETTY FOLK.
"BECAUSE YOU DON'T FLY AND CATCH PEOPLE WHO ARE FALLING. YOU DON'T MOVE MOUNTAINS WITH YOUR BARE HANDS.
"NO KID ANYWHERE IN THE WORLD'S GOT A POSTER OF YOU TAPED TO THEIR WALL, STARING AT IT EVERY DAY, WISHING THEY COULD GROW UP TO BE JUST LIKE YOU.
"YOU'RE NOT ONE OF EARTH'S MIGHTIEST HEROES.
"ALL YOU'VE EVER BEEN IS A KILLER--"

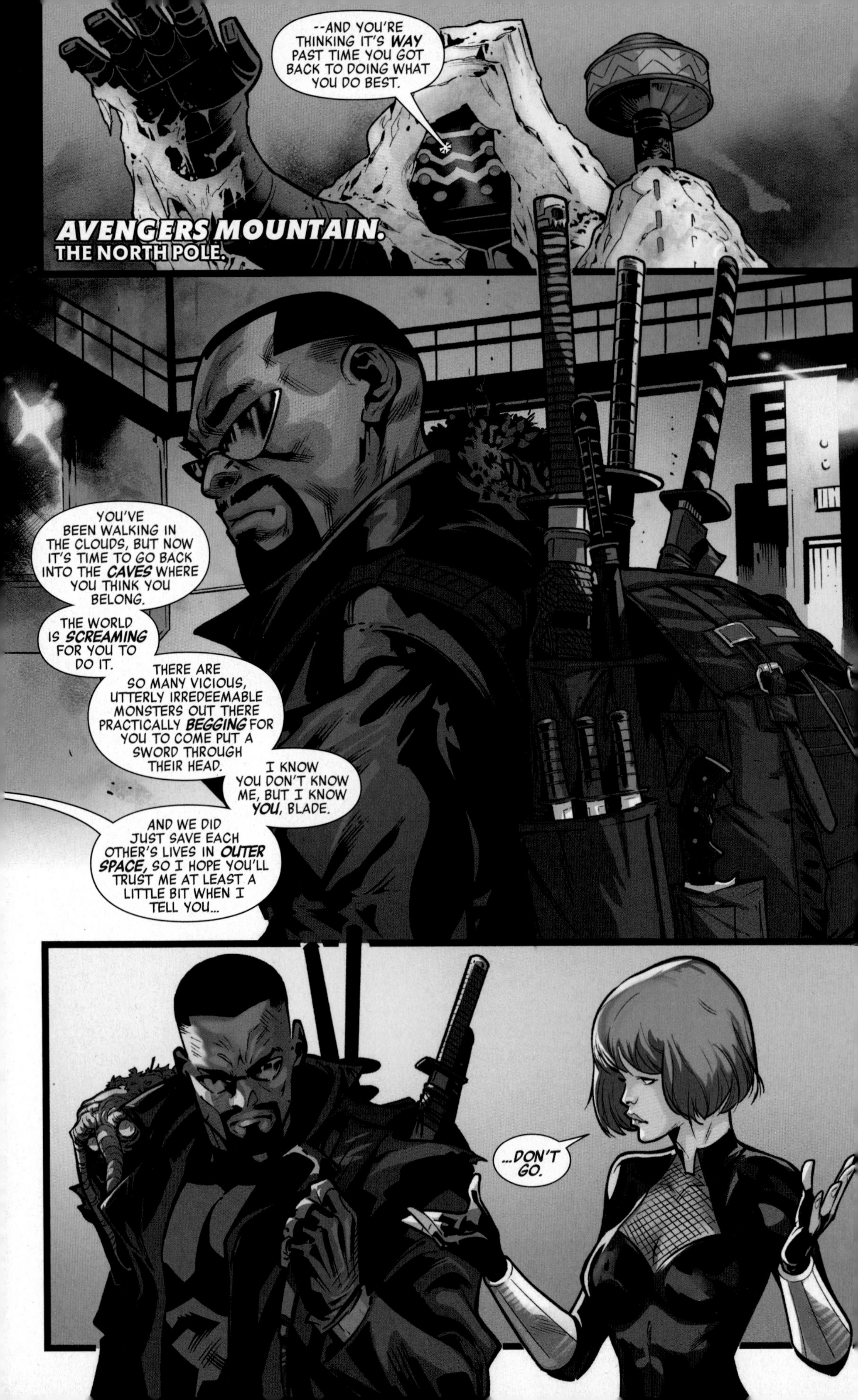
--AND YOU'RE THINKING IT'S WAY PAST TIME YOU GOT BACK TO DOING WHAT YOU DO BEST.
AVENGERS MOUNTAIN. THE NORTH POLE.
YOU'VE BEEN WALKING IN THE CLOUDS, BUT NOW IT'S TIME TO GO BACK INTO THE CAVES WHERE YOU THINK YOU BELONG.
THE WORLD IS SCREAMING FOR YOU TO DO IT.
THERE ARE SO MANY VICIOUS, UTTERLY IRREDEEMABLE MONSTERS OUT THERE PRACTICALLY BEGGING FOR YOU TO COME PUT A SWORD THROUGH THEIR HEAD.
I KNOW YOU DON'T KNOW ME, BUT I KNOW YOU, BLADE.
AND WE DID JUST SAVE EACH OTHER'S LIVES IN OUTER SPACE, SO I HOPE YOU'LL TRUST ME AT LEAST A LITTLE BIT WHEN I TELL YOU...
...DON'T GO.

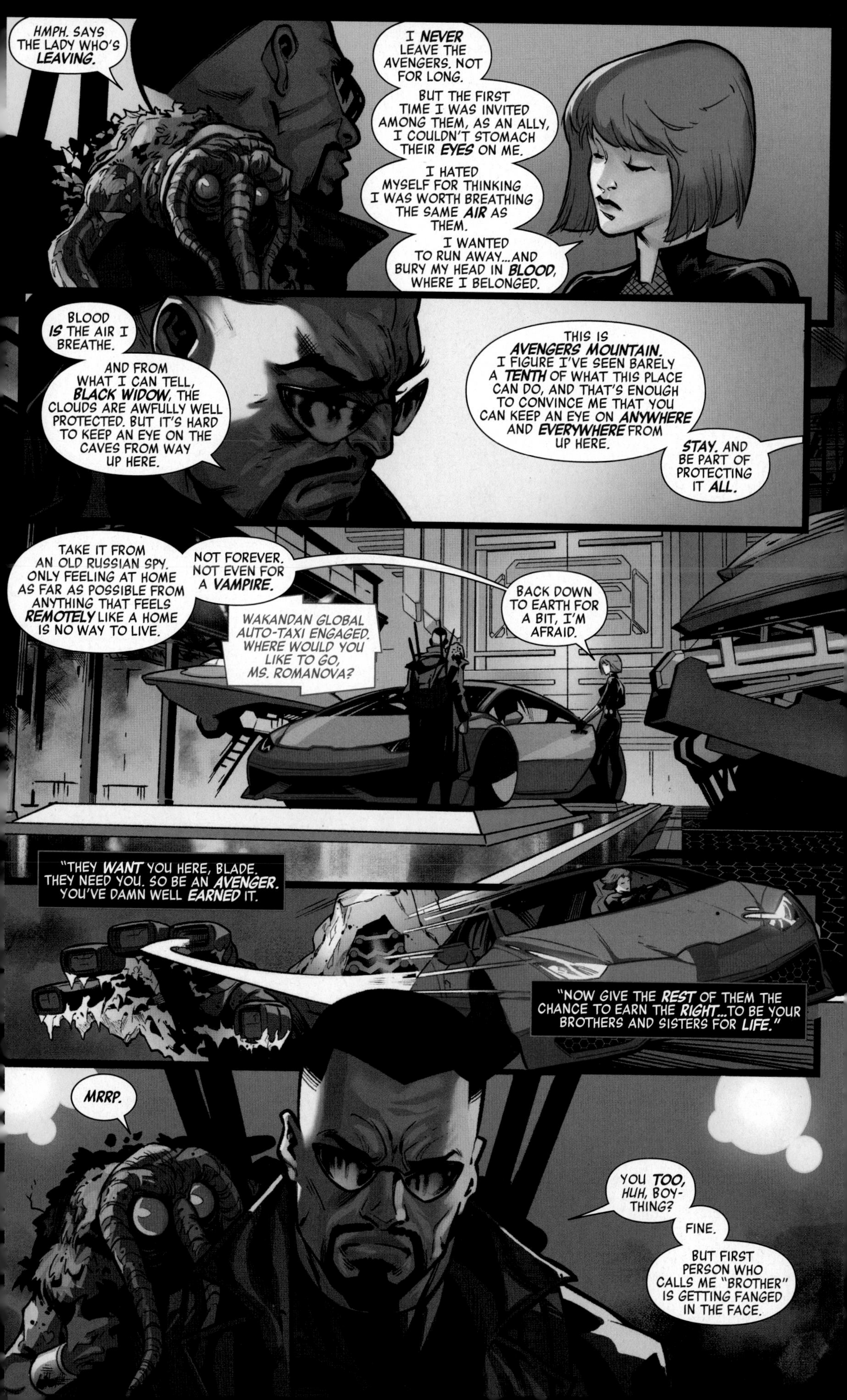
HMPH. SAYS THE LADY WHO'S LEAVING.
I NEVER LEAVE THE AVENGERS. NOT FOR LONG.
BUT THE FIRST TIME I WAS INVITED AMONG THEM, AS AN ALLY, I COULDN'T STOMACH THEIR EYES ON ME.
I HATED MYSELF FOR THINKING I WAS WORTH BREATHING THE SAME AIR AS THEM.
I WANTED TO RUN AWAY...AND BURY MY HEAD IN BLOOD, WHERE I BELONGED.
BLOOD IS THE AIR I BREATHE.
AND FROM WHAT I CAN TELL, BLACK WIDOW, THE CLOUDS ARE AWFULLY WELL PROTECTED. BUT IT'S HARD TO KEEP AN EYE ON THE CAVES FROM WAY UP HERE.
THIS IS AVENGERS MOUNTAIN. I FIGURE I'VE SEEN BARELY A TENTH OF WHAT THIS PLACE CAN DO, AND THAT'S ENOUGH TO CONVINCE ME THAT YOU CAN KEEP AN EYE ON ANYWHERE AND EVERYWHERE FROM UP HERE.
STAY. AND BE PART OF PROTECTING IT ALL.
TAKE IT FROM AN OLD RUSSIAN SPY. ONLY FEELING AT HOME AS FAR AS POSSIBLE FROM ANYTHING THAT FEELS REMOTELY LIKE A HOME IS NO WAY TO LIVE.
NOT FOREVER. NOT EVEN FOR A VAMPIRE.
BACK DOWN TO EARTH FOR A BIT, I'M AFRAID.
WAKANDAN GLOBAL AUTO-TAXI ENGAGED. WHERE WOULD YOU LIKE TO GO, MS. ROMANOVA?
"THEY WANT YOU HERE, BLADE. THEY NEED YOU. SO BE AN AVENGER. YOU'VE DAMN WELL EARNED IT.
"NOW GIVE THE REST OF THEM THE CHANCE TO EARN THE RIGHT...TO BE YOUR BROTHERS AND SISTERS FOR LIFE."
MRRP.
YOU TOO, HUH, BOY-THING?
FINE.
BUT FIRST PERSON WHO CALLS ME "BROTHER" IS GETTING FANGED IN THE FACE.

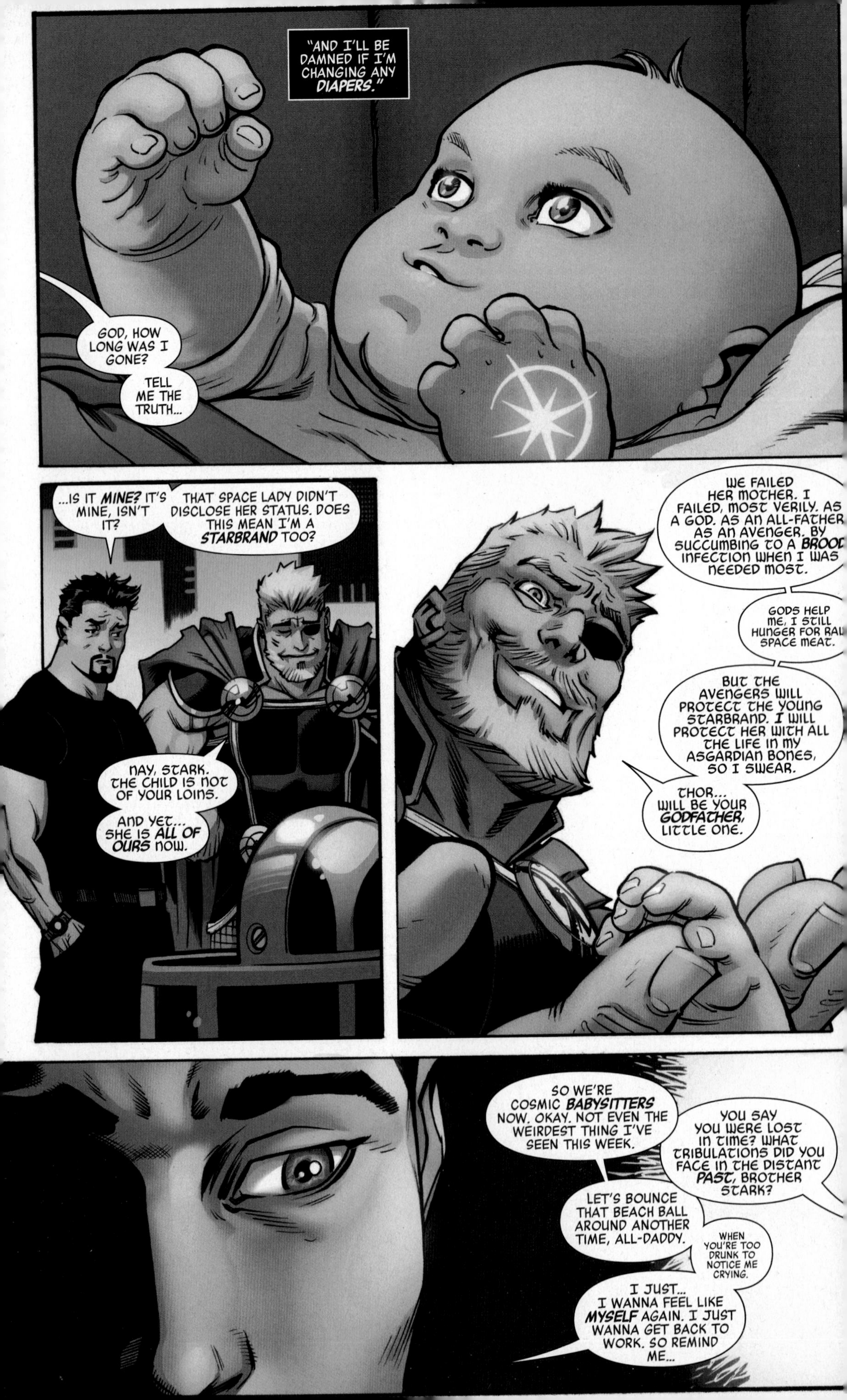
"AND I'LL BE DAMNED IF I'M CHANGING ANY DIAPERS."
GOD, HOW LONG WAS I GONE?
TELL ME THE TRUTH...
...IS IT MINE? IT'S MINE, ISN'T IT?
THAT SPACE LADY DIDN'T DISCLOSE HER STATUS. DOES THIS MEAN I'M A STARBRAND TOO?
NAY, STARK. THE CHILD IS NOT OF YOUR LOINS.
AND YET... SHE IS ALL OF OURS NOW.
WE FAILED HER MOTHER. I FAILED, MOST VERILY. AS A GOD. AS AN ALL-FATHER. AS AN AVENGER. BY SUCCUMBING TO A BROOD INFECTION WHEN I WAS NEEDED MOST.
GODS HELP ME, I STILL HUNGER FOR RAW SPACE MEAT.
BUT THE AVENGERS WILL PROTECT THE YOUNG STARBRAND. I WILL PROTECT HER WITH ALL THE LIFE IN MY ASGARDIAN BONES, SO I SWEAR.
THOR... WILL BE YOUR GODFATHER, LITTLE ONE.
SO WE'RE COSMIC BABYSITTERS NOW. OKAY. NOT EVEN THE WEIRDEST THING I'VE SEEN THIS WEEK.
YOU SAY YOU WERE LOST IN TIME? WHAT TRIBULATIONS DID YOU FACE IN THE DISTANT PAST, BROTHER STARK?
LET'S BOUNCE THAT BEACH BALL AROUND ANOTHER TIME, ALL-DADDY.
WHEN YOU'RE TOO DRUNK TO NOTICE ME CRYING.
I JUST... I WANNA FEEL LIKE MYSELF AGAIN. I JUST WANNA GET BACK TO WORK. SO REMIND ME...

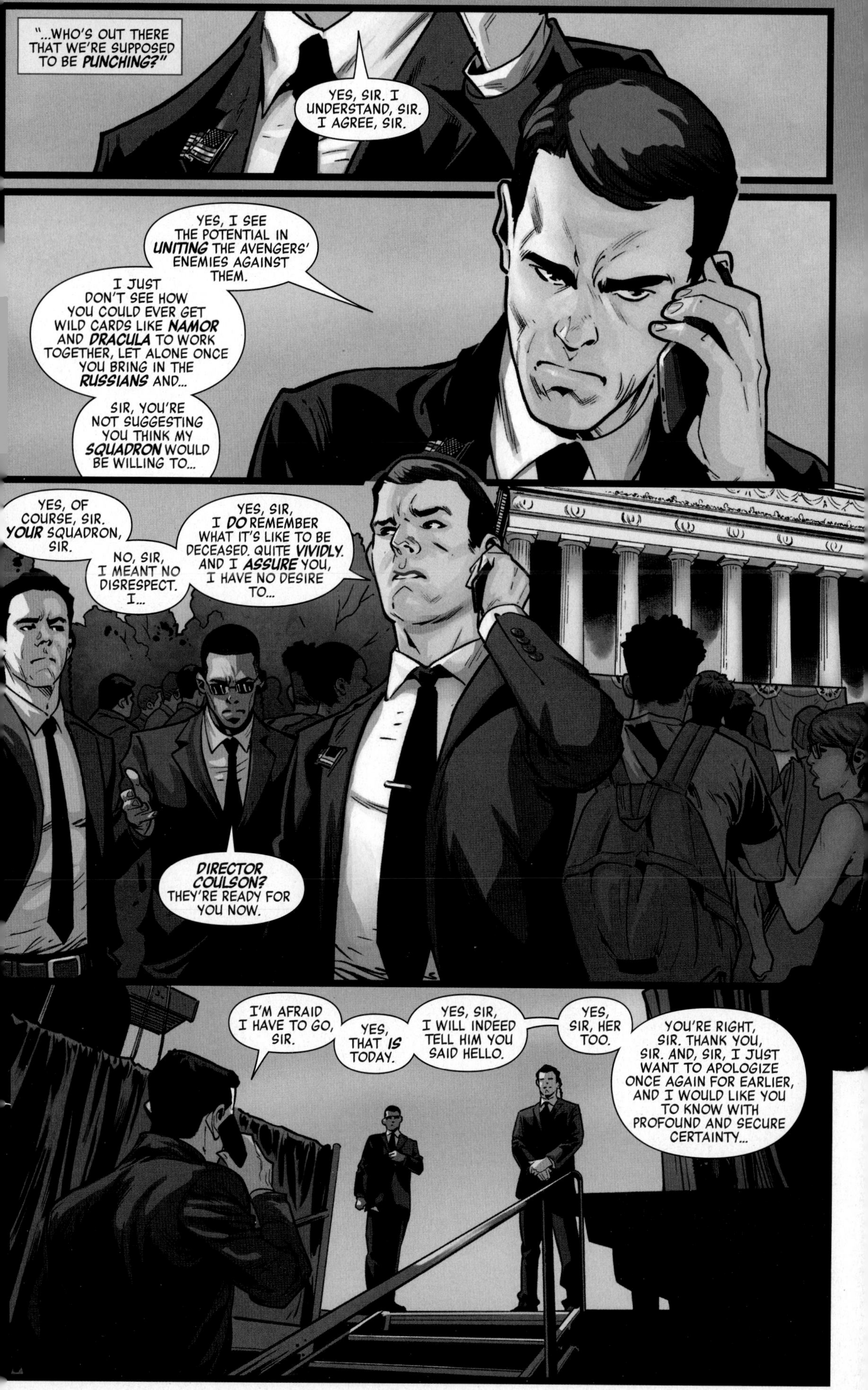
"...WHO'S OUT THERE THAT WE'RE SUPPOSED TO BE PUNCHING?"
YES, SIR. I UNDERSTAND, SIR. I AGREE, SIR.
YES, I SEE THE POTENTIAL IN UNITING THE AVENGERS' ENEMIES AGAINST THEM.
I JUST DON'T SEE HOW YOU COULD EVER GET WILD CARDS LIKE NAMOR AND DRACULA TO WORK TOGETHER, LET ALONE ONCE YOU BRING IN THE RUSSIANS AND...
SIR, YOU'RE NOT SUGGESTING YOU THINK MY SQUADRON WOULD BE WILLING TO...
YES, OF COURSE, SIR. YOUR SQUADRON, SIR.
NO, SIR, I MEANT NO DISRESPECT. I...
YES, SIR, I DO REMEMBER WHAT IT'S LIKE TO BE DECEASED. QUITE VIVIDLY. AND I ASSURE YOU, I HAVE NO DESIRE TO...
DIRECTOR COULSON? THEY'RE READY FOR YOU NOW.
I'M AFRAID I HAVE TO GO, SIR.
YES, THAT IS TODAY.
YES, SIR, I WILL INDEED TELL HIM YOU SAID HELLO.
YES, SIR, HER TOO.
YOU'RE RIGHT, SIR. THANK YOU, SIR. AND, SIR, I JUST WANT TO APOLOGIZE ONCE AGAIN FOR EARLIER, AND I WOULD LIKE YOU TO KNOW WITH PROFOUND AND SECURE CERTAINTY...

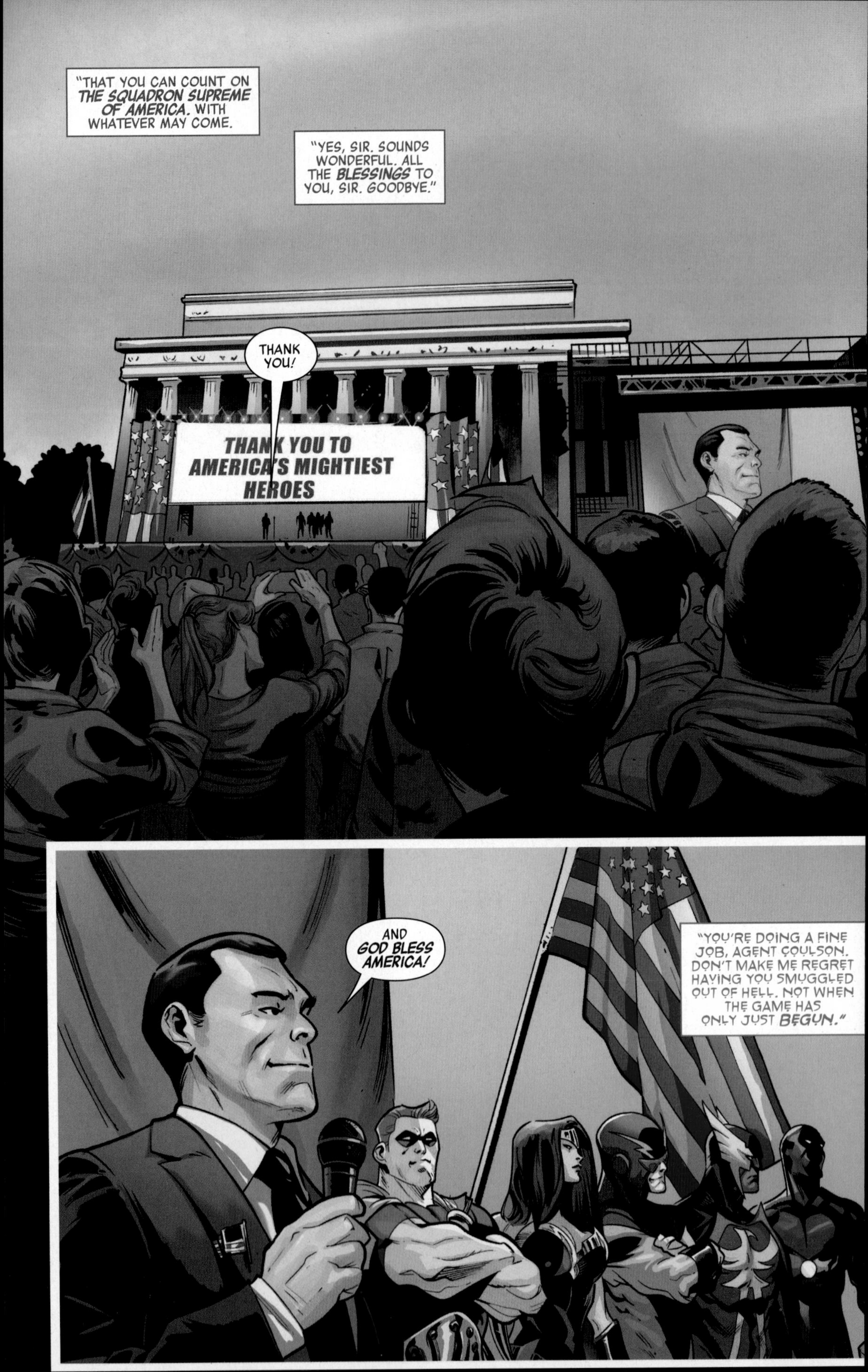
"THAT YOU CAN COUNT ON THE SQUADRON SUPREME OF AMERICA. WITH WHATEVER MAY COME.
"YES, SIR. SOUNDS WONDERFUL. ALL THE BLESSINGS TO YOU, SIR. GOODBYE."
THANK YOU!
THANK YOU TO AMERICA'S MIGHTIEST HEROES
AND GOD BLESS AMERICA!
"YOU'RE DOING A FINE JOB, AGENT COULSON. DON'T MAKE ME REGRET HAVING YOU SMUGGLED OUT OF HELL. NOT WHEN THE GAME HAS ONLY JUST BEGUN."

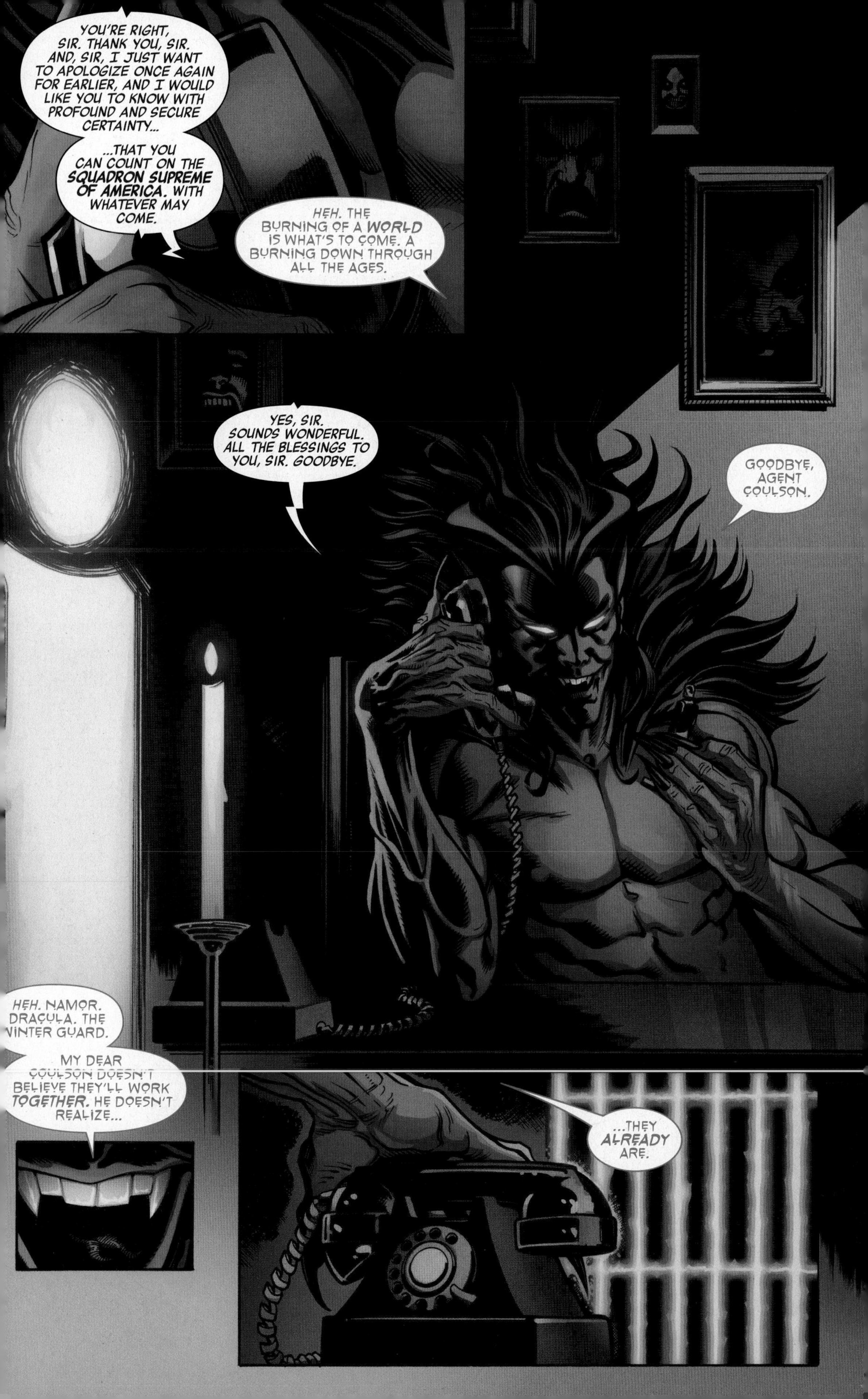
YOU'RE RIGHT, SIR. THANK YOU, SIR. AND, SIR, I JUST WANT TO APOLOGIZE ONCE AGAIN FOR EARLIER, AND I WOULD LIKE YOU TO KNOW WITH PROFOUND AND SECURE CERTAINTY...
...THAT YOU CAN COUNT ON THE SQUADRON SUPREME OF AMERICA. WITH WHATEVER MAY COME.
HEH. THE BURNING OF A WORLD IS WHAT'S TO COME. A BURNING DOWN THROUGH ALL THE AGES.
YES, SIR. SOUNDS WONDERFUL. ALL THE BLESSINGS TO YOU, SIR. GOODBYE.
GOODBYE, AGENT COULSON.
HEH. NAMOR. DRACULA. THE WINTER GUARD.
MY DEAR COULSON DOESN'T BELIEVE THEY'LL WORK TOGETHER. HE DOESN'T REALIZE...
...THEY ALREADY ARE.

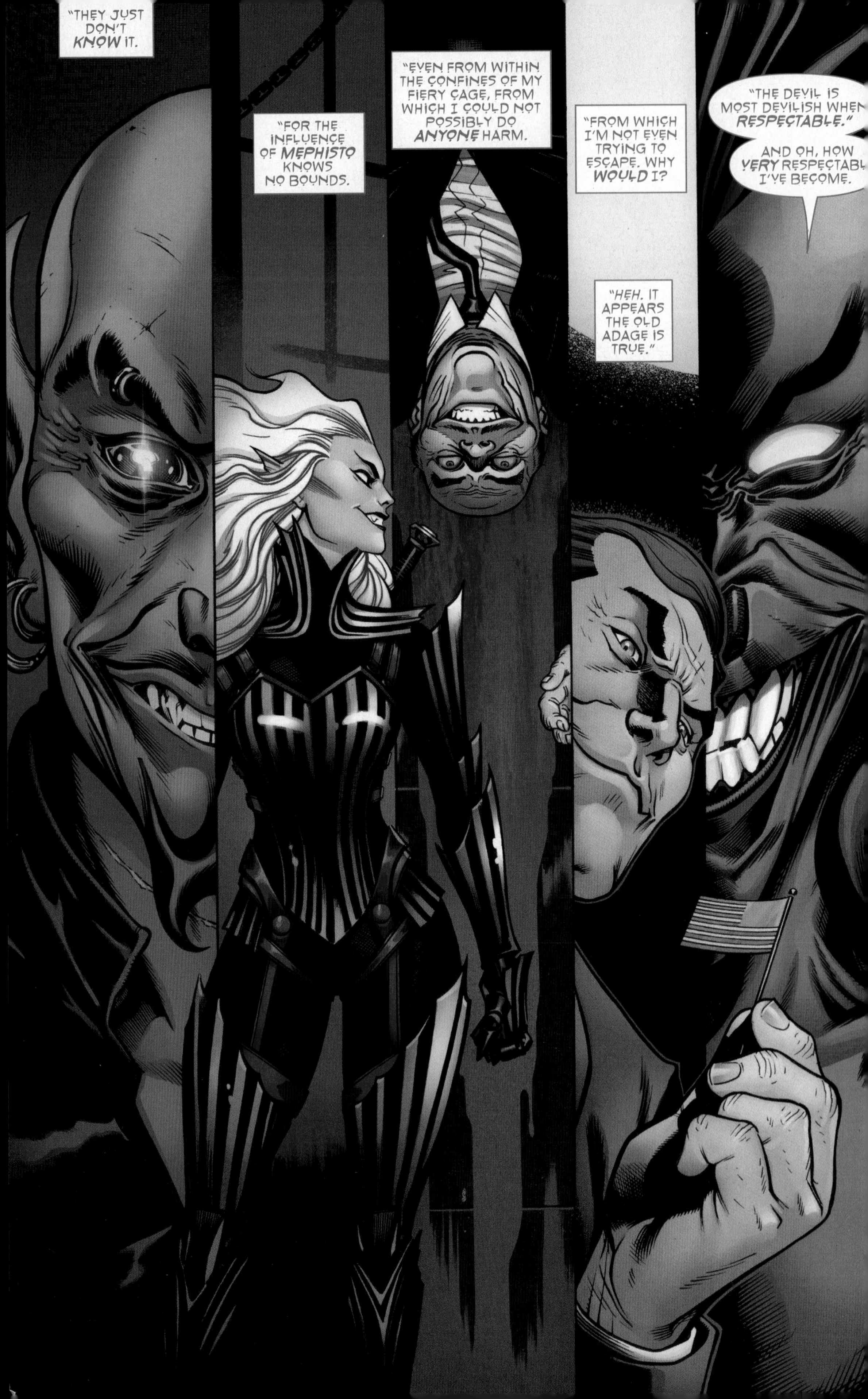
"THEY JUST DON'T KNOW IT.
"FOR THE INFLUENCE OF MEPHISTO KNOWS NO BOUNDS.
"EVEN FROM WITHIN THE CONFINES OF MY FIERY CAGE, FROM WHICH I COULD NOT POSSIBLY DO ANYONE HARM.
"FROM WHICH I'M NOT EVEN TRYING TO ESCAPE. WHY WOULD I?
"HEH. IT APPEARS THE OLD ADAGE IS TRUE."
"THE DEVIL IS MOST DEVILISH WHEN RESPECTABLE."
AND OH, HOW VERY RESPECTABL I'VE BECOME.

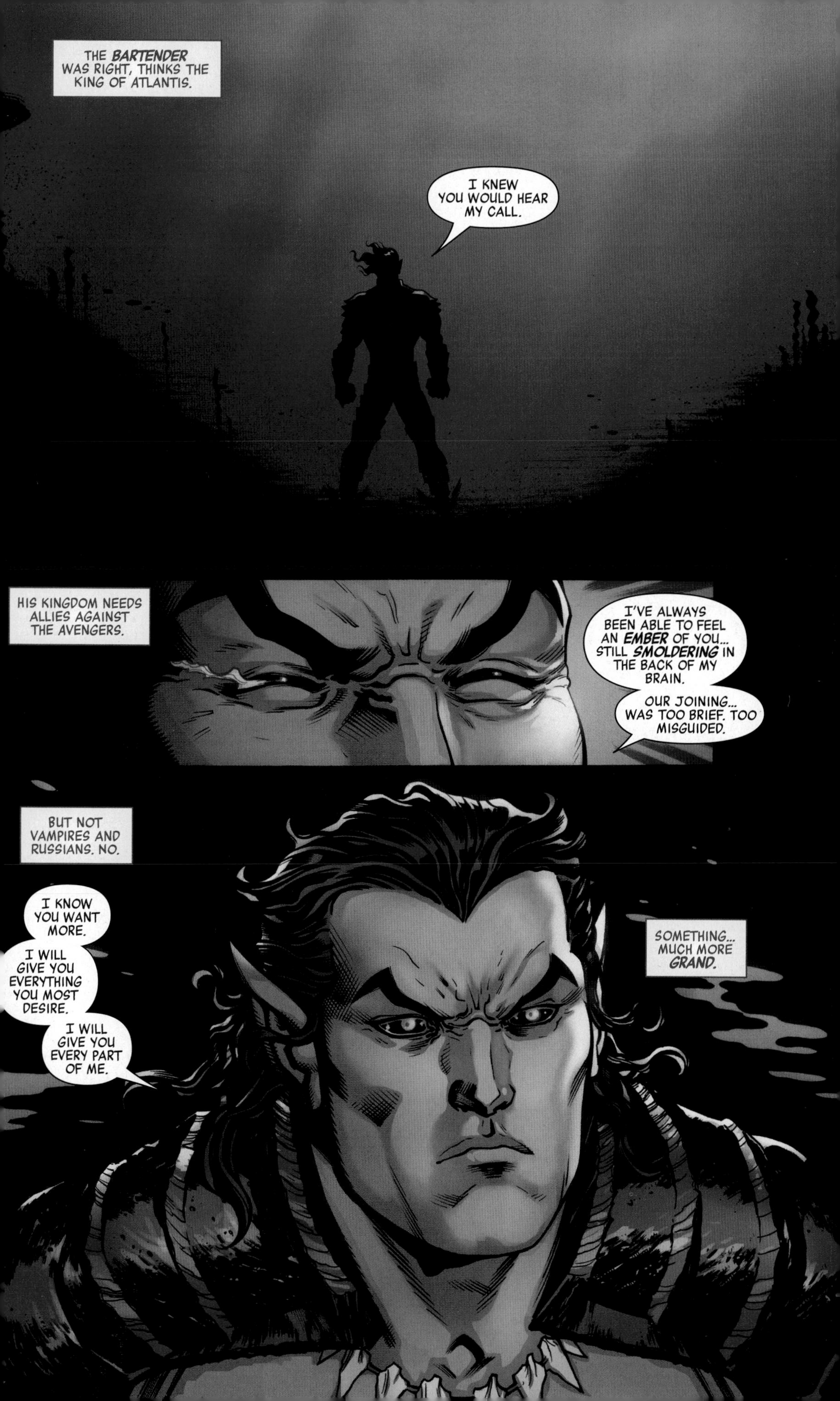
THE BARTENDER WAS RIGHT, THINKS THE KING OF ATLANTIS.
I KNEW YOU WOULD HEAR MY CALL.
HIS KINGDOM NEEDS ALLIES AGAINST THE AVENGERS.
I'VE ALWAYS BEEN ABLE TO FEEL AN EMBER OF YOU... STILL SMOLDERING IN THE BACK OF MY BRAIN.
OUR JOINING... WAS TOO BRIEF. TOO MISGUIDED.
BUT NOT VAMPIRES AND RUSSIANS. NO.
I KNOW YOU WANT MORE.
I WILL GIVE YOU EVERYTHING YOU MOST DESIRE.
I WILL GIVE YOU EVERY PART OF ME.
SOMETHING... MUCH MORE GRAND.

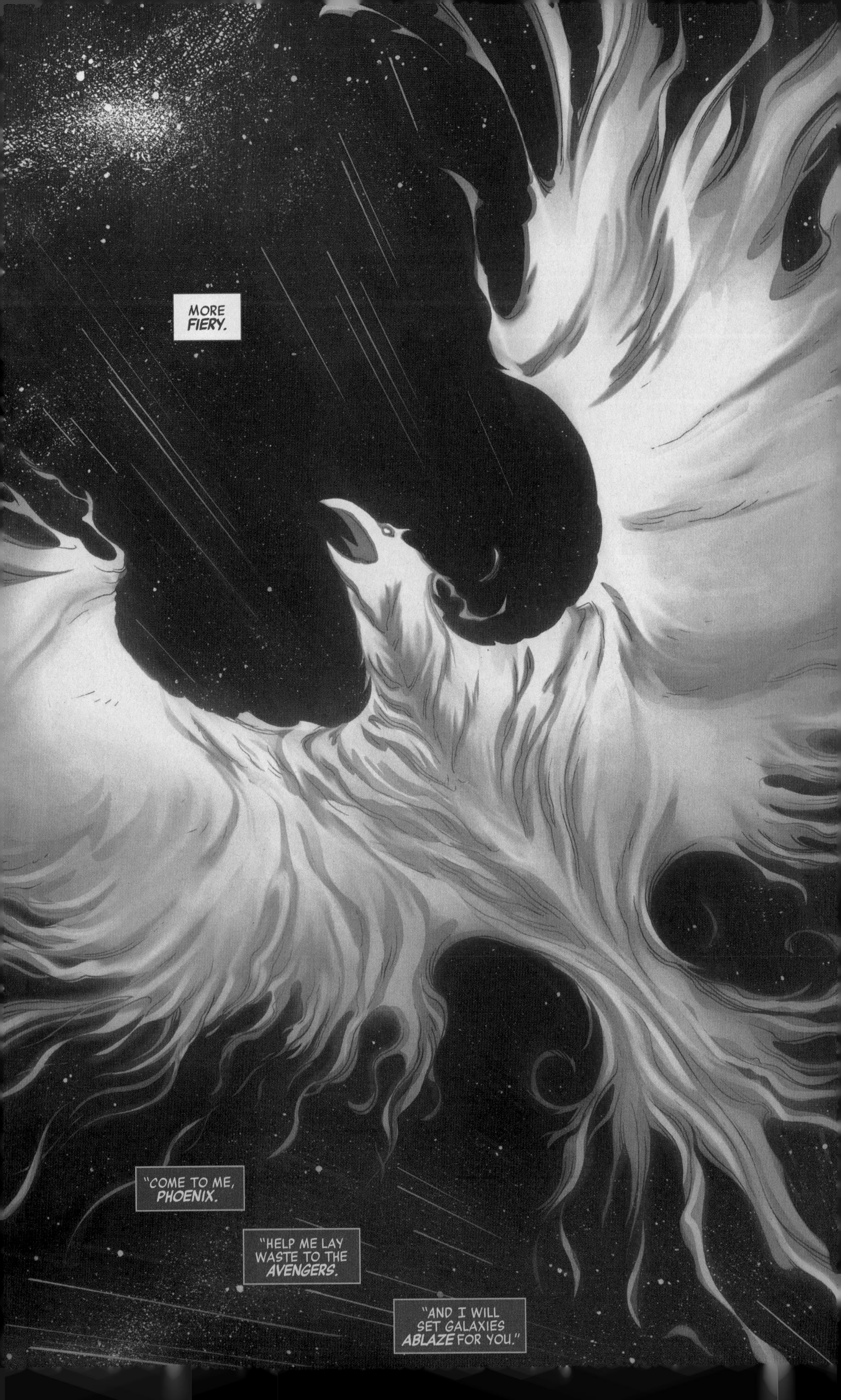
MORE FIERY.
"COME TO ME, PHOENIX.
"HELP ME LAY WASTE TO THE AVENGERS.
"AND I WILL SET GALAXIES ABLAZE FOR YOU."

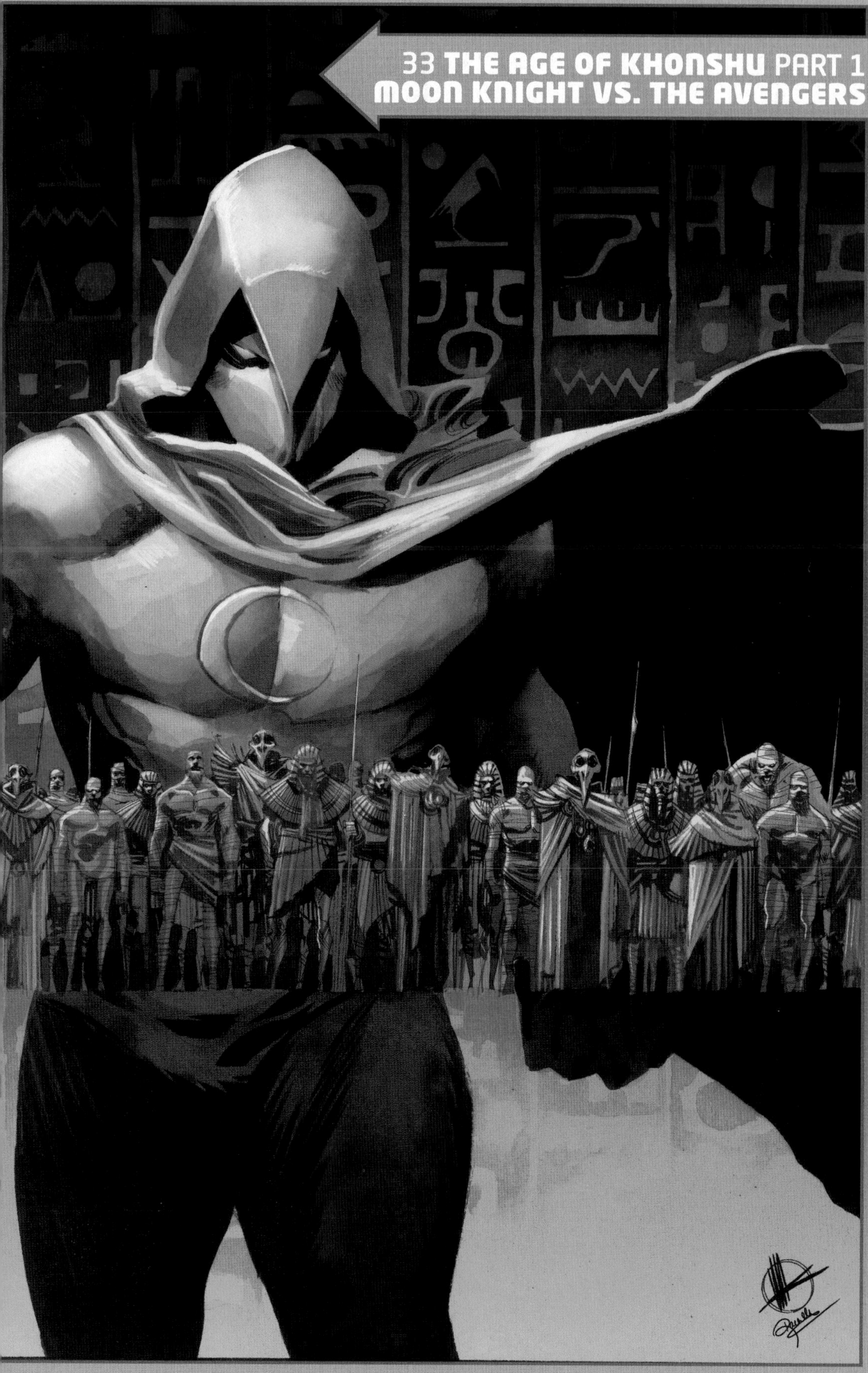
33 THE AGE OF KHONSHU PART 1
MOON KNIGHT VS. THE AVENGERS

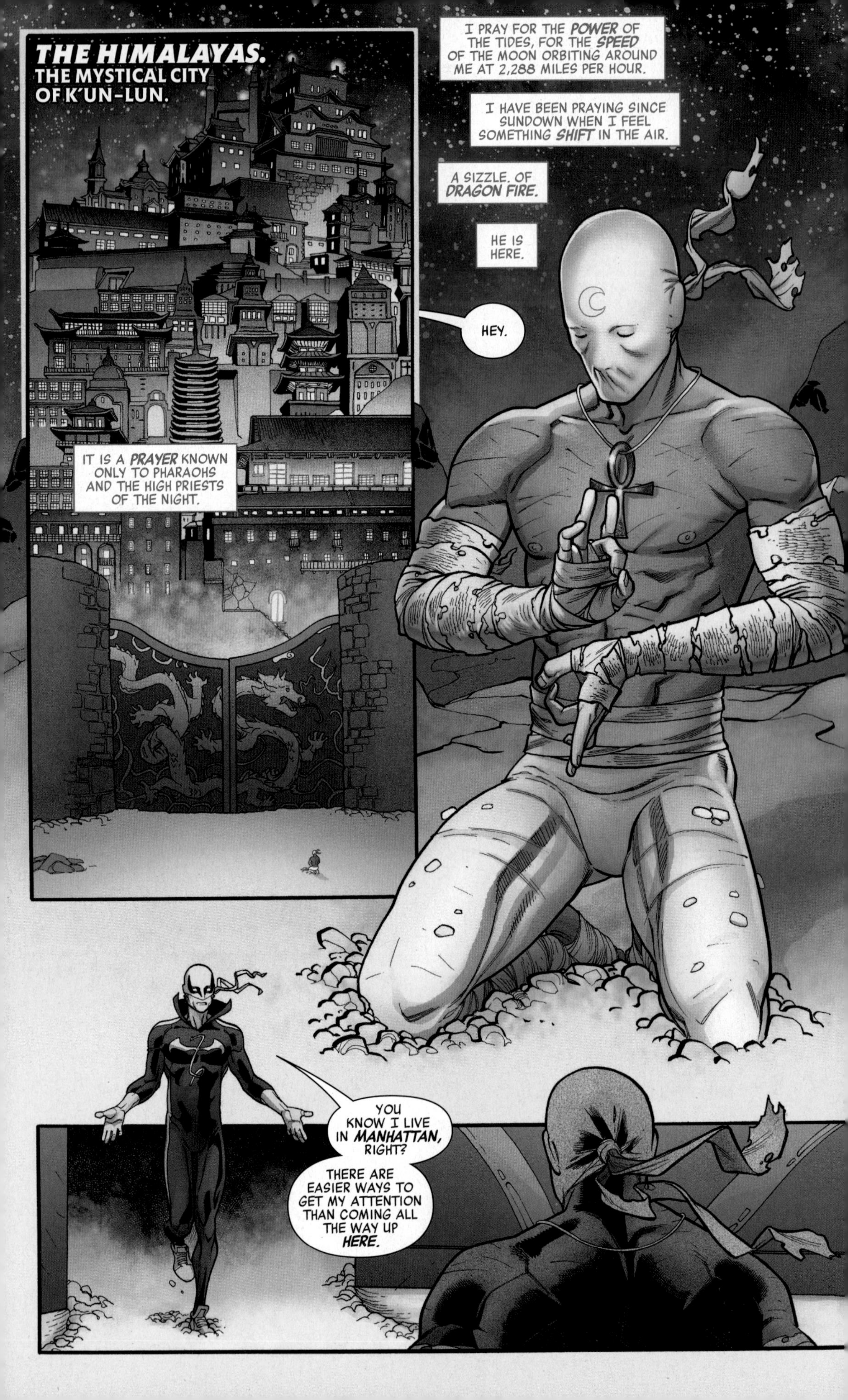
THE HIMALAYAS.
THE MYSTICAL CITY OF K'UN-LUN.
I PRAY FOR THE POWER OF THE TIDES, FOR THE SPEED OF THE MOON ORBITING AROUND ME AT 2,288 MILES PER HOUR.
I HAVE BEEN PRAYING SINCE SUNDOWN WHEN I FEEL SOMETHING SHIFT IN THE AIR.
A SIZZLE. OF DRAGON FIRE.
HE IS HERE.
IT IS A PRAYER KNOWN ONLY TO PHARAOHS AND THE HIGH PRIESTS OF THE NIGHT.
HEY.
YOU KNOW I LIVE IN MANHATTAN, RIGHT?
THERE ARE EASIER WAYS TO GET MY ATTENTION THAN COMING ALL THE WAY UP HERE.

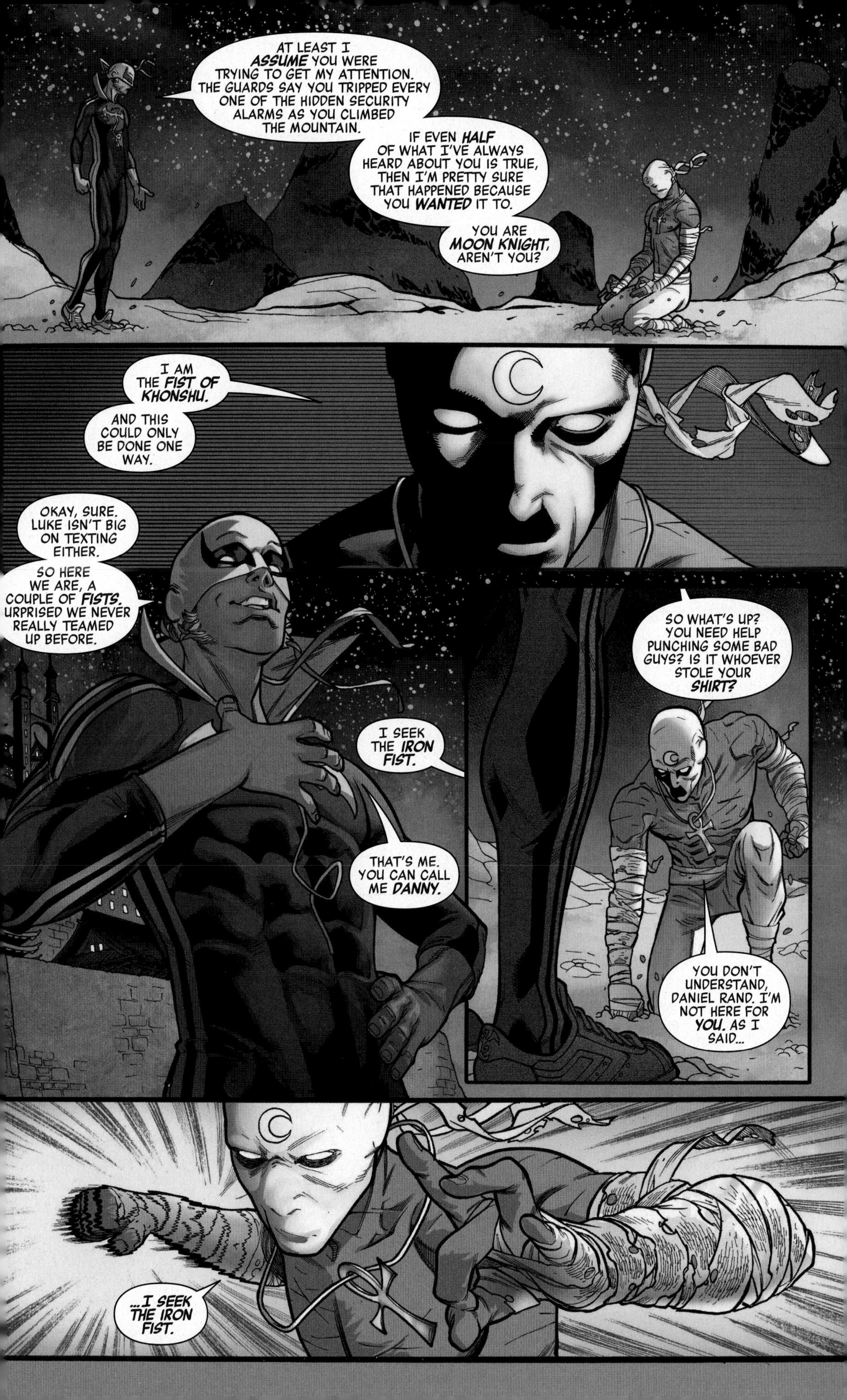
AT LEAST I ASSUME YOU WERE TRYING TO GET MY ATTENTION. THE GUARDS SAY YOU TRIPPED EVERY ONE OF THE HIDDEN SECURITY ALARMS AS YOU CLIMBED THE MOUNTAIN.
IF EVEN HALF OF WHAT I'VE ALWAYS HEARD ABOUT YOU IS TRUE, THEN I'M PRETTY SURE THAT HAPPENED BECAUSE YOU WANTED IT TO.
YOU ARE MOON KNIGHT, AREN'T YOU?
I AM THE FIST OF KHONSHU.
AND THIS COULD ONLY BE DONE ONE WAY.
OKAY, SURE. LUKE ISN'T BIG ON TEXTING EITHER.
SO HERE WE ARE, A COUPLE OF FISTS. URPRISED WE NEVER REALLY TEAMED UP BEFORE.
I SEEK THE IRON FIST.
THAT'S ME. YOU CAN CALL ME DANNY.
SO WHAT'S UP? YOU NEED HELP PUNCHING SOME BAD GUYS? IS IT WHOEVER STOLE YOUR SHIRT?
YOU DON'T UNDERSTAND, DANIEL RAND. I'M NOT HERE FOR YOU. AS I SAID...
...I SEEK THE IRON FIST.

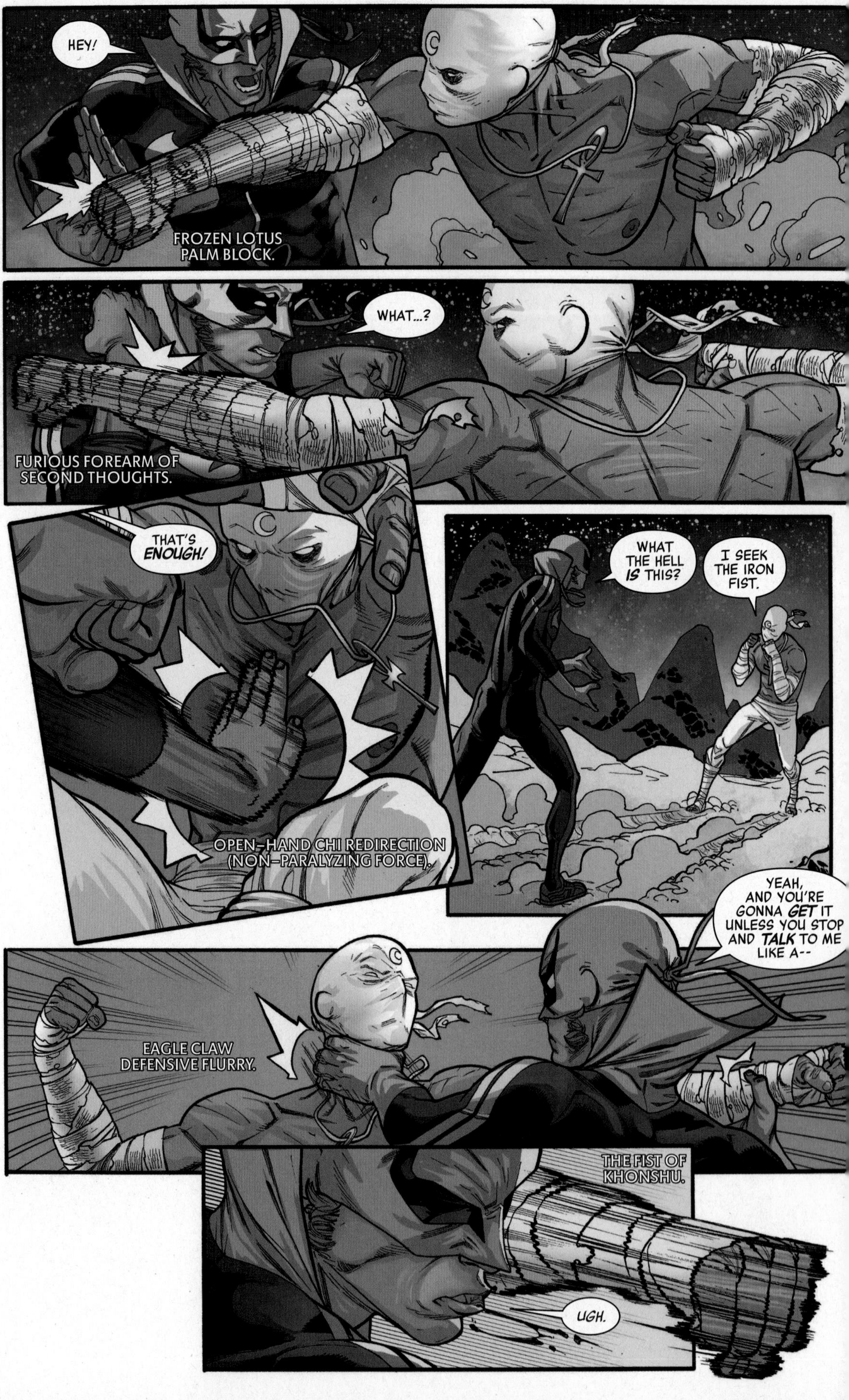
HEY!
FROZEN LOTUS PALM BLOCK.
WHAT...?
FURIOUS FOREARM OF SECOND THOUGHTS.
THAT'S ENOUGH!
OPEN-HAND CHI REDIRECTION (NON-PARALYZING FORCE).
WHAT THE HELL IS THIS?
I SEEK THE IRON FIST.
YEAH, AND YOU'RE GONNA GET IT UNLESS YOU STOP AND TALK TO ME LIKE A--
EAGLE CLAW DEFENSIVE FLURRY.
THE FIST OF KHONSHU.
UGH.

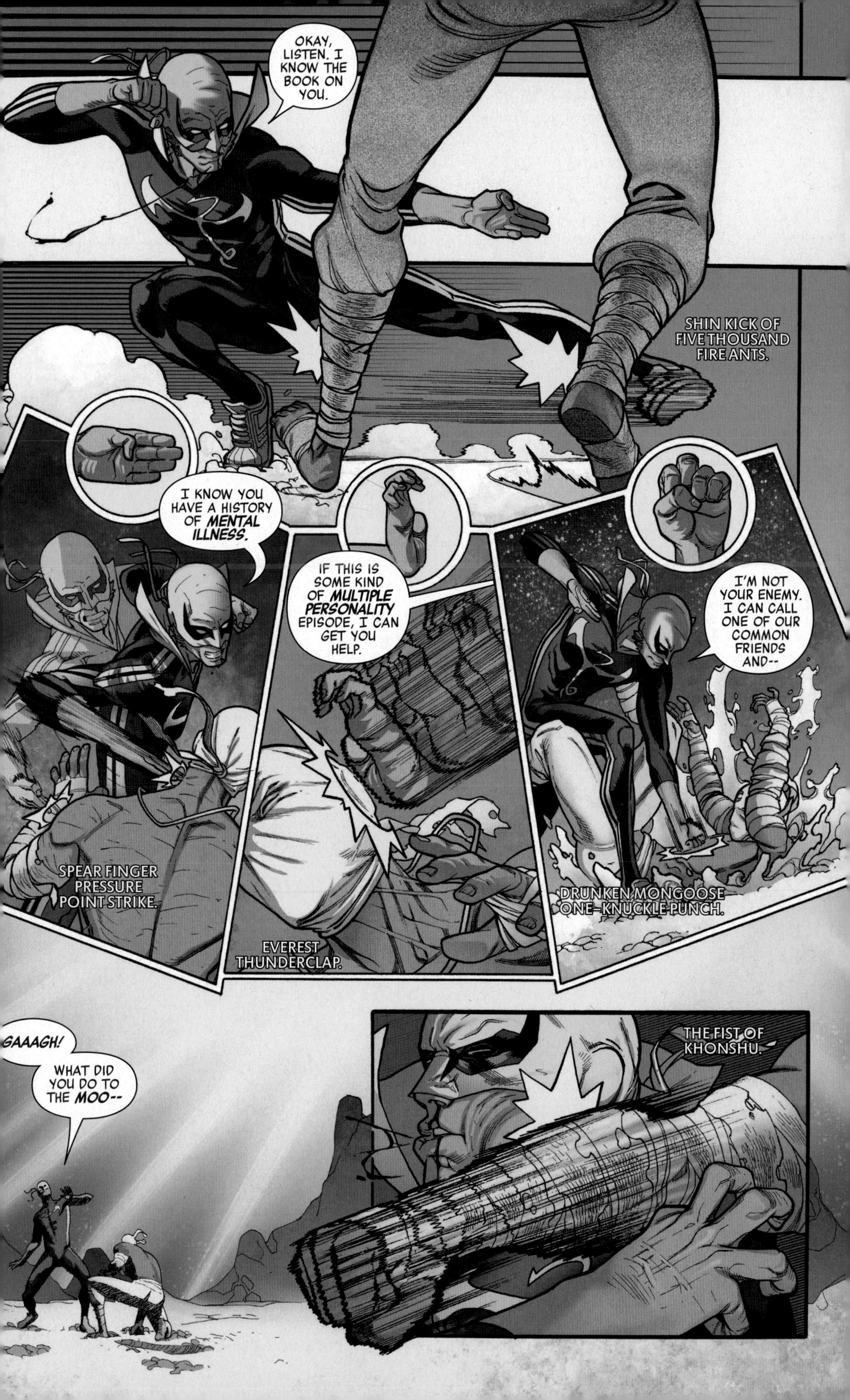
OKAY, LISTEN. I KNOW THE BOOK ON YOU.
SHIN KICK OF FIVE THOUSAND FIRE ANTS.
I KNOW YOU HAVE A HISTORY OF MENTAL ILLNESS.
SPEAR FINGER PRESSURE POINT STRIKE.
IF THIS IS SOME KIND OF MULTIPLE PERSONALITY EPISODE, I CAN GET YOU HELP.
EVEREST THUNDERCLAP.
I'M NOT YOUR ENEMY. I CAN CALL ONE OF OUR COMMON FRIENDS AND--
DRUNKEN MONGOOSE ONE-KNUCKLE PUNCH.
THE FIST OF KHONSHU.
GAAAGH!
WHAT DID YOU DO TO THE MOO--

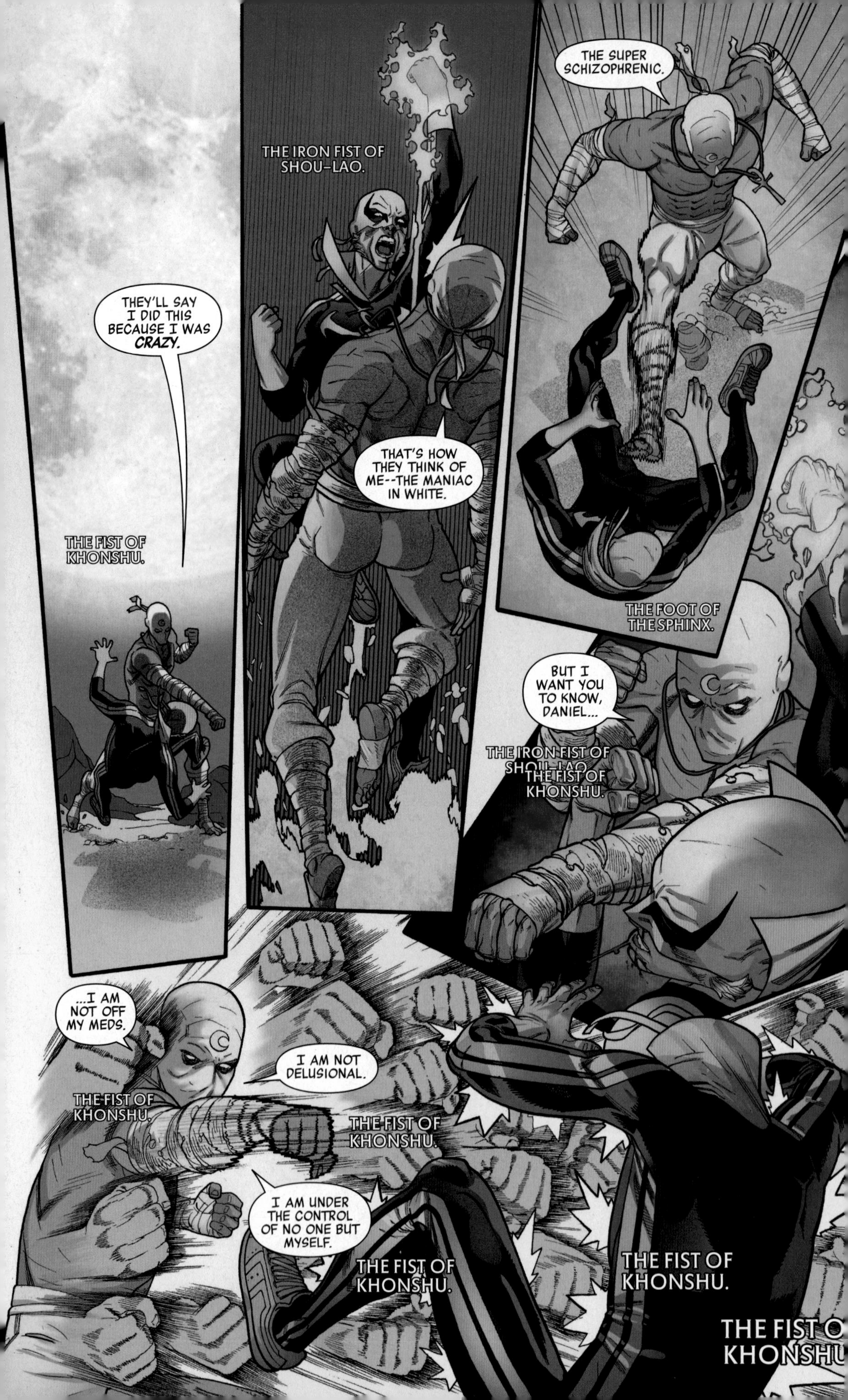
THEY'LL SAY I DID THIS BECAUSE I WAS *CRAZY.*
THE FIST OF KHONSHU.
THE IRON FIST OF SHOU-LAO.
THAT'S HOW THEY THINK OF ME--THE MANIAC IN WHITE.
THE SUPER SCHIZOPHRENIC.
THE FOOT OF THE SPHINX.
BUT I WANT YOU TO KNOW, DANIEL...
THE IRON FIST OF
THE FIST OF KHONSHU.
...I AM NOT OFF MY MEDS.
I AM NOT DELUSIONAL.
THE FIST OF KHONSHU.
THE FIST OF KHONSHU.
I AM UNDER THE CONTROL OF NO ONE BUT MYSELF.
THE FIST OF KHONSHU.
THE FIST OF KHONSHU.
THE FIST O
KHONSHU

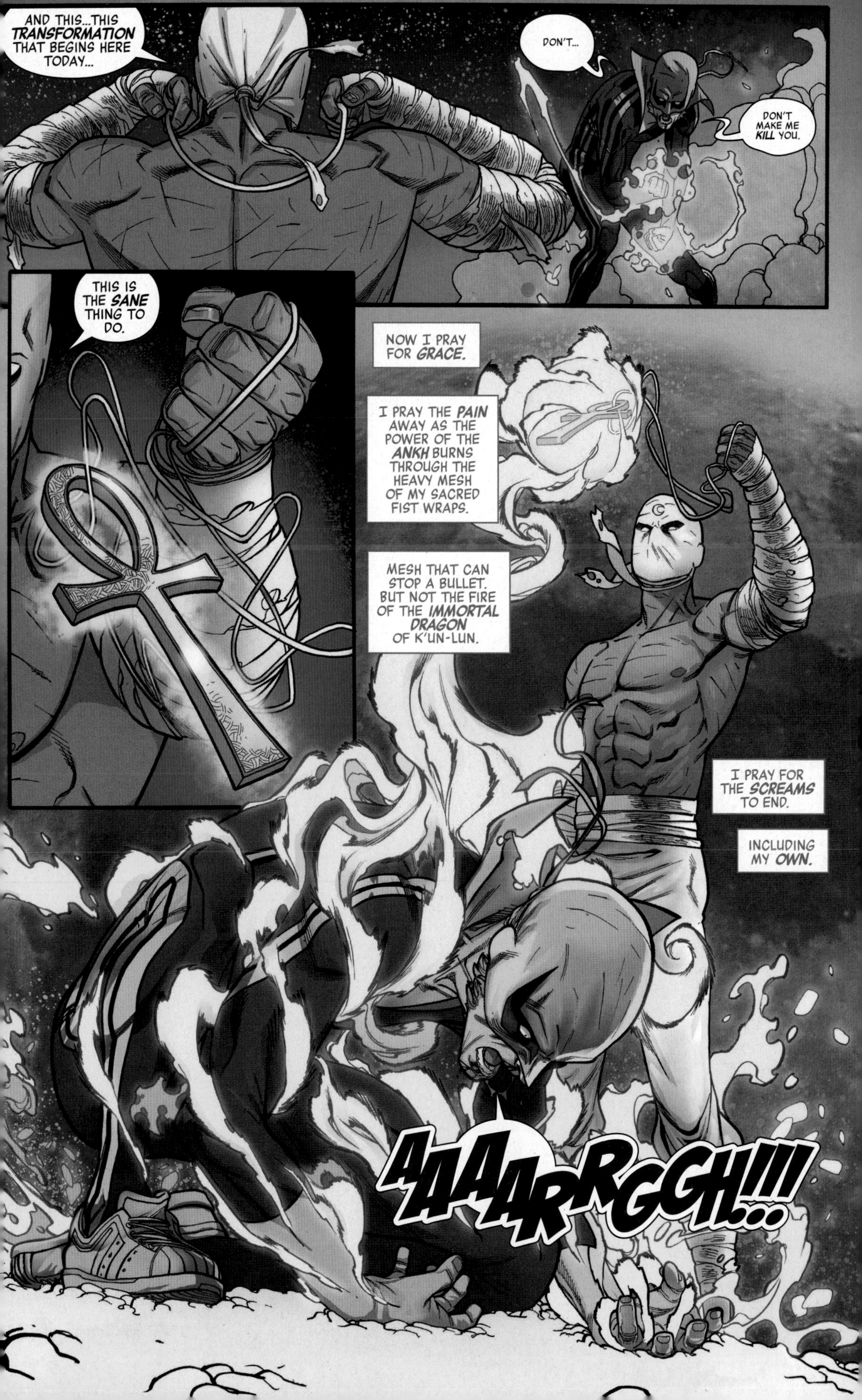
AND THIS...THIS TRANSFORMATION THAT BEGINS HERE TODAY...
DON'T...
DON'T MAKE ME KILL YOU.
THIS IS THE SANE THING TO DO.
NOW I PRAY FOR GRACE.
I PRAY THE PAIN AWAY AS THE POWER OF THE ANKH BURNS THROUGH THE HEAVY MESH OF MY SACRED FIST WRAPS.
MESH THAT CAN STOP A BULLET. BUT NOT THE FIRE OF THE IMMORTAL DRAGON OF K'UN-LUN.
I PRAY FOR THE SCREAMS TO END.
INCLUDING MY OWN.
AAAARRGGH!!!..

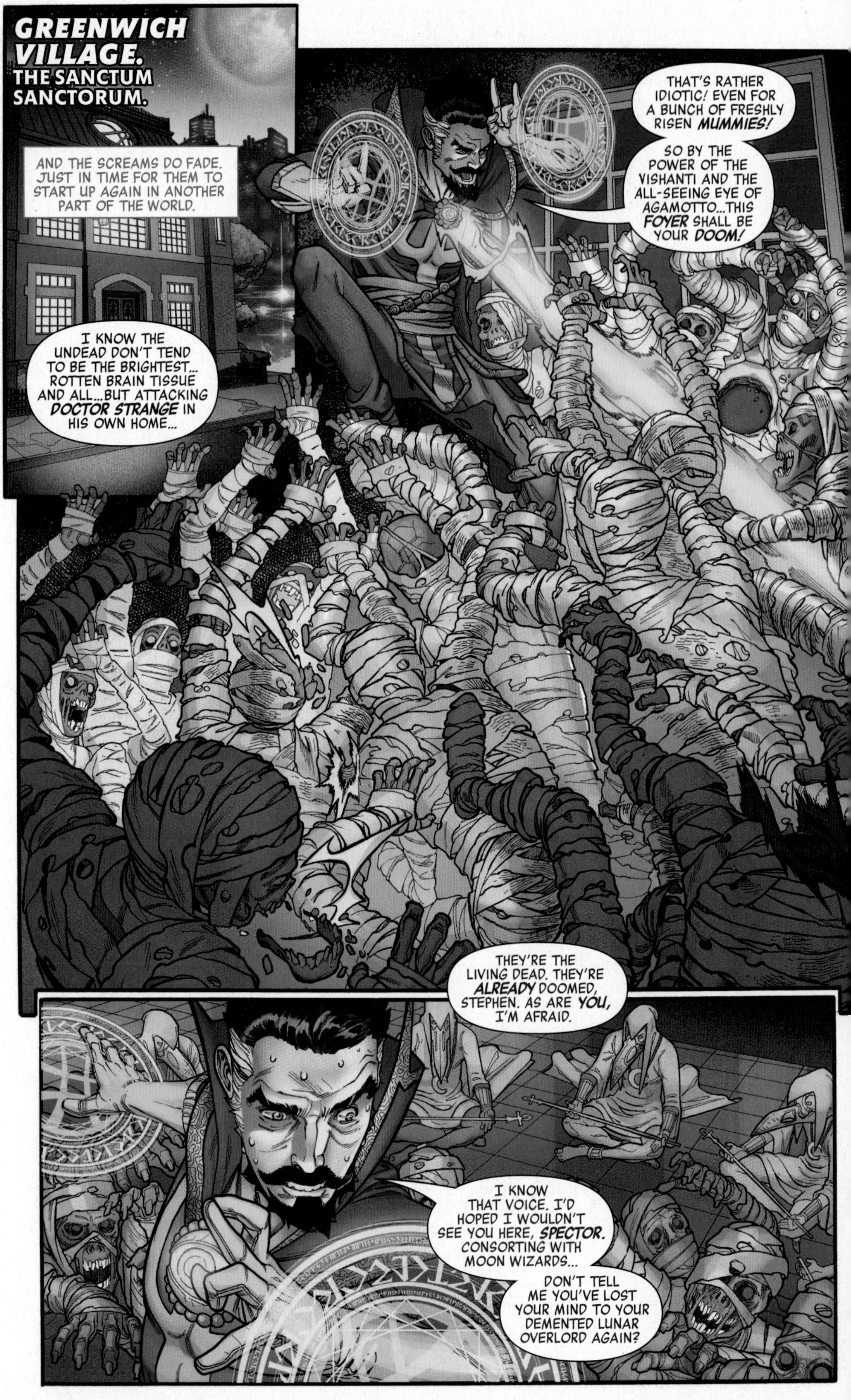

GREENWICH VILLAGE. THE SANCTUM SANCTORUM.
AND THE SCREAMS DO FADE. JUST IN TIME FOR THEM TO START UP AGAIN IN ANOTHER PART OF THE WORLD.
I KNOW THE UNDEAD DON'T TEND TO BE THE BRIGHTEST... ROTTEN BRAIN TISSUE AND ALL...BUT ATTACKING DOCTOR STRANGE IN HIS OWN HOME...
THAT'S RATHER IDIOTIC! EVEN FOR A BUNCH OF FRESHLY RISEN MUMMIES!
SO BY THE POWER OF THE VISHANTI AND THE ALL-SEEING EYE OF AGAMOTTO...THIS FOYER SHALL BE YOUR DOOM!
THEY'RE THE LIVING DEAD. THEY'RE ALREADY DOOMED, STEPHEN. AS ARE YOU, I'M AFRAID.
I KNOW THAT VOICE. I'D HOPED I WOULDN'T SEE YOU HERE, SPECTOR. CONSORTING WITH MOON WIZARDS...
DON'T TELL ME YOU'VE LOST YOUR MIND TO YOUR DEMENTED LUNAR OVERLORD AGAIN?

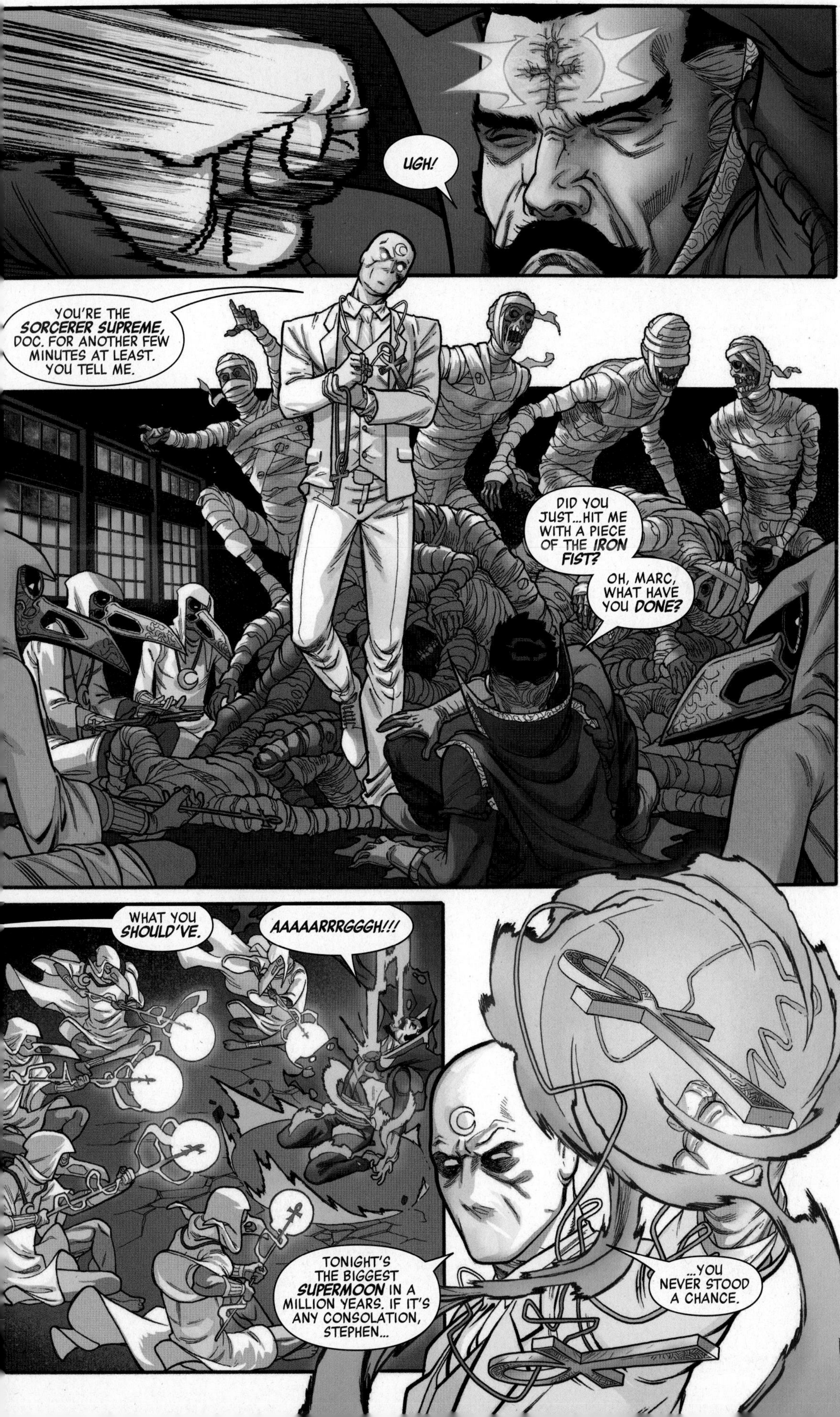
UGH!
YOU'RE THE SORCERER SUPREME, DOC. FOR ANOTHER FEW MINUTES AT LEAST. YOU TELL ME.
DID YOU JUST...HIT ME WITH A PIECE OF THE IRON FIST?
OH, MARC, WHAT HAVE YOU DONE?
WHAT YOU SHOULD'VE.
AAAAARRRGGGH!!!
TONIGHT'S THE BIGGEST SUPERMOON IN A MILLION YEARS. IF IT'S ANY CONSOLATION, STEPHEN...
...YOU NEVER STOOD A CHANCE.

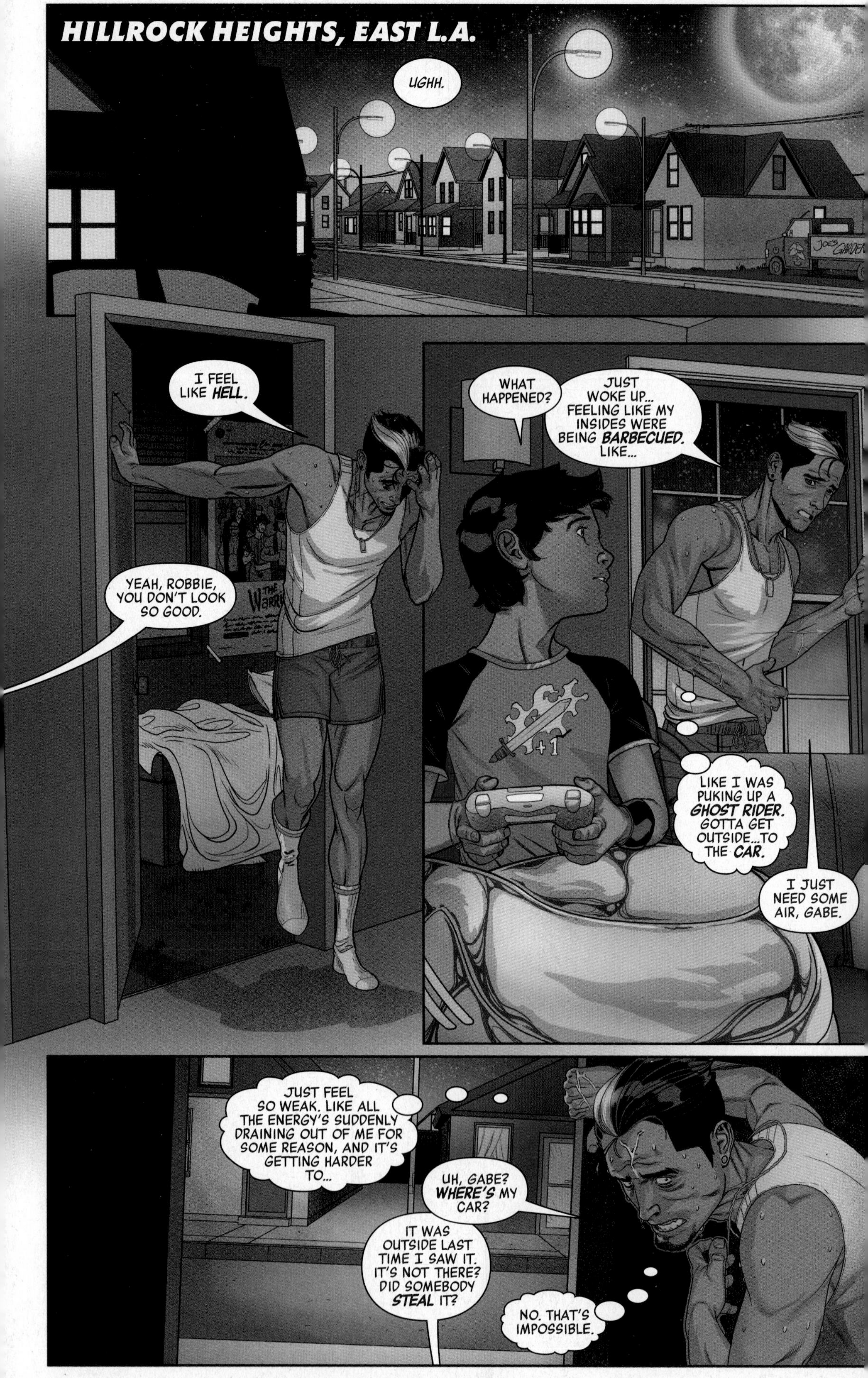
HILLROCK HEIGHTS, EAST L.A.
UGHH.
JOE'S GARDEN
I FEEL LIKE HELL.
YEAH, ROBBIE, YOU DON'T LOOK SO GOOD.
WHAT HAPPENED?
JUST WOKE UP... FEELING LIKE MY INSIDES WERE BEING BARBECUED. LIKE...
LIKE I WAS PUKING UP A GHOST RIDER. GOTTA GET OUTSIDE...TO THE CAR.
I JUST NEED SOME AIR, GABE.
JUST FEEL SO WEAK. LIKE ALL THE ENERGY'S SUDDENLY DRAINING OUT OF ME FOR SOME REASON, AND IT'S GETTING HARDER TO...
UH, GABE? WHERE'S MY CAR?
IT WAS OUTSIDE LAST TIME I SAW IT. IT'S NOT THERE? DID SOMEBODY STEAL IT?
NO. THAT'S IMPOSSIBLE.

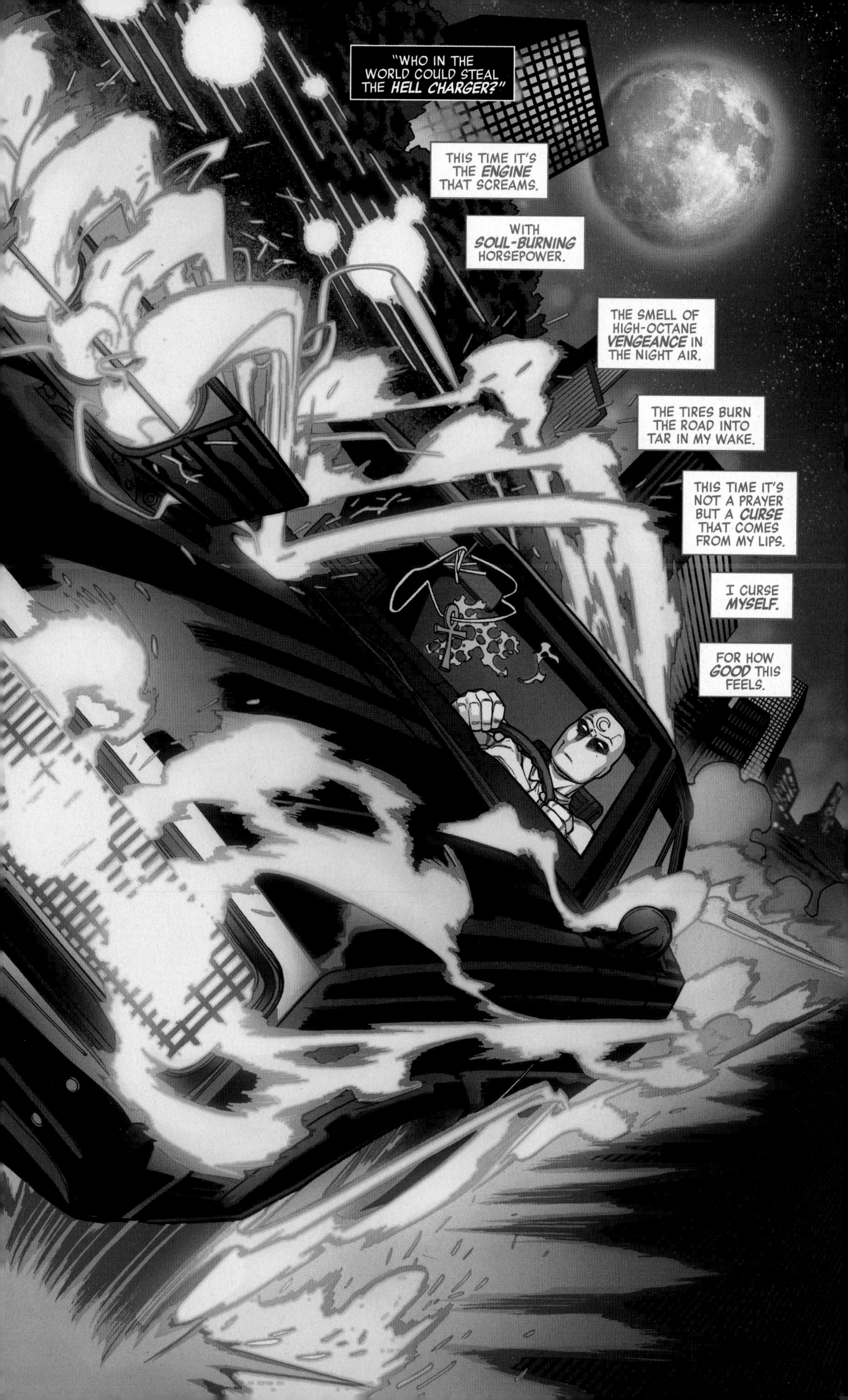
"WHO IN THE WORLD COULD STEAL THE HELL CHARGER?"
THIS TIME IT'S THE ENGINE THAT SCREAMS.
WITH SOUL-BURNING HORSEPOWER.
THE SMELL OF HIGH-OCTANE VENGEANCE IN THE NIGHT AIR.
THE TIRES BURN THE ROAD INTO TAR IN MY WAKE.
THIS TIME IT'S NOT A PRAYER BUT A CURSE THAT COMES FROM MY LIPS.
I CURSE MYSELF.
FOR HOW GOOD THIS FEELS.

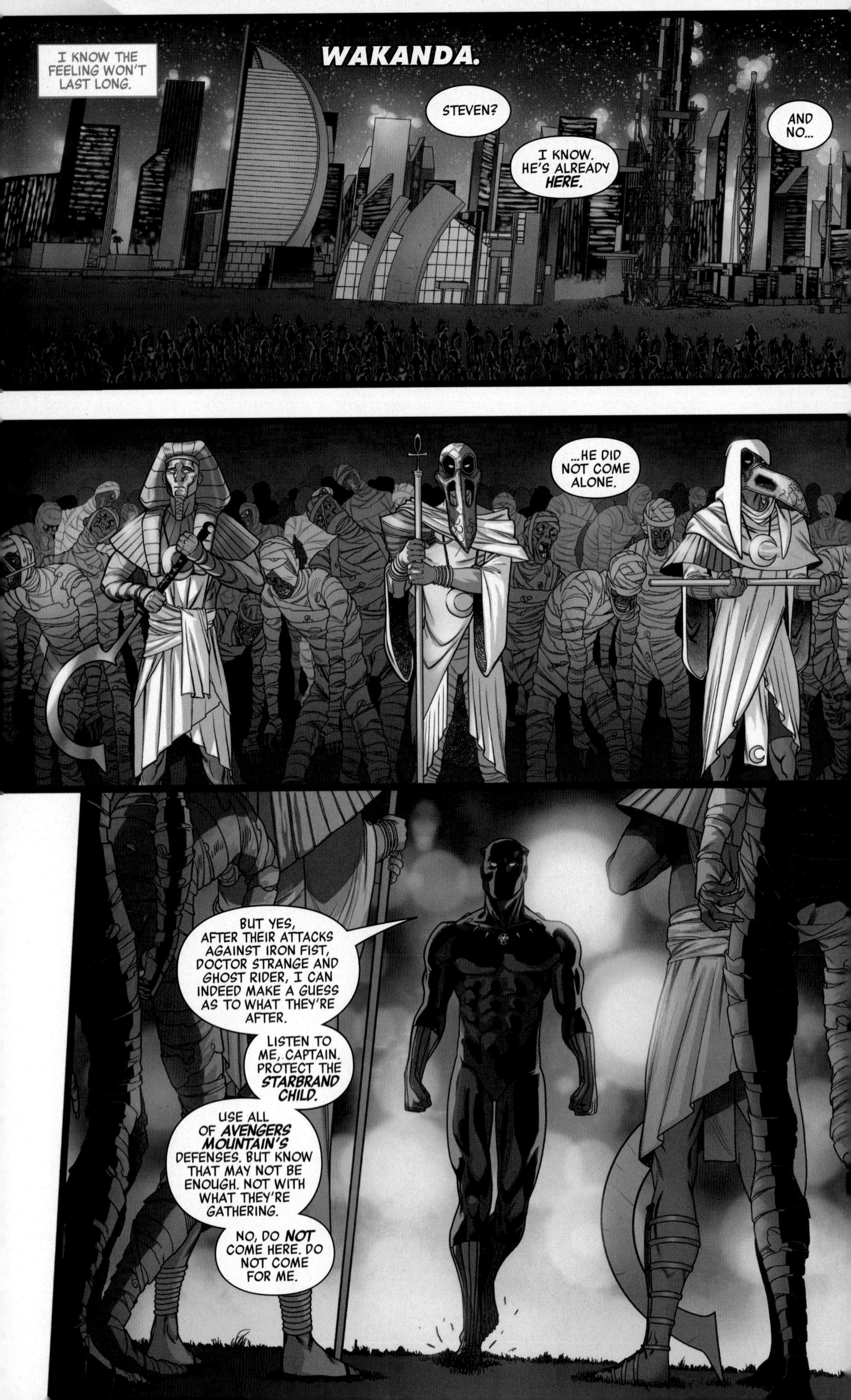
I KNOW THE FEELING WON'T LAST LONG.
WAKANDA.
STEVEN?
I KNOW. HE'S ALREADY HERE.
AND NO...
...HE DID NOT COME ALONE.
BUT YES, AFTER THEIR ATTACKS AGAINST IRON FIST, DOCTOR STRANGE AND GHOST RIDER, I CAN INDEED MAKE A GUESS AS TO WHAT THEY'RE AFTER.
LISTEN TO ME, CAPTAIN. PROTECT THE STARBRAND CHILD.
USE ALL OF AVENGERS MOUNTAIN'S DEFENSES. BUT KNOW THAT MAY NOT BE ENOUGH. NOT WITH WHAT THEY'RE GATHERING.
NO, DO NOT COME HERE. DO NOT COME FOR ME.

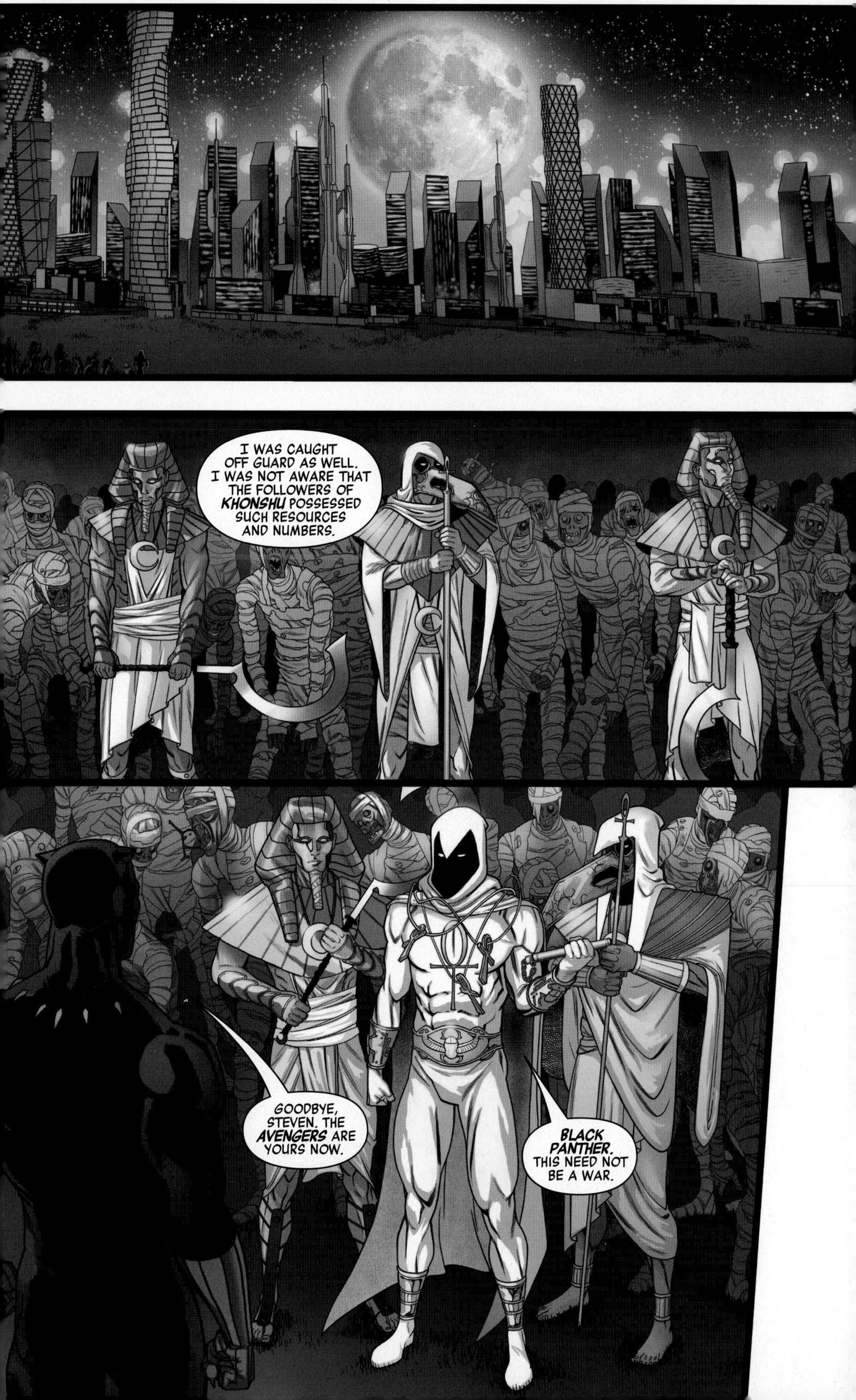
I WAS CAUGHT OFF GUARD AS WELL. I WAS NOT AWARE THAT THE FOLLOWERS OF KHONSHU POSSESSED SUCH RESOURCES AND NUMBERS.
GOODBYE, STEVEN. THE AVENGERS ARE YOURS NOW.
BLACK PANTHER. THIS NEED NOT BE A WAR.

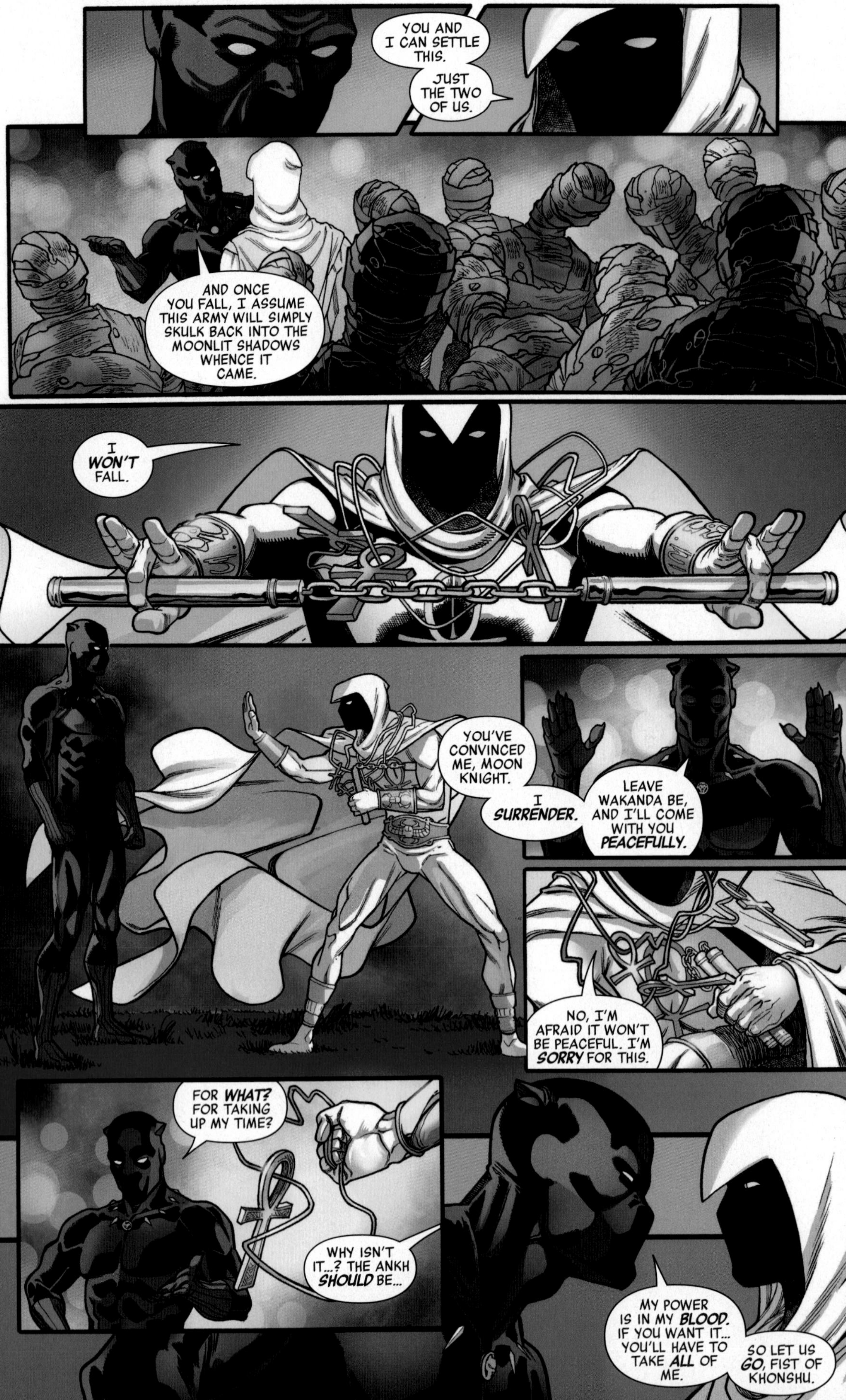
YOU AND I CAN SETTLE THIS.
JUST THE TWO OF US.
AND ONCE YOU FALL, I ASSUME THIS ARMY WILL SIMPLY SKULK BACK INTO THE MOONLIT SHADOWS WHENCE IT CAME.
I WON'T FALL.
YOU'VE CONVINCED ME, MOON KNIGHT.
I SURRENDER.
LEAVE WAKANDA BE, AND I'LL COME WITH YOU PEACEFULLY.
NO, I'M AFRAID IT WON'T BE PEACEFUL. I'M SORRY FOR THIS.
FOR WHAT? FOR TAKING UP MY TIME?
WHY ISN'T IT...? THE ANKH SHOULD BE...
MY POWER IS IN MY BLOOD. IF YOU WANT IT... YOU'LL HAVE TO TAKE ALL OF ME.
SO LET US GO, FIST OF KHONSHU.

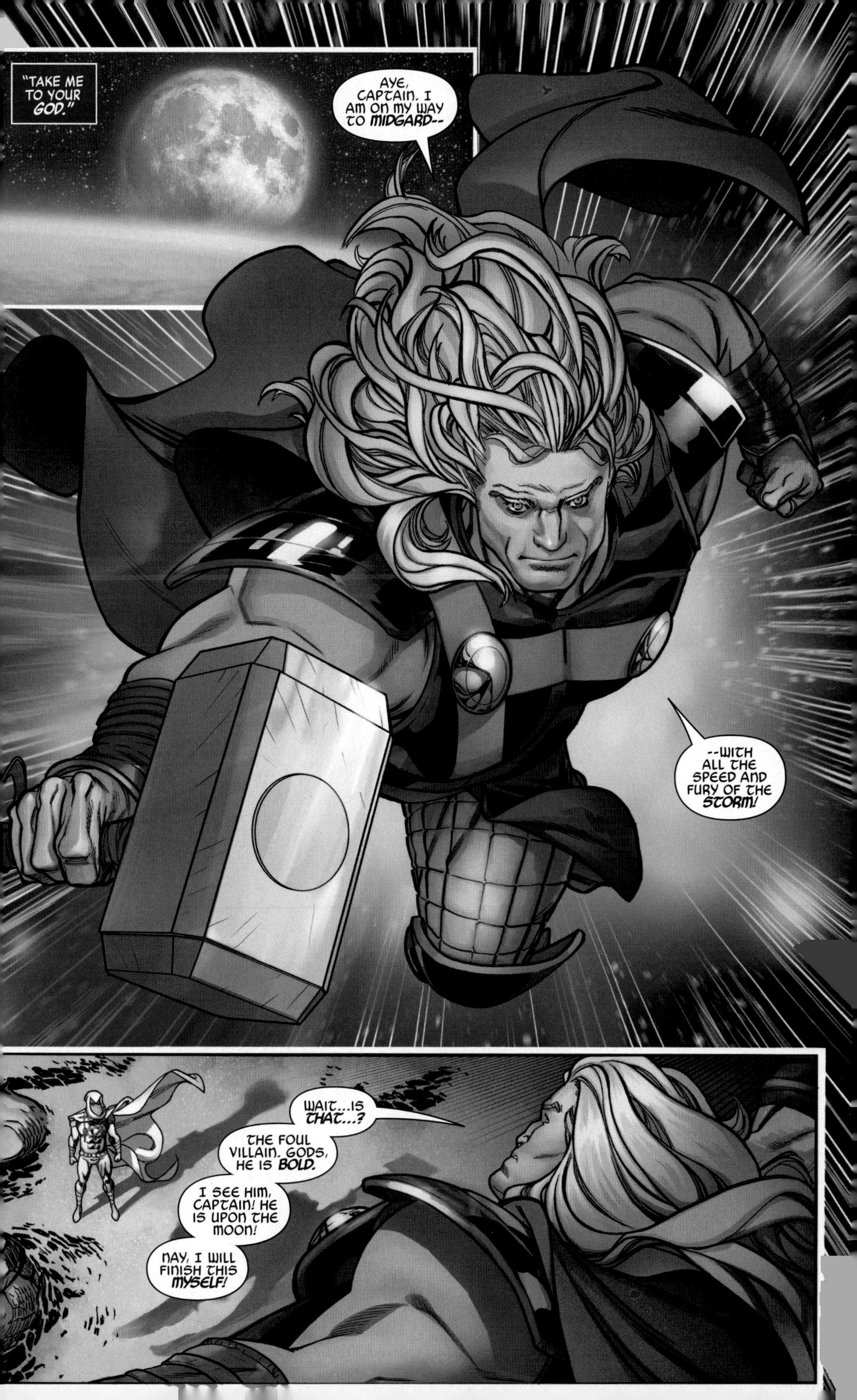
"TAKE ME TO YOUR GOD."
AYE, CAPTAIN. I AM ON MY WAY TO MIDGARD--
--WITH ALL THE SPEED AND FURY OF THE STORM!
WAIT...IS THAT...?
THE FOUL VILLAIN. GODS, HE IS BOLD.
I SEE HIM, CAPTAIN! HE IS UPON THE MOON!
NAY, I WILL FINISH THIS MYSELF!

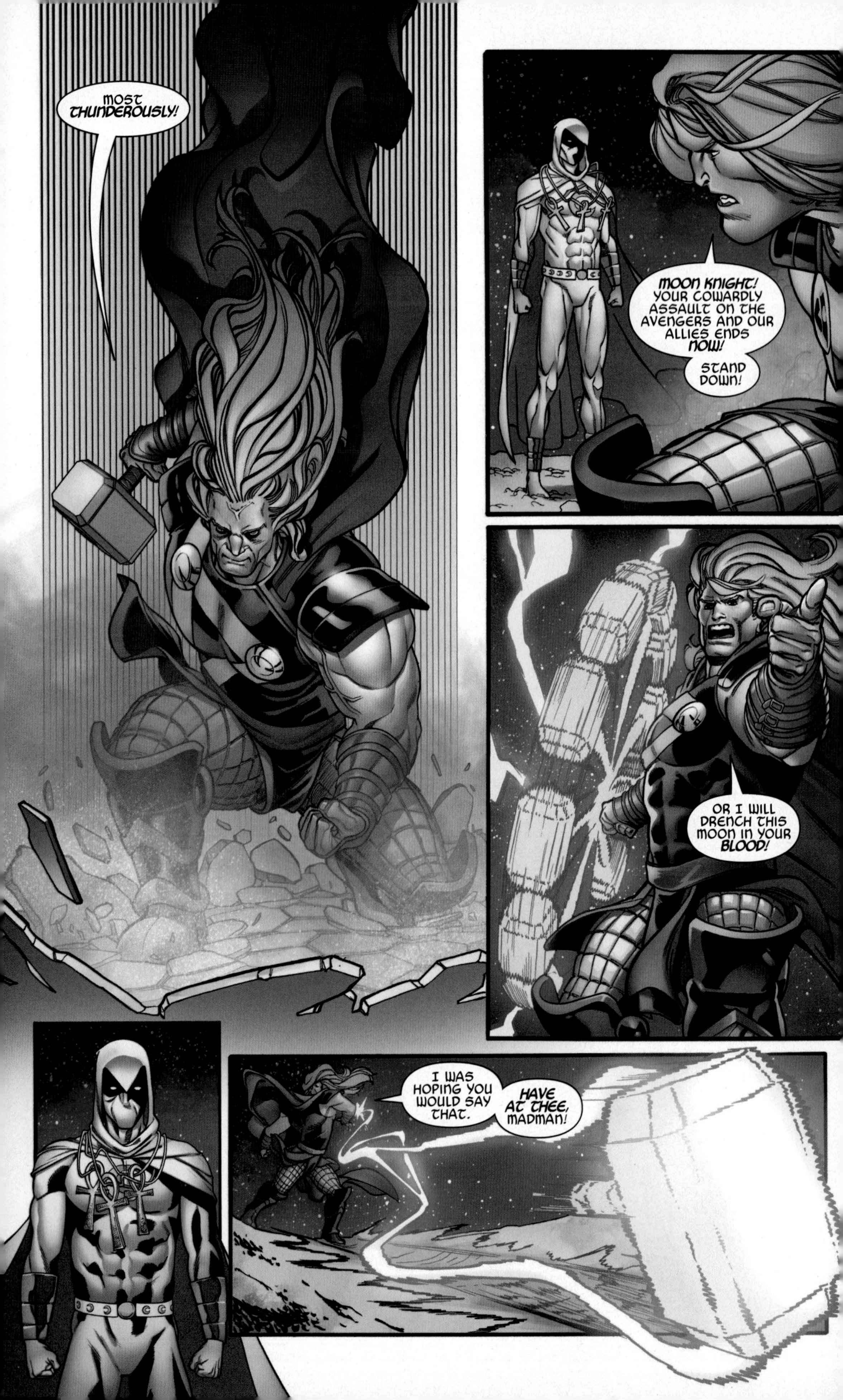
MOST THUNDEROUSLY!
MOON KNIGHT! YOUR COWARDLY ASSAULT ON THE AVENGERS AND OUR ALLIES ENDS NOW!
STAND DOWN!
OR I WILL DRENCH THIS MOON IN YOUR BLOOD!
I WAS HOPING YOU WOULD SAY THAT.
HAVE AT THEE, MADMAN!

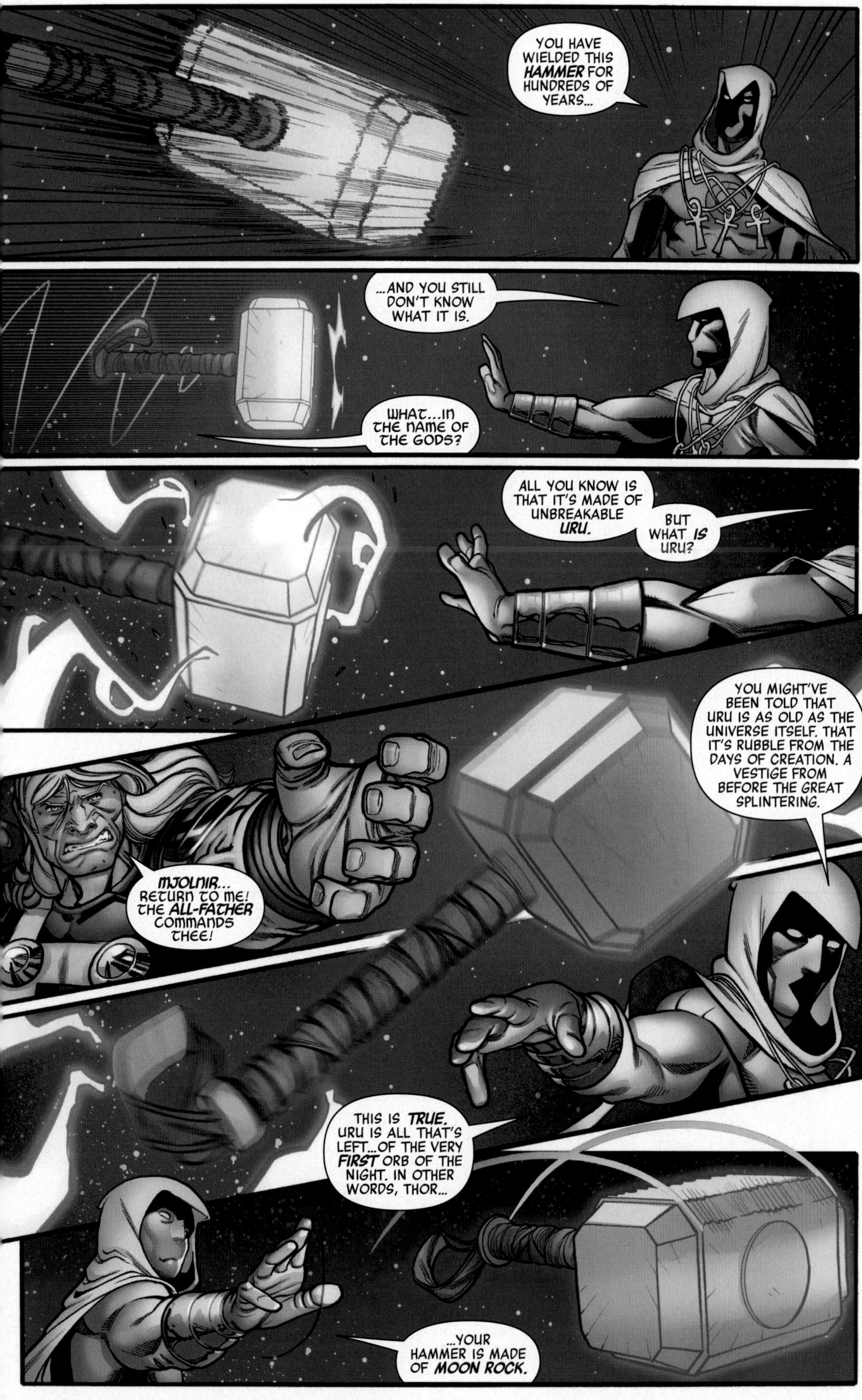

YOU HAVE WIELDED THIS HAMMER FOR HUNDREDS OF YEARS...
...AND YOU STILL DON'T KNOW WHAT IT IS.
WHAT...IN THE NAME OF THE GODS?
ALL YOU KNOW IS THAT IT'S MADE OF UNBREAKABLE URU.
BUT WHAT IS URU?
YOU MIGHT'VE BEEN TOLD THAT URU IS AS OLD AS THE UNIVERSE ITSELF. THAT IT'S RUBBLE FROM THE DAYS OF CREATION. A VESTIGE FROM BEFORE THE GREAT SPLINTERING.
MJOLNIR... RETURN TO ME! THE ALL-FATHER COMMANDS THEE!
THIS IS TRUE. URU IS ALL THAT'S LEFT...OF THE VERY FIRST ORB OF THE NIGHT. IN OTHER WORDS, THOR...
...YOUR HAMMER IS MADE OF MOON ROCK.

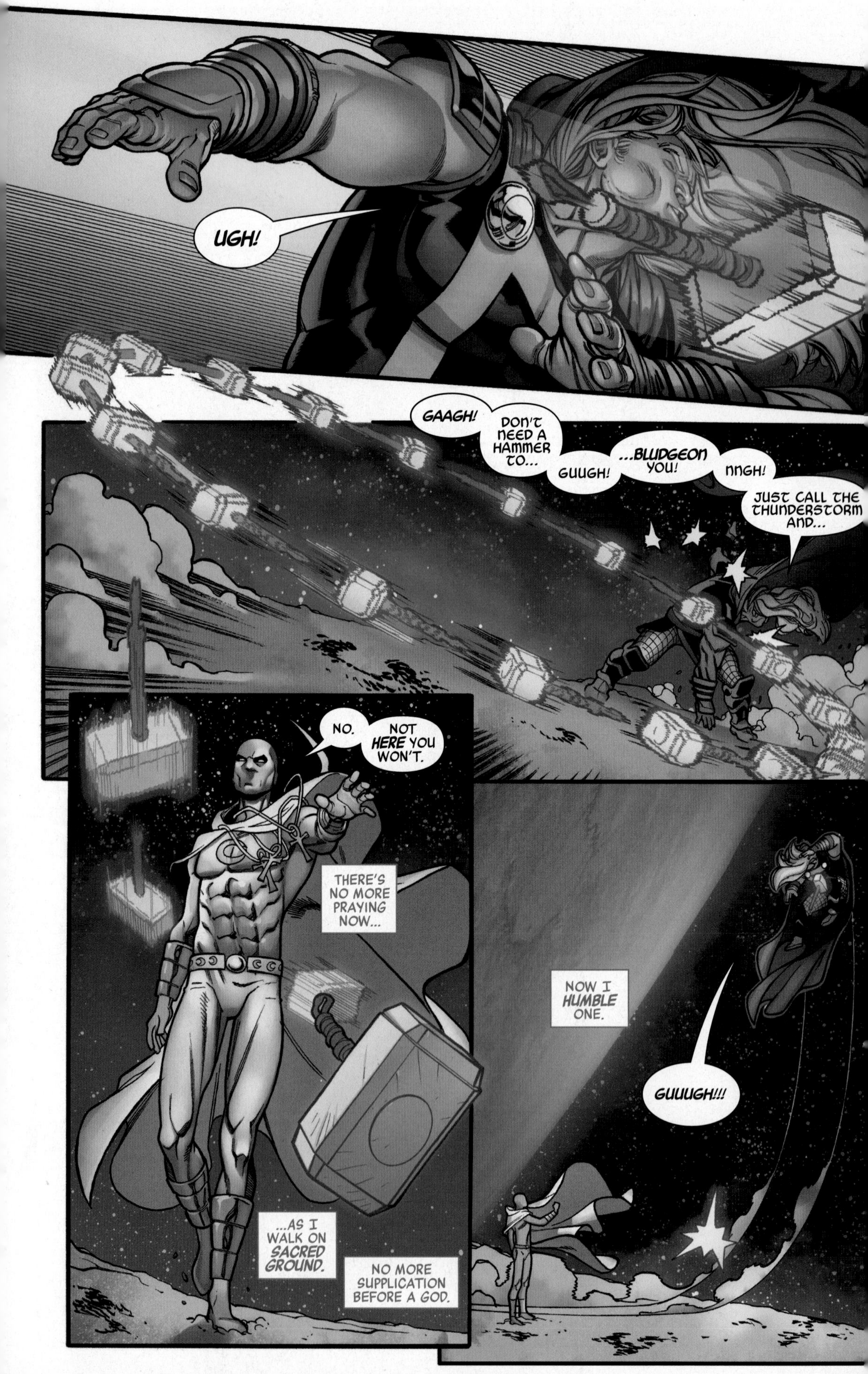
UGH!
GAAGH!
DON'T NEED A HAMMER TO...
GUUGH!
...BLUDGEON YOU!
NNGH!
JUST CALL THE THUNDERSTORM AND...
NO.
NOT HERE YOU WON'T.
THERE'S NO MORE PRAYING NOW...
...AS I WALK ON SACRED GROUND.
NO MORE SUPPLICATION BEFORE A GOD.
NOW I HUMBLE ONE.
GUUUGH!!!

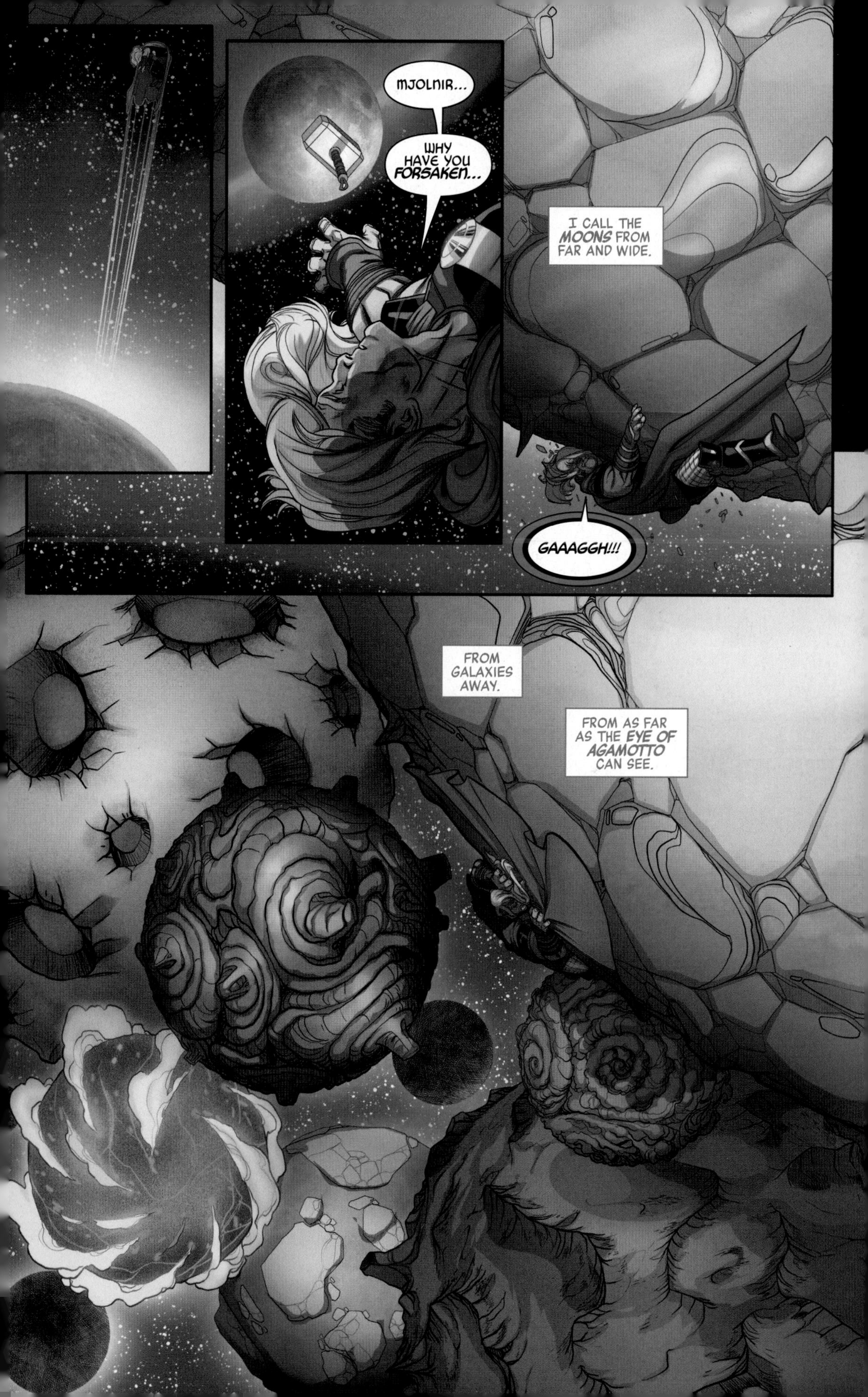
MJOLNIR...
WHY HAVE YOU FORSAKEN...
I CALL THE MOONS FROM FAR AND WIDE.
GAAAGGH!!!
FROM GALAXIES AWAY.
FROM AS FAR AS THE EYE OF AGAMOTTO CAN SEE.

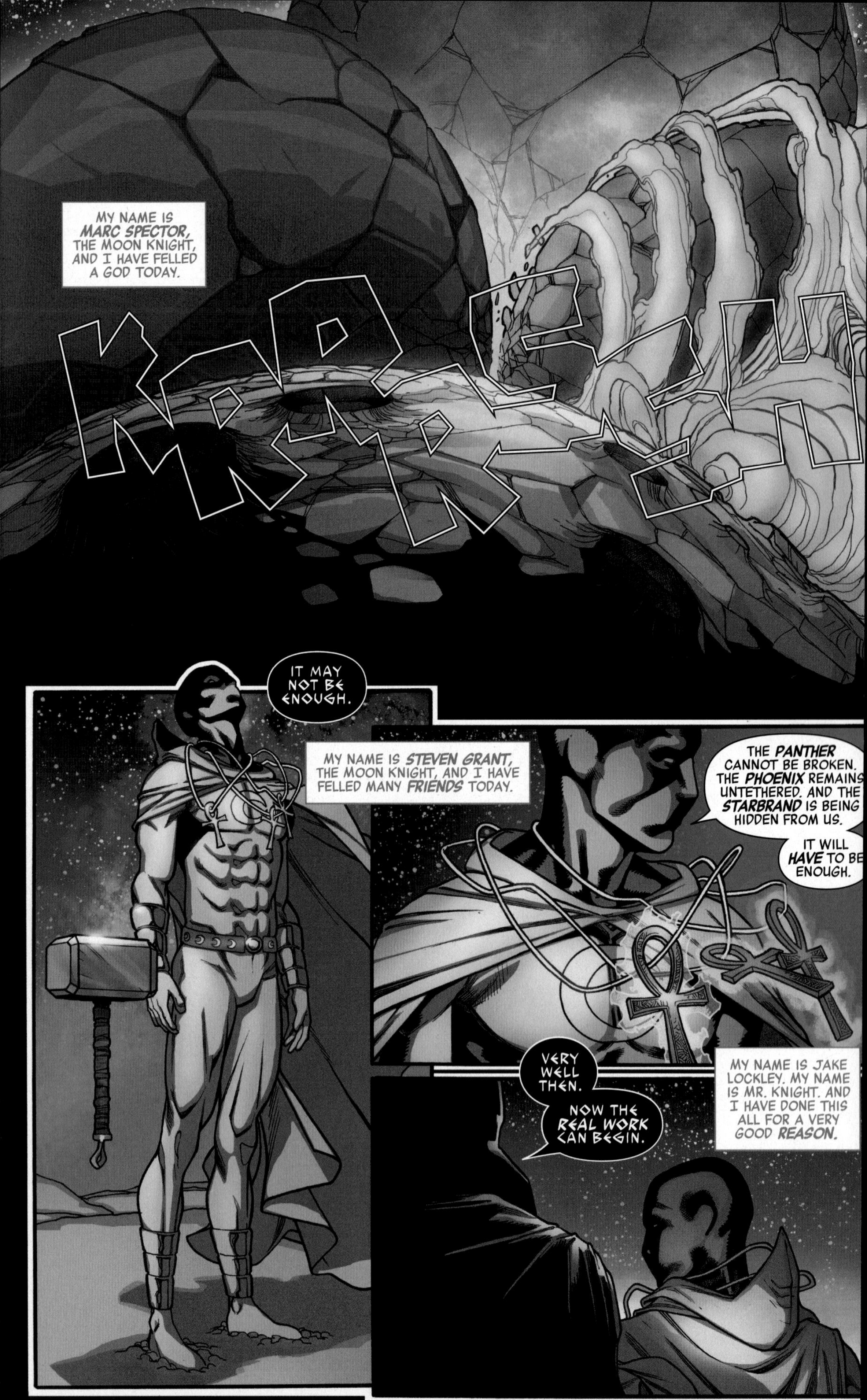
MY NAME IS MARC SPECTOR, THE MOON KNIGHT, AND I HAVE FELLED A GOD TODAY.
IT MAY NOT BE ENOUGH.
MY NAME IS STEVEN GRANT, THE MOON KNIGHT, AND I HAVE FELLED MANY FRIENDS TODAY.
THE PANTHER CANNOT BE BROKEN. THE PHOENIX REMAINS UNTETHERED. AND THE STARBRAND IS BEING HIDDEN FROM US.
IT WILL HAVE TO BE ENOUGH.
VERY WELL THEN.
NOW THE REAL WORK CAN BEGIN.
MY NAME IS JAKE LOCKLEY. MY NAME IS MR. KNIGHT. AND I HAVE DONE THIS ALL FOR A VERY GOOD REASON.

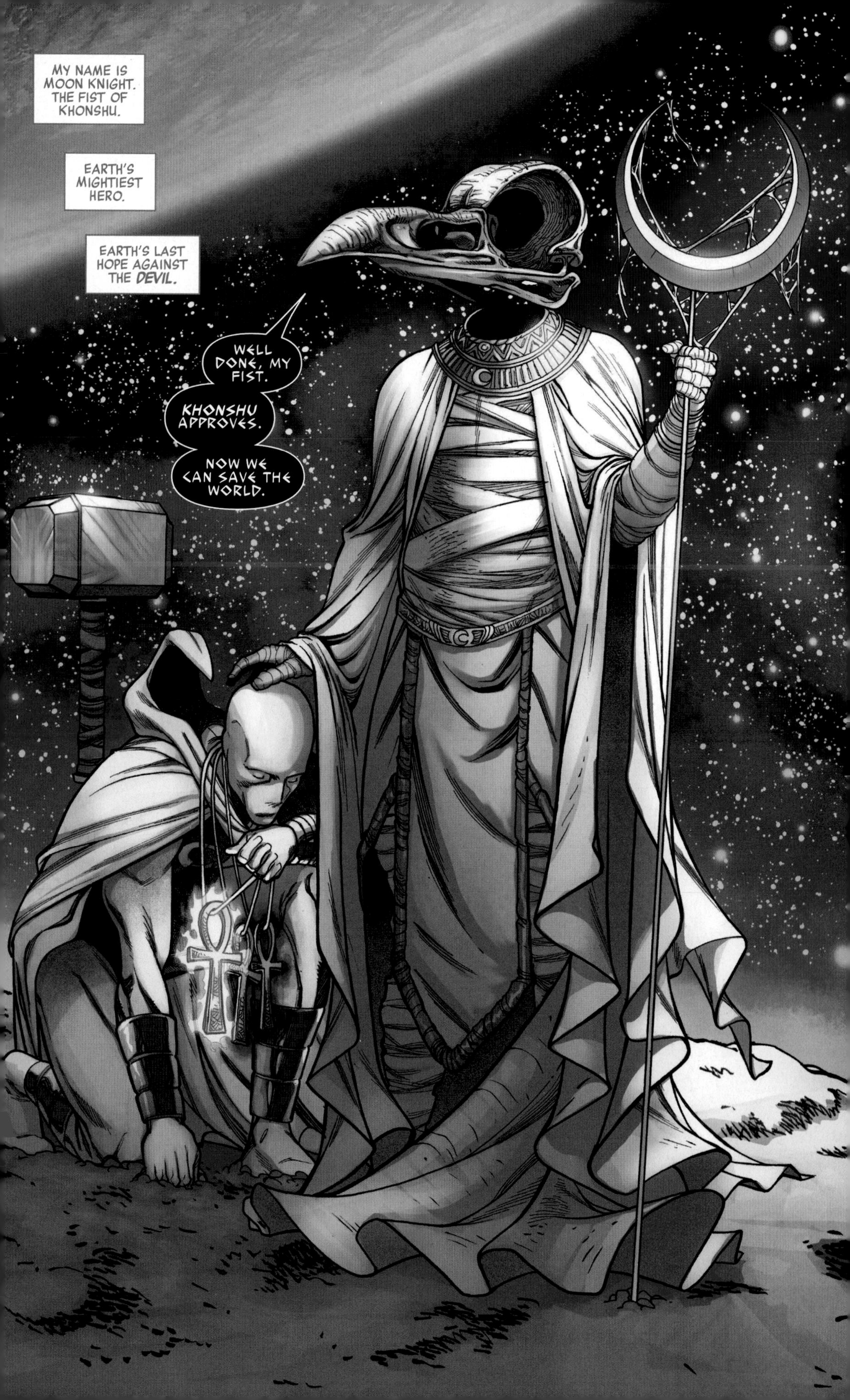
MY NAME IS MOON KNIGHT. THE FIST OF KHONSHU.
EARTH'S MIGHTIEST HERO.
EARTH'S LAST HOPE AGAINST THE *DEVIL.*
WELL DONE, MY FIST.
KHONSHU APPROVES.
NOW WE CAN SAVE THE WORLD.

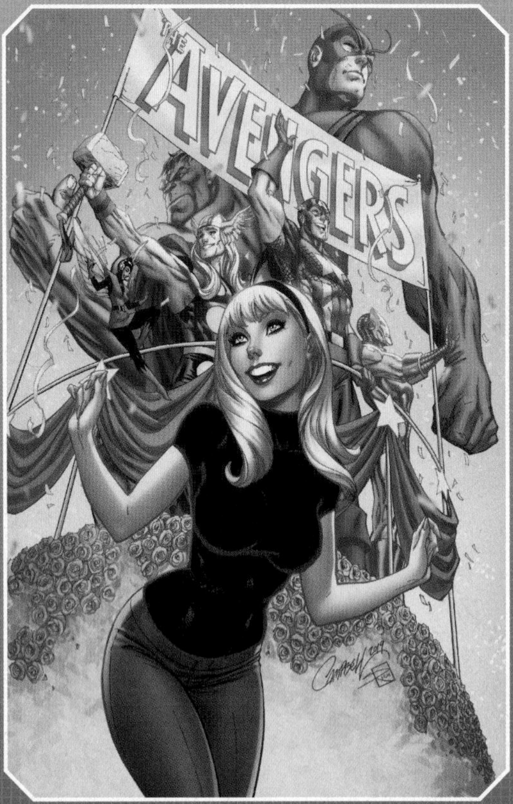
THE AVENGERS

J. SCOTT CAMPBELL & SABINE RICH
31 GWEN STACY VARIANT

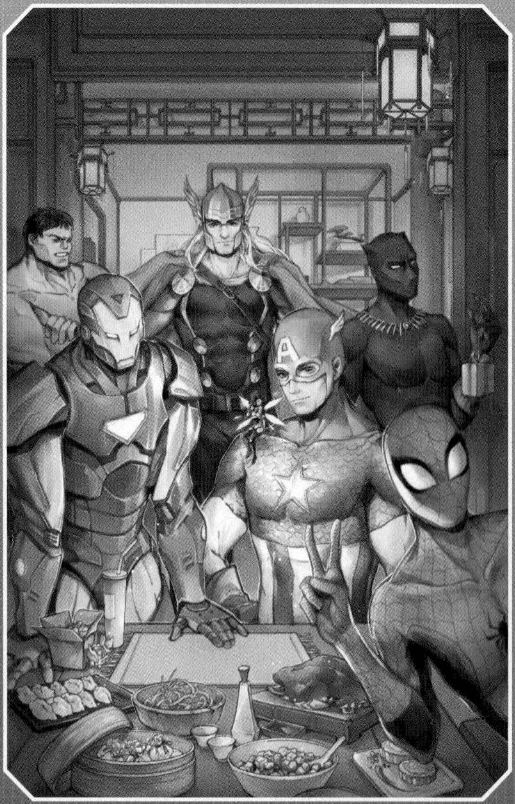

TIANQI HU
31 CHINESE NEW YEAR VARIANT

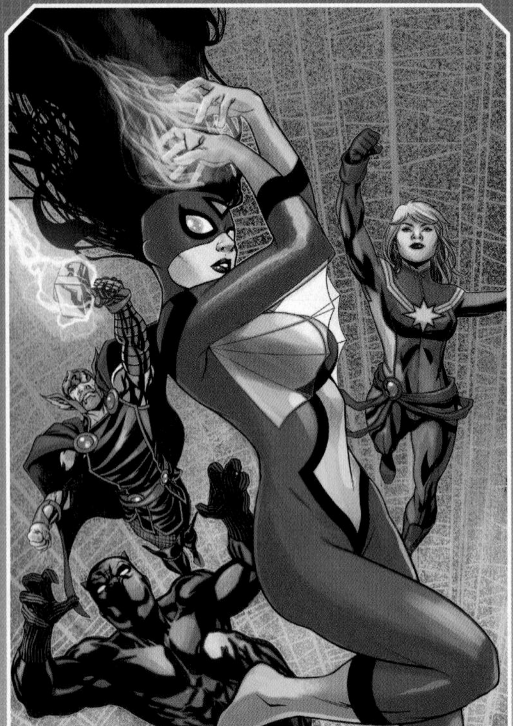

MIKE MCKONE & ANDRES MOSSA
32 SPIDER-WOMAN VARIANT

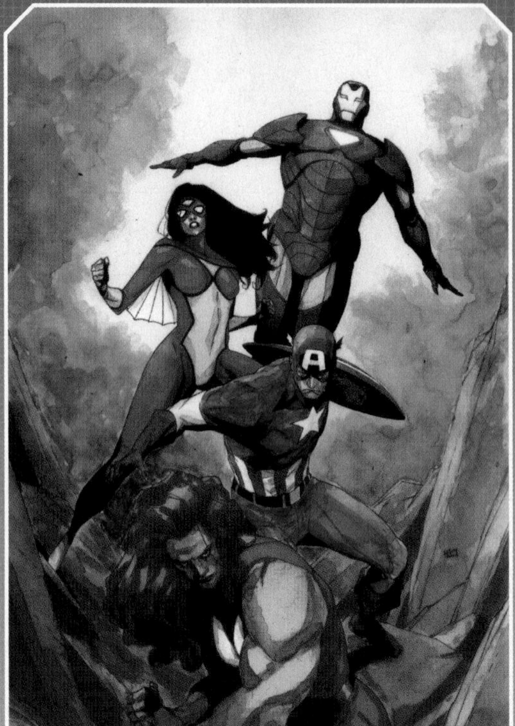

KHOI PHAM & MORRY HOLLOWELL
33 SPIDER-WOMAN VARIANT

34 THE AGE OF KHONSHU PART 2
THE FIST OF VENGEANCE

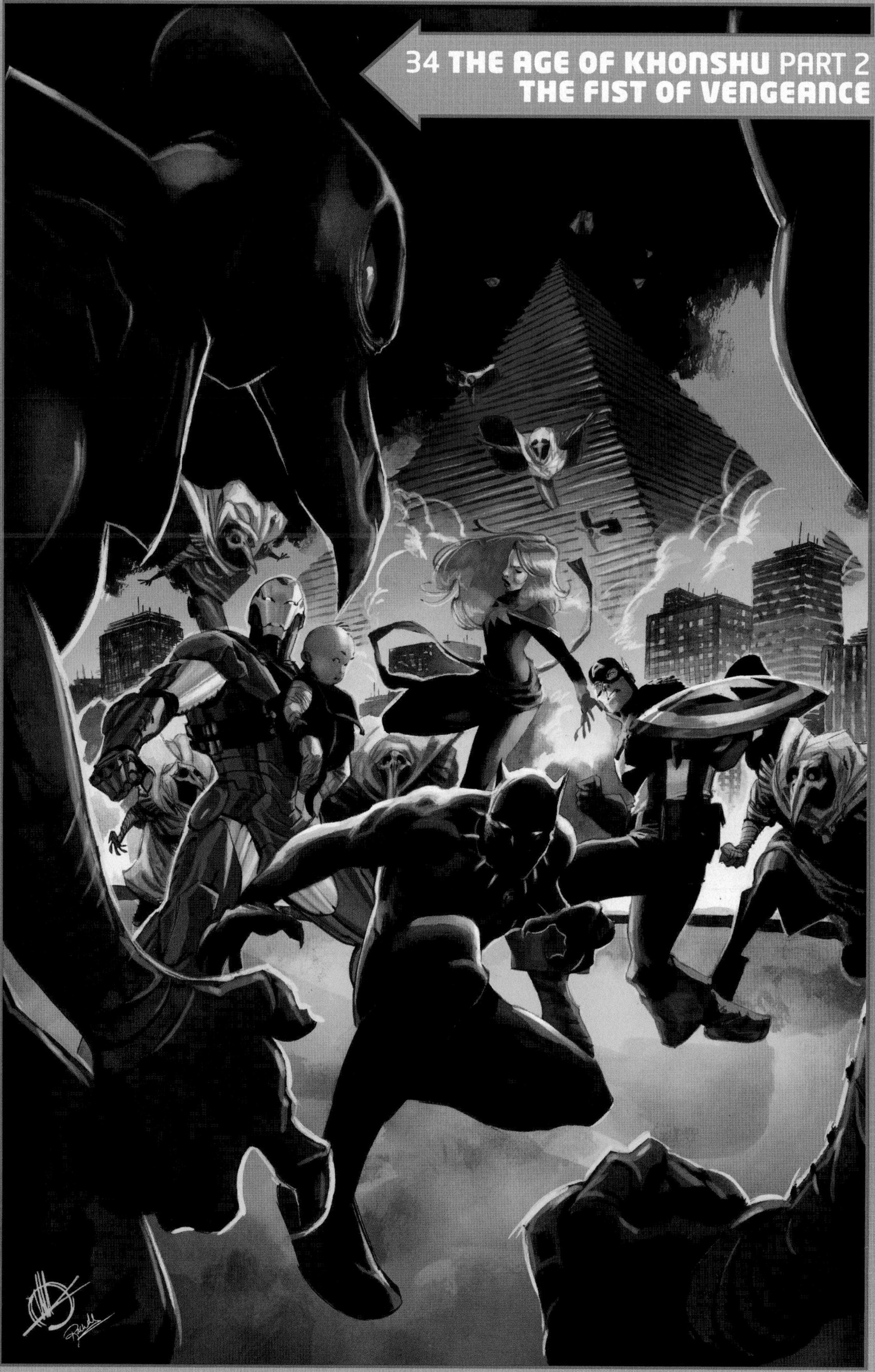

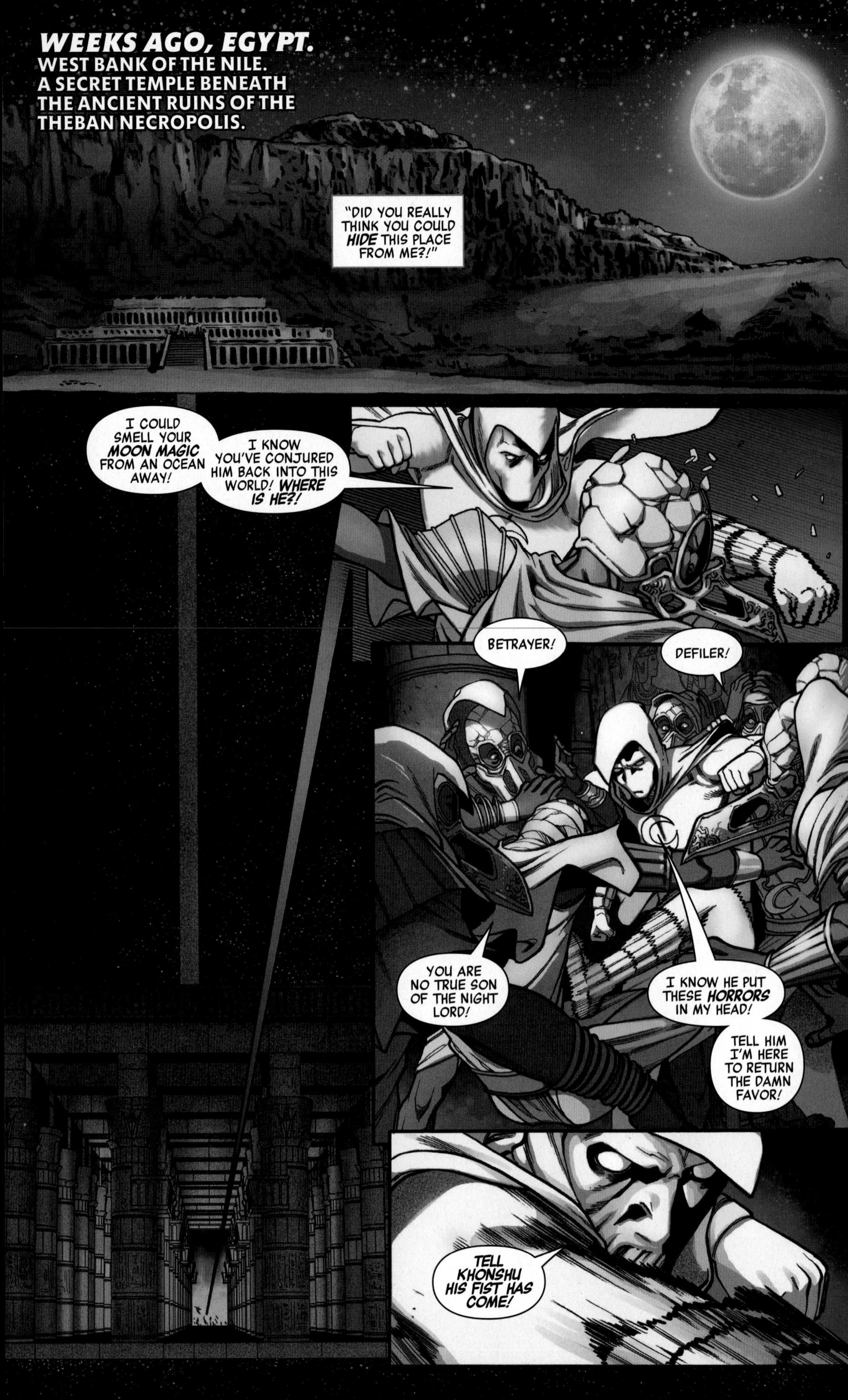
WEEKS AGO, EGYPT.
WEST BANK OF THE NILE. A SECRET TEMPLE BENEATH THE ANCIENT RUINS OF THE THEBAN NECROPOLIS.
"DID YOU REALLY THINK YOU COULD HIDE THIS PLACE FROM ME?!"
I COULD SMELL YOUR MOON MAGIC FROM AN OCEAN AWAY!
I KNOW YOU'VE CONJURED HIM BACK INTO THIS WORLD! WHERE IS HE?!
BETRAYER!
DEFILER!
YOU ARE NO TRUE SON OF THE NIGHT LORD!
I KNOW HE PUT THESE HORRORS IN MY HEAD!
TELL HIM I'M HERE TO RETURN THE DAMN FAVOR!
TELL KHONSHU HIS FIST HAS COME!

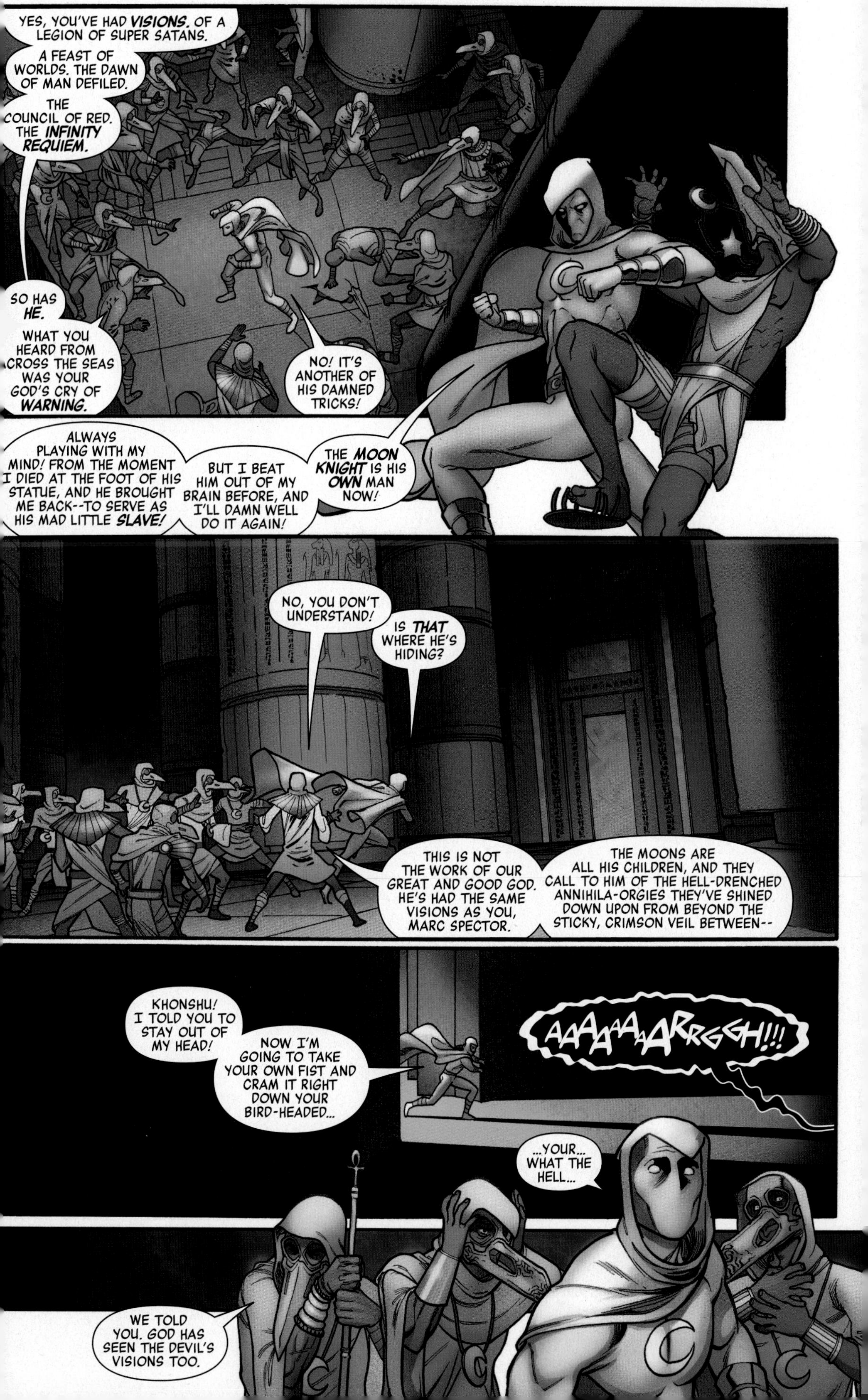

YES, YOU'VE HAD VISIONS. OF A LEGION OF SUPER SATANS.
A FEAST OF WORLDS. THE DAWN OF MAN DEFILED.
THE COUNCIL OF RED. THE INFINITY REQUIEM.
SO HAS HE.
WHAT YOU HEARD FROM CROSS THE SEAS WAS YOUR GOD'S CRY OF WARNING.
NO! IT'S ANOTHER OF HIS DAMNED TRICKS!
ALWAYS PLAYING WITH MY MIND! FROM THE MOMENT I DIED AT THE FOOT OF HIS STATUE, AND HE BROUGHT ME BACK--TO SERVE AS HIS MAD LITTLE SLAVE!
BUT I BEAT HIM OUT OF MY BRAIN BEFORE, AND I'LL DAMN WELL DO IT AGAIN!
THE MOON KNIGHT IS HIS OWN MAN NOW!
NO, YOU DON'T UNDERSTAND!
IS THAT WHERE HE'S HIDING?
THIS IS NOT THE WORK OF OUR GREAT AND GOOD GOD. HE'S HAD THE SAME VISIONS AS YOU, MARC SPECTOR.
THE MOONS ARE ALL HIS CHILDREN, AND THEY CALL TO HIM OF THE HELL-DRENCHED ANNIHILA-ORGIES THEY'VE SHINED DOWN UPON FROM BEYOND THE STICKY, CRIMSON VEIL BETWEEN--
KHONSHU! I TOLD YOU TO STAY OUT OF MY HEAD!
NOW I'M GOING TO TAKE YOUR OWN FIST AND CRAM IT RIGHT DOWN YOUR BIRD-HEADED...
AAAAAAARRGGH!!!
...YOUR... WHAT THE HELL...
WE TOLD YOU. GOD HAS SEEN THE DEVIL'S VISIONS TOO.

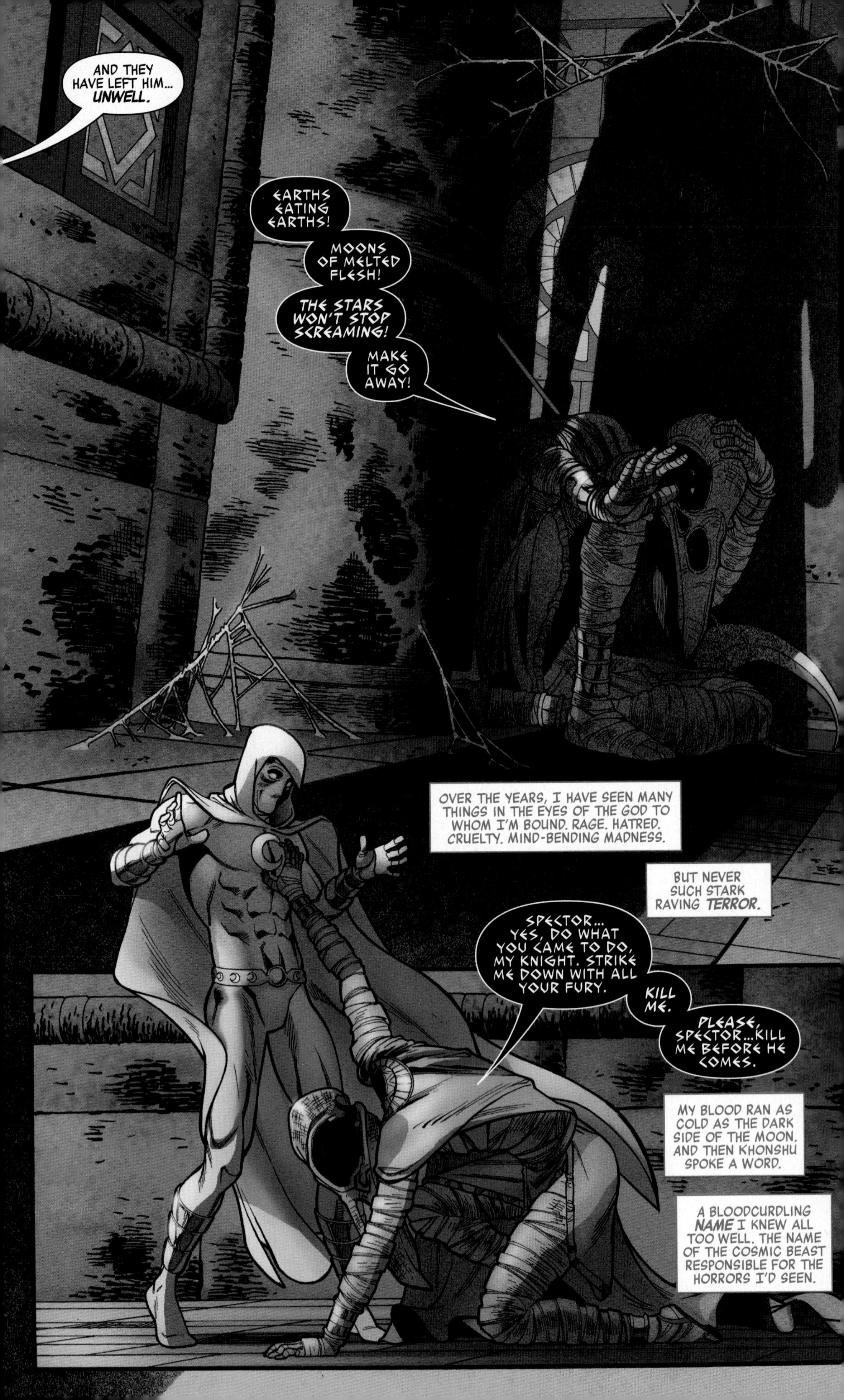
AND THEY HAVE LEFT HIM... UNWELL.
EARTHS EATING EARTHS!
MOONS OF MELTED FLESH!
THE STARS WON'T STOP SCREAMING!
MAKE IT GO AWAY!
OVER THE YEARS, I HAVE SEEN MANY THINGS IN THE EYES OF THE GOD TO WHOM I'M BOUND. RAGE. HATRED. CRUELTY. MIND-BENDING MADNESS.
BUT NEVER SUCH STARK RAVING TERROR.
SPECTOR... YES, DO WHAT YOU CAME TO DO, MY KNIGHT. STRIKE ME DOWN WITH ALL YOUR FURY.
KILL ME.
PLEASE, SPECTOR...KILL ME BEFORE HE COMES.
MY BLOOD RAN AS COLD AS THE DARK SIDE OF THE MOON. AND THEN KHONSHU SPOKE A WORD.
A BLOODCURDLING NAME I KNEW ALL TOO WELL. THE NAME OF THE COSMIC BEAST RESPONSIBLE FOR THE HORRORS I'D SEEN.

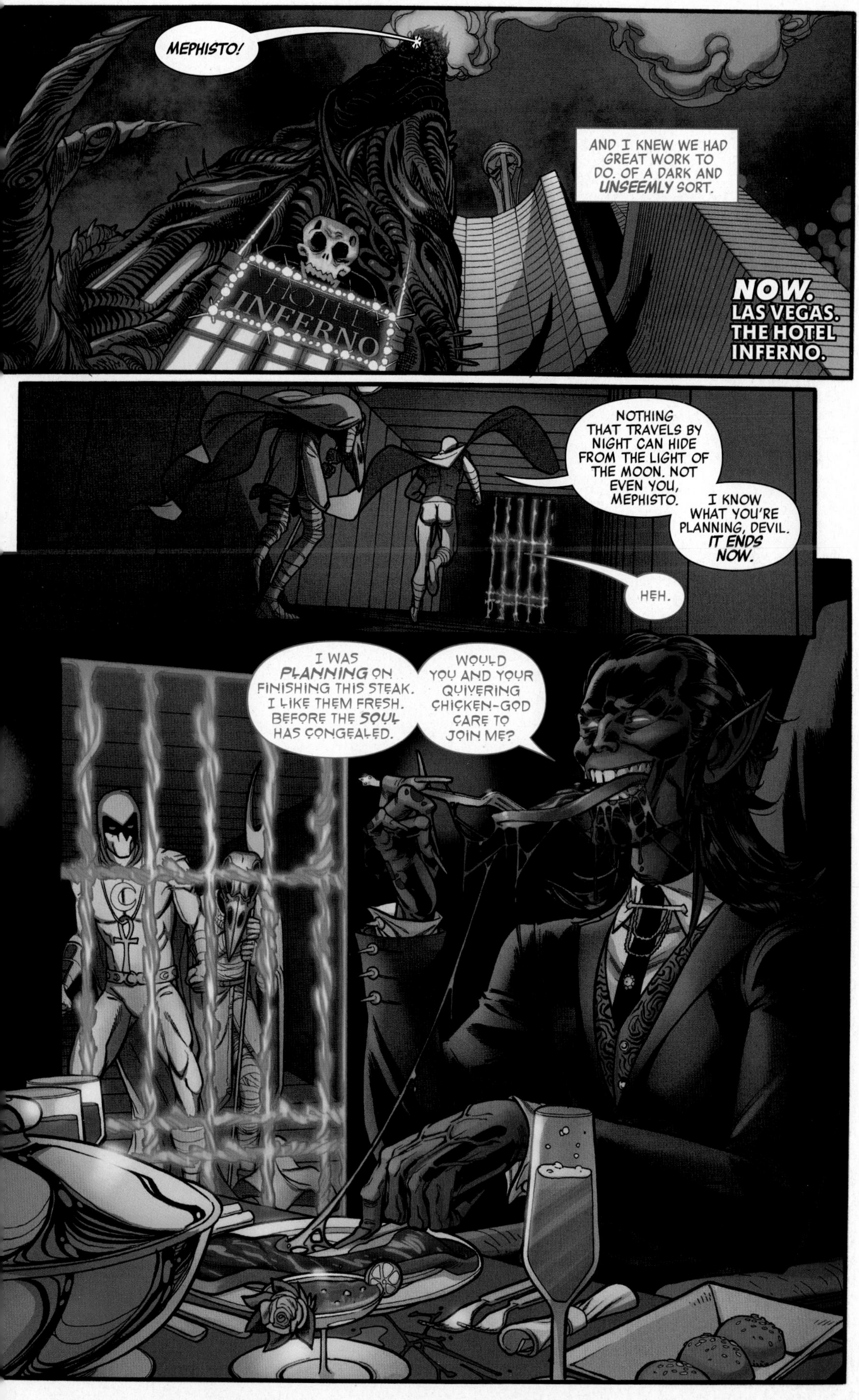
MEPHISTO!
AND I KNEW WE HAD GREAT WORK TO DO. OF A DARK AND UNSEEMLY SORT.
HOTEL INFERNO
NOW. LAS VEGAS. THE HOTEL INFERNO.
NOTHING THAT TRAVELS BY NIGHT CAN HIDE FROM THE LIGHT OF THE MOON. NOT EVEN YOU, MEPHISTO.
I KNOW WHAT YOU'RE PLANNING, DEVIL. IT ENDS NOW.
HEH.
I WAS PLANNING ON FINISHING THIS STEAK. I LIKE THEM FRESH. BEFORE THE SOUL HAS CONGEALED.
WOULD YOU AND YOUR QUIVERING CHICKEN-GOD CARE TO JOIN ME?

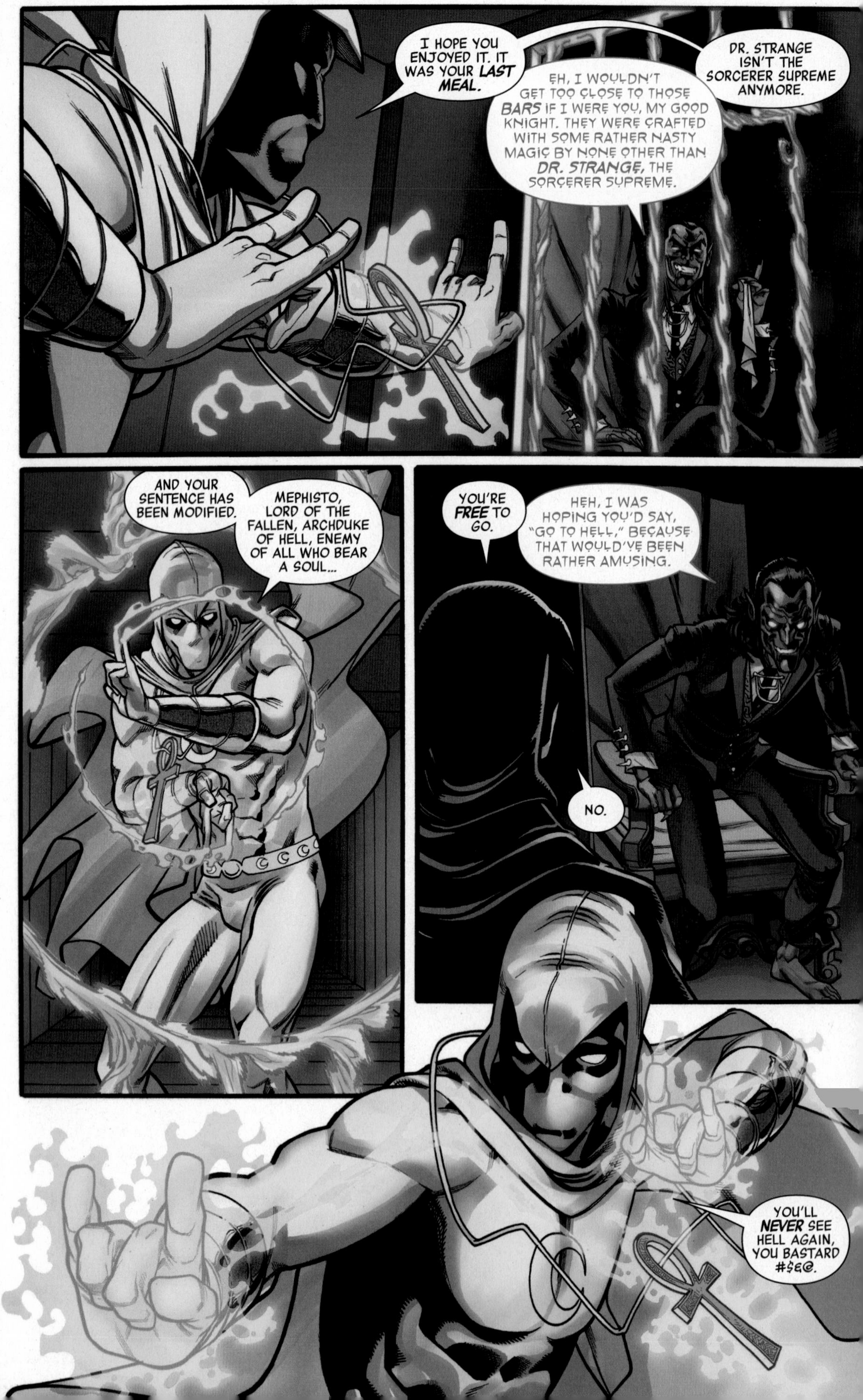

I HOPE YOU ENJOYED IT. IT WAS YOUR LAST MEAL.
DR. STRANGE ISN'T THE SORCERER SUPREME ANYMORE.
EH, I WOULDN'T GET TOO CLOSE TO THOSE BARS IF I WERE YOU, MY GOOD KNIGHT. THEY WERE CRAFTED WITH SOME RATHER NASTY MAGIC BY NONE OTHER THAN DR. STRANGE, THE SORCERER SUPREME.
AND YOUR SENTENCE HAS BEEN MODIFIED.
MEPHISTO, LORD OF THE FALLEN, ARCHDUKE OF HELL, ENEMY OF ALL WHO BEAR A SOUL...
YOU'RE FREE TO GO.
HEH, I WAS HOPING YOU'D SAY, "GO TO HELL," BECAUSE THAT WOULD'VE BEEN RATHER AMUSING.
NO.
YOU'LL NEVER SEE HELL AGAIN, YOU BASTARD #$&@.

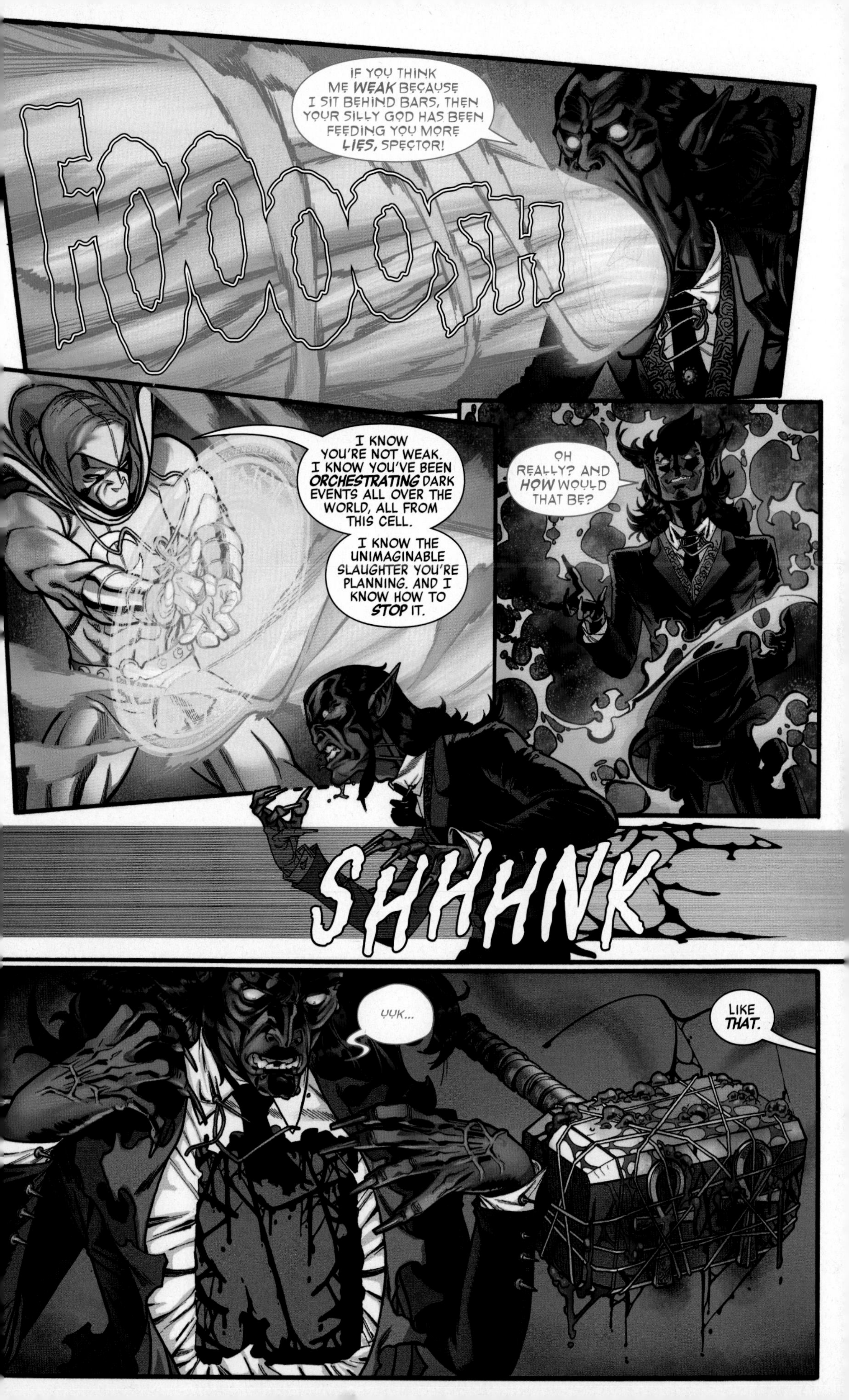
IF YOU THINK ME WEAK BECAUSE I SIT BEHIND BARS, THEN YOUR SILLY GOD HAS BEEN FEEDING YOU MORE LIES, SPECTOR!
FOOOOOSH
I KNOW YOU'RE NOT WEAK. I KNOW YOU'VE BEEN ORCHESTRATING DARK EVENTS ALL OVER THE WORLD, ALL FROM THIS CELL.
I KNOW THE UNIMAGINABLE SLAUGHTER YOU'RE PLANNING. AND I KNOW HOW TO STOP IT.
OH REALLY? AND HOW WOULD THAT BE?
SHHHNK
UUK...
LIKE THAT.

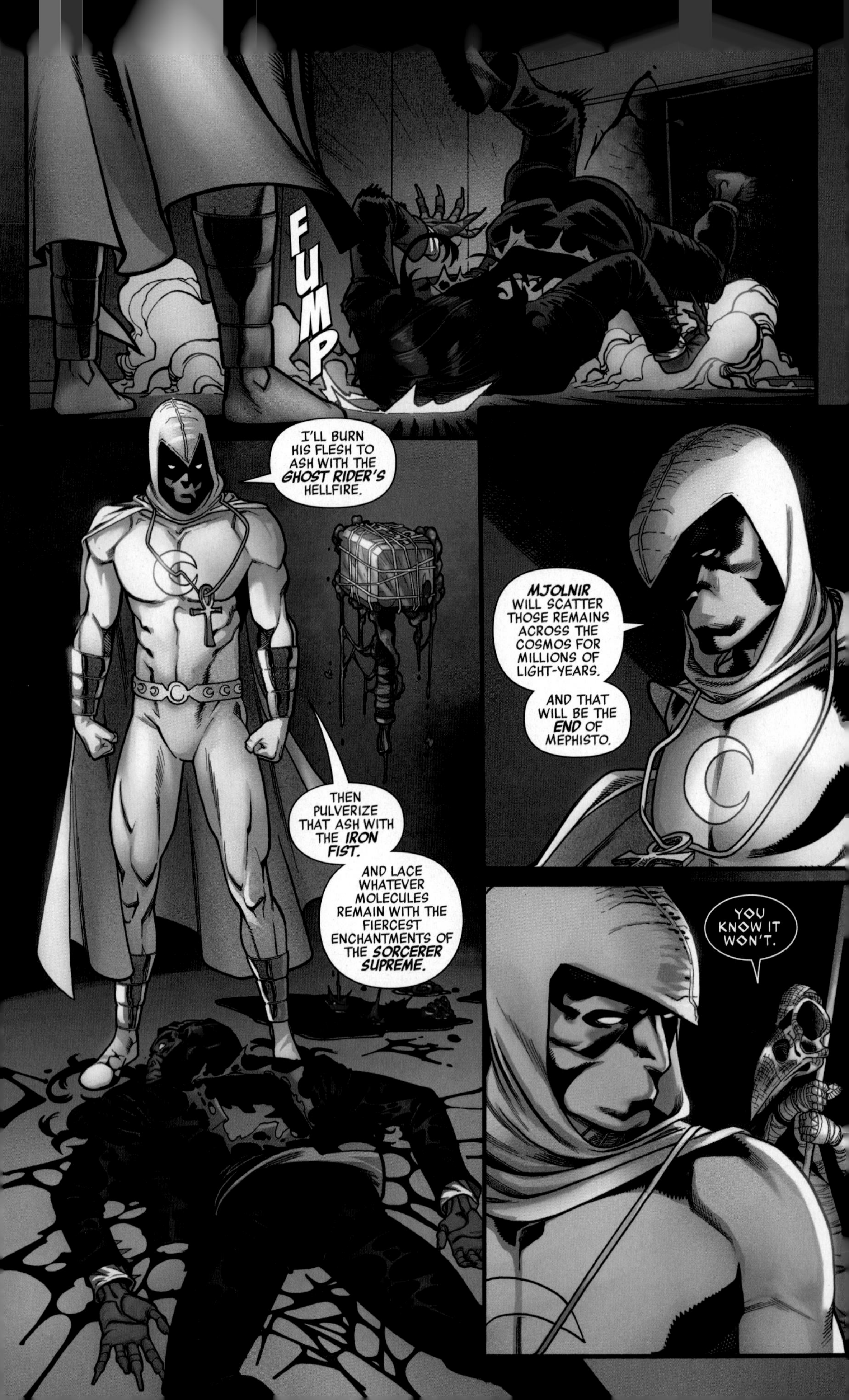
FUMP
I'LL BURN HIS FLESH TO ASH WITH THE GHOST RIDER'S HELLFIRE.
MJOLNIR WILL SCATTER THOSE REMAINS ACROSS THE COSMOS FOR MILLIONS OF LIGHT-YEARS.
AND THAT WILL BE THE END OF MEPHISTO.
THEN PULVERIZE THAT ASH WITH THE IRON FIST.
AND LACE WHATEVER MOLECULES REMAIN WITH THE FIERCEST ENCHANTMENTS OF THE SORCERER SUPREME.
YOU KNOW IT WON'T.

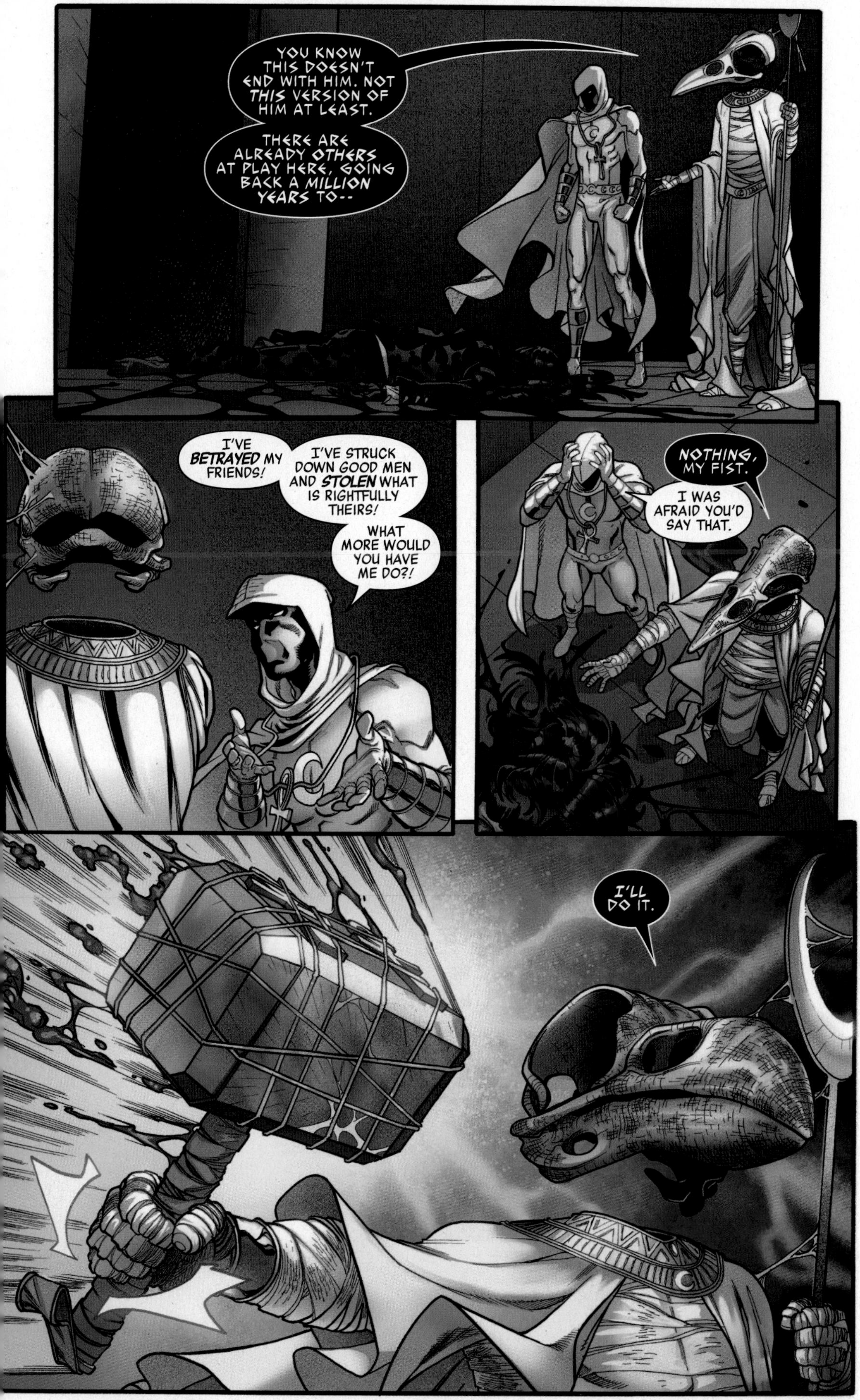
YOU KNOW THIS DOESN'T END WITH HIM. NOT THIS VERSION OF HIM AT LEAST.
THERE ARE ALREADY OTHERS AT PLAY HERE, GOING BACK A MILLION YEARS TO--
I'VE BETRAYED MY FRIENDS!
I'VE STRUCK DOWN GOOD MEN AND STOLEN WHAT IS RIGHTFULLY THEIRS!
WHAT MORE WOULD YOU HAVE ME DO?!
NOTHING, MY FIST.
I WAS AFRAID YOU'D SAY THAT.
I'LL DO IT.

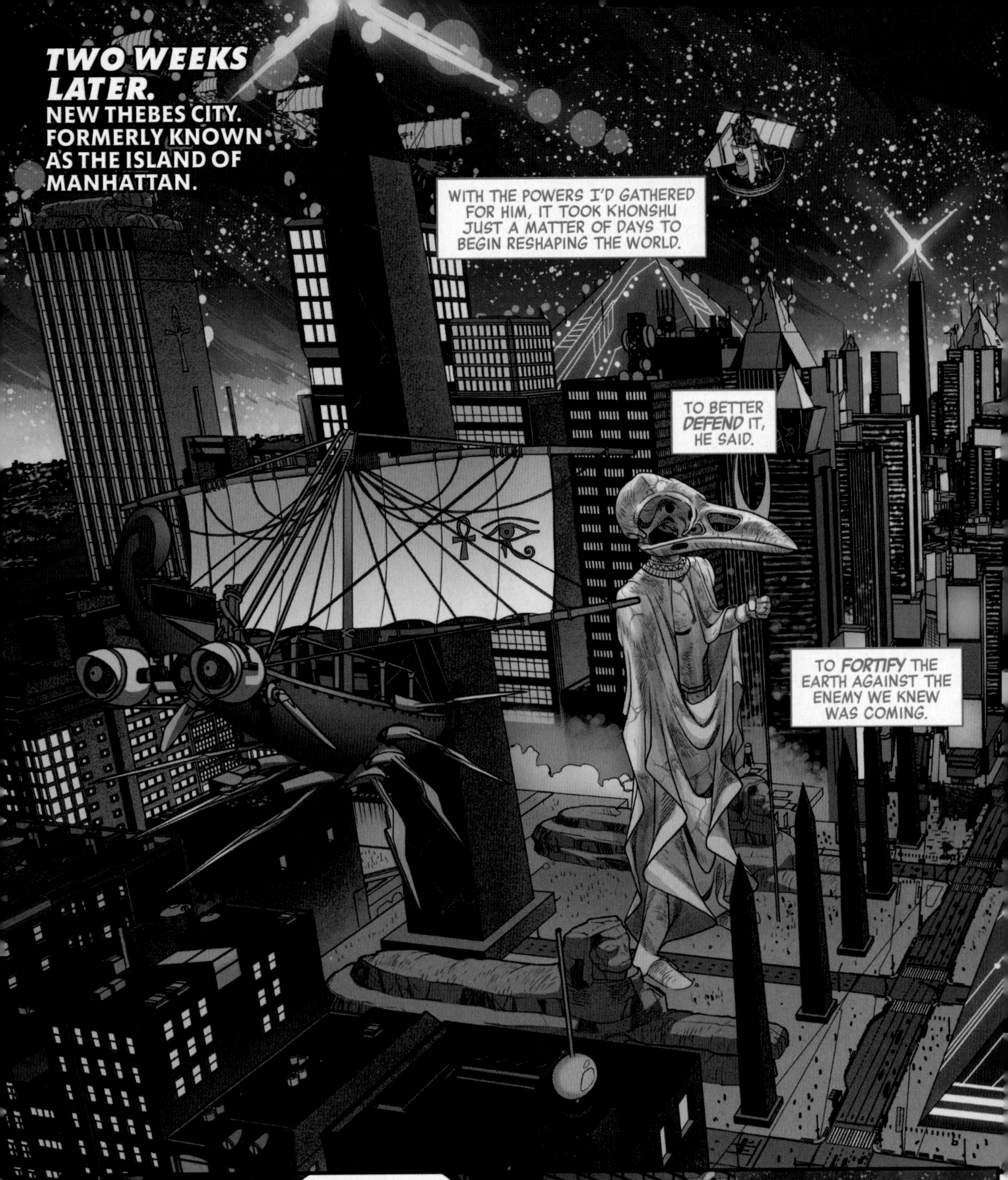
TWO WEEKS LATER.
NEW THEBES CITY. FORMERLY KNOWN AS THE ISLAND OF MANHATTAN.
WITH THE POWERS I'D GATHERED FOR HIM, IT TOOK KHONSHU JUST A MATTER OF DAYS TO BEGIN RESHAPING THE WORLD.
TO BETTER DEFEND IT, HE SAID.
TO FORTIFY THE EARTH AGAINST THE ENEMY WE KNEW WAS COMING.

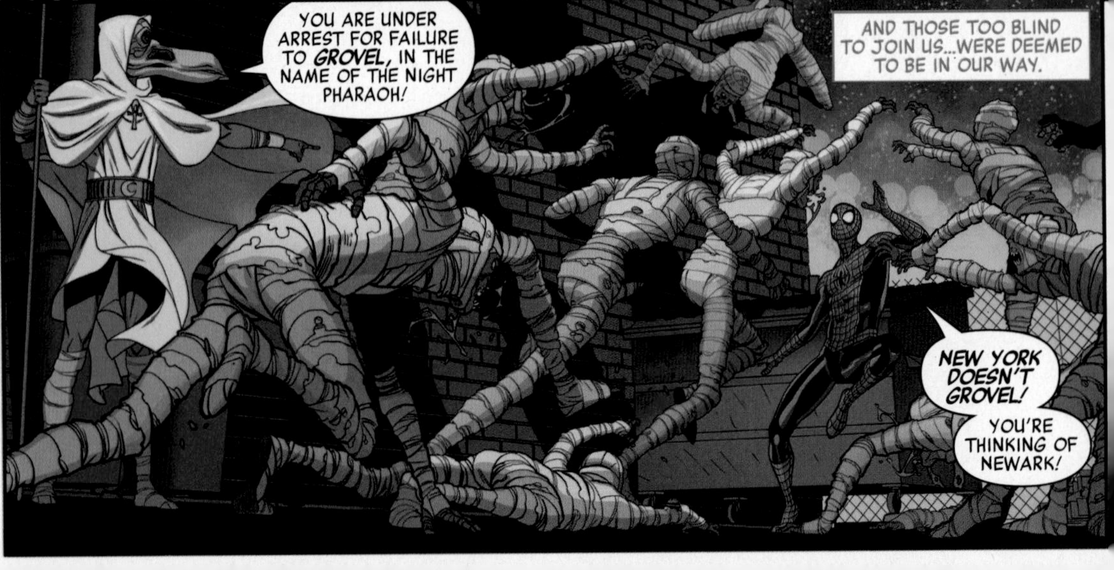
YOU ARE UNDER ARREST FOR FAILURE TO GROVEL, IN THE NAME OF THE NIGHT PHARAOH!
AND THOSE TOO BLIND TO JOIN US...WERE DEEMED TO BE IN OUR WAY.
NEW YORK DOESN'T GROVEL!
YOU'RE THINKING OF NEWARK!

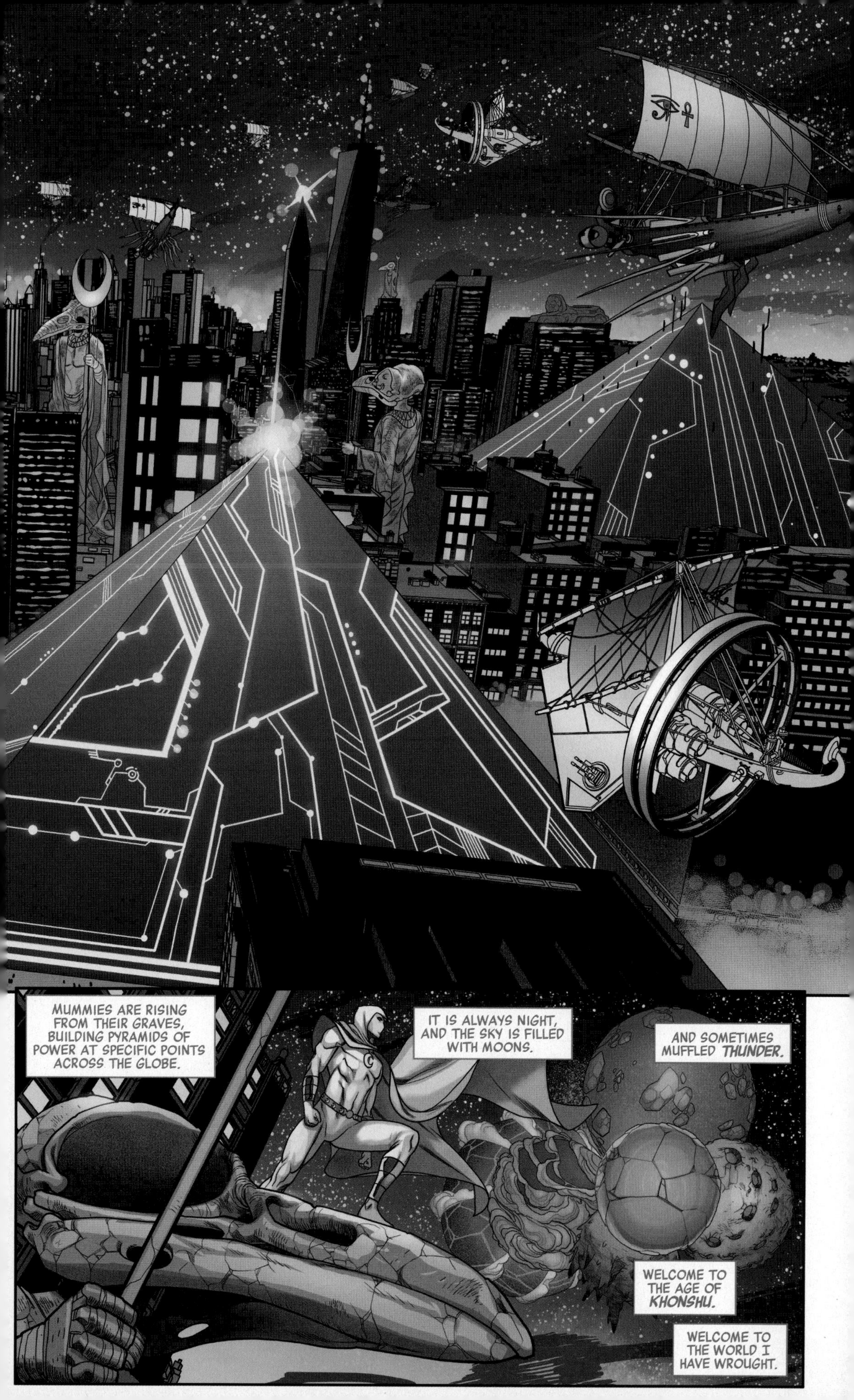
MUMMIES ARE RISING FROM THEIR GRAVES, BUILDING PYRAMIDS OF POWER AT SPECIFIC POINTS ACROSS THE GLOBE.
IT IS ALWAYS NIGHT, AND THE SKY IS FILLED WITH MOONS.
AND SOMETIMES MUFFLED THUNDER.
WELCOME TO THE AGE OF KHONSHU.
WELCOME TO THE WORLD I HAVE WROUGHT.

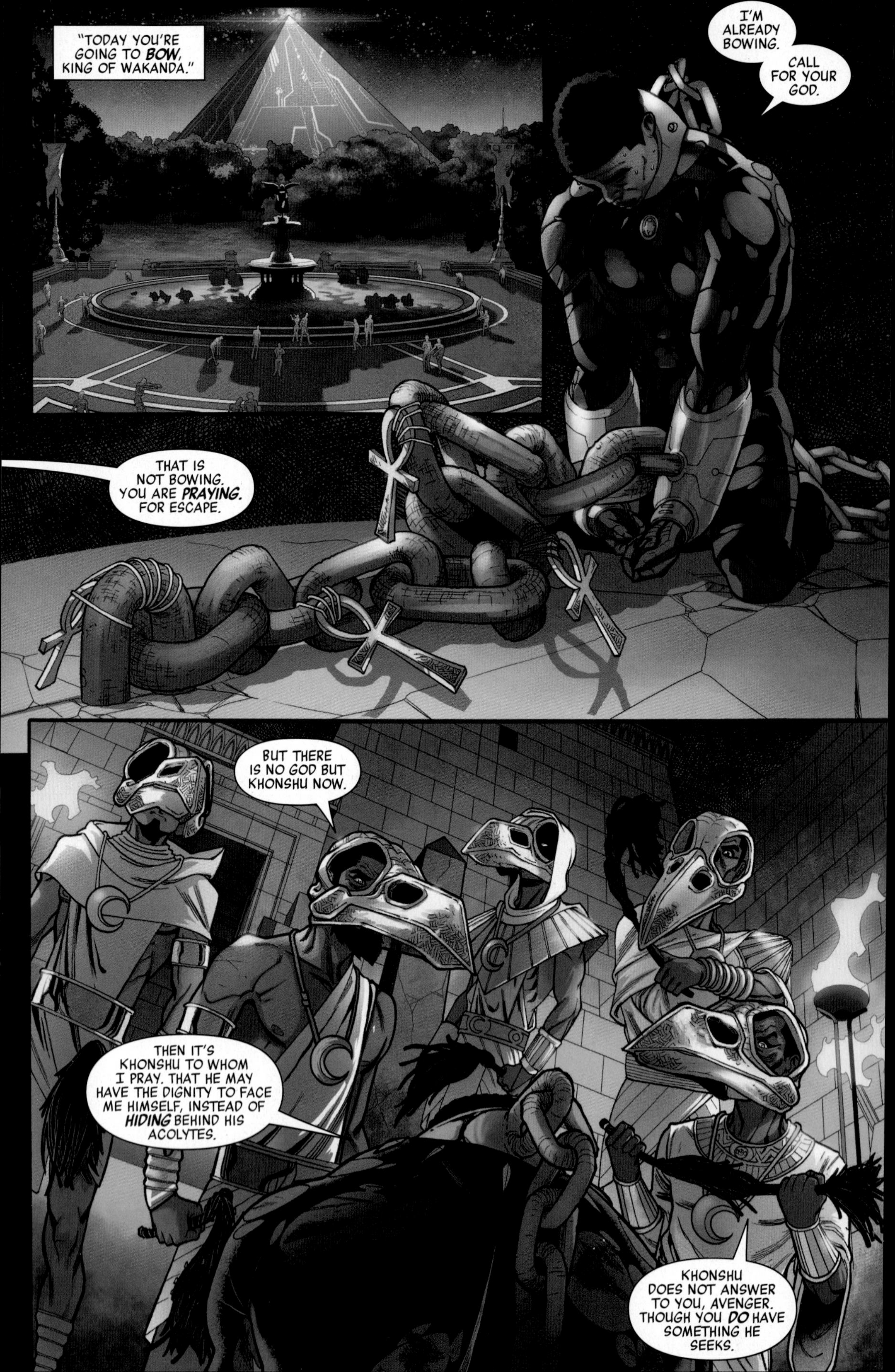
"TODAY YOU'RE GOING TO BOW, KING OF WAKANDA."
I'M ALREADY BOWING.
CALL FOR YOUR GOD.
THAT IS NOT BOWING. YOU ARE PRAYING. FOR ESCAPE.
BUT THERE IS NO GOD BUT KHONSHU NOW.
THEN IT'S KHONSHU TO WHOM I PRAY. THAT HE MAY HAVE THE DIGNITY TO FACE ME HIMSELF, INSTEAD OF HIDING BEHIND HIS ACOLYTES.
KHONSHU DOES NOT ANSWER TO YOU, AVENGER. THOUGH YOU DO HAVE SOMETHING HE SEEKS.

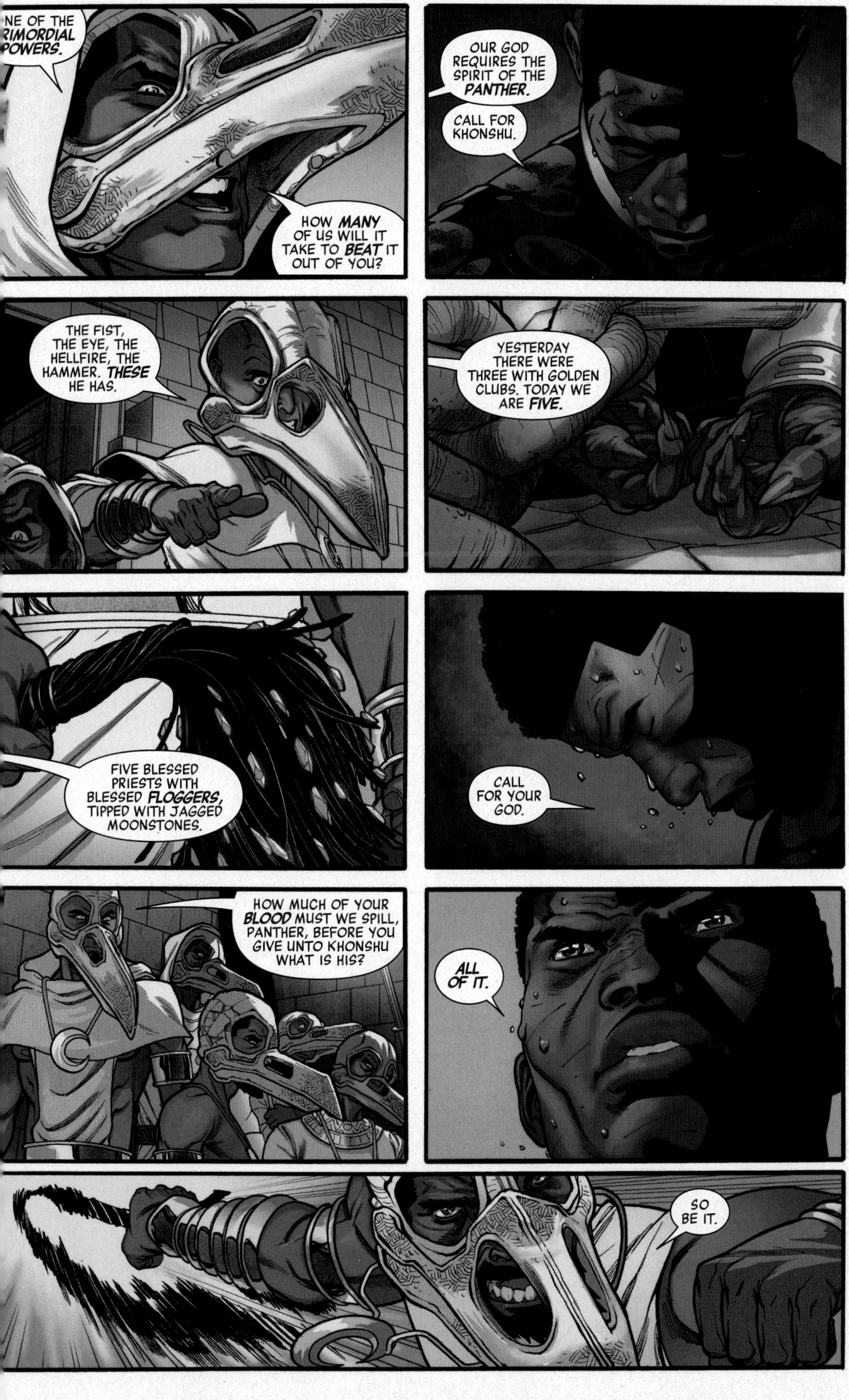
NE OF THE
RIMORDIAL
POWERS.
HOW MANY OF US WILL IT TAKE TO BEAT IT OUT OF YOU?
OUR GOD REQUIRES THE SPIRIT OF THE PANTHER.
CALL FOR KHONSHU.
THE FIST, THE EYE, THE HELLFIRE, THE HAMMER. THESE HE HAS.
YESTERDAY THERE WERE THREE WITH GOLDEN CLUBS. TODAY WE ARE FIVE.
FIVE BLESSED PRIESTS WITH BLESSED FLOGGERS, TIPPED WITH JAGGED MOONSTONES.
CALL FOR YOUR GOD.
HOW MUCH OF YOUR BLOOD MUST WE SPILL, PANTHER, BEFORE YOU GIVE UNTO KHONSHU WHAT IS HIS?
ALL OF IT.
SO BE IT.

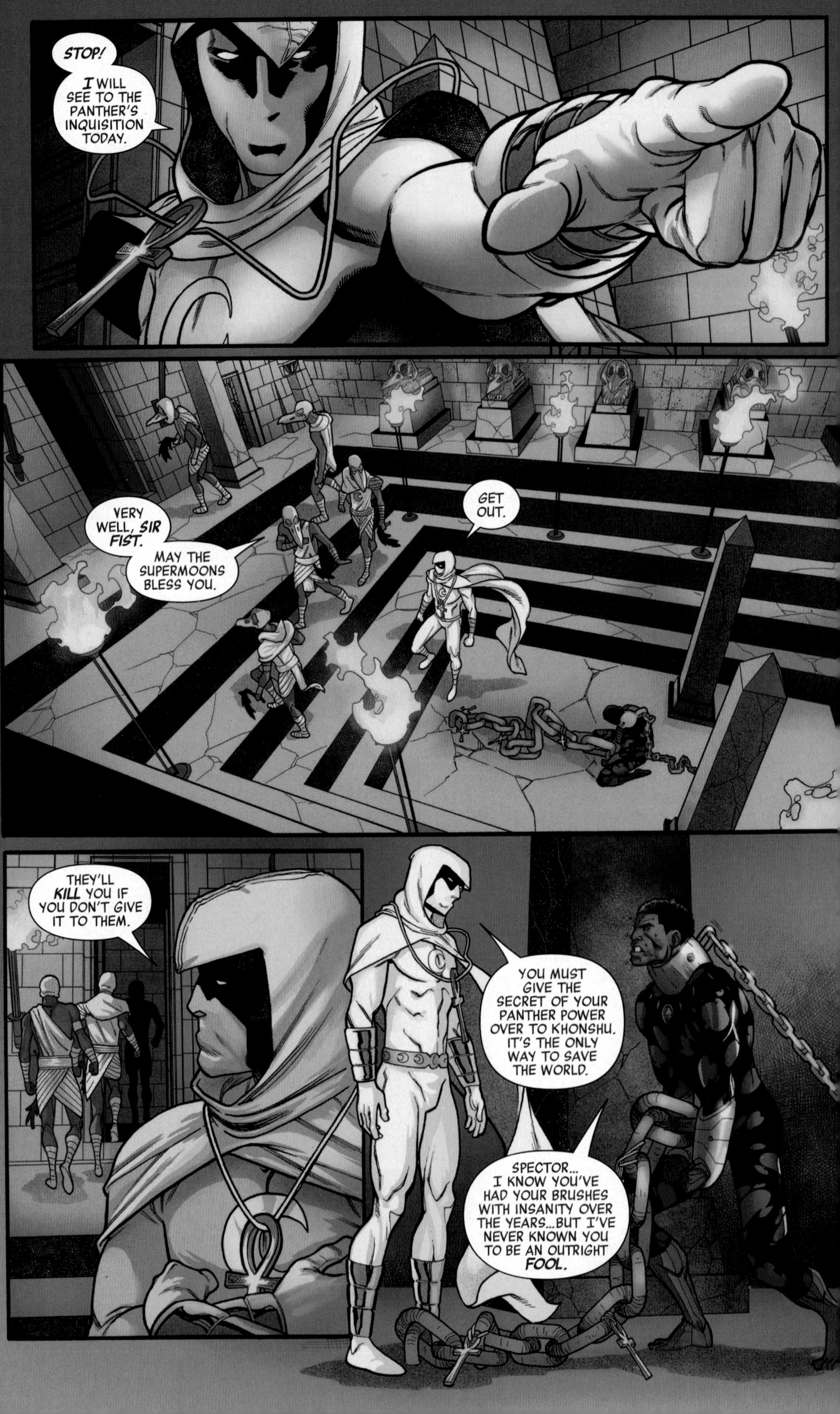
STOP!
I WILL SEE TO THE PANTHER'S INQUISITION TODAY.
VERY WELL, SIR FIST.
MAY THE SUPERMOONS BLESS YOU.
GET OUT.
THEY'LL KILL YOU IF YOU DON'T GIVE IT TO THEM.
YOU MUST GIVE THE SECRET OF YOUR PANTHER POWER OVER TO KHONSHU. IT'S THE ONLY WAY TO SAVE THE WORLD.
SPECTOR... I KNOW YOU'VE HAD YOUR BRUSHES WITH INSANITY OVER THE YEARS...BUT I'VE NEVER KNOWN YOU TO BE AN OUTRIGHT FOOL.

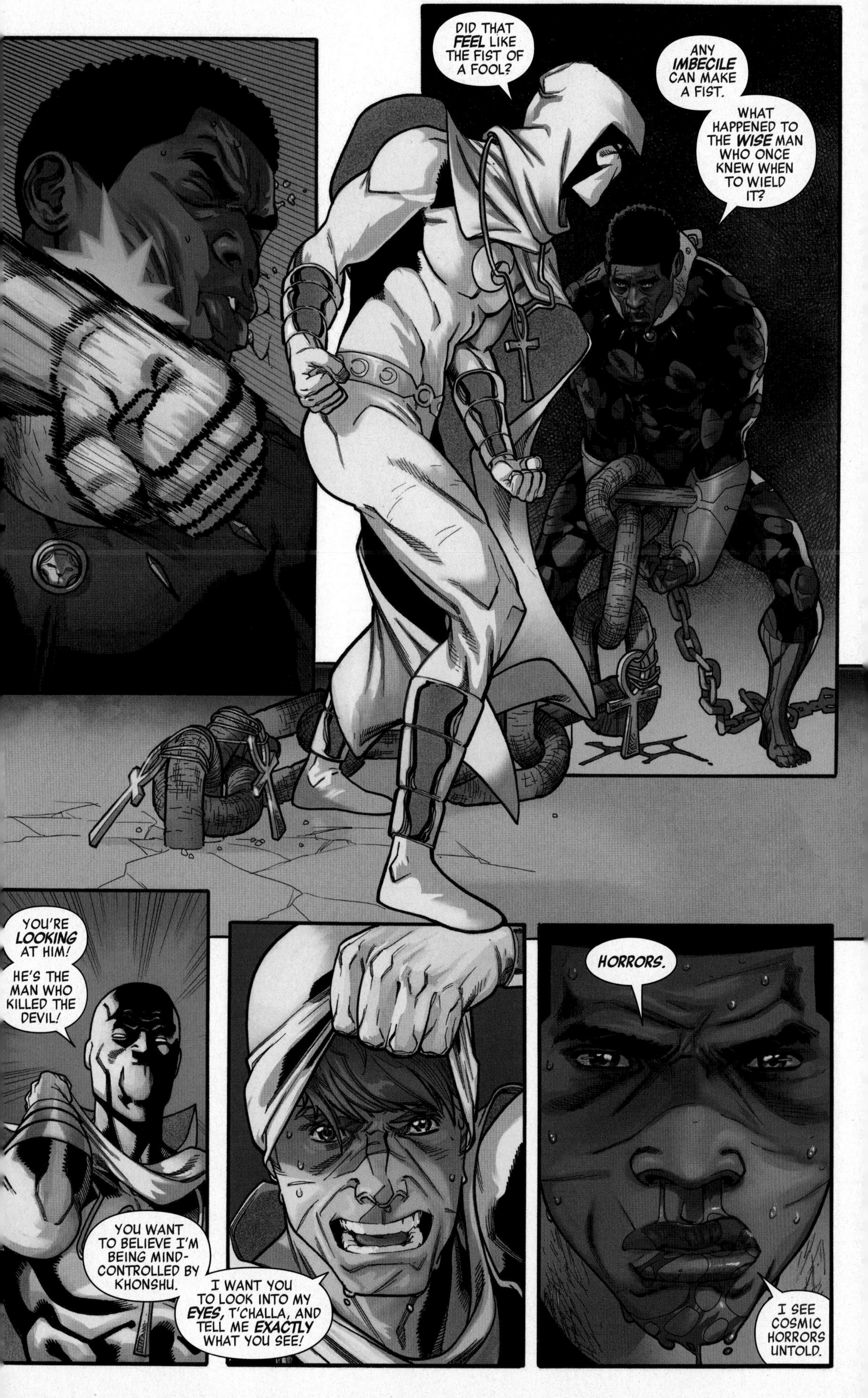
DID THAT FEEL LIKE THE FIST OF A FOOL?
ANY IMBECILE CAN MAKE A FIST.
WHAT HAPPENED TO THE WISE MAN WHO ONCE KNEW WHEN TO WIELD IT?
YOU'RE LOOKING AT HIM!
HE'S THE MAN WHO KILLED THE DEVIL!
YOU WANT TO BELIEVE I'M BEING MIND-CONTROLLED BY KHONSHU.
I WANT YOU TO LOOK INTO MY EYES, T'CHALLA, AND TELL ME EXACTLY WHAT YOU SEE!
HORRORS.
I SEE COSMIC HORRORS UNTOLD.

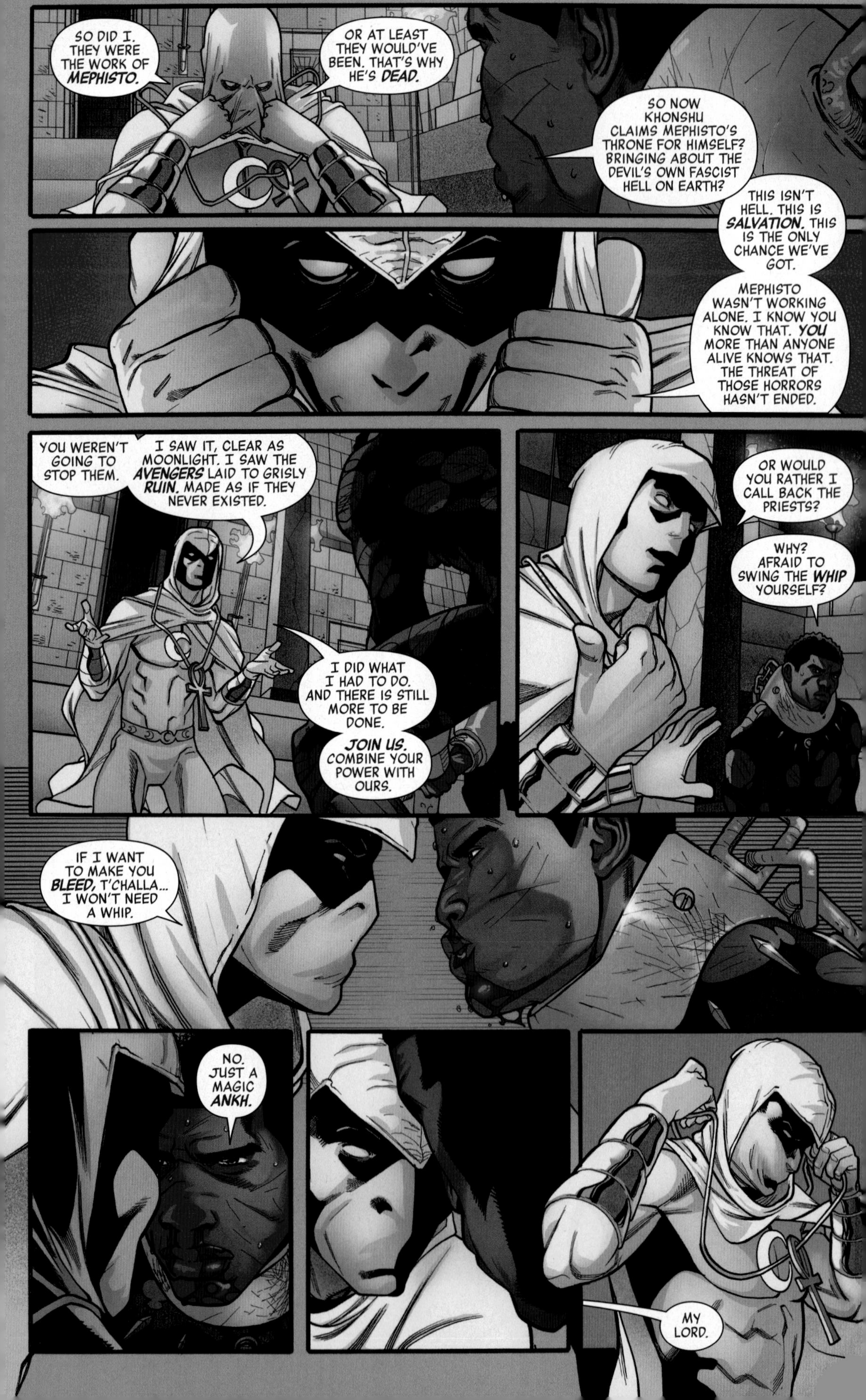
SO DID I. THEY WERE THE WORK OF MEPHISTO.
OR AT LEAST THEY WOULD'VE BEEN. THAT'S WHY HE'S DEAD.
SO NOW KHONSHU CLAIMS MEPHISTO'S THRONE FOR HIMSELF? BRINGING ABOUT THE DEVIL'S OWN FASCIST HELL ON EARTH?
THIS ISN'T HELL. THIS IS SALVATION. THIS IS THE ONLY CHANCE WE'VE GOT.
MEPHISTO WASN'T WORKING ALONE. I KNOW YOU KNOW THAT. YOU MORE THAN ANYONE ALIVE KNOWS THAT. THE THREAT OF THOSE HORRORS HASN'T ENDED.
YOU WEREN'T GOING TO STOP THEM.
I SAW IT, CLEAR AS MOONLIGHT. I SAW THE AVENGERS LAID TO GRISLY RUIN. MADE AS IF THEY NEVER EXISTED.
I DID WHAT I HAD TO DO. AND THERE IS STILL MORE TO BE DONE.
JOIN US. COMBINE YOUR POWER WITH OURS.
OR WOULD YOU RATHER I CALL BACK THE PRIESTS?
WHY? AFRAID TO SWING THE WHIP YOURSELF?
IF I WANT TO MAKE YOU BLEED, T'CHALLA... I WON'T NEED A WHIP.
NO. JUST A MAGIC ANKH.
MY LORD.

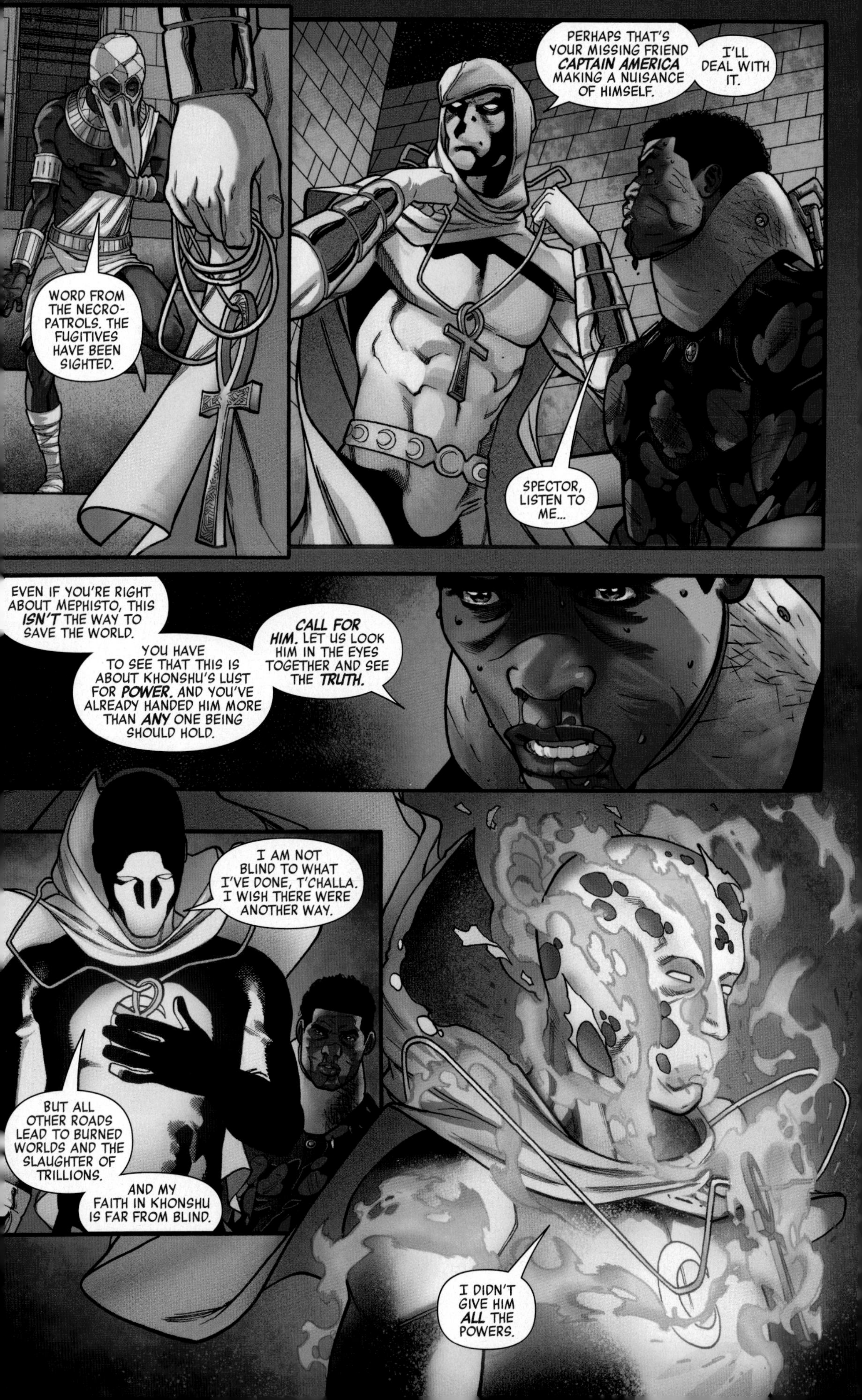

WORD FROM THE NECRO-PATROLS. THE FUGITIVES HAVE BEEN SIGHTED.
PERHAPS THAT'S YOUR MISSING FRIEND CAPTAIN AMERICA MAKING A NUISANCE OF HIMSELF.
I'LL DEAL WITH IT.
SPECTOR, LISTEN TO ME...
EVEN IF YOU'RE RIGHT ABOUT MEPHISTO, THIS ISN'T THE WAY TO SAVE THE WORLD.
YOU HAVE TO SEE THAT THIS IS ABOUT KHONSHU'S LUST FOR POWER. AND YOU'VE ALREADY HANDED HIM MORE THAN ANY ONE BEING SHOULD HOLD.
CALL FOR HIM. LET US LOOK HIM IN THE EYES TOGETHER AND SEE THE TRUTH.
I AM NOT BLIND TO WHAT I'VE DONE, T'CHALLA. I WISH THERE WERE ANOTHER WAY.
BUT ALL OTHER ROADS LEAD TO BURNED WORLDS AND THE SLAUGHTER OF TRILLIONS.
AND MY FAITH IN KHONSHU IS FAR FROM BLIND.
I DIDN'T GIVE HIM ALL THE POWERS.

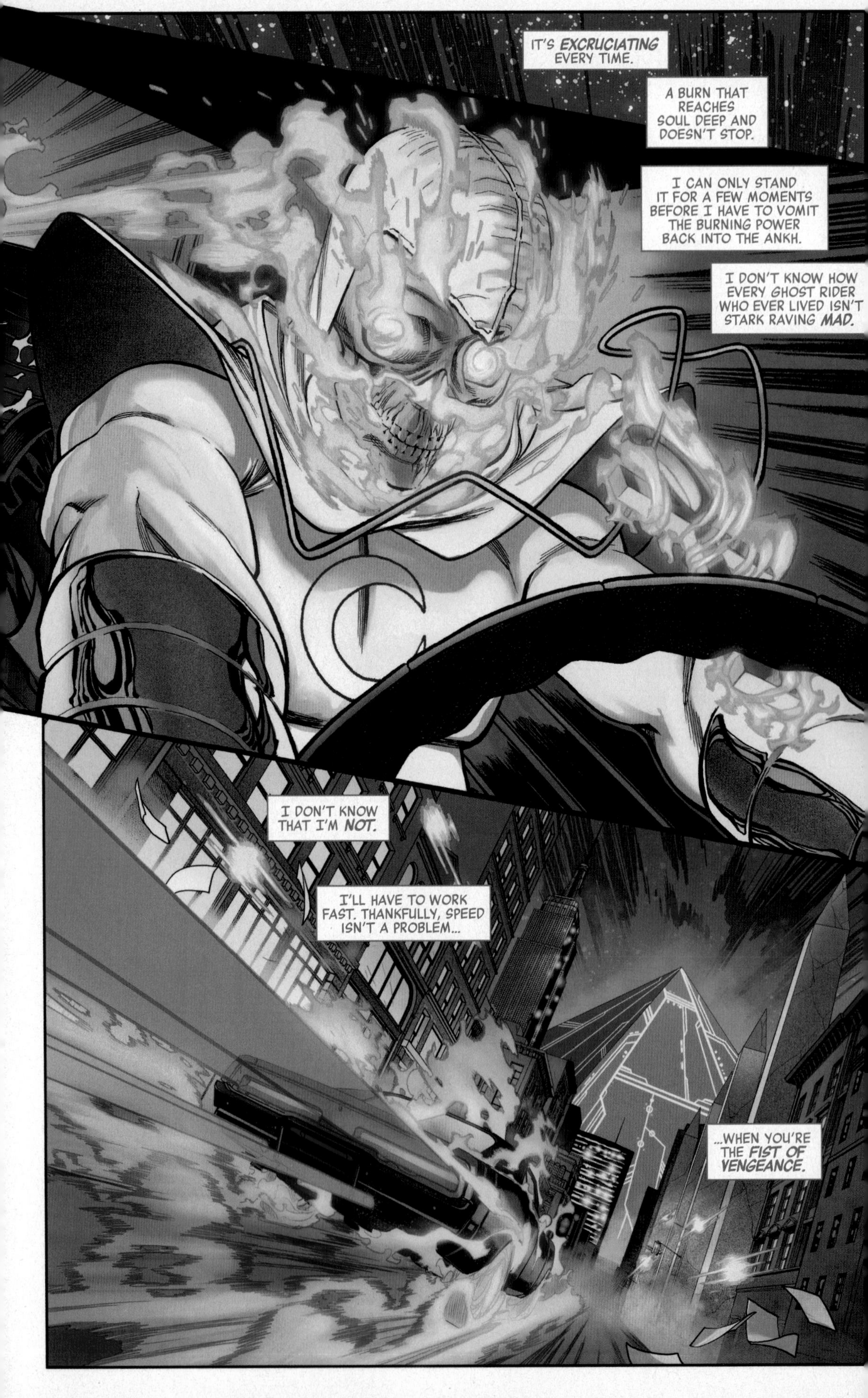
IT'S *EXCRUCIATING* EVERY TIME.
A BURN THAT REACHES SOUL DEEP AND DOESN'T STOP.
I CAN ONLY STAND IT FOR A FEW MOMENTS BEFORE I HAVE TO VOMIT THE BURNING POWER BACK INTO THE ANKH.
I DON'T KNOW HOW EVERY *GHOST RIDER* WHO EVER LIVED ISN'T STARK RAVING *MAD*.
I DON'T KNOW THAT I'M *NOT*.
I'LL HAVE TO WORK FAST. THANKFULLY, SPEED ISN'T A PROBLEM...
...WHEN YOU'RE THE *FIST OF VENGEANCE*.

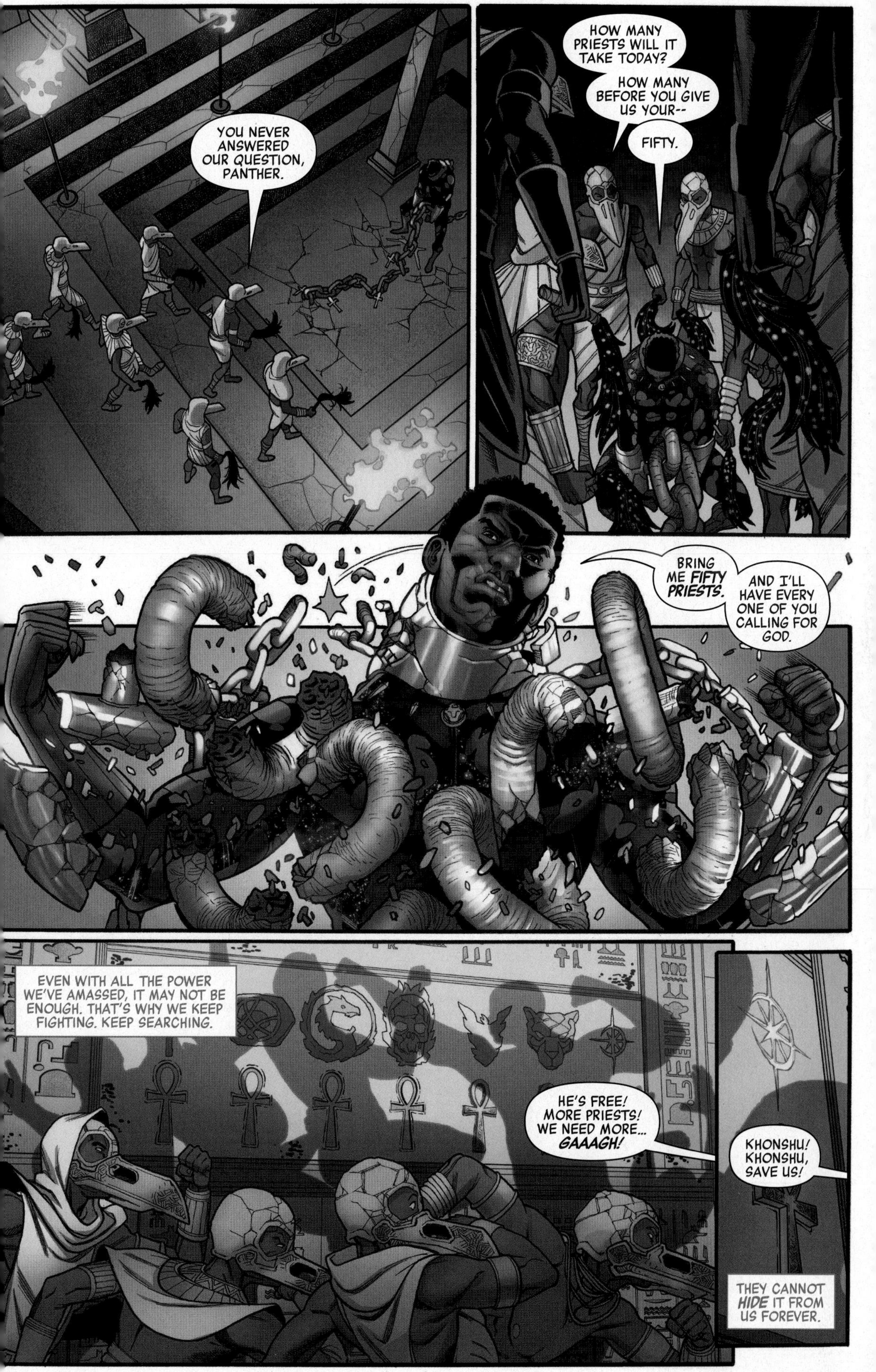
YOU NEVER ANSWERED OUR QUESTION, PANTHER.
HOW MANY PRIESTS WILL IT TAKE TODAY?
HOW MANY BEFORE YOU GIVE US YOUR--
FIFTY.
BRING ME FIFTY PRIESTS.
AND I'LL HAVE EVERY ONE OF YOU CALLING FOR GOD.
EVEN WITH ALL THE POWER WE'VE AMASSED, IT MAY NOT BE ENOUGH. THAT'S WHY WE KEEP FIGHTING. KEEP SEARCHING.
HE'S FREE! MORE PRIESTS! WE NEED MORE... GAAAGH!
KHONSHU! KHONSHU, SAVE US!
THEY CANNOT HIDE IT FROM US FOREVER.

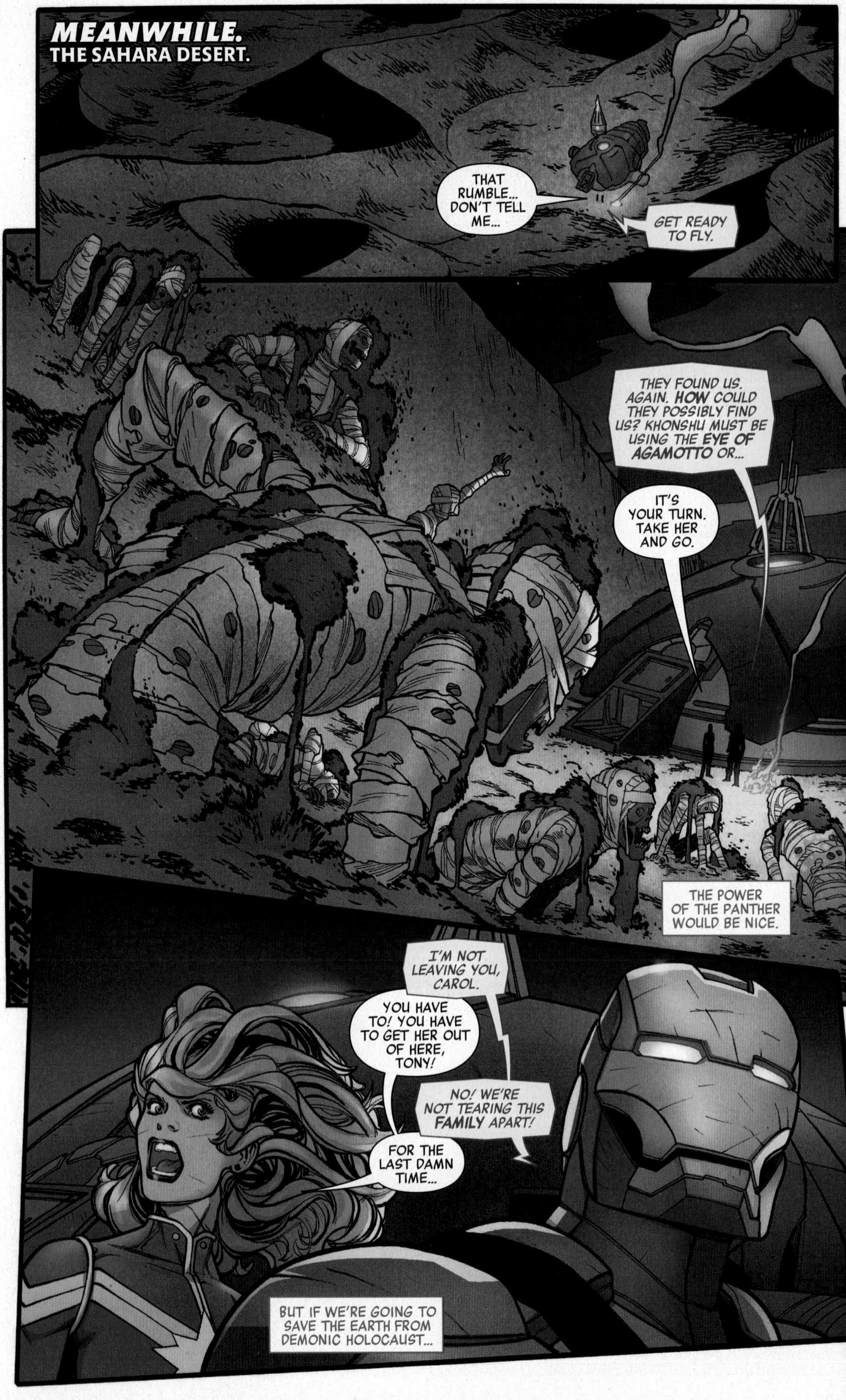
MEANWHILE.
THE SAHARA DESERT.
THAT RUMBLE... DON'T TELL ME...
GET READY TO FLY.
THEY FOUND US. AGAIN. HOW COULD THEY POSSIBLY FIND US? KHONSHU MUST BE USING THE EYE OF AGAMOTTO OR...
IT'S YOUR TURN. TAKE HER AND GO.
THE POWER OF THE PANTHER WOULD BE NICE.
I'M NOT LEAVING YOU, CAROL.
YOU HAVE TO! YOU HAVE TO GET HER OUT OF HERE, TONY!
NO! WE'RE NOT TEARING THIS FAMILY APART!
FOR THE LAST DAMN TIME...
BUT IF WE'RE GOING TO SAVE THE EARTH FROM DEMONIC HOLOCAUST...

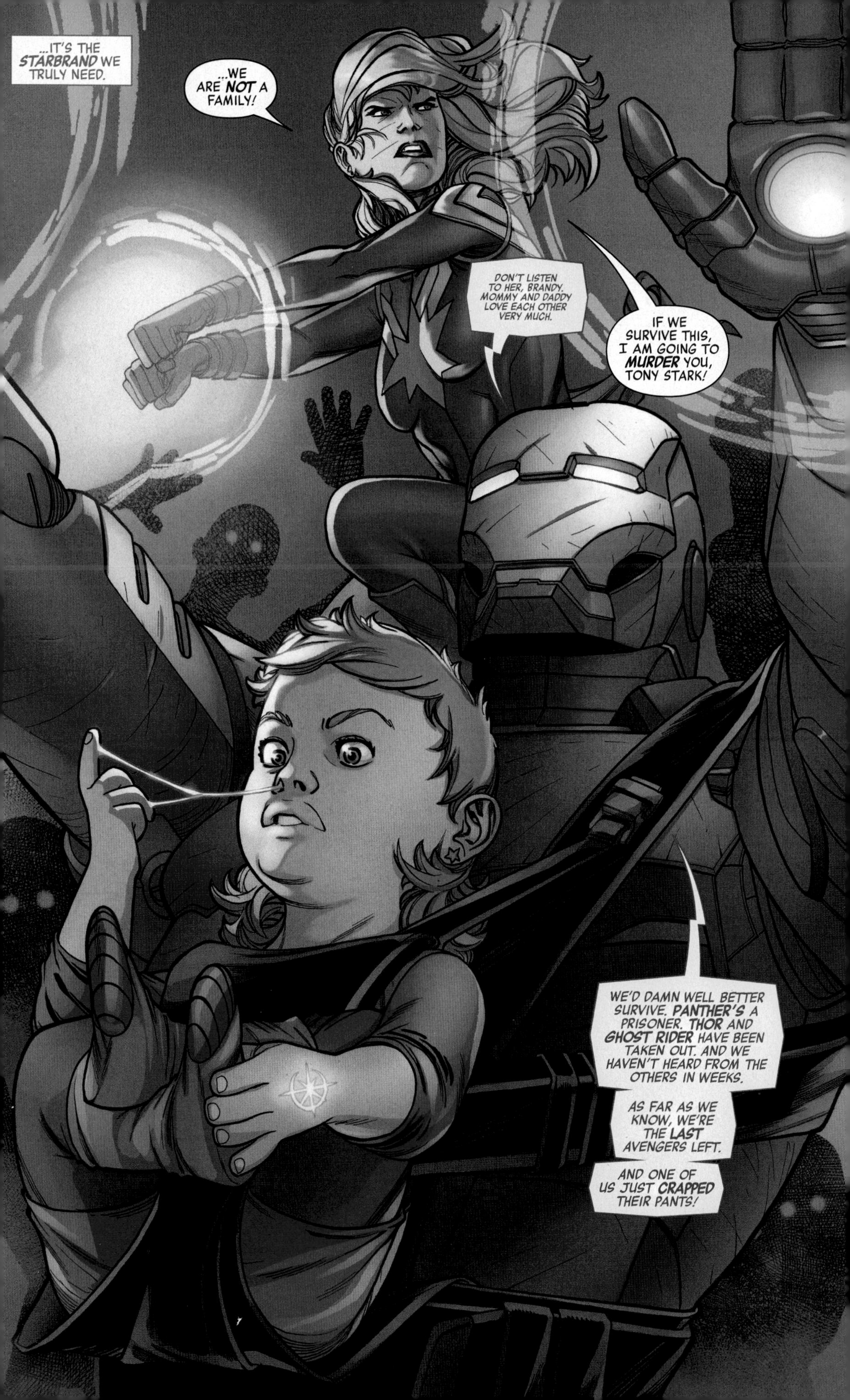
...IT'S THE STARBRAND WE TRULY NEED.
...WE ARE NOT A FAMILY!
DON'T LISTEN TO HER, BRANDY. MOMMY AND DADDY LOVE EACH OTHER VERY MUCH.
IF WE SURVIVE THIS, I AM GOING TO MURDER YOU, TONY STARK!
WE'D DAMN WELL BETTER SURVIVE. PANTHER'S A PRISONER. THOR AND GHOST RIDER HAVE BEEN TAKEN OUT. AND WE HAVEN'T HEARD FROM THE OTHERS IN WEEKS.
AS FAR AS WE KNOW, WE'RE THE LAST AVENGERS LEFT.
AND ONE OF US JUST CRAPPED THEIR PANTS!

35 THE AGE OF KHONSHU PART 3
YOU DON'T BEAT THE DEVIL BY BEING AN ANGEL

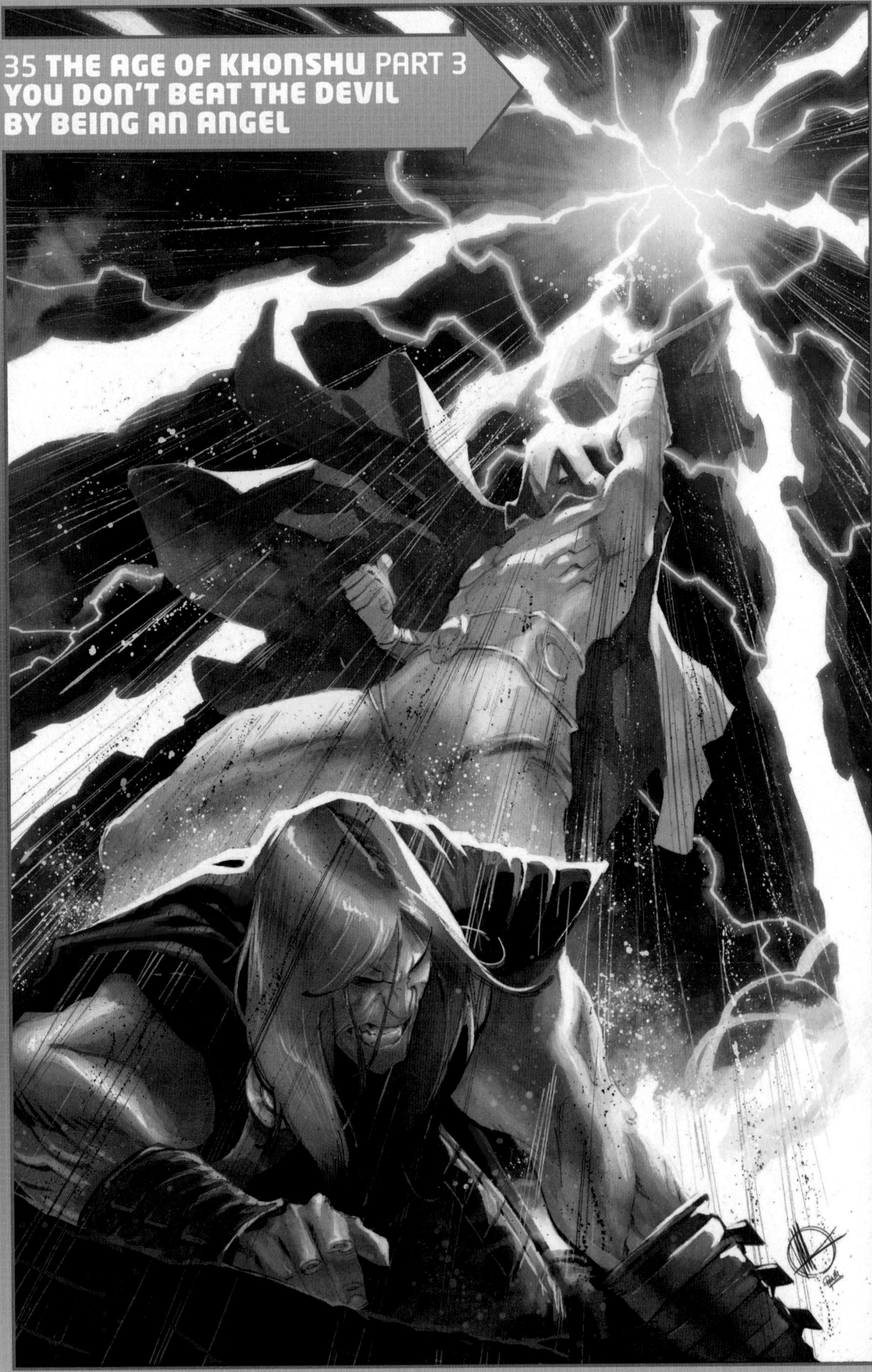

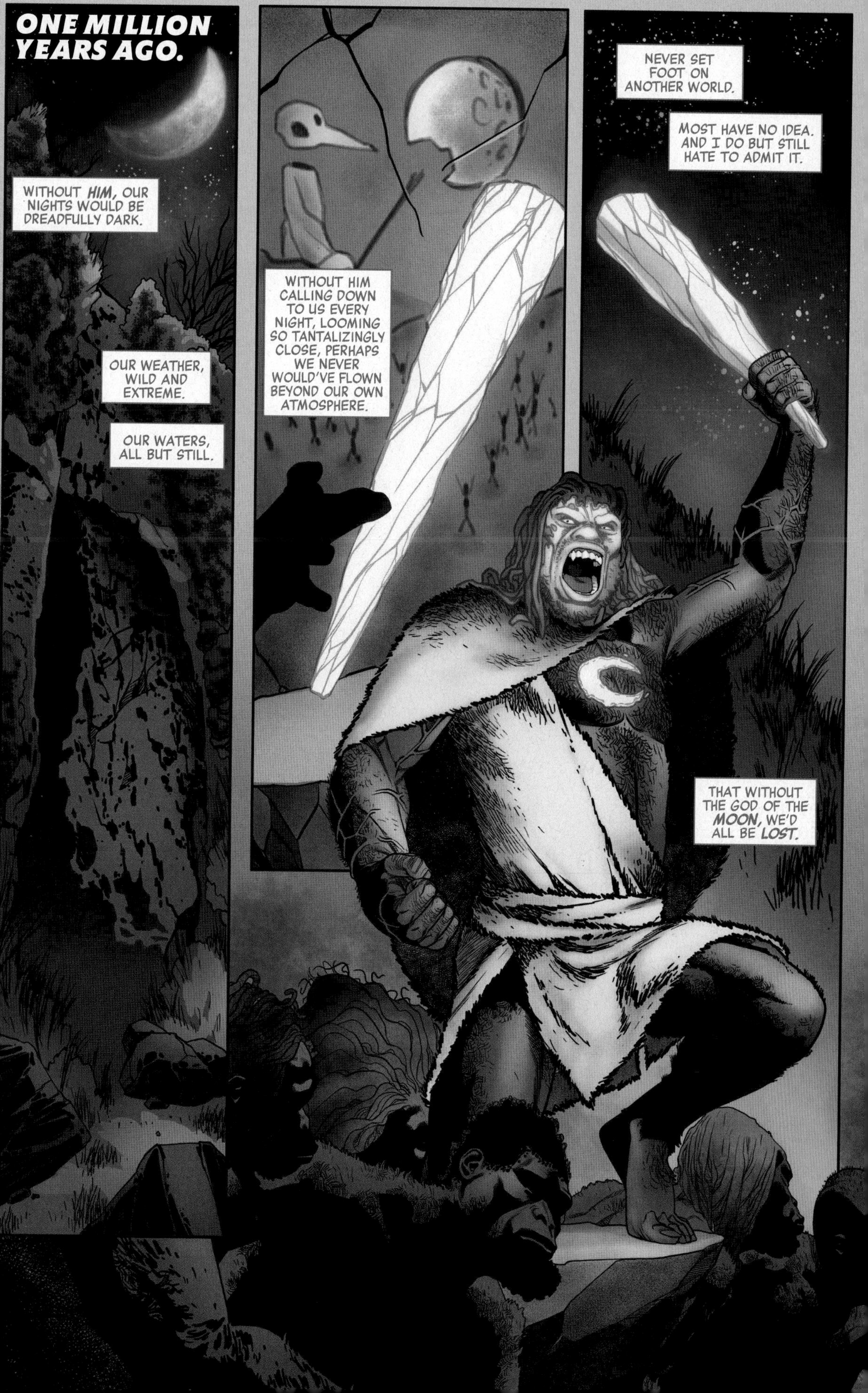
ONE MILLION YEARS AGO.
WITHOUT HIM, OUR NIGHTS WOULD BE DREADFULLY DARK.
OUR WEATHER, WILD AND EXTREME.
OUR WATERS, ALL BUT STILL.
WITHOUT HIM CALLING DOWN TO US EVERY NIGHT, LOOMING SO TANTALIZINGLY CLOSE, PERHAPS WE NEVER WOULD'VE FLOWN BEYOND OUR OWN ATMOSPHERE.
NEVER SET FOOT ON ANOTHER WORLD.
MOST HAVE NO IDEA. AND I DO BUT STILL HATE TO ADMIT IT.
THAT WITHOUT THE GOD OF THE MOON, WE'D ALL BE LOST.

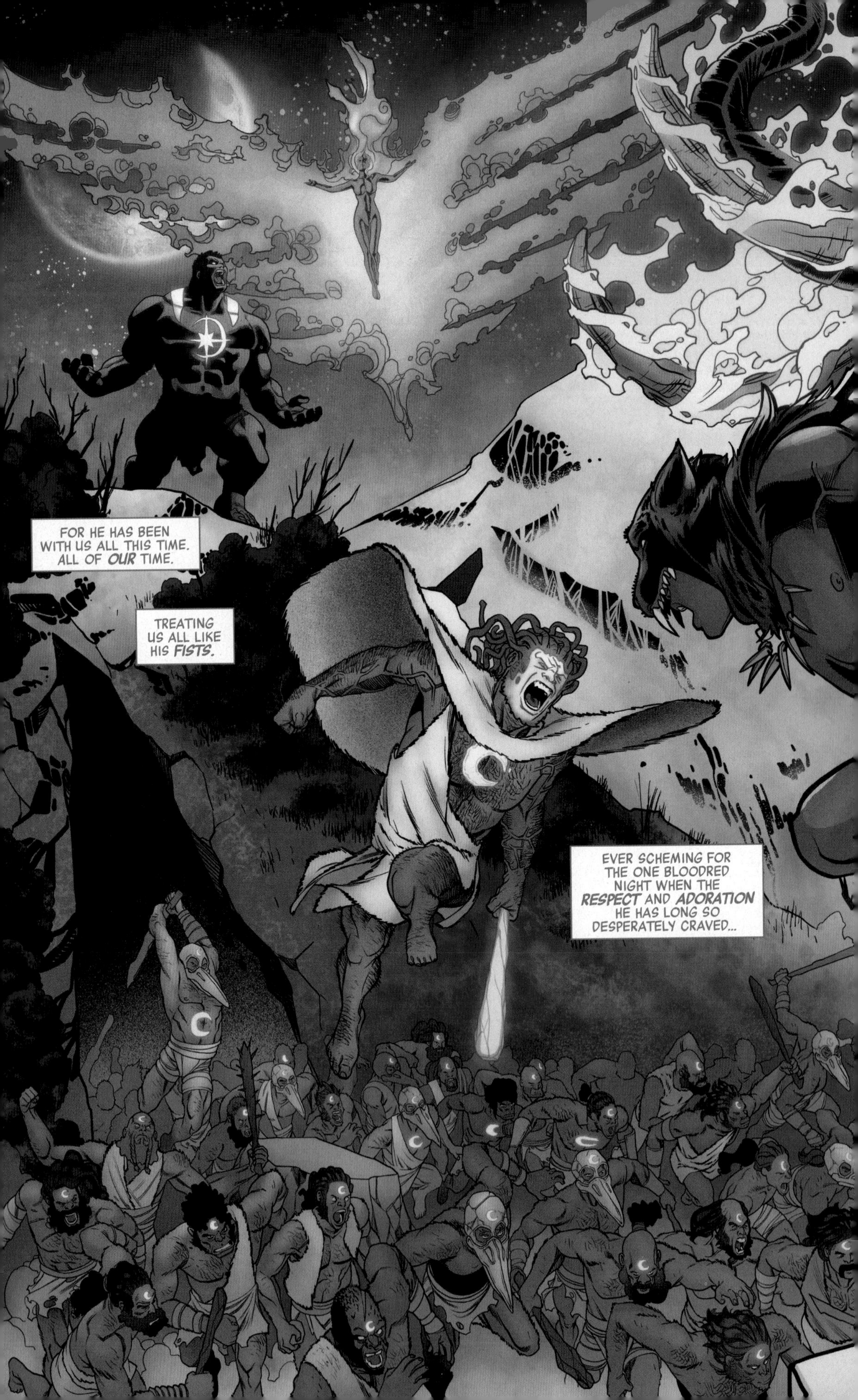
FOR HE HAS BEEN WITH US ALL THIS TIME. ALL OF OUR TIME.
TREATING US ALL LIKE HIS FISTS.
EVER SCHEMING FOR THE ONE BLOODRED NIGHT WHEN THE RESPECT AND ADORATION HE HAS LONG SO DESPERATELY CRAVED...

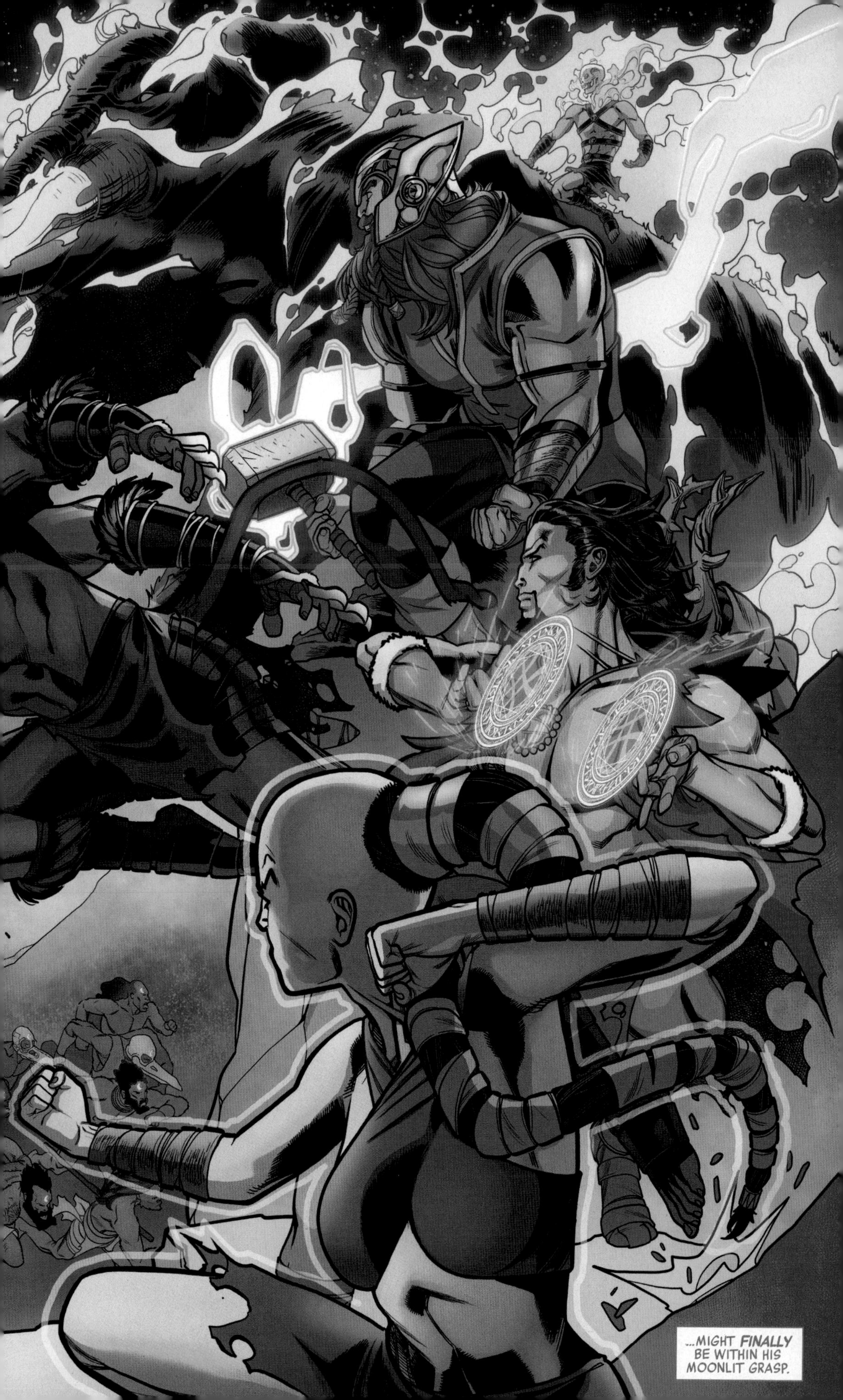
...MIGHT FINALLY BE WITHIN HIS MOONLIT GRASP.

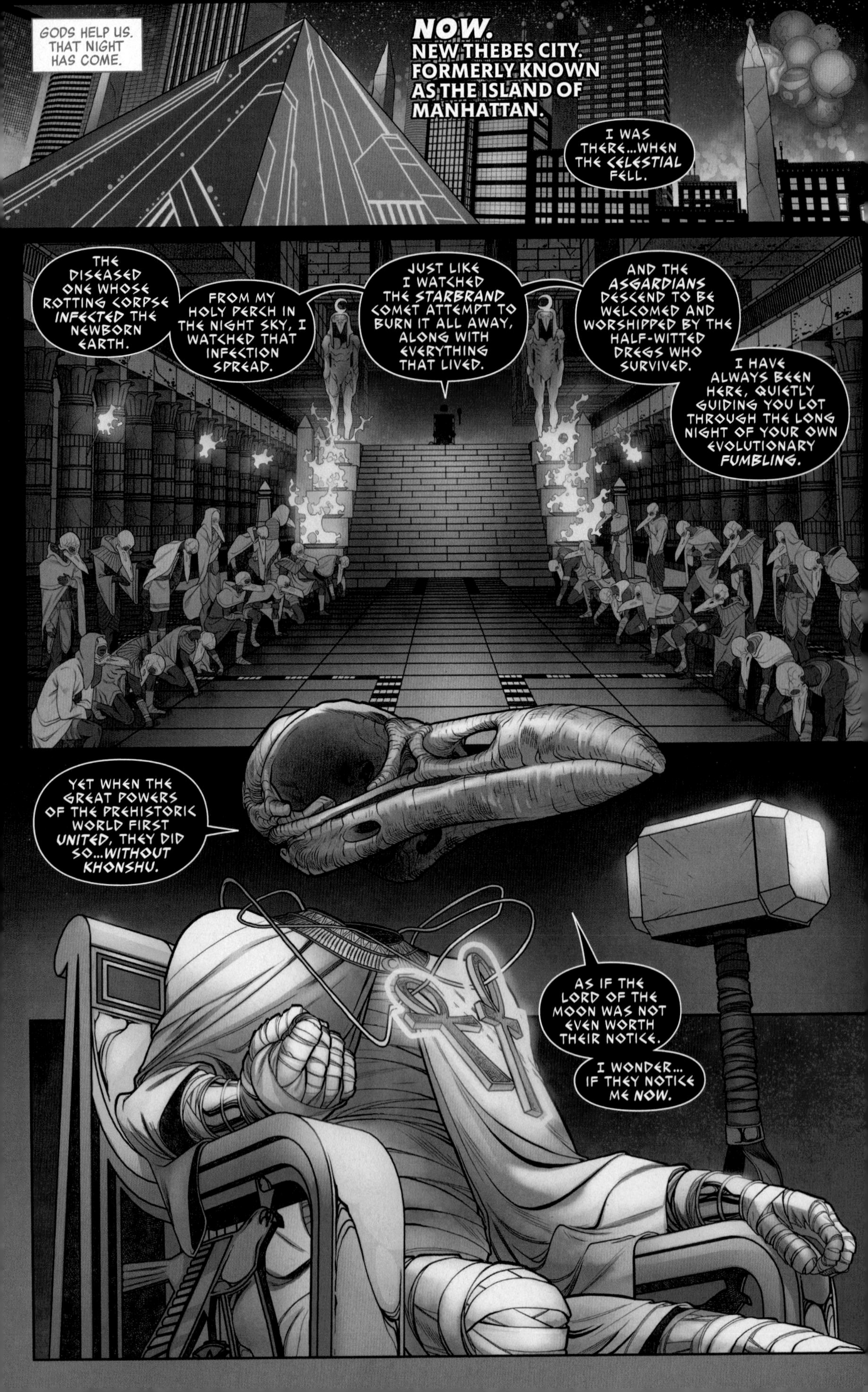
GODS HELP US. THAT NIGHT HAS COME.
NOW. NEW THEBES CITY. FORMERLY KNOWN AS THE ISLAND OF MANHATTAN.
I WAS THERE...WHEN THE CELESTIAL FELL.
THE DISEASED ONE WHOSE ROTTING CORPSE INFECTED THE NEWBORN EARTH.
FROM MY HOLY PERCH IN THE NIGHT SKY, I WATCHED THAT INFECTION SPREAD.
JUST LIKE I WATCHED THE STARBRAND COMET ATTEMPT TO BURN IT ALL AWAY, ALONG WITH EVERYTHING THAT LIVED.
AND THE ASGARDIANS DESCEND TO BE WELCOMED AND WORSHIPPED BY THE HALF-WITTED DREGS WHO SURVIVED.
I HAVE ALWAYS BEEN HERE, QUIETLY GUIDING YOU LOT THROUGH THE LONG NIGHT OF YOUR OWN EVOLUTIONARY FUMBLING.
YET WHEN THE GREAT POWERS OF THE PREHISTORIC WORLD FIRST UNITED, THEY DID SO...WITHOUT KHONSHU.
AS IF THE LORD OF THE MOON WAS NOT EVEN WORTH THEIR NOTICE.
I WONDER... IF THEY NOTICE ME NOW.

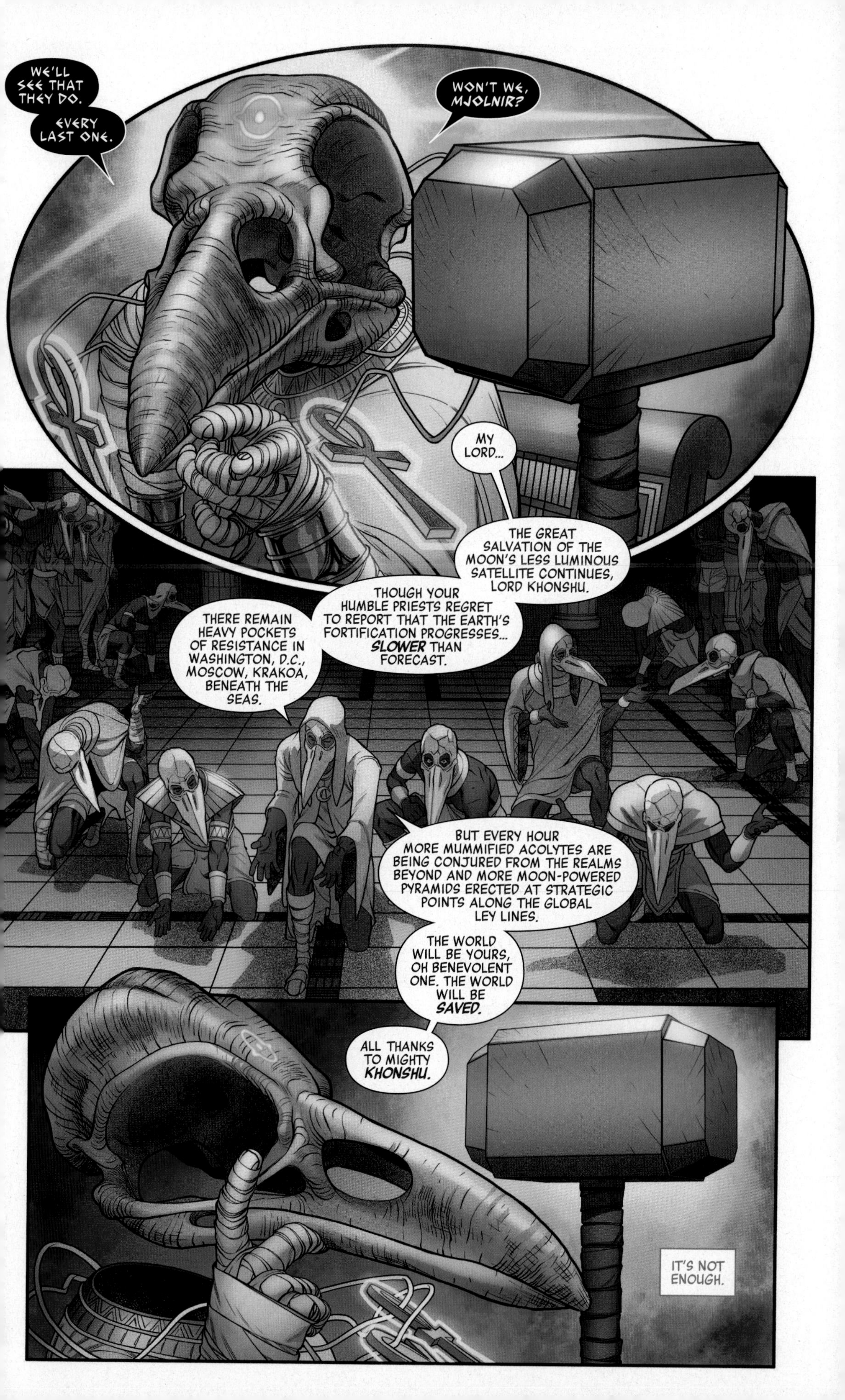
WE'LL SEE THAT THEY DO.
EVERY LAST ONE.
WON'T WE, MJOLNIR?
MY LORD...
THE GREAT SALVATION OF THE MOON'S LESS LUMINOUS SATELLITE CONTINUES, LORD KHONSHU.
THOUGH YOUR HUMBLE PRIESTS REGRET TO REPORT THAT THE EARTH'S FORTIFICATION PROGRESSES... SLOWER THAN FORECAST.
THERE REMAIN HEAVY POCKETS OF RESISTANCE IN WASHINGTON, D.C., MOSCOW, KRAKOA, BENEATH THE SEAS.
BUT EVERY HOUR MORE MUMMIFIED ACOLYTES ARE BEING CONJURED FROM THE REALMS BEYOND AND MORE MOON-POWERED PYRAMIDS ERECTED AT STRATEGIC POINTS ALONG THE GLOBAL LEY LINES.
THE WORLD WILL BE YOURS, OH BENEVOLENT ONE. THE WORLD WILL BE SAVED.
ALL THANKS TO MIGHTY KHONSHU.
IT'S NOT ENOUGH.

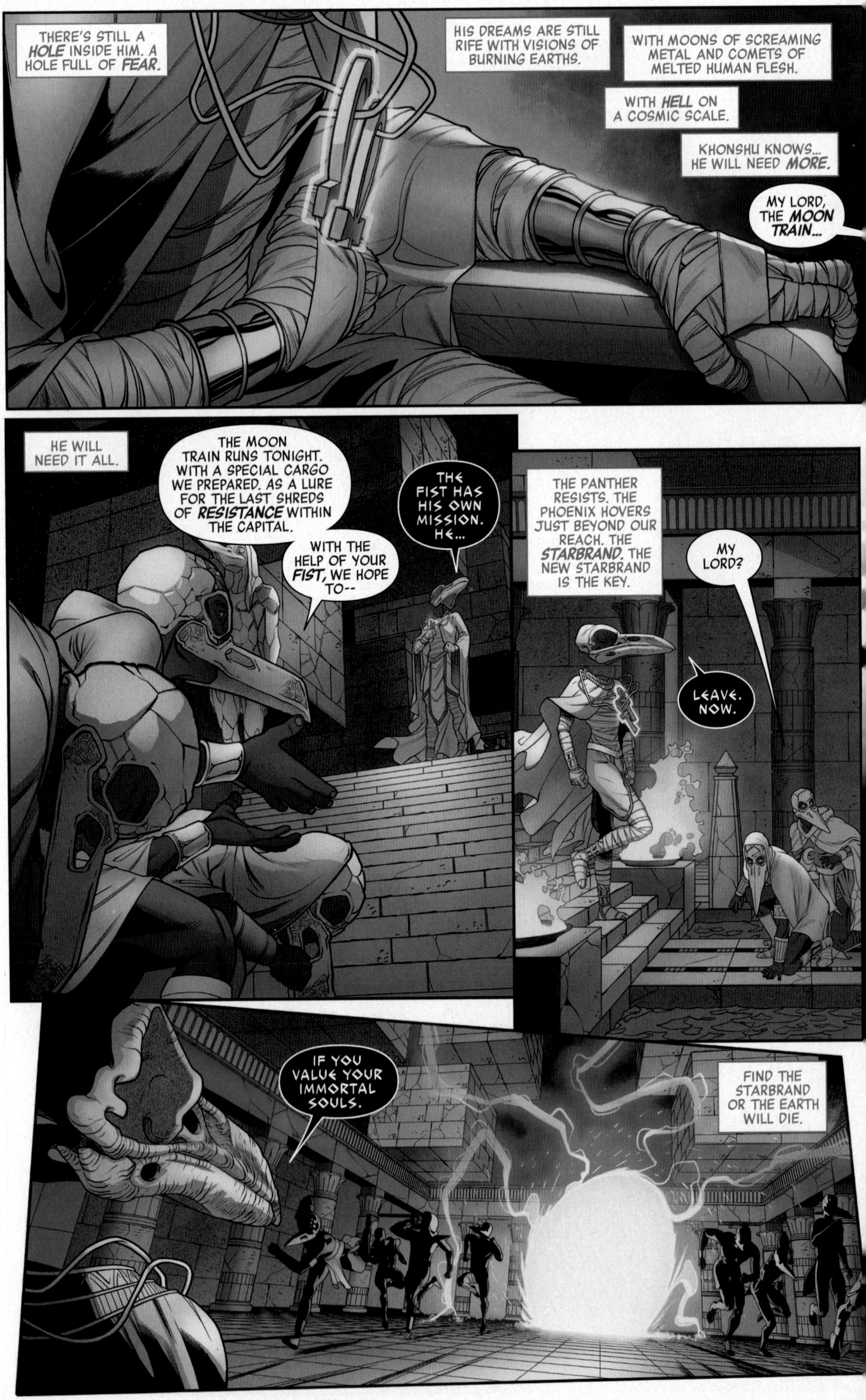
THERE'S STILL A HOLE INSIDE HIM. A HOLE FULL OF FEAR.
HIS DREAMS ARE STILL RIFE WITH VISIONS OF BURNING EARTHS.
WITH MOONS OF SCREAMING METAL AND COMETS OF MELTED HUMAN FLESH.
WITH HELL ON A COSMIC SCALE.
KHONSHU KNOWS... HE WILL NEED MORE.
MY LORD, THE MOON TRAIN...
HE WILL NEED IT ALL.
THE MOON TRAIN RUNS TONIGHT. WITH A SPECIAL CARGO WE PREPARED. AS A LURE FOR THE LAST SHREDS OF RESISTANCE WITHIN THE CAPITAL.
WITH THE HELP OF YOUR FIST, WE HOPE TO--
THE FIST HAS HIS OWN MISSION. HE...
THE PANTHER RESISTS. THE PHOENIX HOVERS JUST BEYOND OUR REACH. THE STARBRAND. THE NEW STARBRAND IS THE KEY.
MY LORD?
LEAVE. NOW.
IF YOU VALUE YOUR IMMORTAL SOULS.
FIND THE STARBRAND OR THE EARTH WILL DIE.

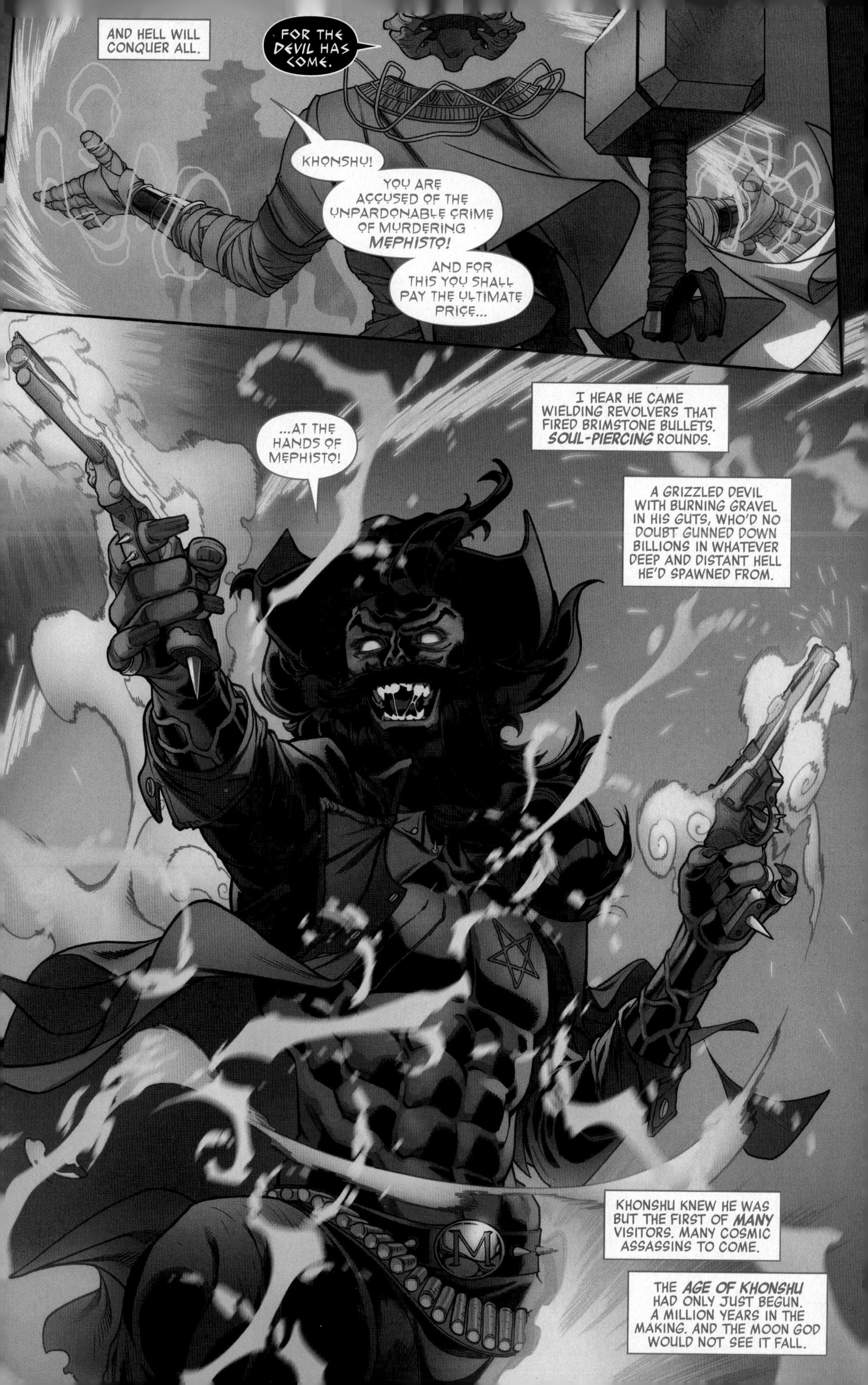
AND HELL WILL CONQUER ALL.
FOR THE DEVIL HAS COME.
KHONSHU!
YOU ARE ACCUSED OF THE UNPARDONABLE CRIME OF MURDERING MEPHISTO!
AND FOR THIS YOU SHALL PAY THE ULTIMATE PRICE...
...AT THE HANDS OF MEPHISTO!
I HEAR HE CAME WIELDING REVOLVERS THAT FIRED BRIMSTONE BULLETS. SOUL-PIERCING ROUNDS.
A GRIZZLED DEVIL WITH BURNING GRAVEL IN HIS GUTS, WHO'D NO DOUBT GUNNED DOWN BILLIONS IN WHATEVER DEEP AND DISTANT HELL HE'D SPAWNED FROM.
KHONSHU KNEW HE WAS BUT THE FIRST OF MANY VISITORS. MANY COSMIC ASSASSINS TO COME.
THE AGE OF KHONSHU HAD ONLY JUST BEGUN. A MILLION YEARS IN THE MAKING. AND THE MOON GOD WOULD NOT SEE IT FALL.

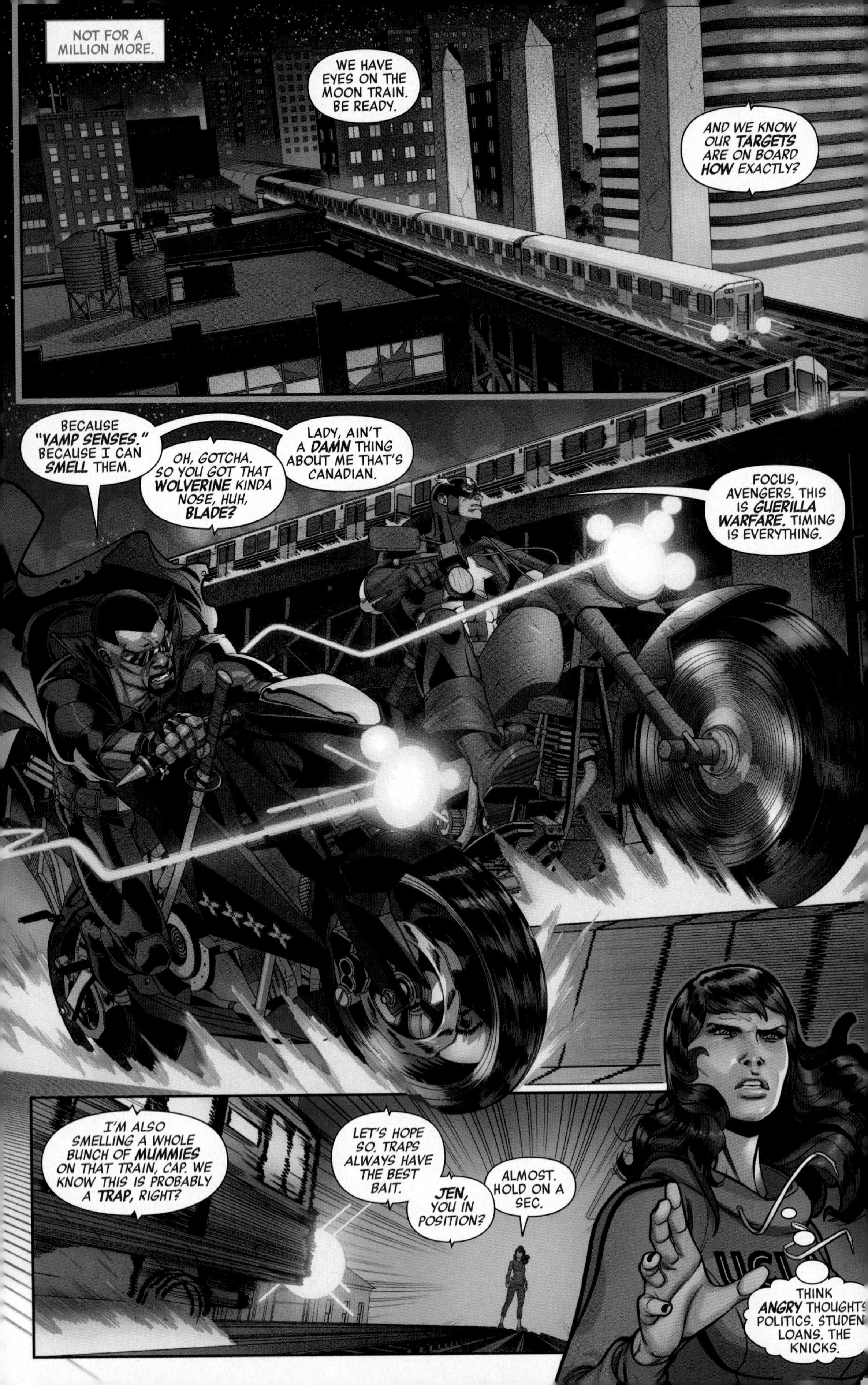
NOT FOR A MILLION MORE.
WE HAVE EYES ON THE MOON TRAIN. BE READY.
AND WE KNOW OUR TARGETS ARE ON BOARD HOW EXACTLY?
BECAUSE "VAMP SENSES." BECAUSE I CAN SMELL THEM.
OH, GOTCHA. SO YOU GOT THAT WOLVERINE KINDA NOSE, HUH, BLADE?
LADY, AIN'T A DAMN THING ABOUT ME THAT'S CANADIAN.
FOCUS, AVENGERS. THIS IS GUERILLA WARFARE. TIMING IS EVERYTHING.
I'M ALSO SMELLING A WHOLE BUNCH OF MUMMIES ON THAT TRAIN, CAP. WE KNOW THIS IS PROBABLY A TRAP, RIGHT?
LET'S HOPE SO. TRAPS ALWAYS HAVE THE BEST BAIT.
JEN, YOU IN POSITION?
ALMOST. HOLD ON A SEC.
THINK ANGRY THOUGHTS. POLITICS. STUDEN LOANS. THE KNICKS.

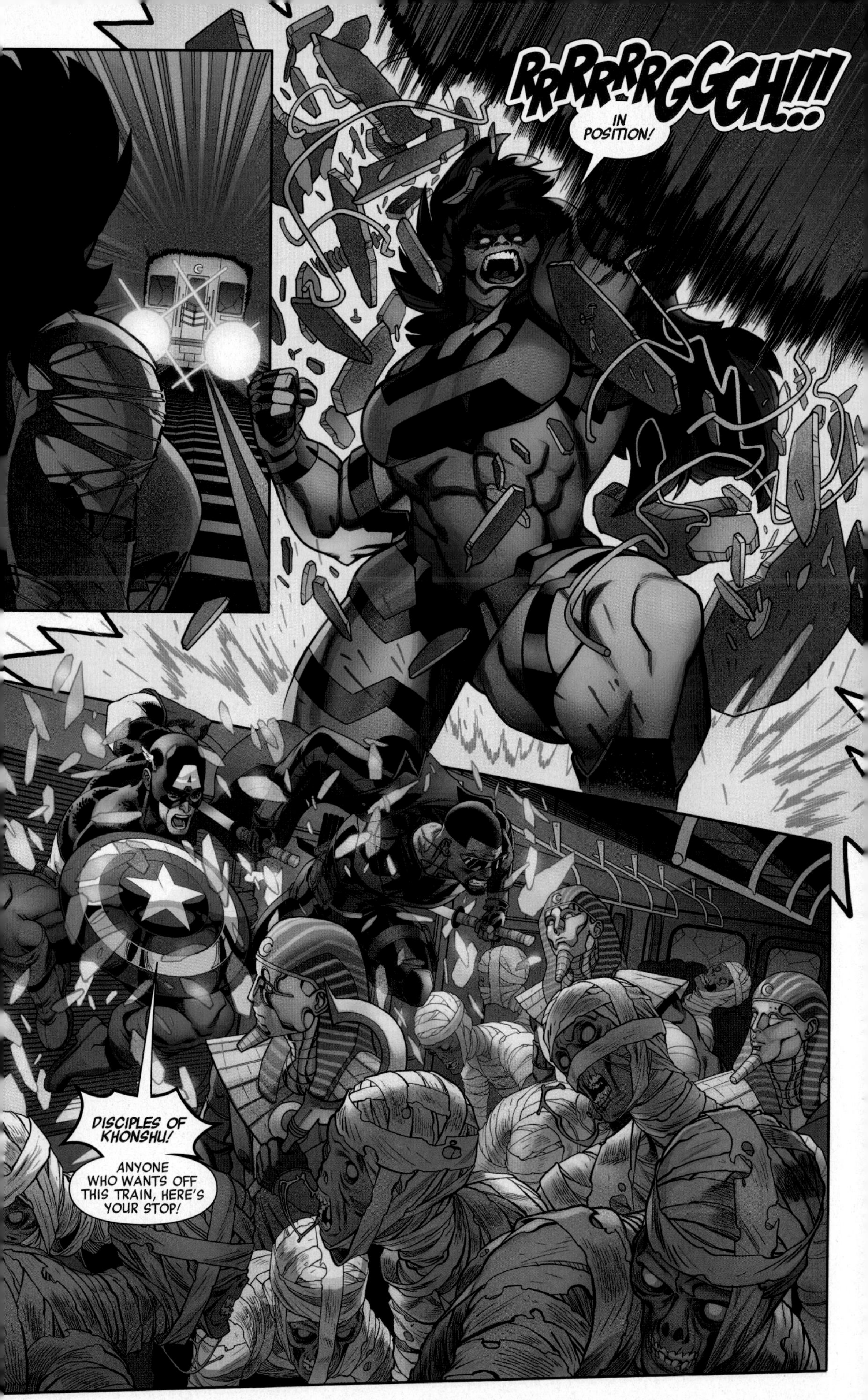
RRRRRRGGGH!!!!...
IN POSITION!
DISCIPLES OF KHONSHU!
ANYONE WHO WANTS OFF THIS TRAIN, HERE'S YOUR STOP!

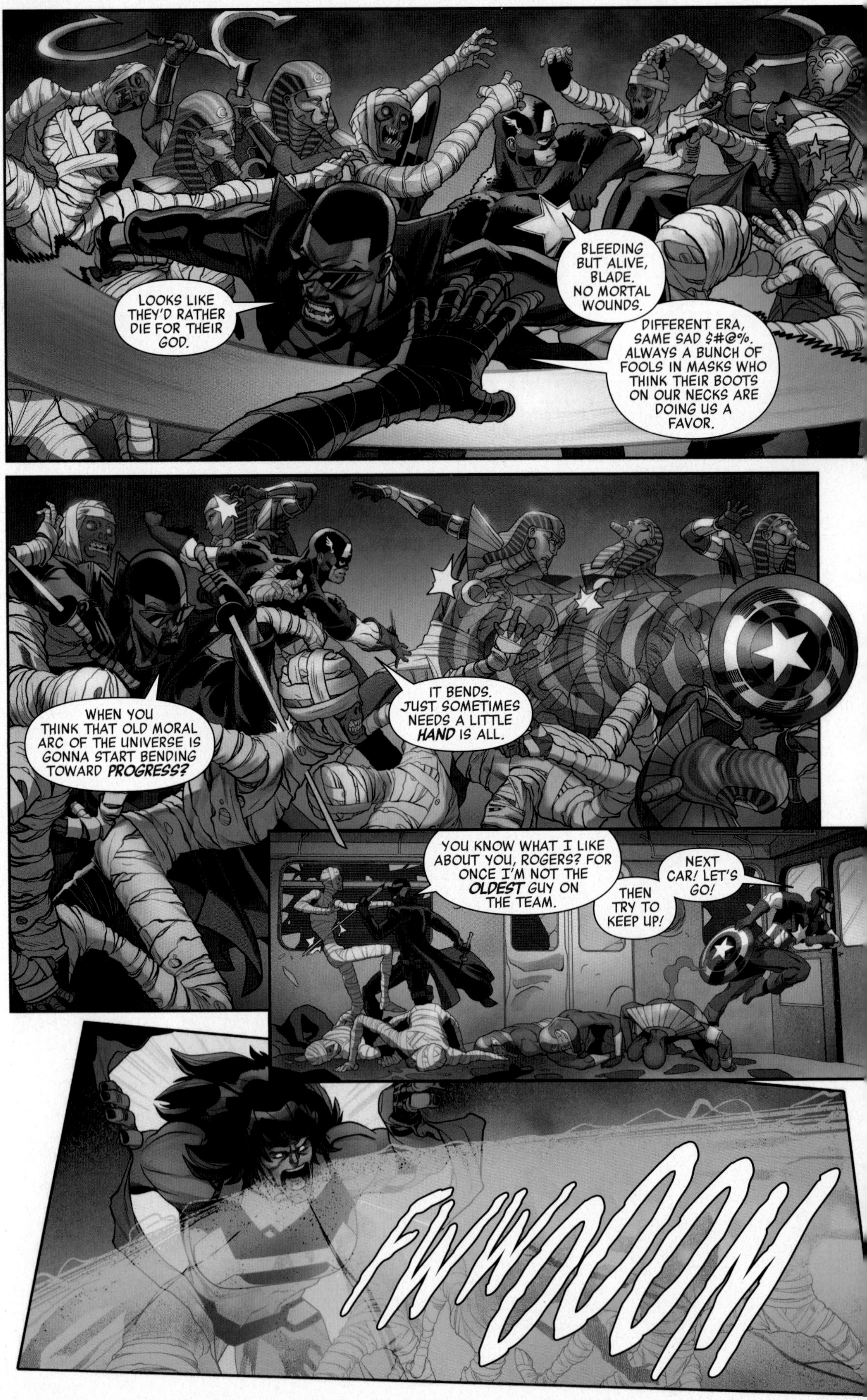
LOOKS LIKE THEY'D RATHER DIE FOR THEIR GOD.
BLEEDING BUT ALIVE, BLADE. NO MORTAL WOUNDS.
DIFFERENT ERA, SAME SAD $#@%. ALWAYS A BUNCH OF FOOLS IN MASKS WHO THINK THEIR BOOTS ON OUR NECKS ARE DOING US A FAVOR.
WHEN YOU THINK THAT OLD MORAL ARC OF THE UNIVERSE IS GONNA START BENDING TOWARD PROGRESS?
IT BENDS. JUST SOMETIMES NEEDS A LITTLE HAND IS ALL.
YOU KNOW WHAT I LIKE ABOUT YOU, ROGERS? FOR ONCE I'M NOT THE OLDEST GUY ON THE TEAM.
THEN TRY TO KEEP UP!
NEXT CAR! LET'S GO!
FWWOOOM

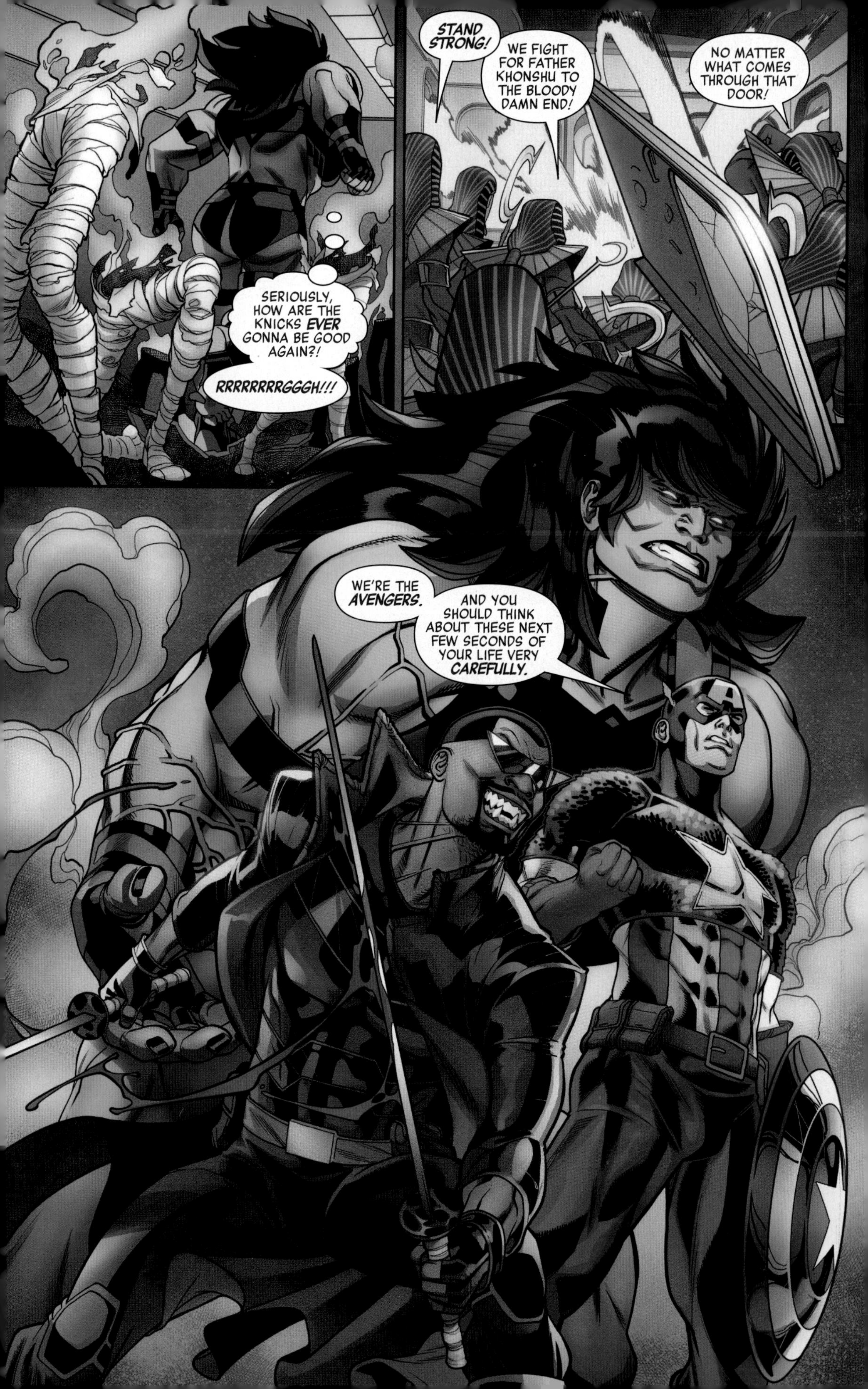
SERIOUSLY, HOW ARE THE KNICKS EVER GONNA BE GOOD AGAIN?!
RRRRRRRRGGGH!!!
STAND STRONG!
WE FIGHT FOR FATHER KHONSHU TO THE BLOODY DAMN END!
NO MATTER WHAT COMES THROUGH THAT DOOR!
WE'RE THE AVENGERS.
AND YOU SHOULD THINK ABOUT THESE NEXT FEW SECONDS OF YOUR LIFE VERY CAREFULLY.

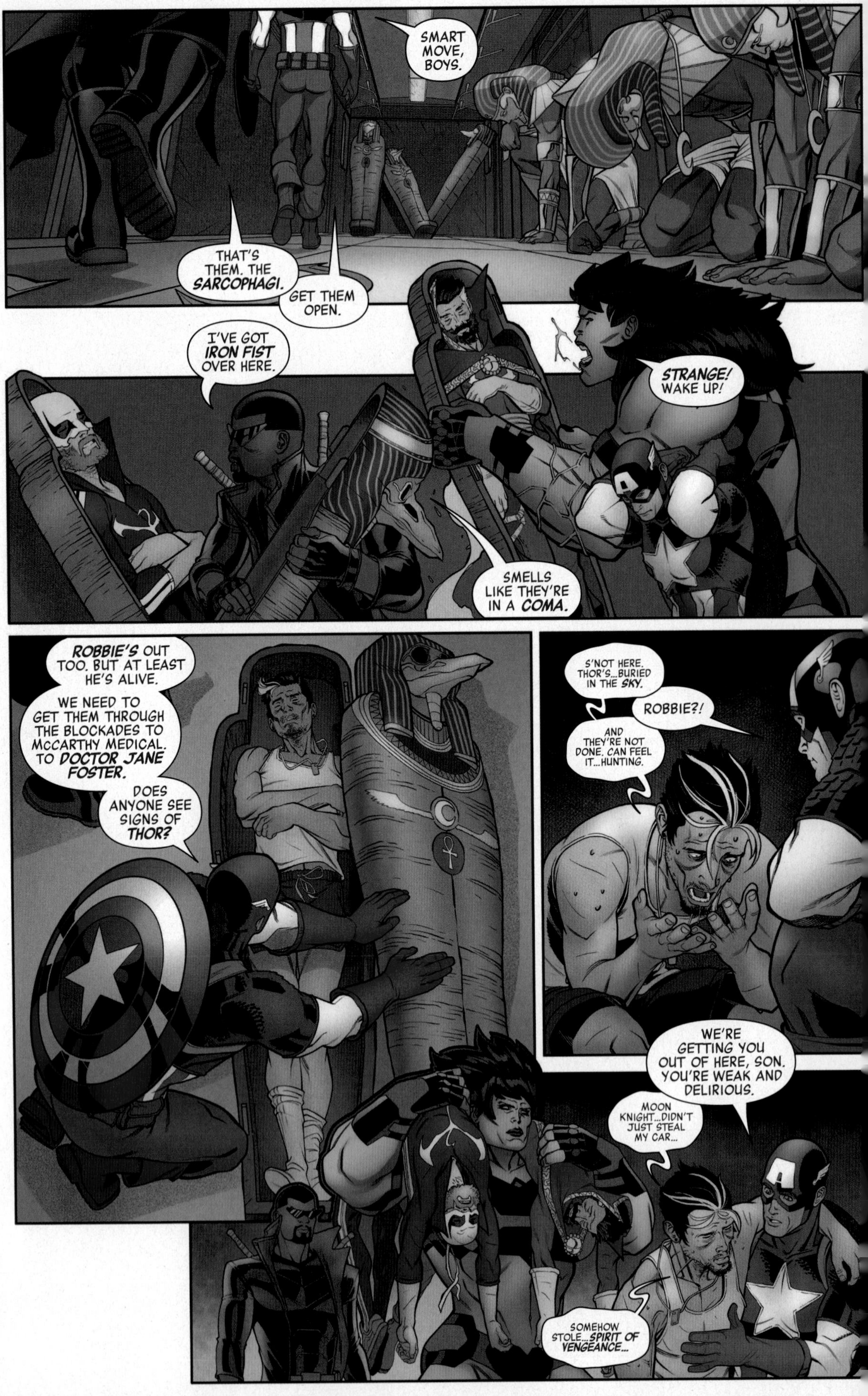
SMART MOVE, BOYS.
THAT'S THEM. THE SARCOPHAGI.
GET THEM OPEN.
I'VE GOT IRON FIST OVER HERE.
STRANGE! WAKE UP!
SMELLS LIKE THEY'RE IN A COMA.
ROBBIE'S OUT TOO. BUT AT LEAST HE'S ALIVE.
WE NEED TO GET THEM THROUGH THE BLOCKADES TO McCARTHY MEDICAL. TO DOCTOR JANE FOSTER.
DOES ANYONE SEE SIGNS OF THOR?
S'NOT HERE. THOR'S...BURIED IN THE SKY.
ROBBIE?!
AND THEY'RE NOT DONE. CAN FEEL IT...HUNTING.
WE'RE GETTING YOU OUT OF HERE, SON. YOU'RE WEAK AND DELIRIOUS.
MOON KNIGHT...DIDN'T JUST STEAL MY CAR...
SOMEHOW STOLE...SPIRIT OF VENGEANCE...

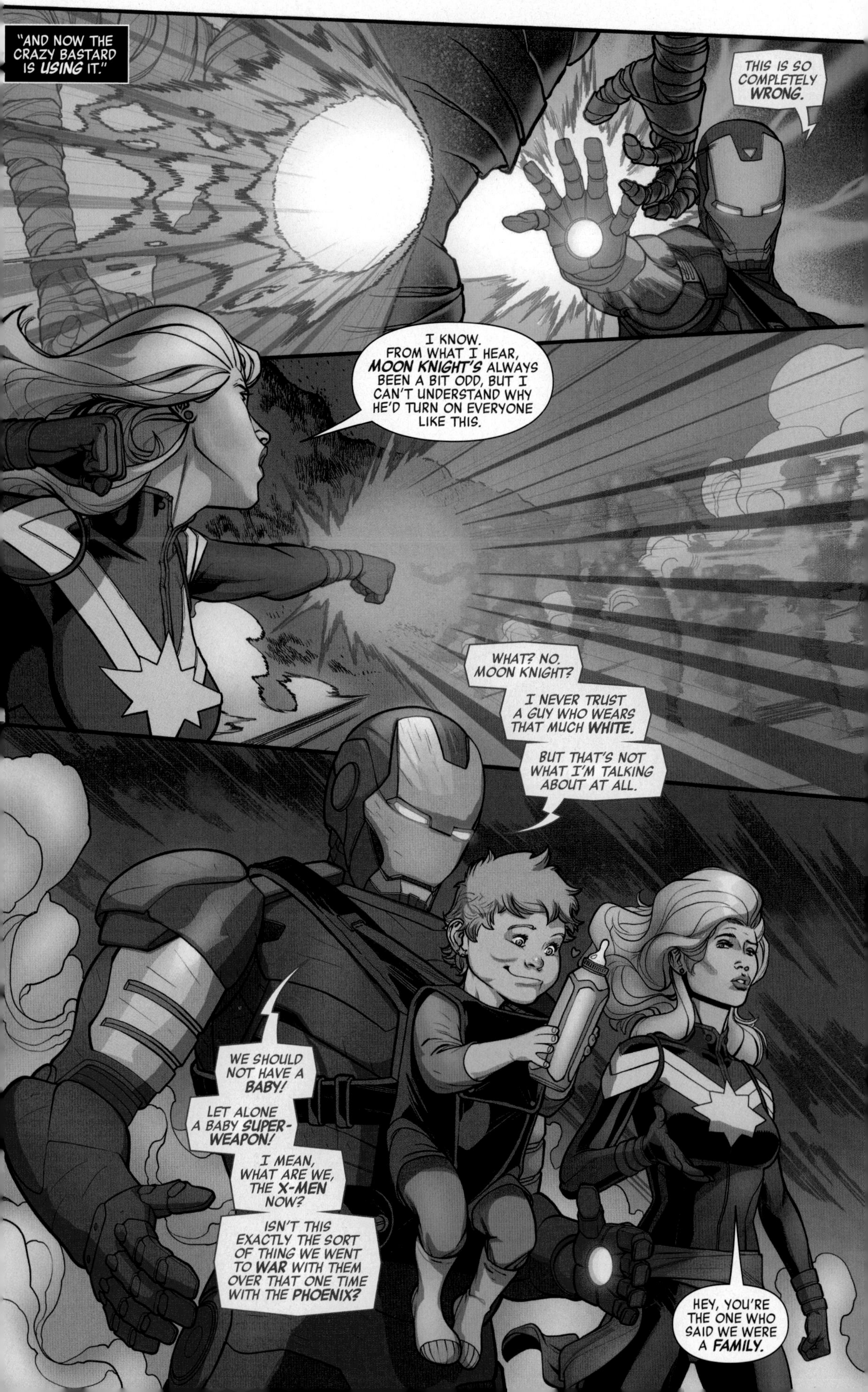
"AND NOW THE CRAZY BASTARD IS USING IT."
THIS IS SO COMPLETELY WRONG.
I KNOW. FROM WHAT I HEAR, MOON KNIGHT'S ALWAYS BEEN A BIT ODD, BUT I CAN'T UNDERSTAND WHY HE'D TURN ON EVERYONE LIKE THIS.
WHAT? NO. MOON KNIGHT?
I NEVER TRUST A GUY WHO WEARS THAT MUCH WHITE.
BUT THAT'S NOT WHAT I'M TALKING ABOUT AT ALL.
WE SHOULD NOT HAVE A BABY!
LET ALONE A BABY SUPER-WEAPON!
I MEAN, WHAT ARE WE, THE X-MEN NOW?
ISN'T THIS EXACTLY THE SORT OF THING WE WENT TO WAR WITH THEM OVER THAT ONE TIME WITH THE PHOENIX?
HEY, YOU'RE THE ONE WHO SAID WE WERE A FAMILY.

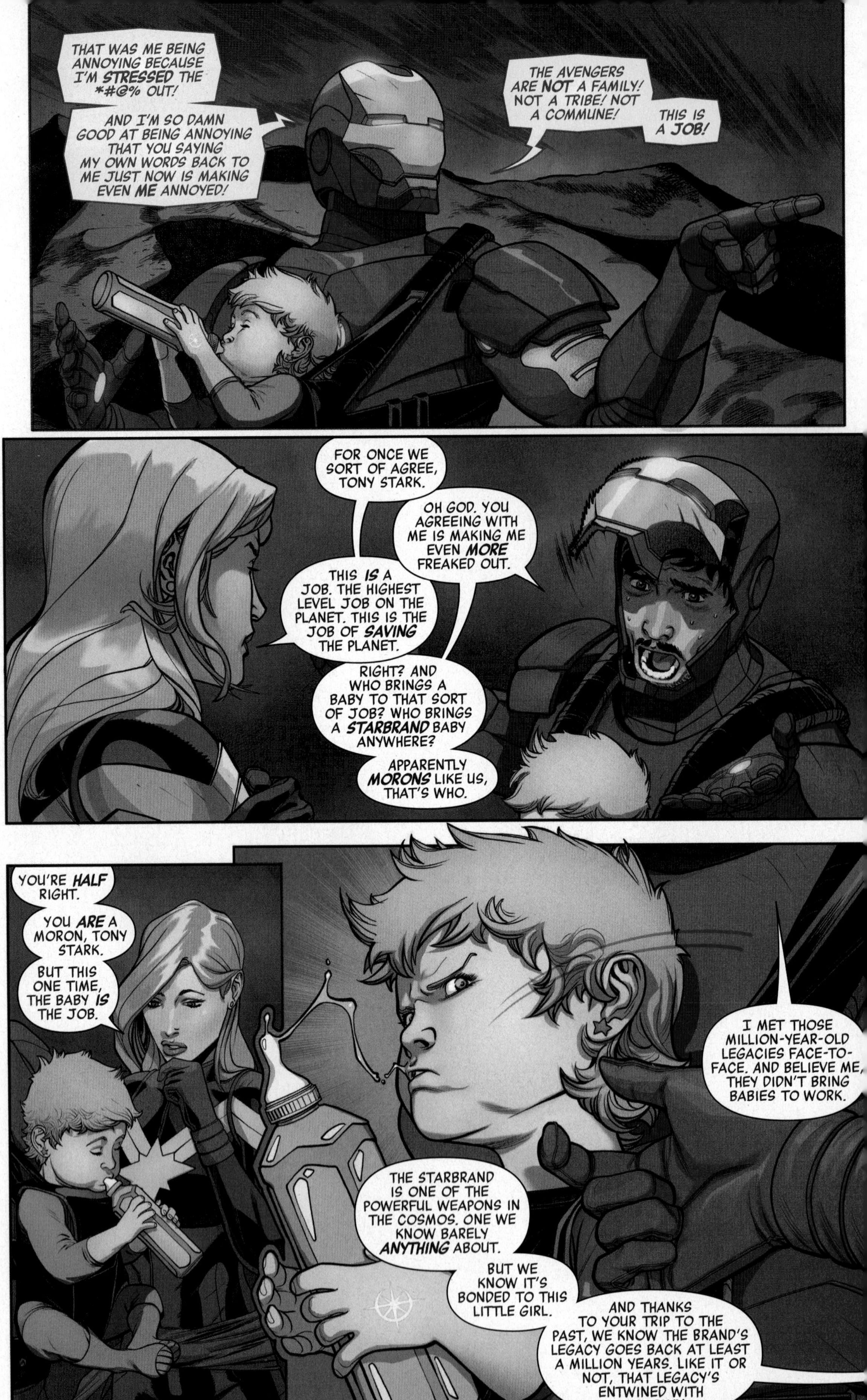

THAT WAS ME BEING ANNOYING BECAUSE I'M STRESSED THE *#@% OUT!
AND I'M SO DAMN GOOD AT BEING ANNOYING THAT YOU SAYING MY OWN WORDS BACK TO ME JUST NOW IS MAKING EVEN ME ANNOYED!
THE AVENGERS ARE NOT A FAMILY! NOT A TRIBE! NOT A COMMUNE!
THIS IS A JOB!
FOR ONCE WE SORT OF AGREE, TONY STARK.
OH GOD. YOU AGREEING WITH ME IS MAKING ME EVEN MORE FREAKED OUT.
THIS IS A JOB. THE HIGHEST LEVEL JOB ON THE PLANET. THIS IS THE JOB OF SAVING THE PLANET.
RIGHT? AND WHO BRINGS A BABY TO THAT SORT OF JOB? WHO BRINGS A STARBRAND BABY ANYWHERE?
APPARENTLY MORONS LIKE US, THAT'S WHO.
YOU'RE HALF RIGHT.
YOU ARE A MORON, TONY STARK.
BUT THIS ONE TIME, THE BABY IS THE JOB.
I MET THOSE MILLION-YEAR-OLD LEGACIES FACE-TO-FACE. AND BELIEVE ME, THEY DIDN'T BRING BABIES TO WORK.
THE STARBRAND IS ONE OF THE POWERFUL WEAPONS IN THE COSMOS. ONE WE KNOW BARELY ANYTHING ABOUT.
BUT WE KNOW IT'S BONDED TO THIS LITTLE GIRL.
AND THANKS TO YOUR TRIP TO THE PAST, WE KNOW THE BRAND'S LEGACY GOES BACK AT LEAST A MILLION YEARS. LIKE IT OR NOT, THAT LEGACY'S ENTWINED WITH OUR OWN.

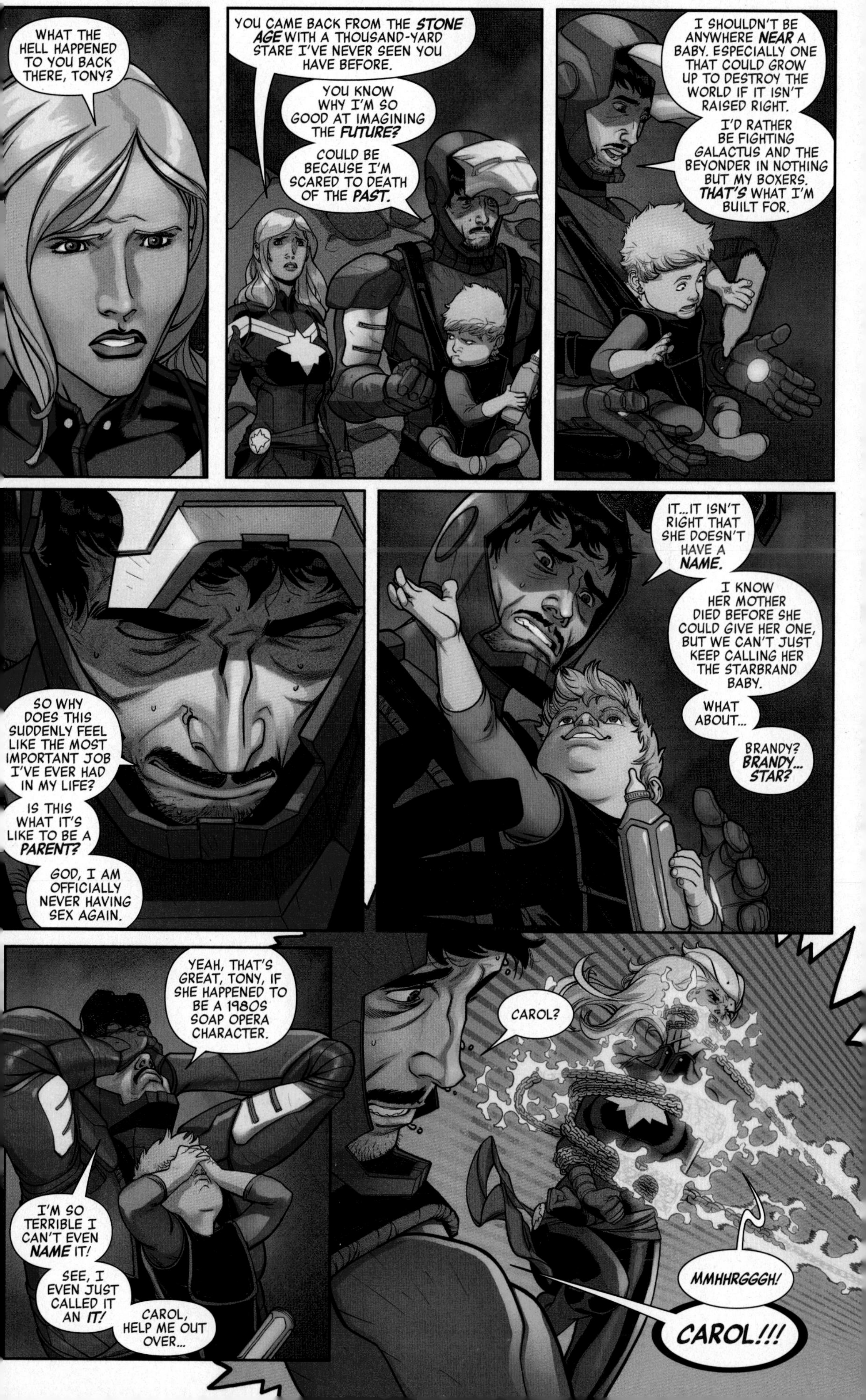
WHAT THE HELL HAPPENED TO YOU BACK THERE, TONY?
YOU CAME BACK FROM THE STONE AGE WITH A THOUSAND-YARD STARE I'VE NEVER SEEN YOU HAVE BEFORE.
YOU KNOW WHY I'M SO GOOD AT IMAGINING THE FUTURE?
COULD BE BECAUSE I'M SCARED TO DEATH OF THE PAST.
I SHOULDN'T BE ANYWHERE NEAR A BABY. ESPECIALLY ONE THAT COULD GROW UP TO DESTROY THE WORLD IF IT ISN'T RAISED RIGHT.
I'D RATHER BE FIGHTING GALACTUS AND THE BEYONDER IN NOTHING BUT MY BOXERS. THAT'S WHAT I'M BUILT FOR.
SO WHY DOES THIS SUDDENLY FEEL LIKE THE MOST IMPORTANT JOB I'VE EVER HAD IN MY LIFE?
IS THIS WHAT IT'S LIKE TO BE A PARENT?
GOD, I AM OFFICIALLY NEVER HAVING SEX AGAIN.
IT...IT ISN'T RIGHT THAT SHE DOESN'T HAVE A NAME.
I KNOW HER MOTHER DIED BEFORE SHE COULD GIVE HER ONE, BUT WE CAN'T JUST KEEP CALLING HER THE STARBRAND BABY.
WHAT ABOUT...
BRANDY? BRANDY... STAR?
YEAH, THAT'S GREAT, TONY, IF SHE HAPPENED TO BE A 1980S SOAP OPERA CHARACTER.
I'M SO TERRIBLE I CAN'T EVEN NAME IT!
SEE, I EVEN JUST CALLED IT AN IT!
CAROL, HELP ME OUT OVER...
CAROL?
MMHHRGGGH!
CAROL!!!

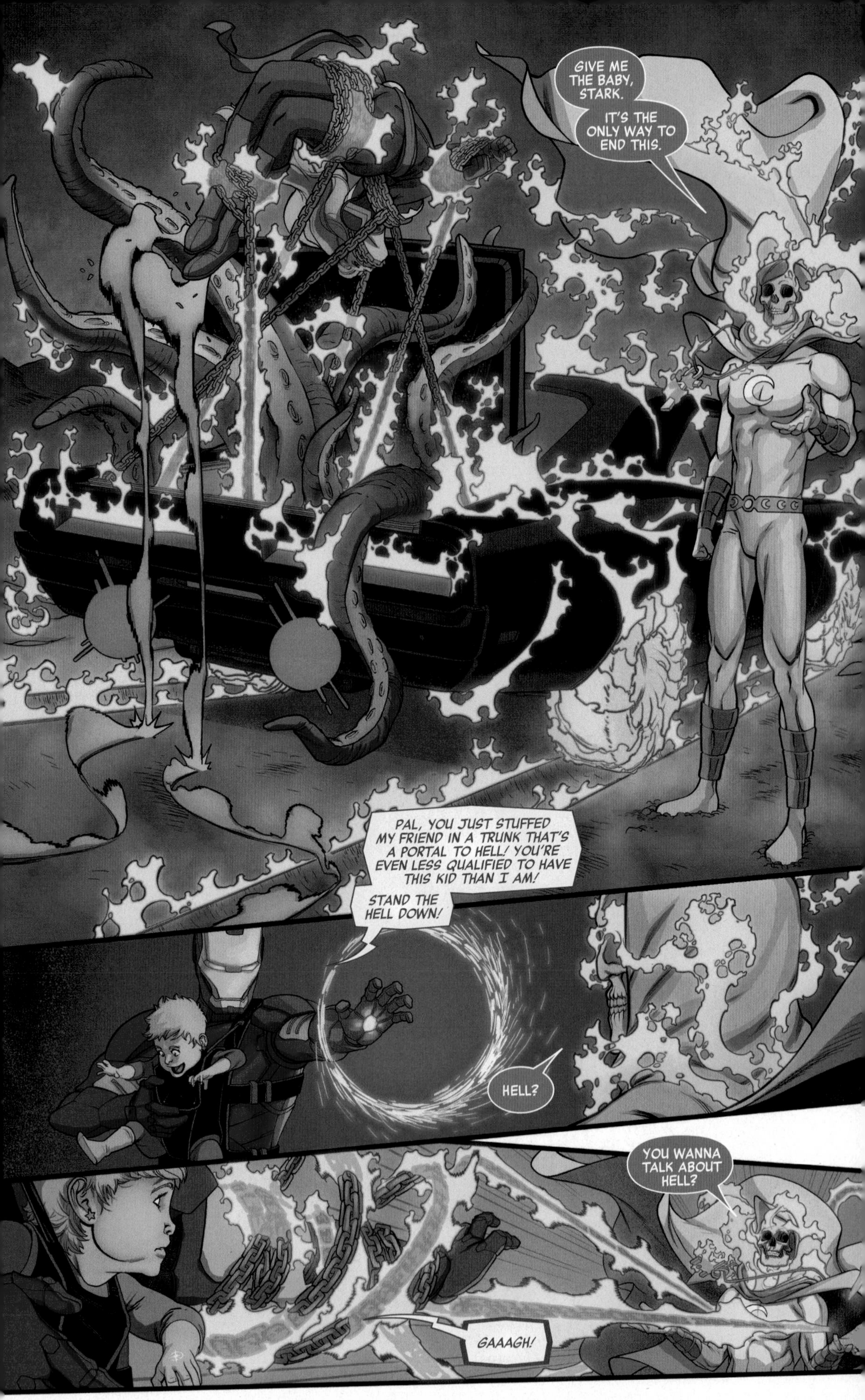
GIVE ME THE BABY, STARK.
IT'S THE ONLY WAY TO END THIS.
PAL, YOU JUST STUFFED MY FRIEND IN A TRUNK THAT'S A PORTAL TO HELL! YOU'RE EVEN LESS QUALIFIED TO HAVE THIS KID THAN I AM!
STAND THE HELL DOWN!
HELL?
YOU WANNA TALK ABOUT HELL?
GAAAGH!

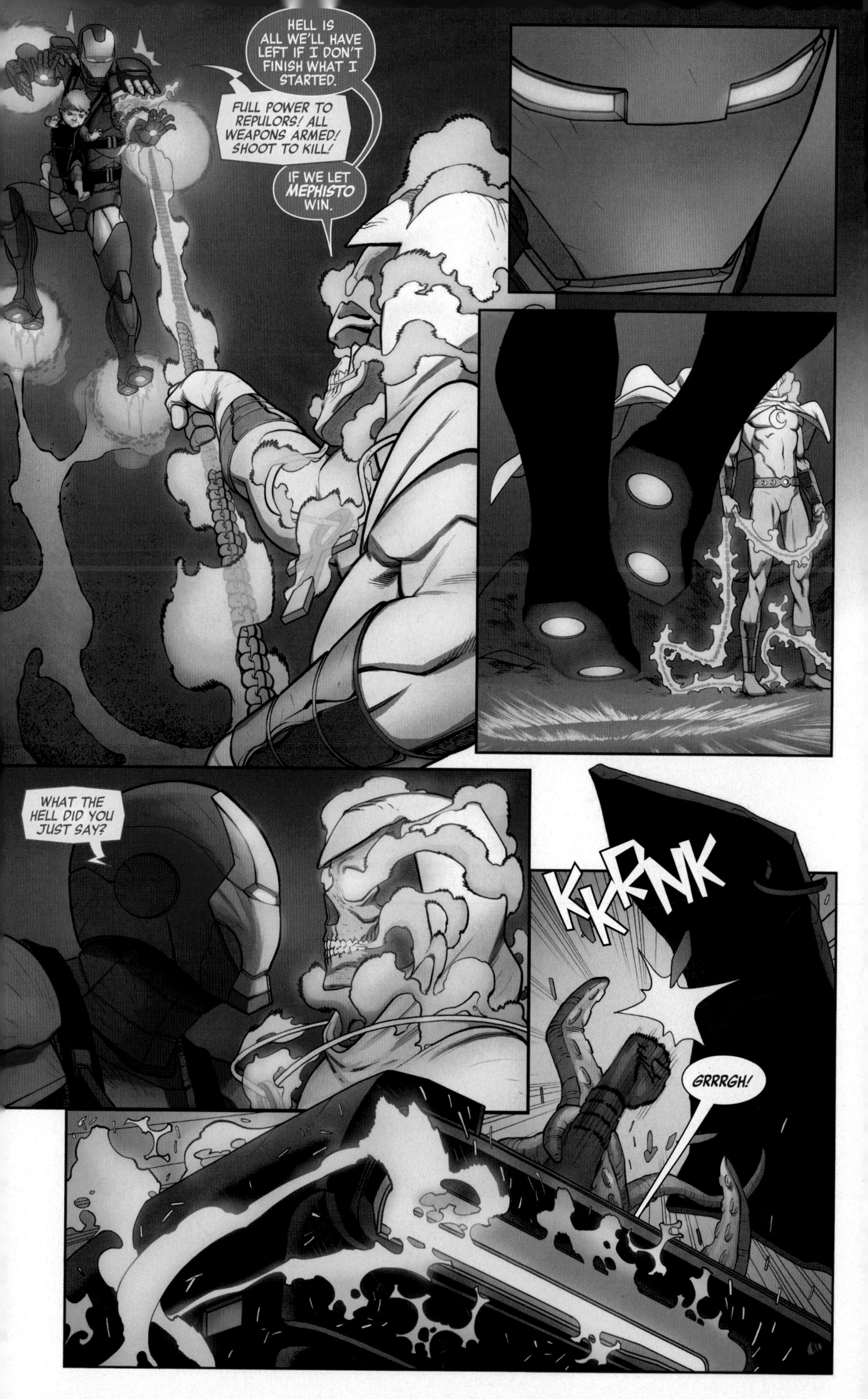
HELL IS ALL WE'LL HAVE LEFT IF I DON'T FINISH WHAT I STARTED.
FULL POWER TO REPULSORS! ALL WEAPONS ARMED! SHOOT TO KILL!
IF WE LET MEPHISTO WIN.
WHAT THE HELL DID YOU JUST SAY?
KKRNK
GRRRGH!

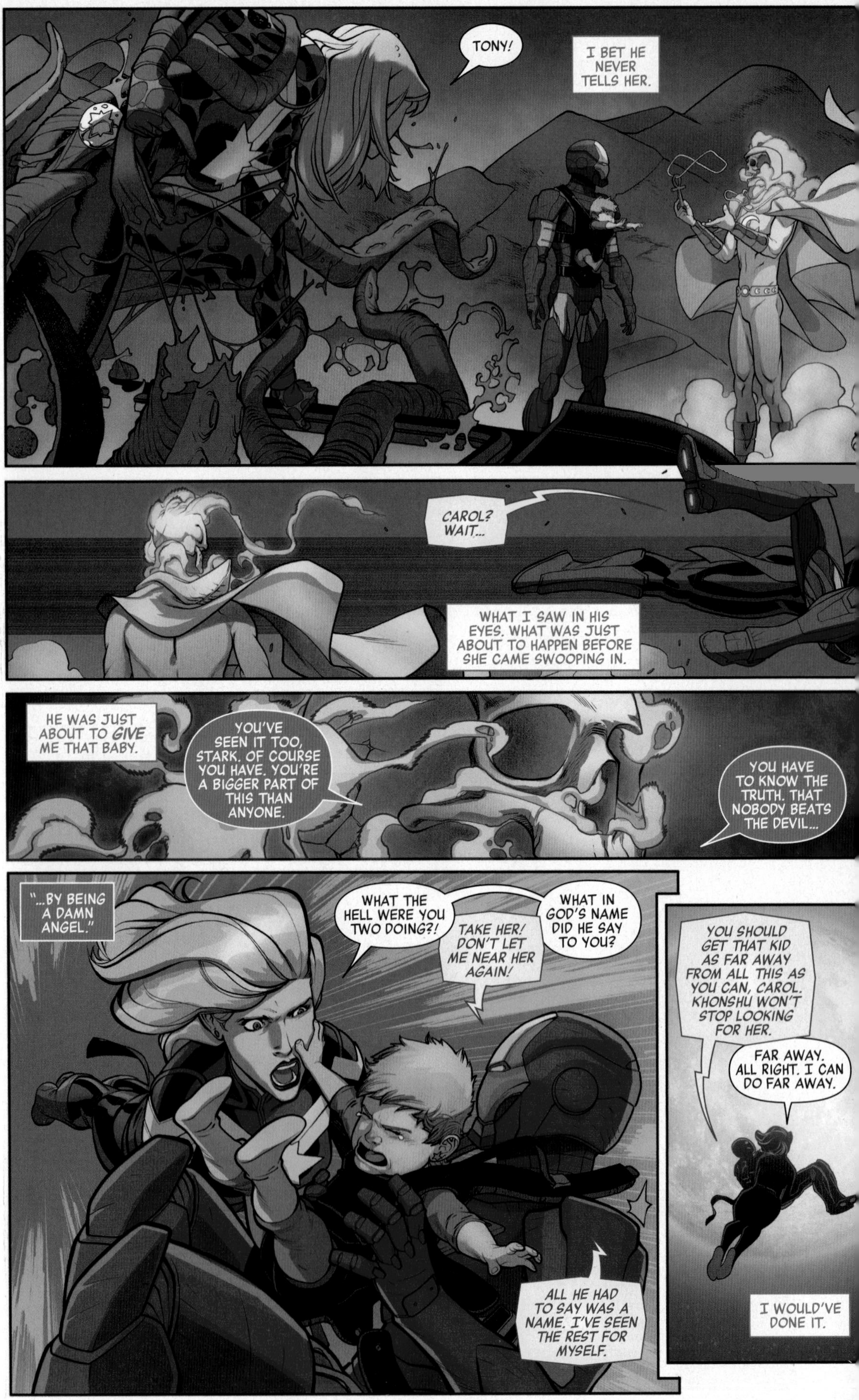
TONY!
I BET HE NEVER TELLS HER.
CAROL? WAIT...
WHAT I SAW IN HIS EYES. WHAT WAS JUST ABOUT TO HAPPEN BEFORE SHE CAME SWOOPING IN.
HE WAS JUST ABOUT TO GIVE ME THAT BABY.
YOU'VE SEEN IT TOO, STARK, OF COURSE YOU HAVE. YOU'RE A BIGGER PART OF THIS THAN ANYONE.
YOU HAVE TO KNOW THE TRUTH. THAT NOBODY BEATS THE DEVIL...
"...BY BEING A DAMN ANGEL."
WHAT THE HELL WERE YOU TWO DOING?!
WHAT IN GOD'S NAME DID HE SAY TO YOU?
TAKE HER! DON'T LET ME NEAR HER AGAIN!
ALL HE HAD TO SAY WAS A NAME. I'VE SEEN THE REST FOR MYSELF.
YOU SHOULD GET THAT KID AS FAR AWAY FROM ALL THIS AS YOU CAN, CAROL. KHONSHU WON'T STOP LOOKING FOR HER.
FAR AWAY. ALL RIGHT. I CAN DO FAR AWAY.
I WOULD'VE DONE IT.

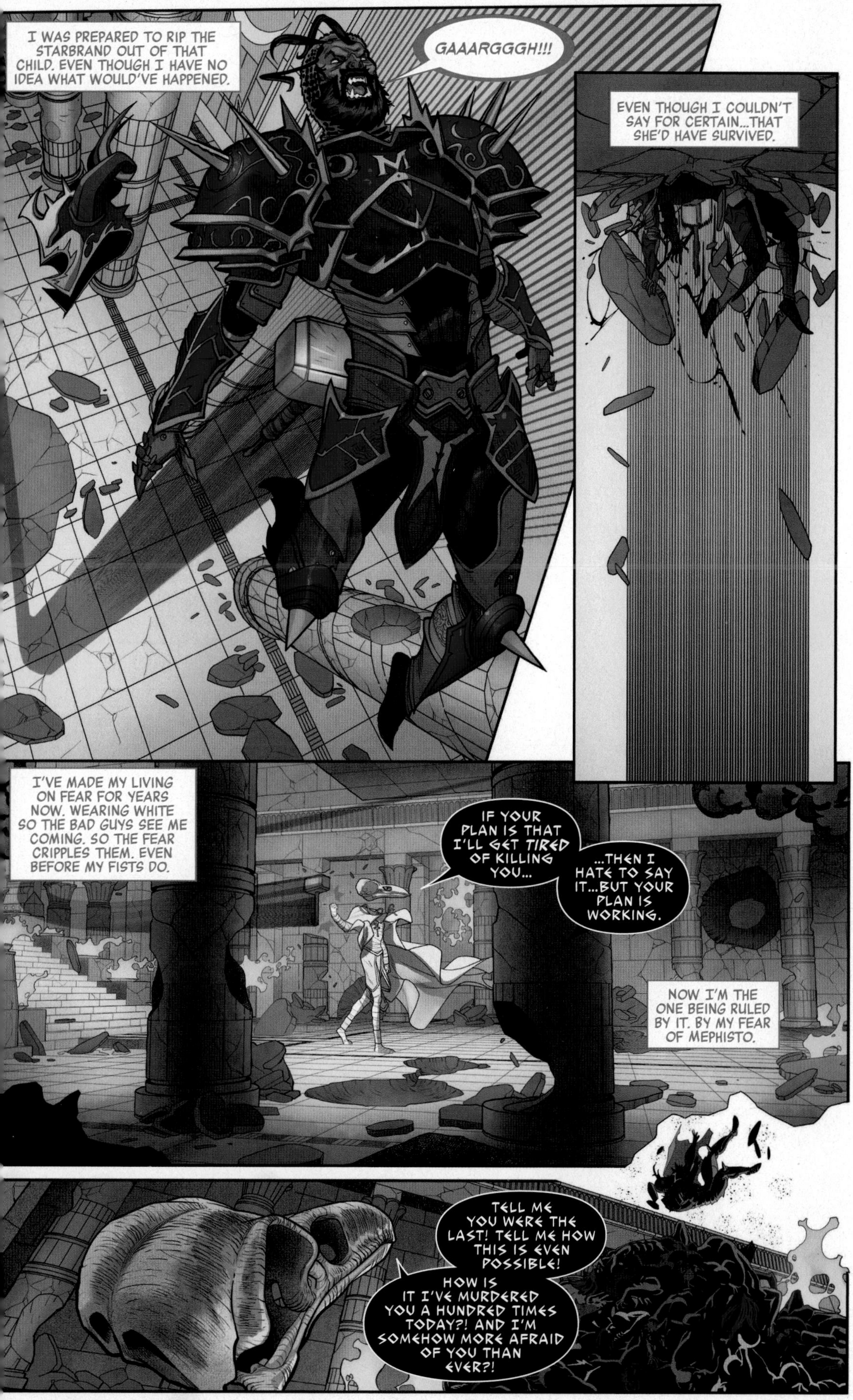
I WAS PREPARED TO RIP THE STARBRAND OUT OF THAT CHILD. EVEN THOUGH I HAVE NO IDEA WHAT WOULD'VE HAPPENED.
GAAARGGGH!!!
EVEN THOUGH I COULDN'T SAY FOR CERTAIN...THAT SHE'D HAVE SURVIVED.
I'VE MADE MY LIVING ON FEAR FOR YEARS NOW. WEARING WHITE SO THE BAD GUYS SEE ME COMING. SO THE FEAR CRIPPLES THEM. EVEN BEFORE MY FISTS DO.
IF YOUR PLAN IS THAT I'LL GET TIRED OF KILLING YOU...
...THEN I HATE TO SAY IT...BUT YOUR PLAN IS WORKING.
NOW I'M THE ONE BEING RULED BY IT. BY MY FEAR OF MEPHISTO.
TELL ME YOU WERE THE LAST! TELL ME HOW THIS IS EVEN POSSIBLE!
HOW IS IT I'VE MURDERED YOU A HUNDRED TIMES TODAY?! AND I'M SOMEHOW MORE AFRAID OF YOU THAN EVER?!

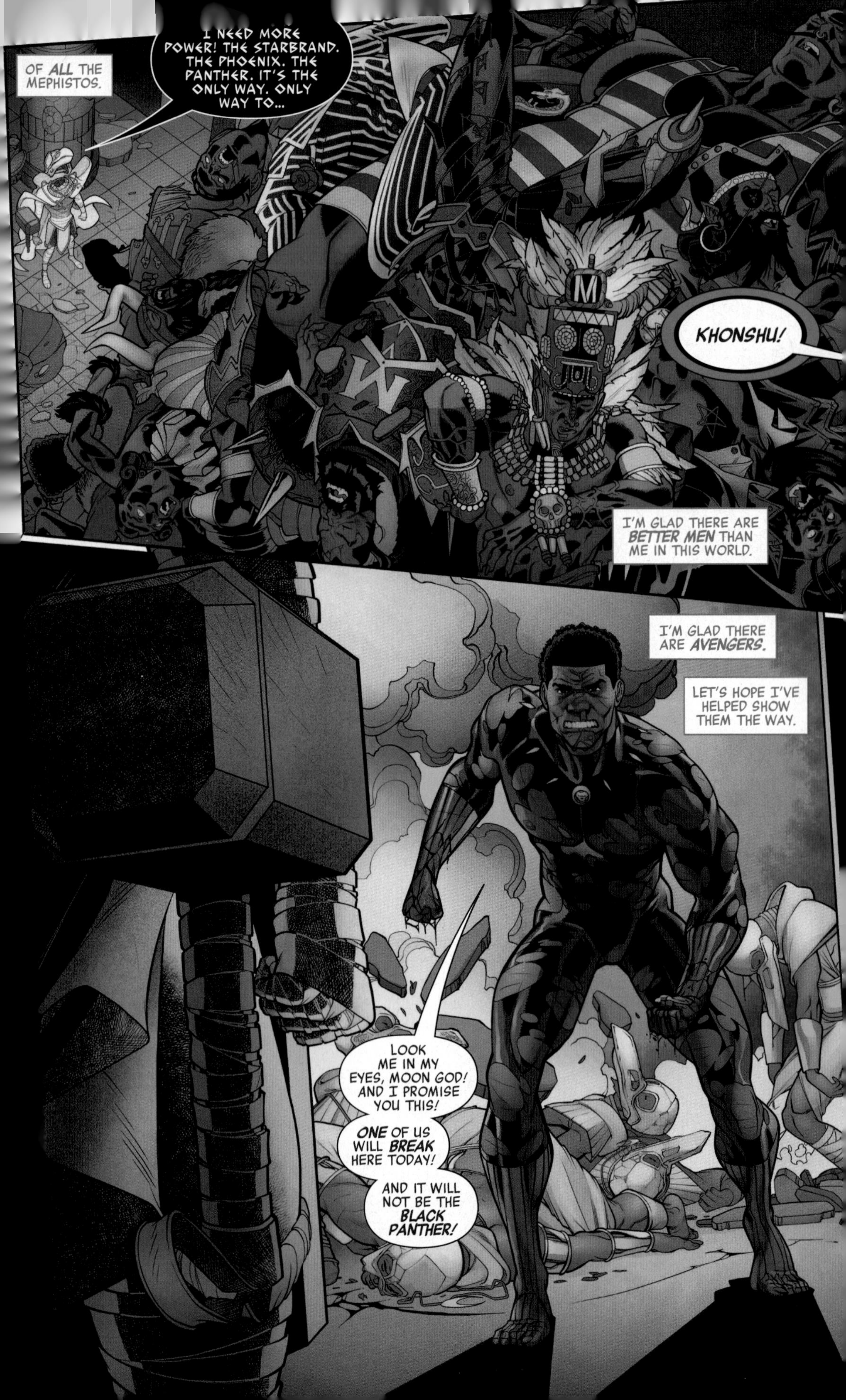

OF ALL THE MEPHISTOS.
I NEED MORE POWER! THE STARBRAND. THE PHOENIX. THE PANTHER. IT'S THE ONLY WAY. ONLY WAY TO...
KHONSHU!
I'M GLAD THERE ARE BETTER MEN THAN ME IN THIS WORLD.
I'M GLAD THERE ARE AVENGERS.
LET'S HOPE I'VE HELPED SHOW THEM THE WAY.
LOOK ME IN MY EYES, MOON GOD! AND I PROMISE YOU THIS!
ONE OF US WILL BREAK HERE TODAY!
AND IT WILL NOT BE THE BLACK PANTHER!

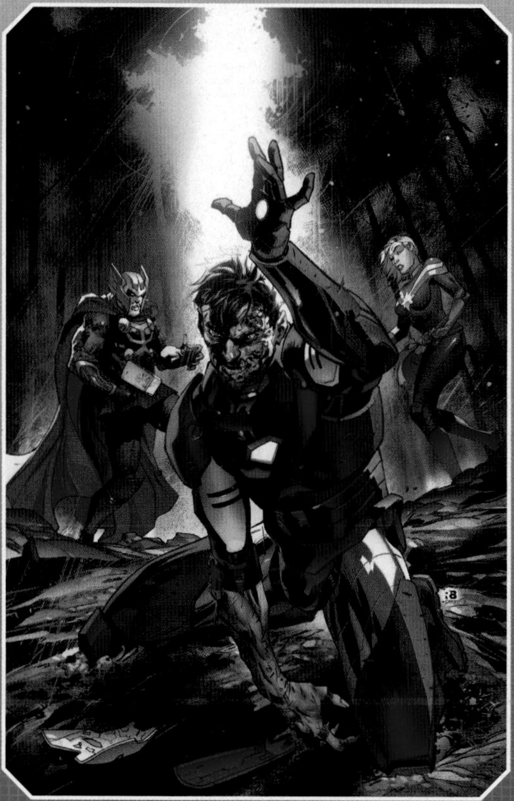

RYAN BENJAMIN & DAVID CURIEL
33 ZOMBIES VARIANT

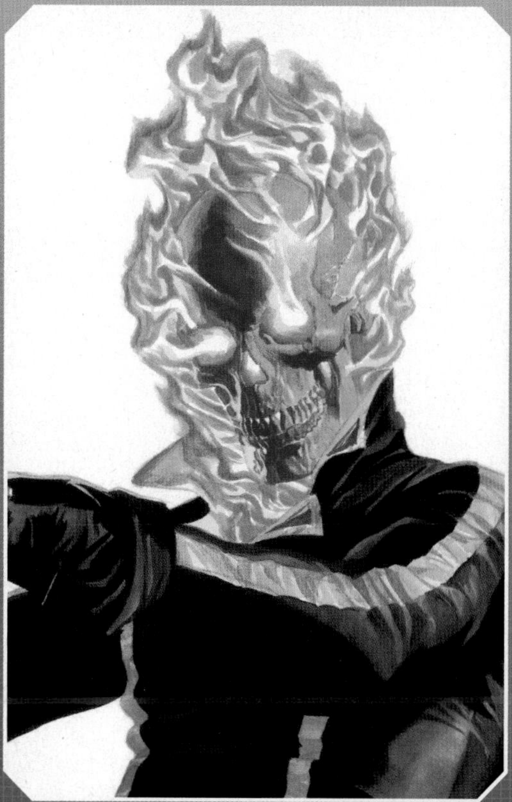

ALEX ROSS
36 TIMELESS VARIANT

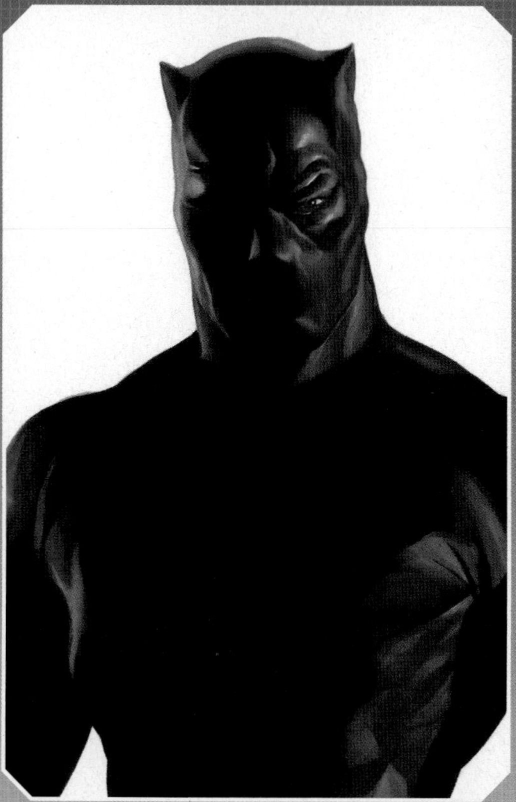

ALEX ROSS
37 TIMELESS VARIANT

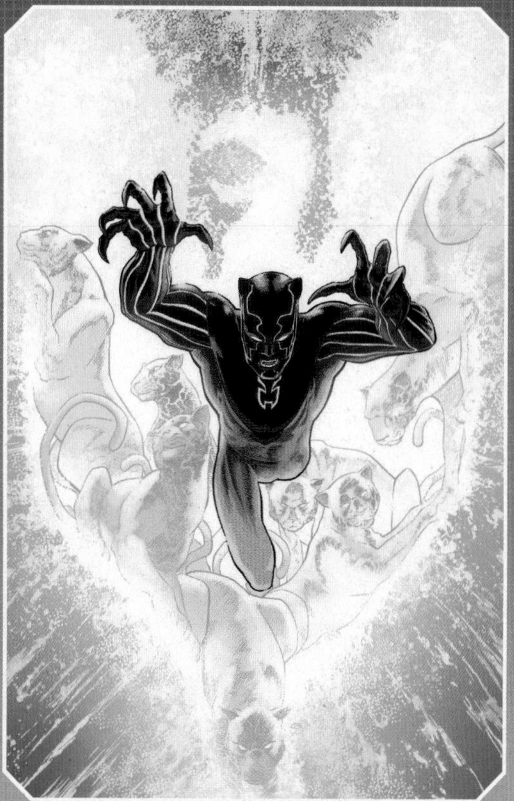

AARON KUDER & MATTHEW WILSON
38 PHOENIX VARIANT

36 THE AGE OF KHONSHU PART 4
MOONS OF FIRE, STARS OF BLOOD, PANTHERS OF BLACK

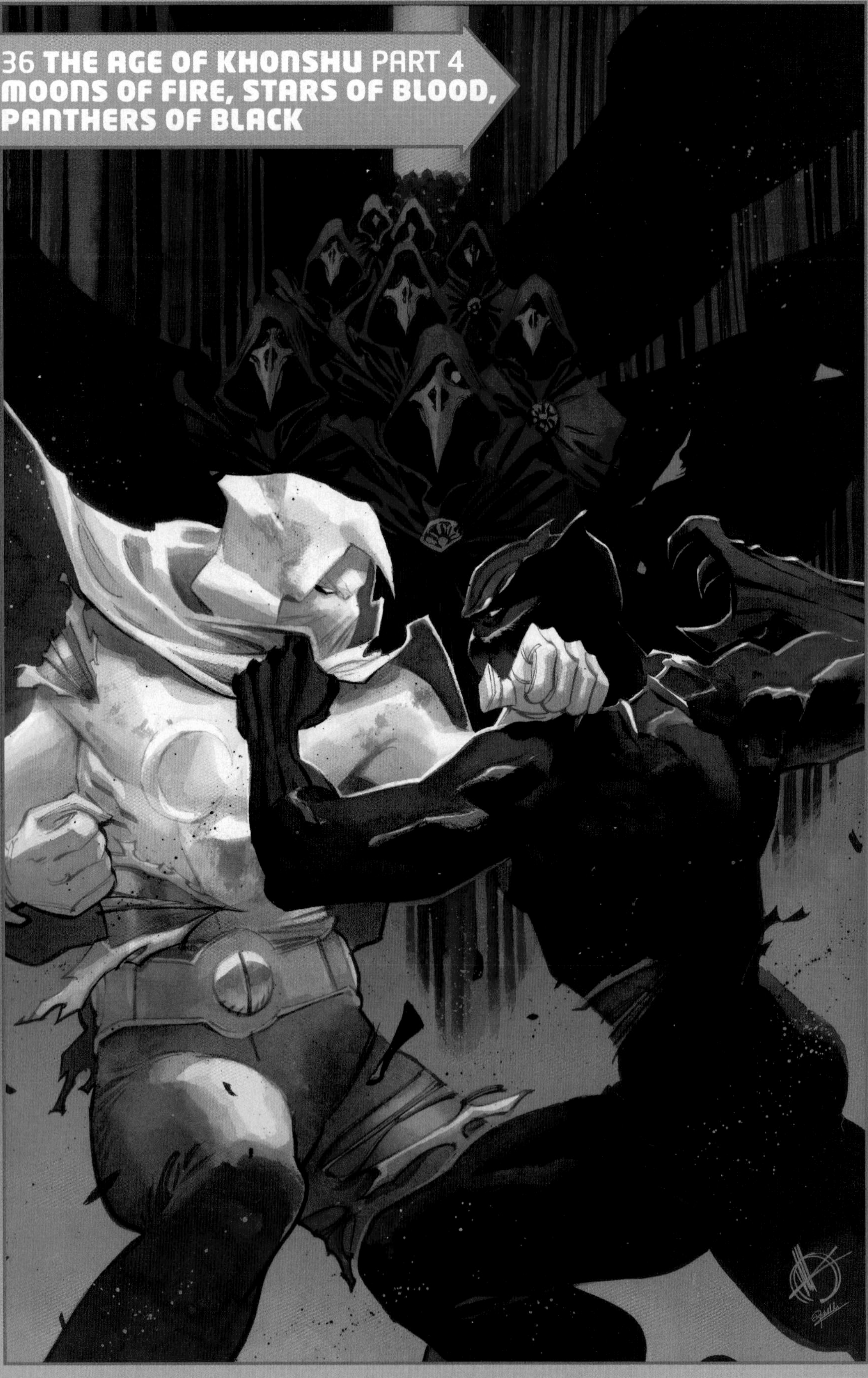

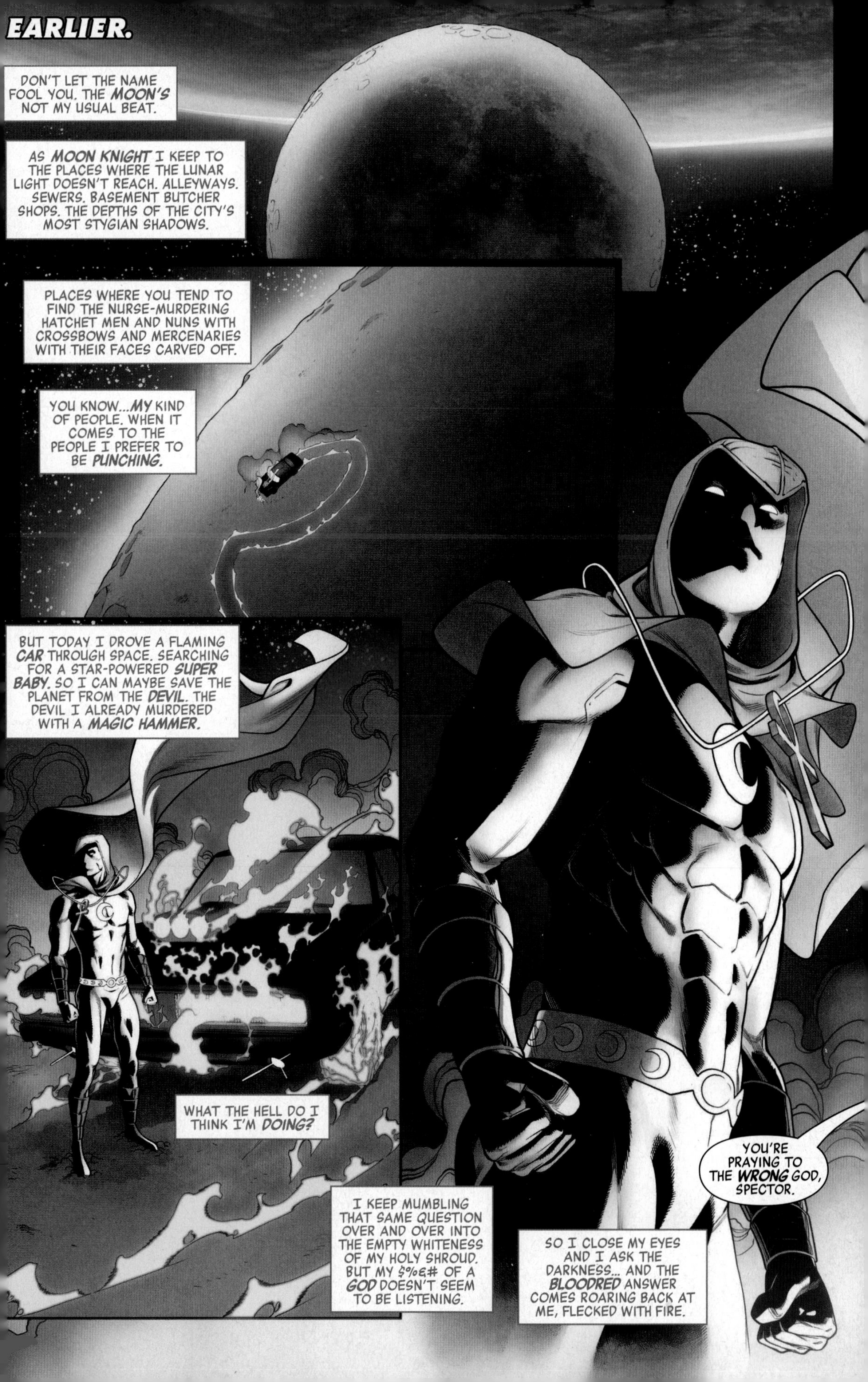
EARLIER.
DON'T LET THE NAME FOOL YOU. THE MOON'S NOT MY USUAL BEAT.
AS MOON KNIGHT I KEEP TO THE PLACES WHERE THE LUNAR LIGHT DOESN'T REACH. ALLEYWAYS. SEWERS. BASEMENT BUTCHER SHOPS. THE DEPTHS OF THE CITY'S MOST STYGIAN SHADOWS.
PLACES WHERE YOU TEND TO FIND THE NURSE-MURDERING HATCHET MEN AND NUNS WITH CROSSBOWS AND MERCENARIES WITH THEIR FACES CARVED OFF.
YOU KNOW...MY KIND OF PEOPLE. WHEN IT COMES TO THE PEOPLE I PREFER TO BE PUNCHING.
BUT TODAY I DROVE A FLAMING CAR THROUGH SPACE. SEARCHING FOR A STAR-POWERED SUPER BABY. SO I CAN MAYBE SAVE THE PLANET FROM THE DEVIL. THE DEVIL I ALREADY MURDERED WITH A MAGIC HAMMER.
WHAT THE HELL DO I THINK I'M DOING?
I KEEP MUMBLING THAT SAME QUESTION OVER AND OVER INTO THE EMPTY WHITENESS OF MY HOLY SHROUD. BUT MY $%&# OF A GOD DOESN'T SEEM TO BE LISTENING.
YOU'RE PRAYING TO THE WRONG GOD, SPECTOR.
SO I CLOSE MY EYES AND I ASK THE DARKNESS... AND THE BLOODRED ANSWER COMES ROARING BACK AT ME, FLECKED WITH FIRE.

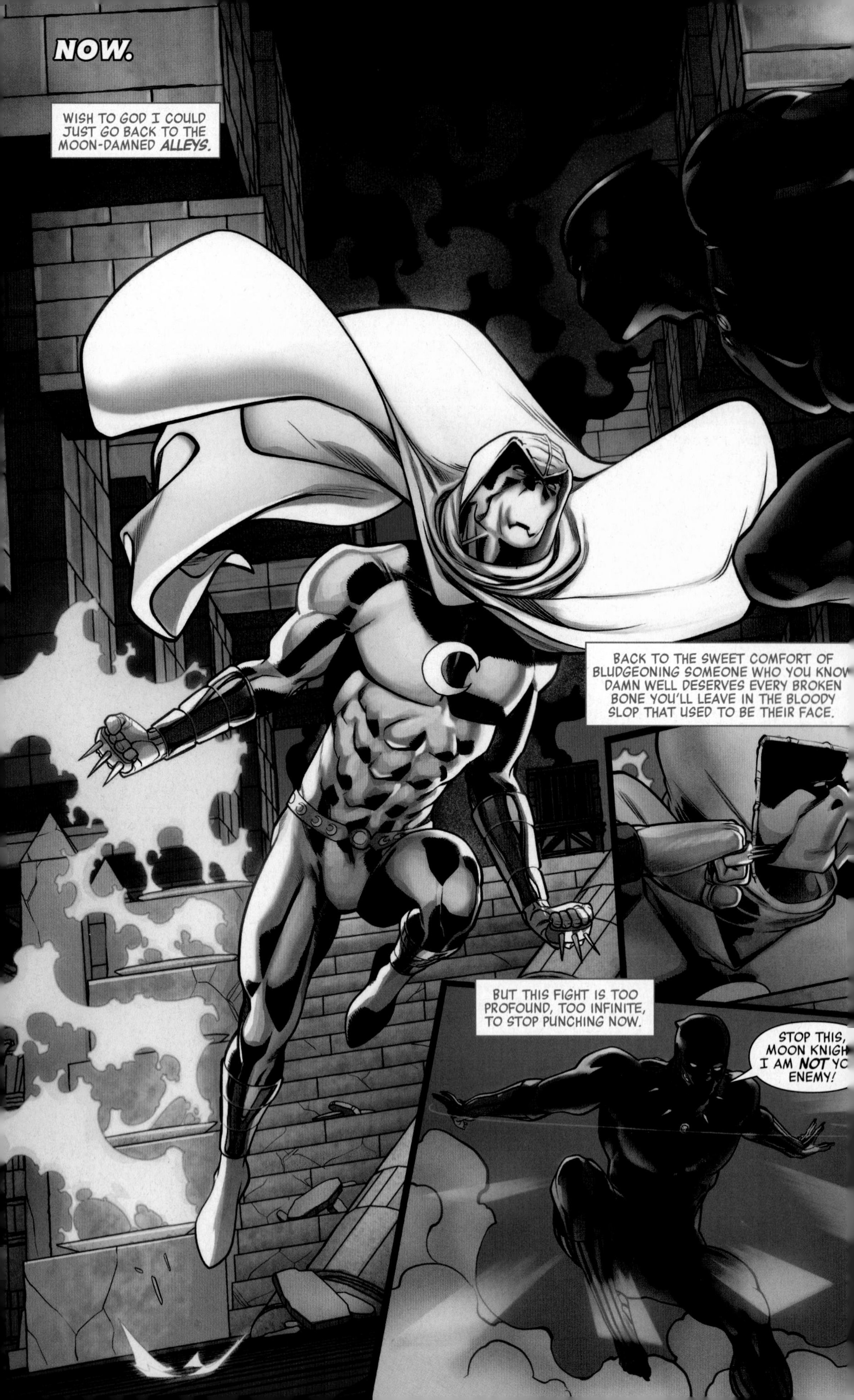
NOW.
WISH TO GOD I COULD JUST GO BACK TO THE MOON-DAMNED ALLEYS.
BACK TO THE SWEET COMFORT OF BLUDGEONING SOMEONE WHO YOU KNOW DAMN WELL DESERVES EVERY BROKEN BONE YOU'LL LEAVE IN THE BLOODY SLOP THAT USED TO BE THEIR FACE.
BUT THIS FIGHT IS TOO PROFOUND, TOO INFINITE, TO STOP PUNCHING NOW.
STOP THIS, MOON KNIGH I AM NOT YO ENEMY!

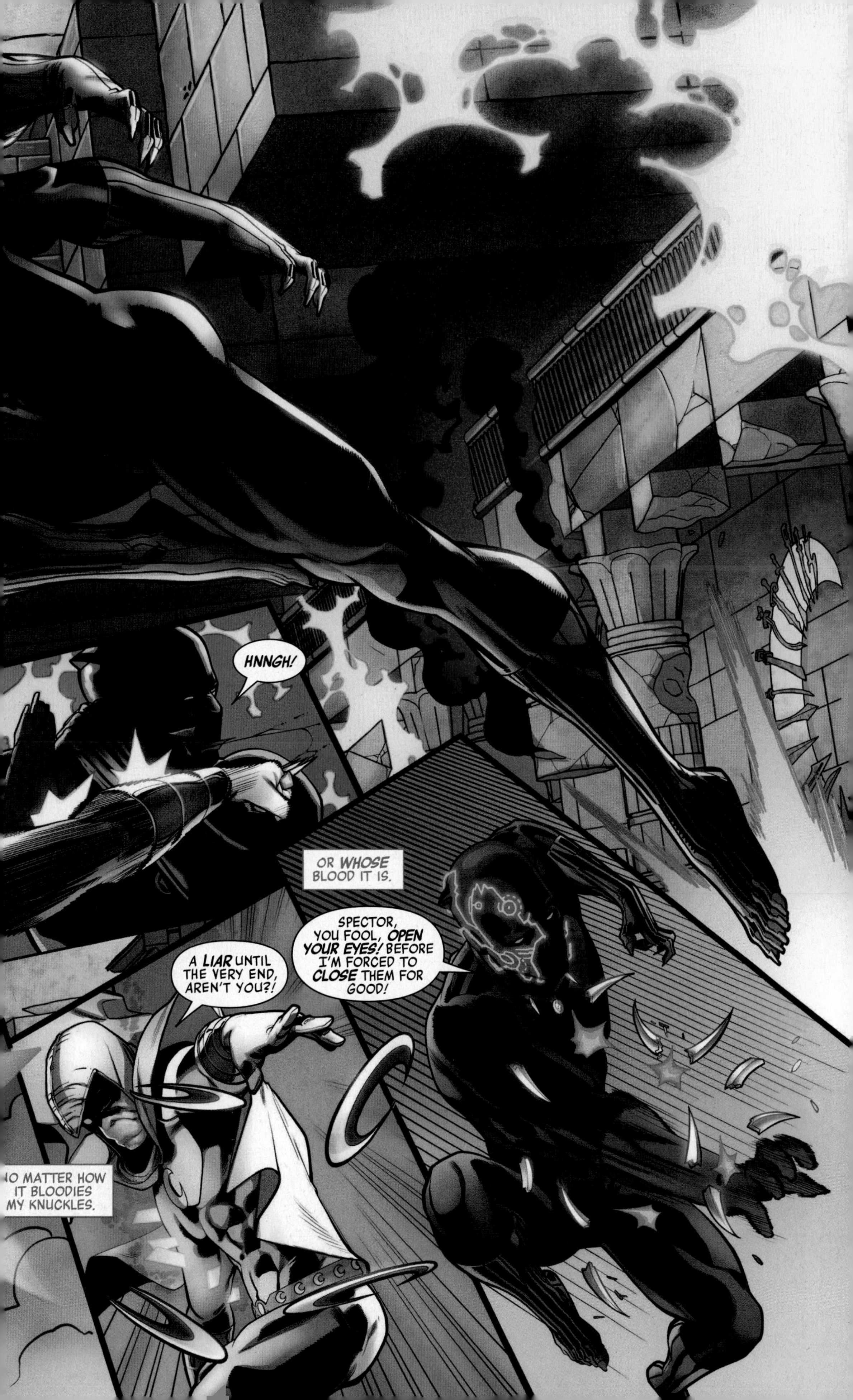

HNNGH!
OR WHOSE BLOOD IT IS.
NO MATTER HOW IT BLOODIES MY KNUCKLES.
A LIAR UNTIL THE VERY END, AREN'T YOU?!
SPECTOR, YOU FOOL, OPEN YOUR EYES! BEFORE I'M FORCED TO CLOSE THEM FOR GOOD!

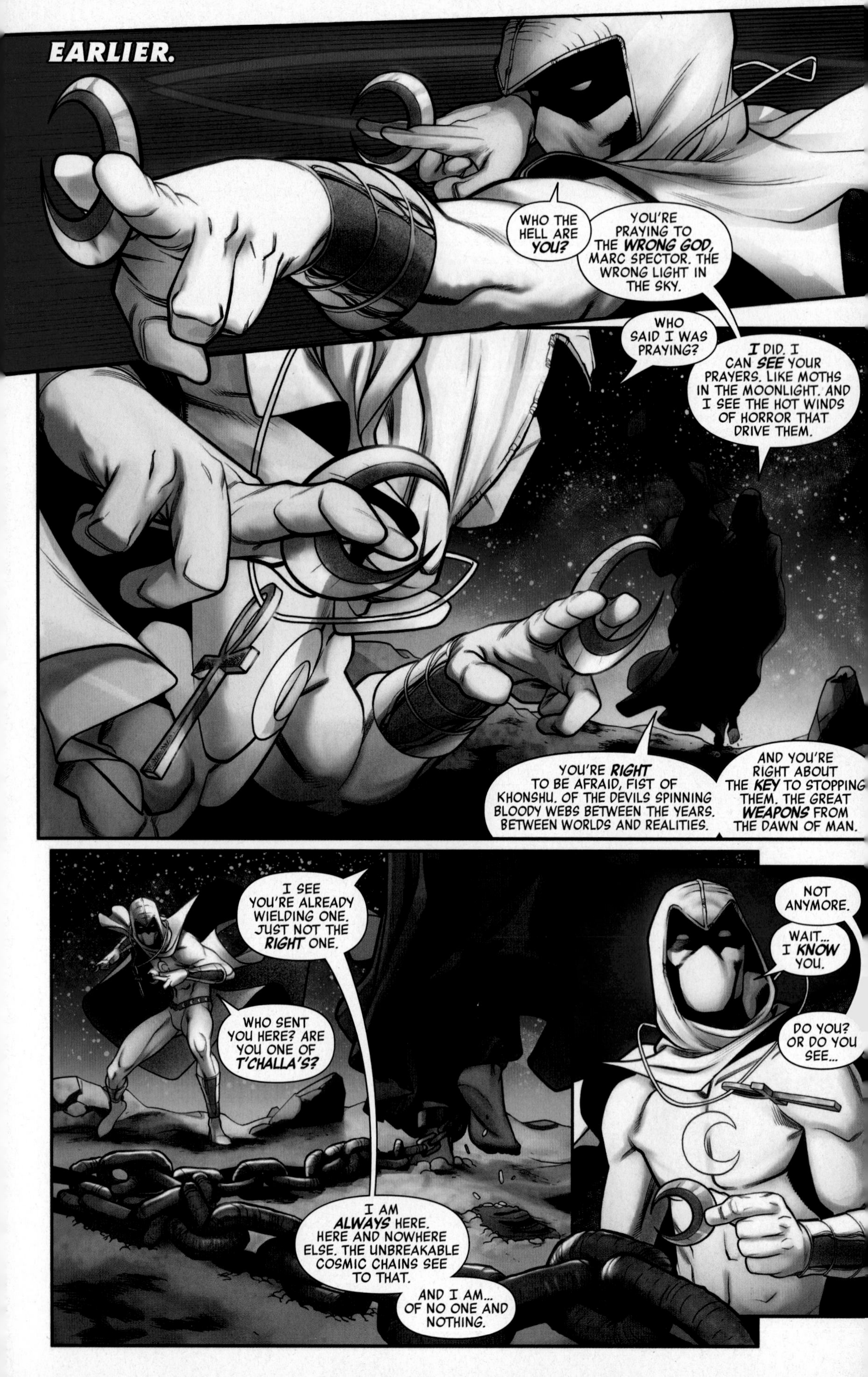
EARLIER.
WHO THE HELL ARE YOU?
YOU'RE PRAYING TO THE WRONG GOD, MARC SPECTOR. THE WRONG LIGHT IN THE SKY.
WHO SAID I WAS PRAYING?
I DID. I CAN SEE YOUR PRAYERS. LIKE MOTHS IN THE MOONLIGHT. AND I SEE THE HOT WINDS OF HORROR THAT DRIVE THEM.
YOU'RE RIGHT TO BE AFRAID, FIST OF KHONSHU. OF THE DEVILS SPINNING BLOODY WEBS BETWEEN THE YEARS. BETWEEN WORLDS AND REALITIES.
AND YOU'RE RIGHT ABOUT THE KEY TO STOPPING THEM. THE GREAT WEAPONS FROM THE DAWN OF MAN.
I SEE YOU'RE ALREADY WIELDING ONE. JUST NOT THE RIGHT ONE.
NOT ANYMORE.
WAIT... I KNOW YOU.
DO YOU? OR DO YOU SEE...
WHO SENT YOU HERE? ARE YOU ONE OF T'CHALLA'S?
I AM ALWAYS HERE. HERE AND NOWHERE ELSE. THE UNBREAKABLE COSMIC CHAINS SEE TO THAT.
AND I AM... OF NO ONE AND NOTHING.

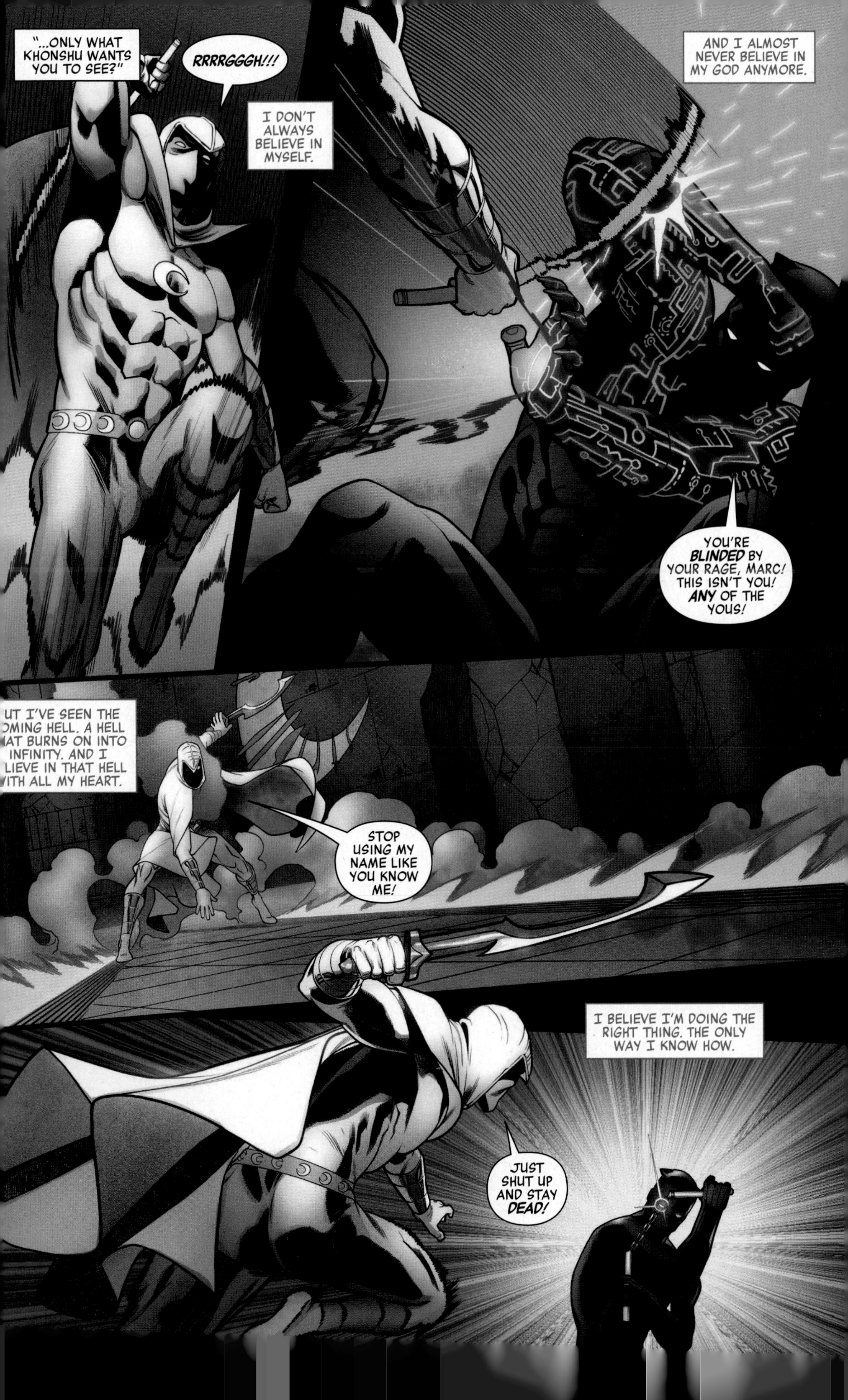
"...ONLY WHAT KHONSHU WANTS YOU TO SEE?"
RRRRGGGH!!!
I DON'T ALWAYS BELIEVE IN MYSELF.
AND I ALMOST NEVER BELIEVE IN MY GOD ANYMORE.
YOU'RE BLINDED BY YOUR RAGE, MARC! THIS ISN'T YOU! ANY OF THE YOUS!
UT I'VE SEEN THE OMING HELL. A HELL AT BURNS ON INTO INFINITY. AND I LIEVE IN THAT HELL VITH ALL MY HEART.
STOP USING MY NAME LIKE YOU KNOW ME!
I BELIEVE I'M DOING THE RIGHT THING. THE ONLY WAY I KNOW HOW.
JUST SHUT UP AND STAY DEAD!

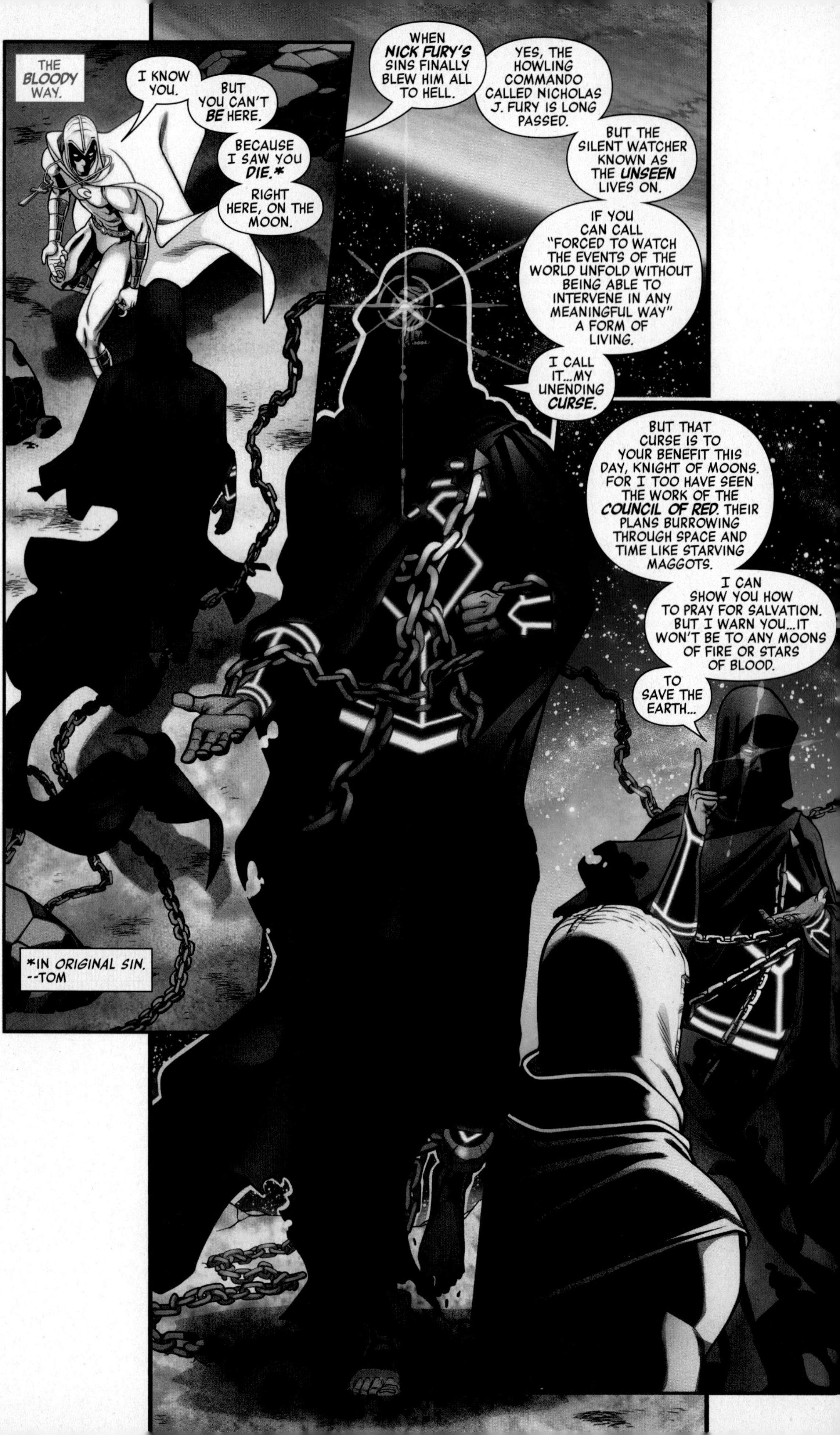
THE BLOODY WAY.
I KNOW YOU.
BUT YOU CAN'T BE HERE.
BECAUSE I SAW YOU DIE.*
RIGHT HERE, ON THE MOON.
*IN ORIGINAL SIN. --TOM
WHEN NICK FURY'S SINS FINALLY BLEW HIM ALL TO HELL.
YES, THE HOWLING COMMANDO CALLED NICHOLAS J. FURY IS LONG PASSED.
BUT THE SILENT WATCHER KNOWN AS THE UNSEEN LIVES ON.
IF YOU CAN CALL "FORCED TO WATCH THE EVENTS OF THE WORLD UNFOLD WITHOUT BEING ABLE TO INTERVENE IN ANY MEANINGFUL WAY" A FORM OF LIVING.
I CALL IT...MY UNENDING CURSE.
BUT THAT CURSE IS TO YOUR BENEFIT THIS DAY, KNIGHT OF MOONS. FOR I TOO HAVE SEEN THE WORK OF THE COUNCIL OF RED. THEIR PLANS BURROWING THROUGH SPACE AND TIME LIKE STARVING MAGGOTS.
I CAN SHOW YOU HOW TO PRAY FOR SALVATION. BUT I WARN YOU...IT WON'T BE TO ANY MOONS OF FIRE OR STARS OF BLOOD.
TO SAVE THE EARTH...

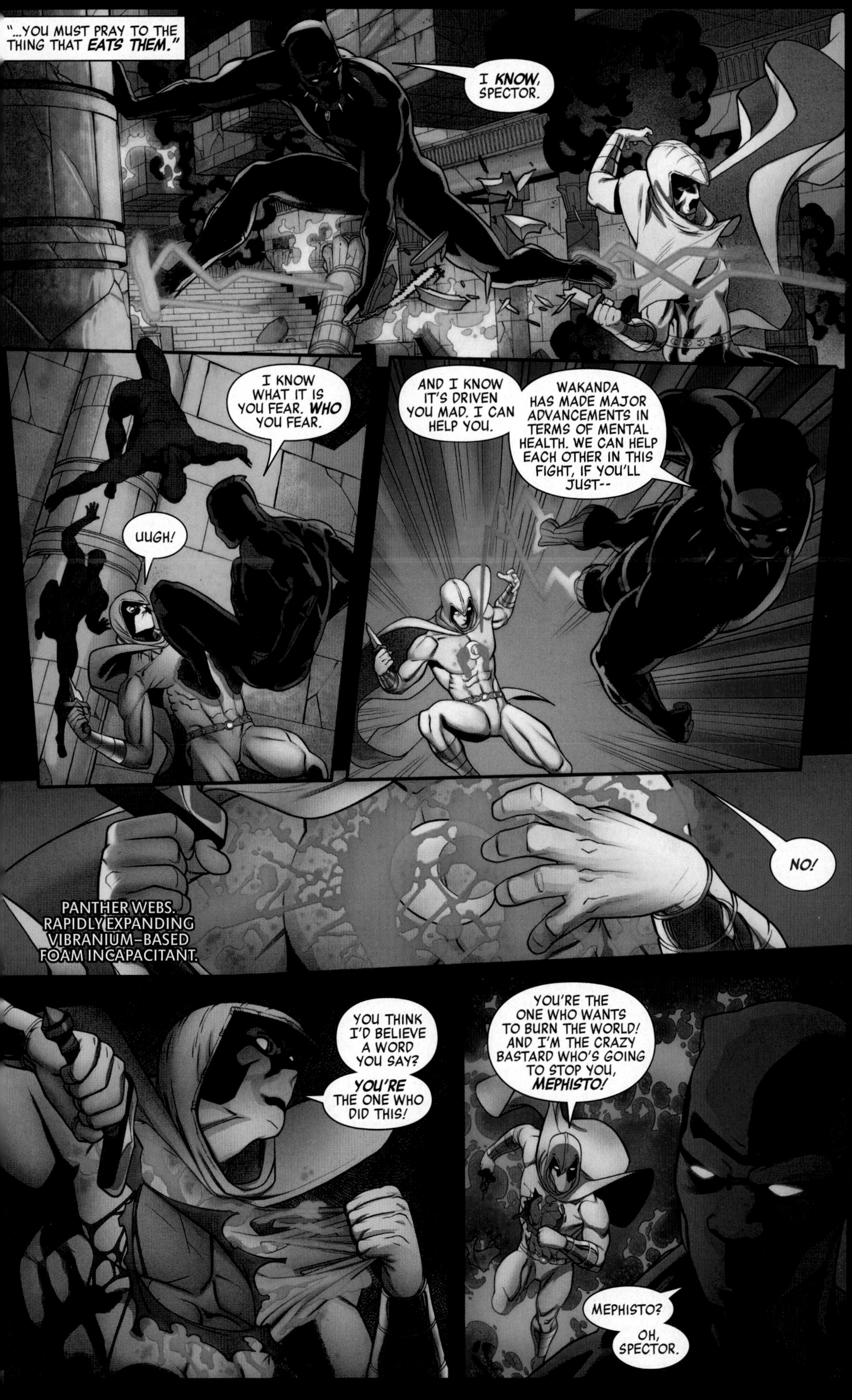
"...YOU MUST PRAY TO THE THING THAT EATS THEM."
I KNOW, SPECTOR.
I KNOW WHAT IT IS YOU FEAR. WHO YOU FEAR.
UUGH!
AND I KNOW IT'S DRIVEN YOU MAD. I CAN HELP YOU.
WAKANDA HAS MADE MAJOR ADVANCEMENTS IN TERMS OF MENTAL HEALTH. WE CAN HELP EACH OTHER IN THIS FIGHT, IF YOU'LL JUST--
NO!
PANTHER WEBS. RAPIDLY EXPANDING VIBRANIUM-BASED FOAM INCAPACITANT.
YOU THINK I'D BELIEVE A WORD YOU SAY?
YOU'RE THE ONE WHO DID THIS!
YOU'RE THE ONE WHO WANTS TO BURN THE WORLD! AND I'M THE CRAZY BASTARD WHO'S GOING TO STOP YOU, MEPHISTO!
MEPHISTO?
OH, SPECTOR.

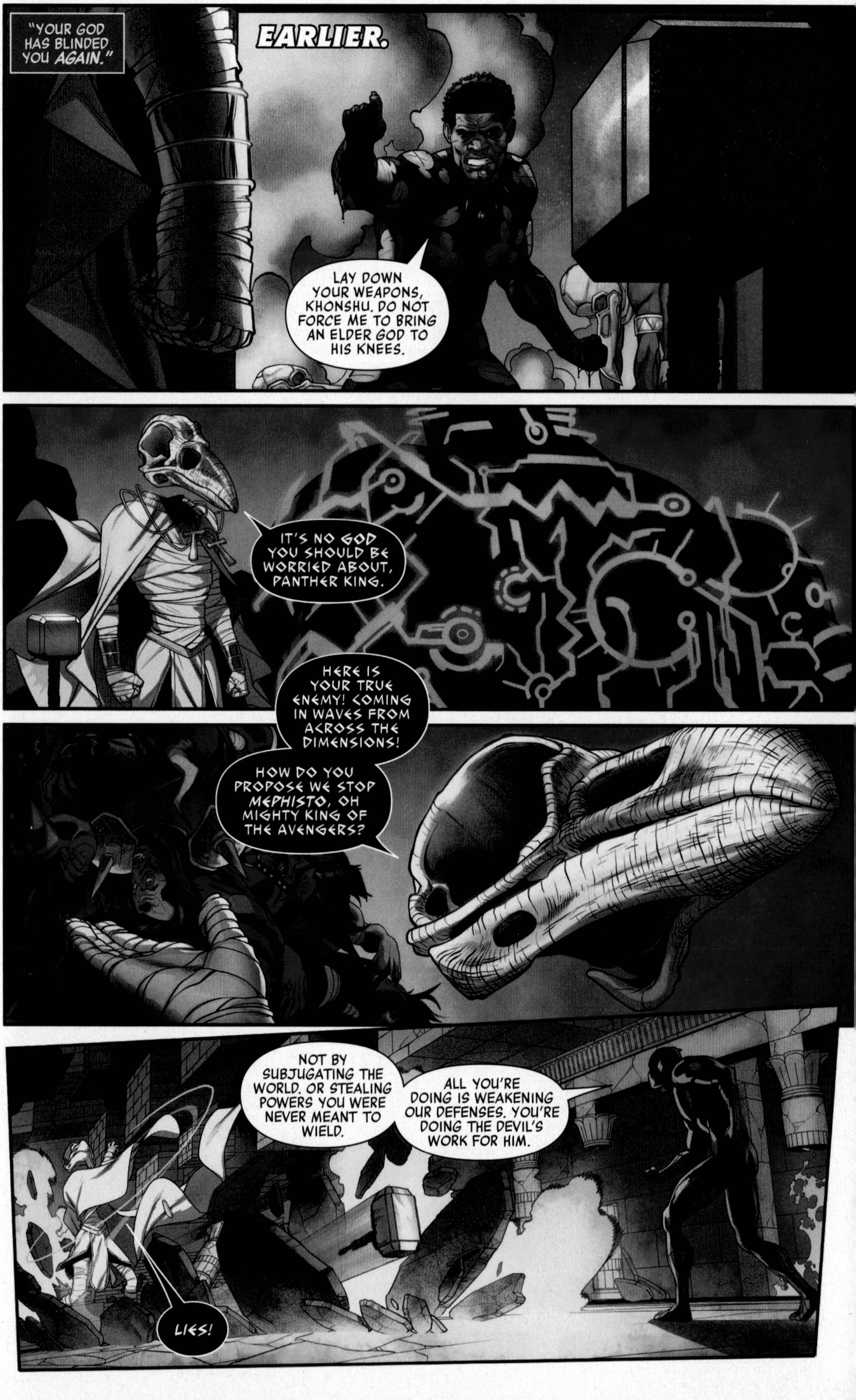
"YOUR GOD HAS BLINDED YOU *AGAIN.*"
EARLIER.
LAY DOWN YOUR WEAPONS, KHONSHU. DO NOT FORCE ME TO BRING AN ELDER GOD TO HIS KNEES.
IT'S NO GOD YOU SHOULD BE WORRIED ABOUT, PANTHER KING.
HERE IS YOUR TRUE ENEMY! COMING IN WAVES FROM ACROSS THE DIMENSIONS!
HOW DO YOU PROPOSE WE STOP *MEPHISTO*, OH MIGHTY KING OF THE AVENGERS?
NOT BY SUBJUGATING THE WORLD. OR STEALING POWERS YOU WERE NEVER MEANT TO WIELD.
ALL YOU'RE DOING IS WEAKENING OUR DEFENSES. YOU'RE DOING THE DEVIL'S WORK FOR HIM.
LIES!

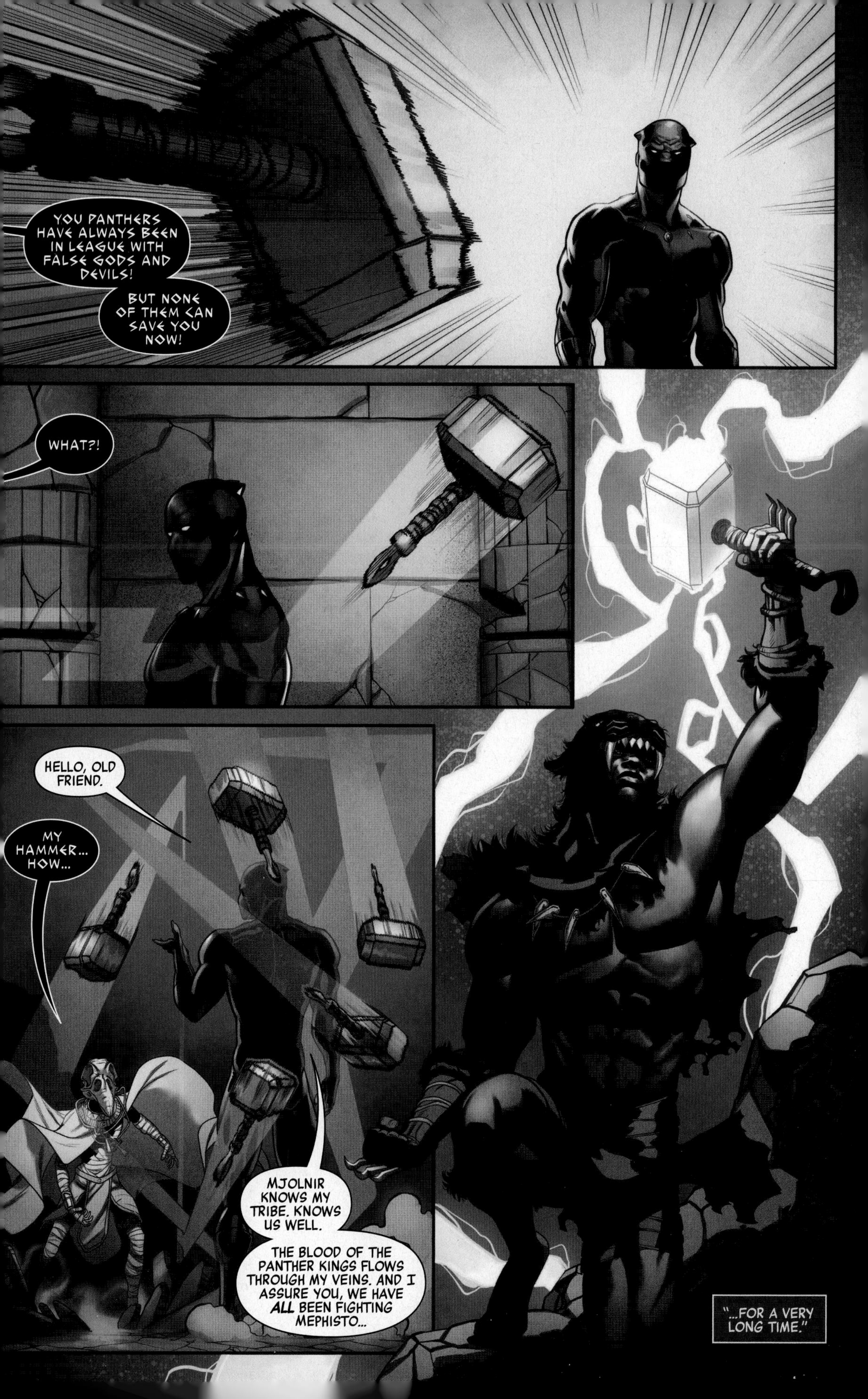
YOU PANTHERS HAVE ALWAYS BEEN IN LEAGUE WITH FALSE GODS AND DEVILS!
BUT NONE OF THEM CAN SAVE YOU NOW!
WHAT?!
HELLO, OLD FRIEND.
MY HAMMER... HOW...
MJOLNIR KNOWS MY TRIBE. KNOWS US WELL.
THE BLOOD OF THE PANTHER KINGS FLOWS THROUGH MY VEINS. AND I ASSURE YOU, WE HAVE ALL BEEN FIGHTING MEPHISTO...
"...FOR A VERY LONG TIME."

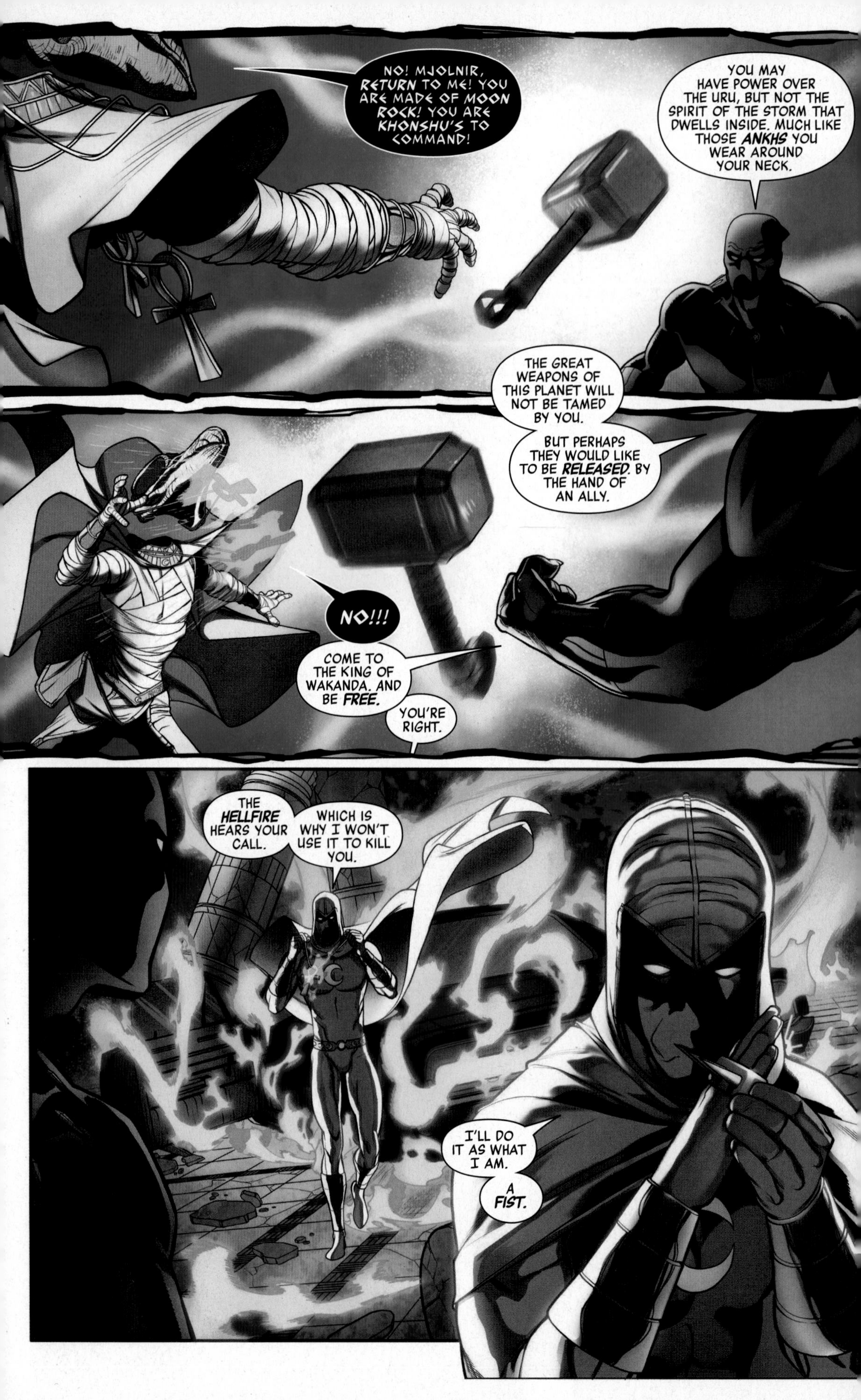
NO! MJOLNIR, RETURN TO ME! YOU ARE MADE OF MOON ROCK! YOU ARE KHONSHU'S TO COMMAND!
YOU MAY HAVE POWER OVER THE URU, BUT NOT THE SPIRIT OF THE STORM THAT DWELLS INSIDE. MUCH LIKE THOSE ANKHS YOU WEAR AROUND YOUR NECK.
THE GREAT WEAPONS OF THIS PLANET WILL NOT BE TAMED BY YOU.
BUT PERHAPS THEY WOULD LIKE TO BE RELEASED. BY THE HAND OF AN ALLY.
NO!!!
COME TO THE KING OF WAKANDA. AND BE FREE.
YOU'RE RIGHT.
THE HELLFIRE HEARS YOUR CALL.
WHICH IS WHY I WON'T USE IT TO KILL YOU.
I'LL DO IT AS WHAT I AM.
A FIST.

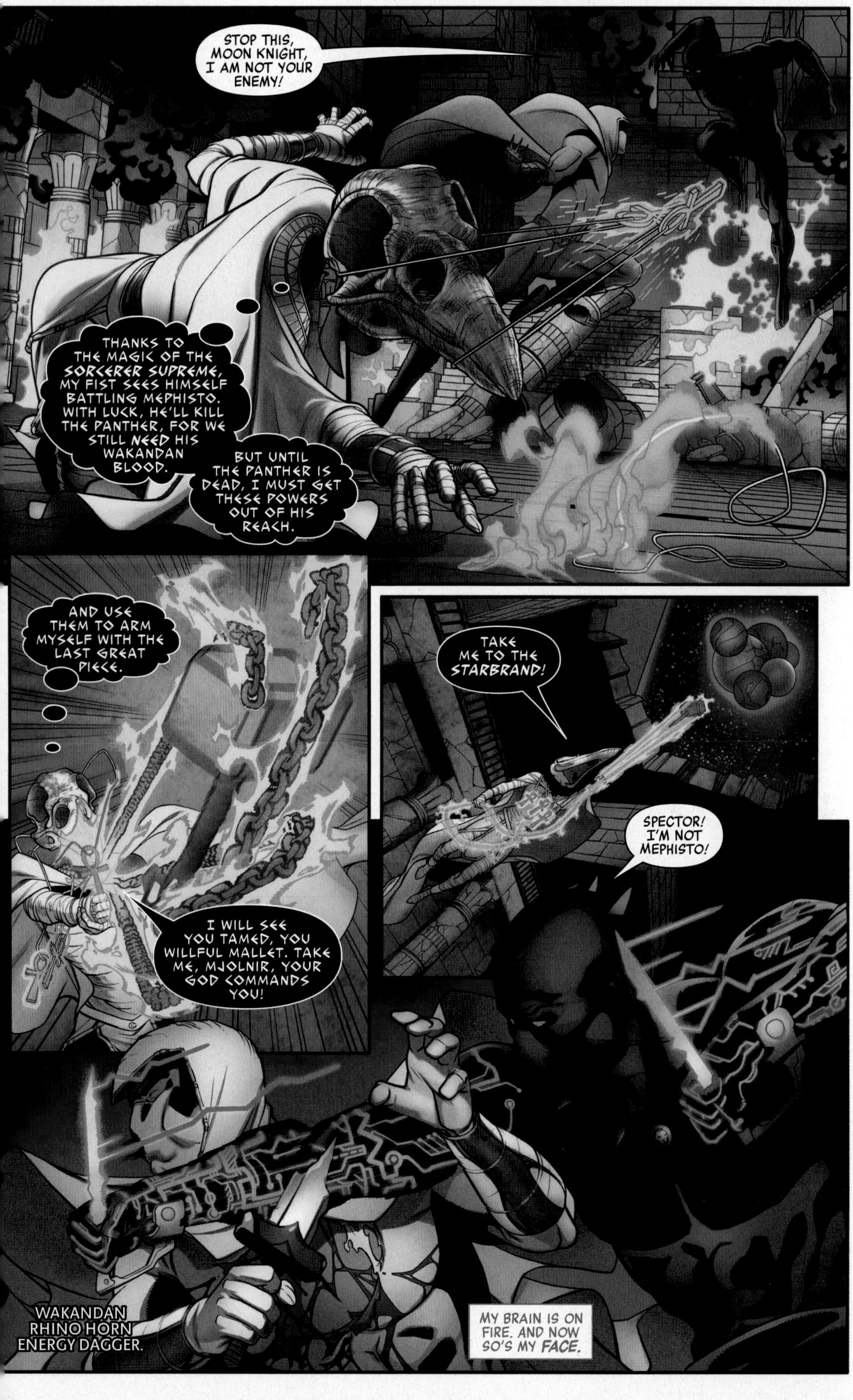
STOP THIS, MOON KNIGHT, I AM NOT YOUR ENEMY!
THANKS TO THE MAGIC OF THE SORCERER SUPREME, MY FIST SEES HIMSELF BATTLING MEPHISTO. WITH LUCK, HE'LL KILL THE PANTHER, FOR WE STILL NEED HIS WAKANDAN BLOOD.
BUT UNTIL THE PANTHER IS DEAD, I MUST GET THESE POWERS OUT OF HIS REACH.
AND USE THEM TO ARM MYSELF WITH THE LAST GREAT PIECE.
I WILL SEE YOU TAMED, YOU WILLFUL MALLET. TAKE ME, MJOLNIR, YOUR GOD COMMANDS YOU!
TAKE ME TO THE STARBRAND!
SPECTOR! I'M NOT MEPHISTO!
WAKANDAN RHINO HORN ENERGY DAGGER.
MY BRAIN IS ON FIRE. AND NOW SO'S MY FACE.

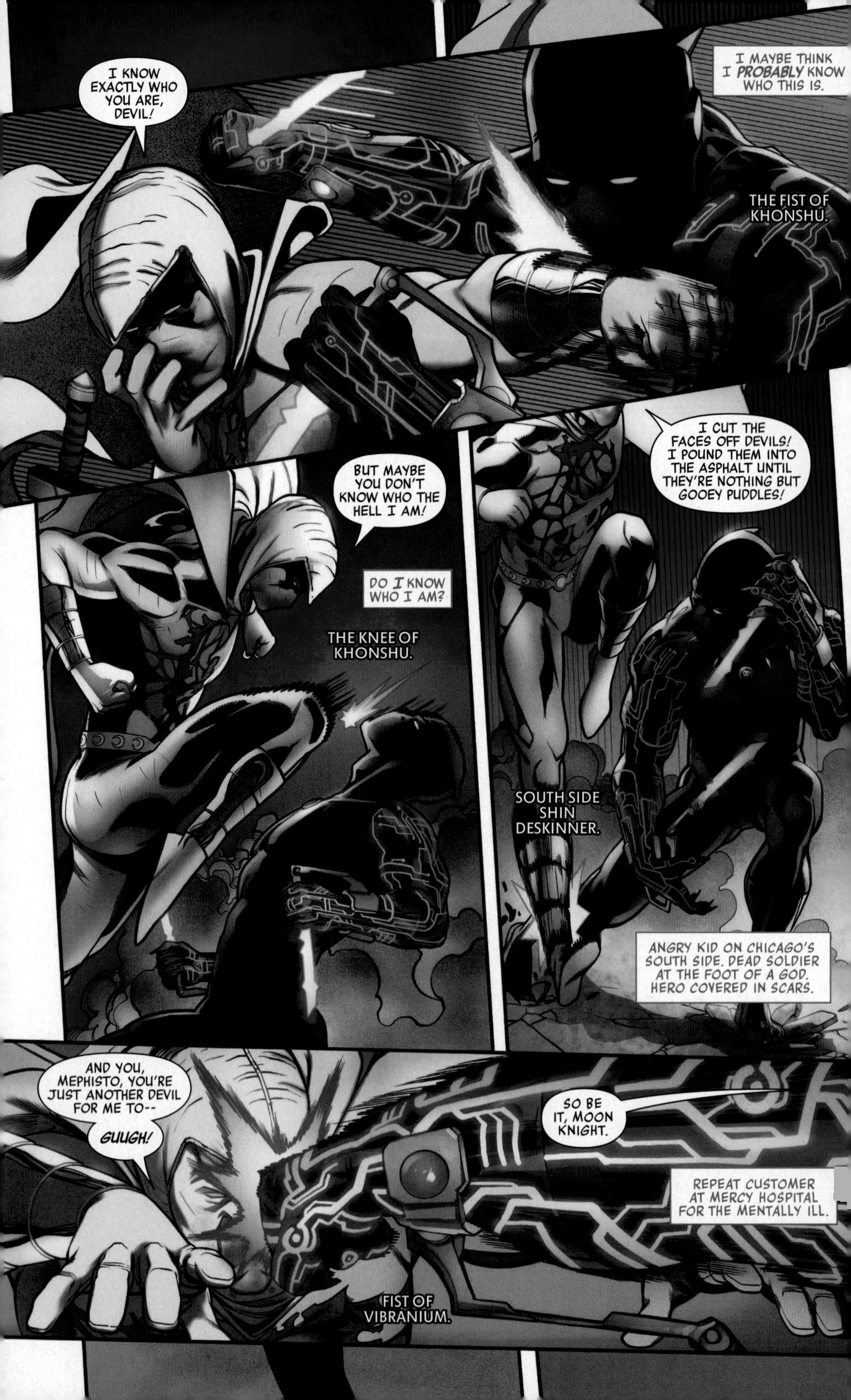

I KNOW EXACTLY WHO YOU ARE, DEVIL!
I MAYBE THINK I *PROBABLY* KNOW WHO THIS IS.
THE FIST OF KHONSHU.
BUT MAYBE YOU DON'T KNOW WHO THE HELL I AM!
DO *I* KNOW WHO I AM?
THE KNEE OF KHONSHU.
I CUT THE FACES OFF DEVILS! I POUND THEM INTO THE ASPHALT UNTIL THEY'RE NOTHING BUT GOOEY PUDDLES!
SOUTH SIDE SHIN DESKINNER.
ANGRY KID ON CHICAGO'S SOUTH SIDE. DEAD SOLDIER AT THE FOOT OF A GOD. HERO COVERED IN SCARS.
AND YOU, MEPHISTO, YOU'RE JUST ANOTHER DEVIL FOR ME TO--
GUUGH!
SO BE IT, MOON KNIGHT.
REPEAT CUSTOMER AT MERCY HOSPITAL FOR THE MENTALLY ILL.
FIST OF VIBRANIUM.

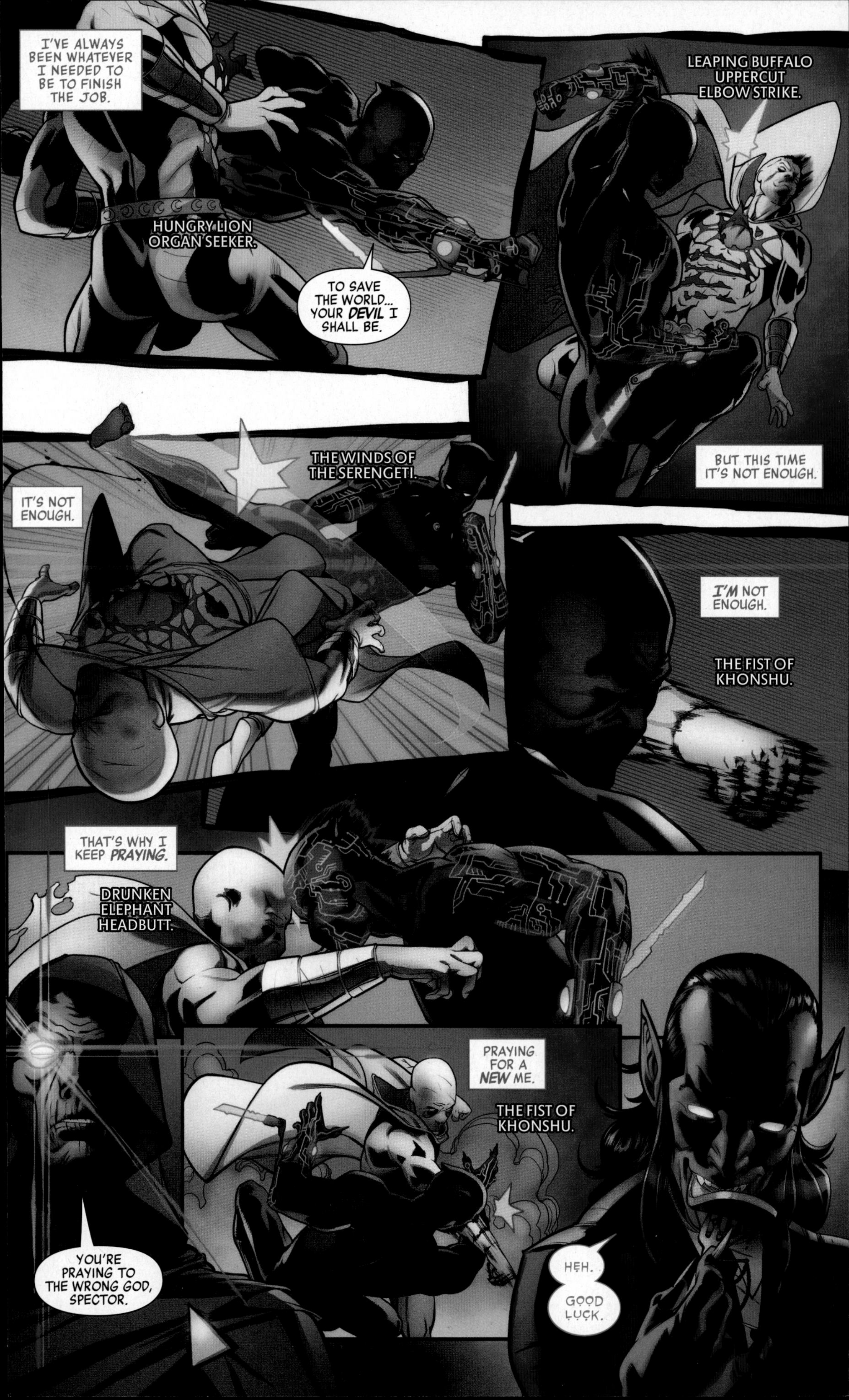
I'VE ALWAYS BEEN WHATEVER I NEEDED TO BE TO FINISH THE JOB.
HUNGRY LION ORGAN SEEKER.
TO SAVE THE WORLD... YOUR DEVIL I SHALL BE.
LEAPING BUFFALO UPPERCUT ELBOW STRIKE.
BUT THIS TIME IT'S NOT ENOUGH.
THE WINDS OF THE SERENGETI.
IT'S NOT ENOUGH.
I'M NOT ENOUGH.
THE FIST OF KHONSHU.
THAT'S WHY I KEEP PRAYING.
DRUNKEN ELEPHANT HEADBUTT.
PRAYING FOR A NEW ME.
THE FIST OF KHONSHU.
YOU'RE PRAYING TO THE WRONG GOD, SPECTOR.
HEH.
GOOD LUCK.

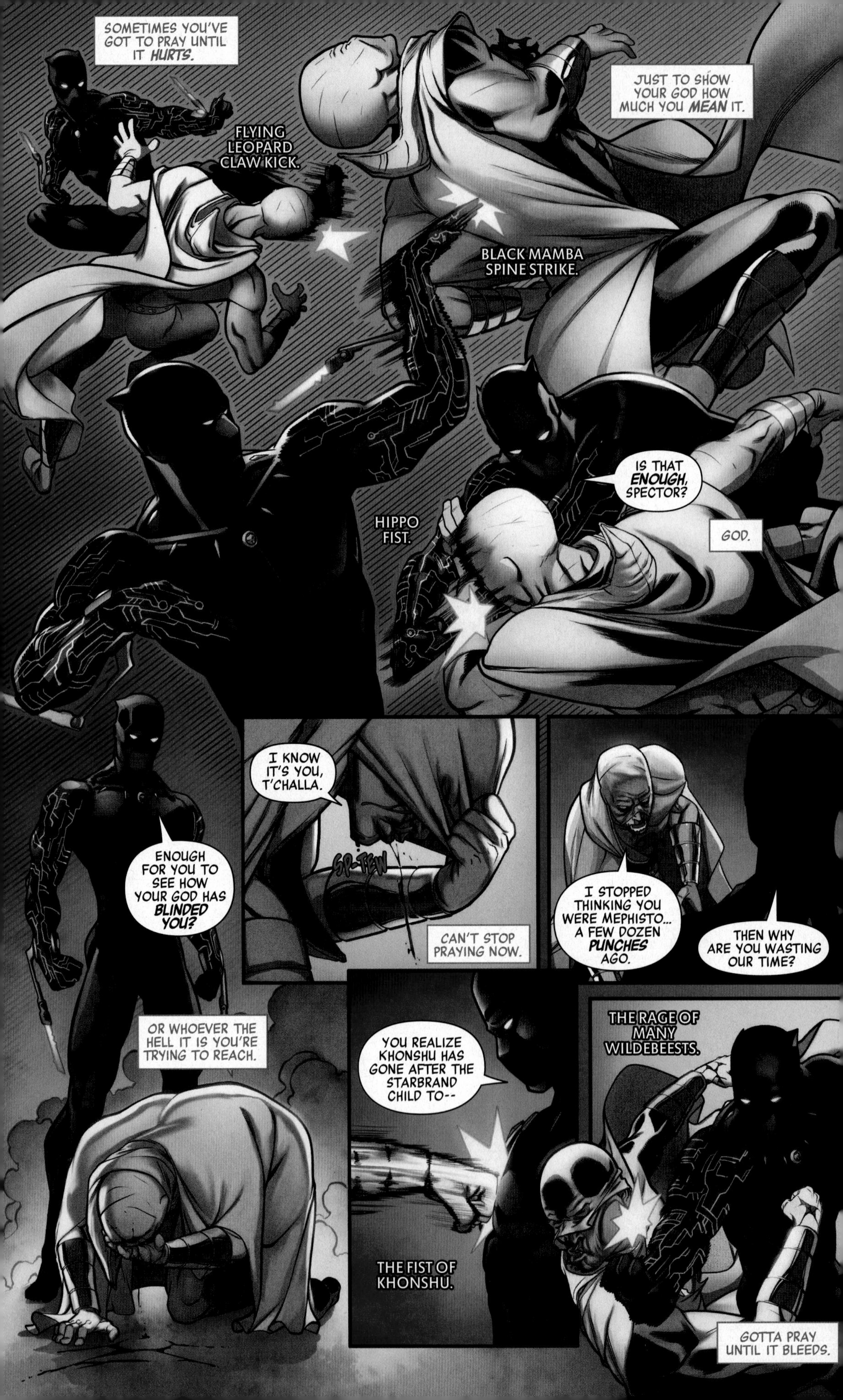
SOMETIMES YOU'VE GOT TO PRAY UNTIL IT HURTS.
FLYING LEOPARD CLAW KICK.
JUST TO SHOW YOUR GOD HOW MUCH YOU MEAN IT.
BLACK MAMBA SPINE STRIKE.
HIPPO FIST.
IS THAT ENOUGH, SPECTOR?
GOD.
ENOUGH FOR YOU TO SEE HOW YOUR GOD HAS BLINDED YOU?
I KNOW IT'S YOU, T'CHALLA.
SP-TEW
CAN'T STOP PRAYING NOW.
I STOPPED THINKING YOU WERE MEPHISTO... A FEW DOZEN PUNCHES AGO.
THEN WHY ARE YOU WASTING OUR TIME?
OR WHOEVER THE HELL IT IS YOU'RE TRYING TO REACH.
YOU REALIZE KHONSHU HAS GONE AFTER THE STARBRAND CHILD TO--
THE FIST OF KHONSHU.
THE RAGE OF MANY WILDEBEESTS.
GOTTA PRAY UNTIL IT BLEEDS.

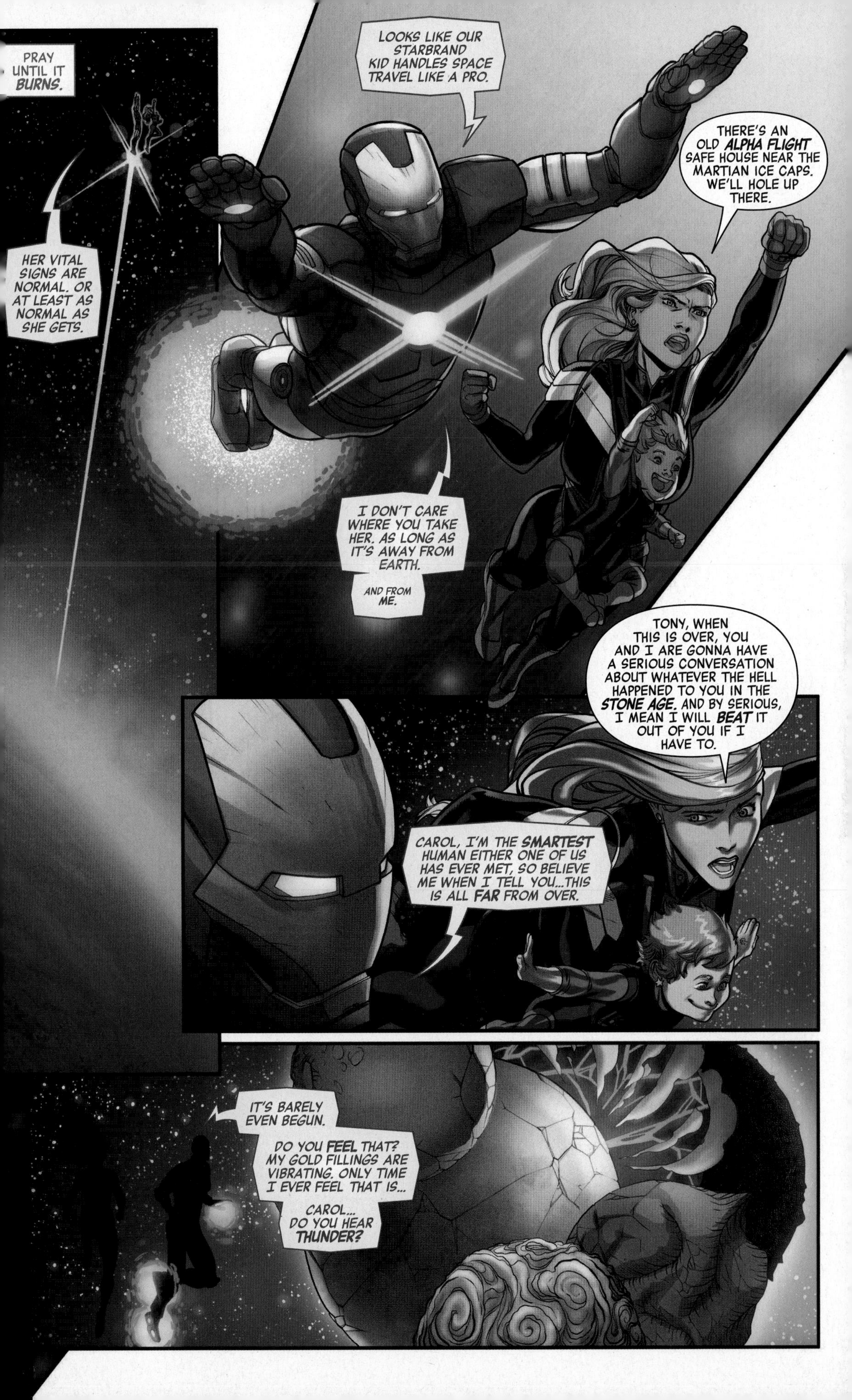
PRAY UNTIL IT BURNS.
LOOKS LIKE OUR STARBRAND KID HANDLES SPACE TRAVEL LIKE A PRO.
THERE'S AN OLD ALPHA FLIGHT SAFE HOUSE NEAR THE MARTIAN ICE CAPS. WE'LL HOLE UP THERE.
HER VITAL SIGNS ARE NORMAL. OR AT LEAST AS NORMAL AS SHE GETS.
I DON'T CARE WHERE YOU TAKE HER. AS LONG AS IT'S AWAY FROM EARTH.
AND FROM ME.
TONY, WHEN THIS IS OVER, YOU AND I ARE GONNA HAVE A SERIOUS CONVERSATION ABOUT WHATEVER THE HELL HAPPENED TO YOU IN THE STONE AGE. AND BY SERIOUS, I MEAN I WILL BEAT IT OUT OF YOU IF I HAVE TO.
CAROL, I'M THE SMARTEST HUMAN EITHER ONE OF US HAS EVER MET, SO BELIEVE ME WHEN I TELL YOU...THIS IS ALL FAR FROM OVER.
IT'S BARELY EVEN BEGUN.
DO YOU FEEL THAT? MY GOLD FILLINGS ARE VIBRATING. ONLY TIME I EVER FEEL THAT IS...
CAROL... DO YOU HEAR THUNDER?

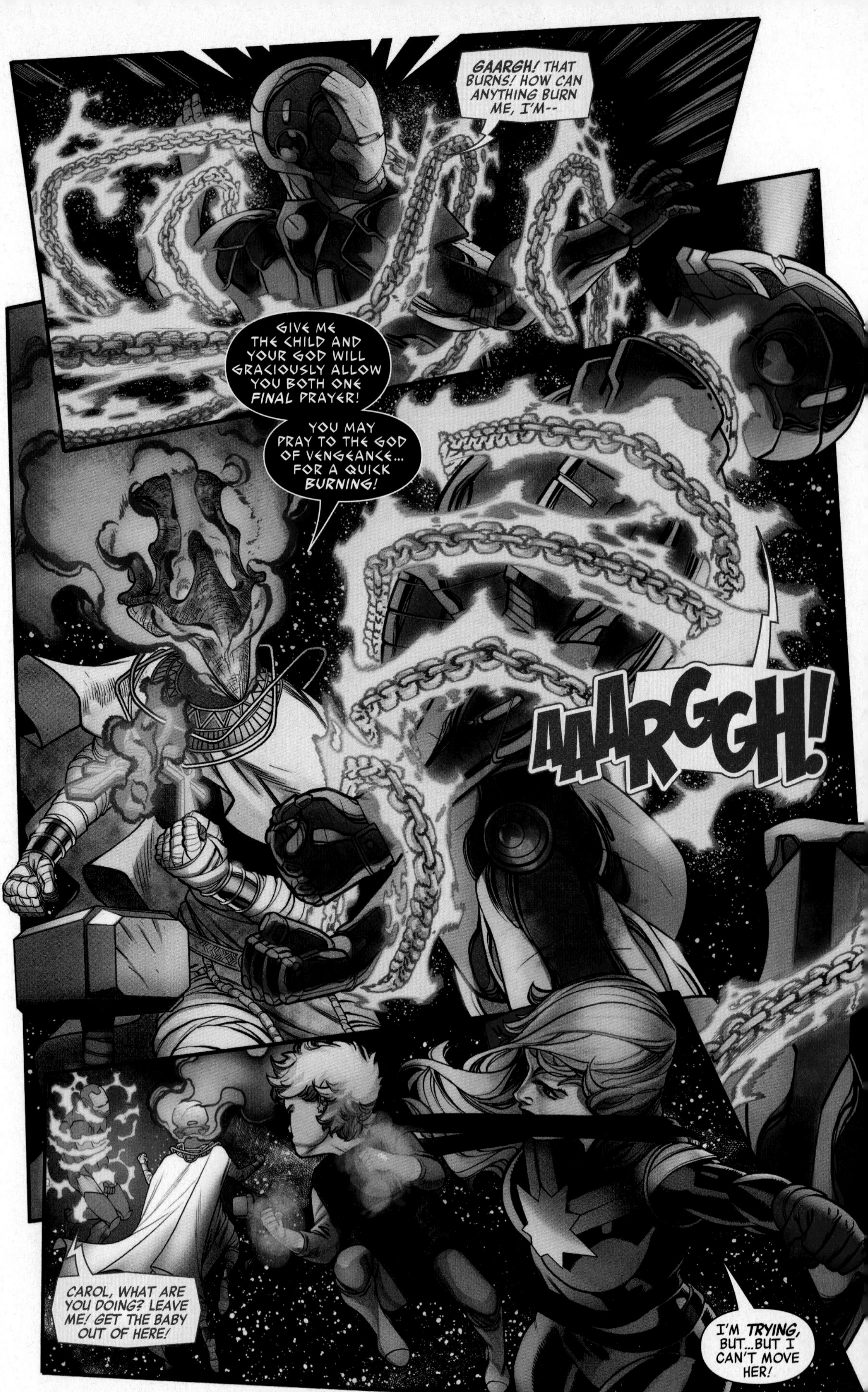
GAARGH! THAT BURNS! HOW CAN ANYTHING BURN ME, I'M--
GIVE ME THE CHILD AND YOUR GOD WILL GRACIOUSLY ALLOW YOU BOTH ONE FINAL PRAYER!
YOU MAY PRAY TO THE GOD OF VENGEANCE... FOR A QUICK BURNING!
AAARGGH!
CAROL, WHAT ARE YOU DOING? LEAVE ME! GET THE BABY OUT OF HERE!
I'M TRYING, BUT...BUT I CAN'T MOVE HER!

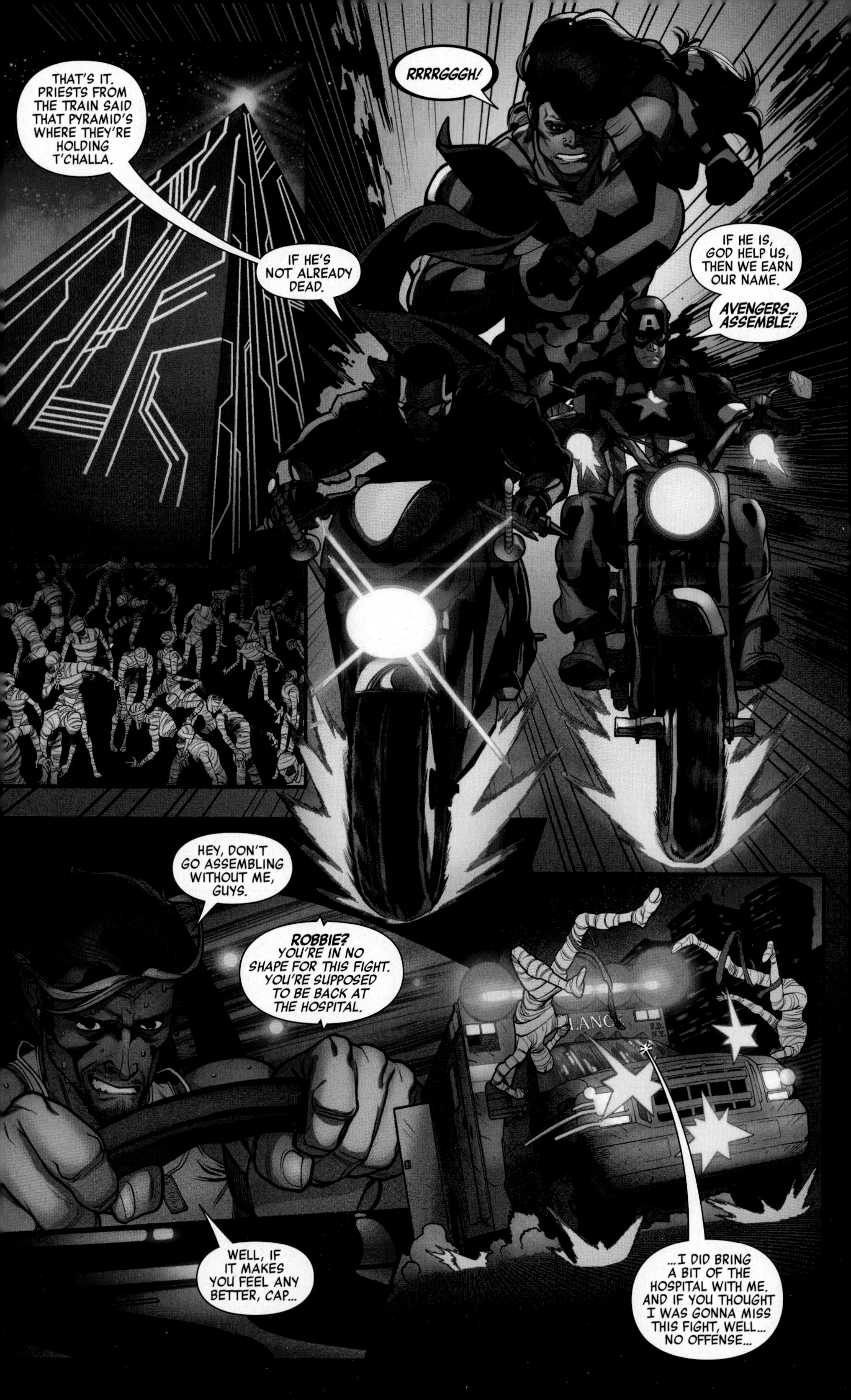
THAT'S IT. PRIESTS FROM THE TRAIN SAID THAT PYRAMID'S WHERE THEY'RE HOLDING T'CHALLA.
RRRRGGGH!
IF HE'S NOT ALREADY DEAD.
IF HE IS, GOD HELP US, THEN WE EARN OUR NAME.
AVENGERS... ASSEMBLE!
HEY, DON'T GO ASSEMBLING WITHOUT ME, GUYS.
ROBBIE? YOU'RE IN NO SHAPE FOR THIS FIGHT. YOU'RE SUPPOSED TO BE BACK AT THE HOSPITAL.
WELL, IF IT MAKES YOU FEEL ANY BETTER, CAP...
...I DID BRING A BIT OF THE HOSPITAL WITH ME. AND IF YOU THOUGHT I WAS GONNA MISS THIS FIGHT, WELL... NO OFFENSE...

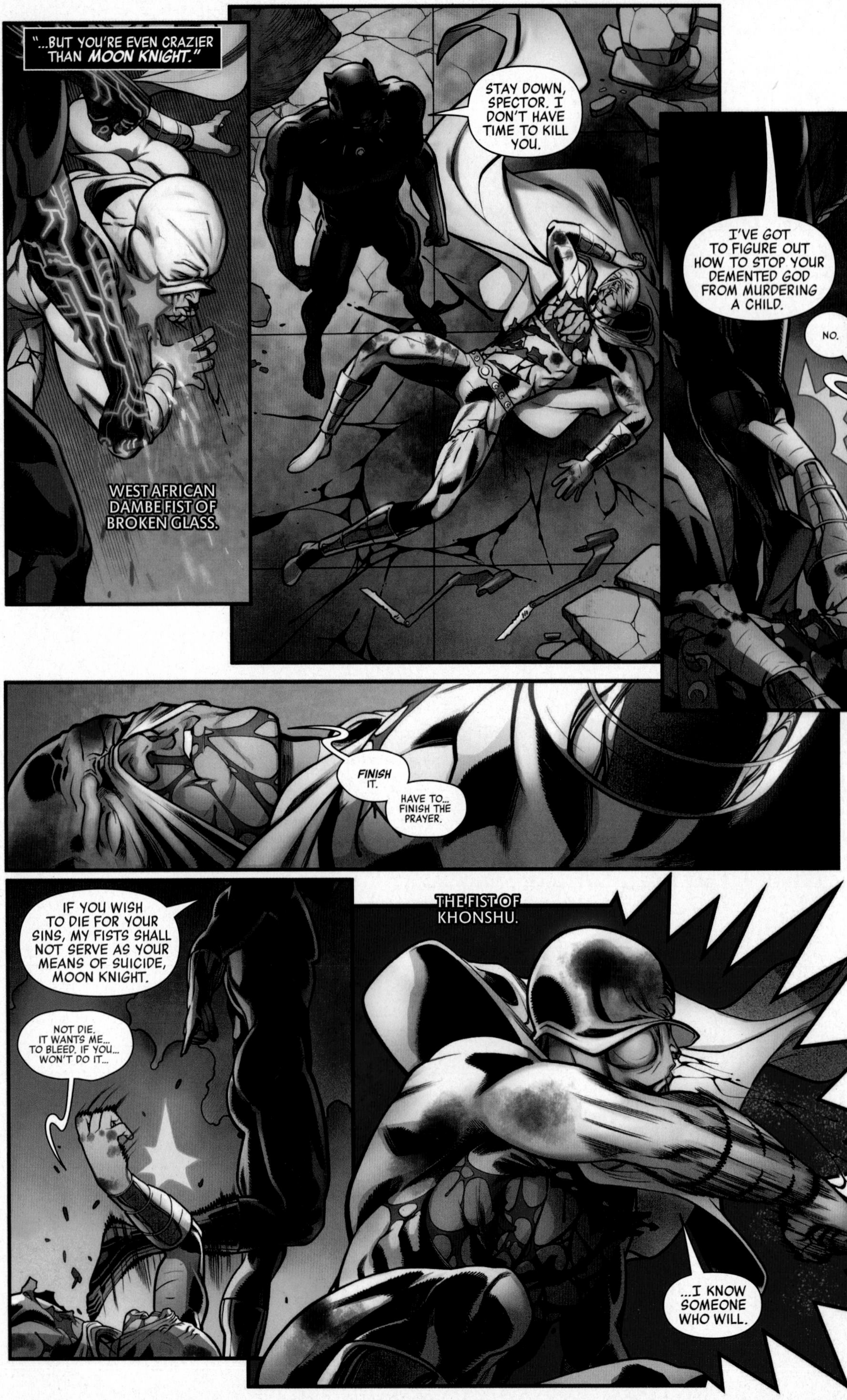
"...BUT YOU'RE EVEN CRAZIER THAN MOON KNIGHT."
WEST AFRICAN DAMBE FIST OF BROKEN GLASS.
STAY DOWN, SPECTOR. I DON'T HAVE TIME TO KILL YOU.
I'VE GOT TO FIGURE OUT HOW TO STOP YOUR DEMENTED GOD FROM MURDERING A CHILD.
NO.
FINISH IT.
HAVE TO... FINISH THE PRAYER.
IF YOU WISH TO DIE FOR YOUR SINS, MY FISTS SHALL NOT SERVE AS YOUR MEANS OF SUICIDE, MOON KNIGHT.
NOT DIE. IT WANTS ME... TO BLEED. IF YOU... WON'T DO IT...
THE FIST OF KHONSHU.
...I KNOW SOMEONE WHO WILL.

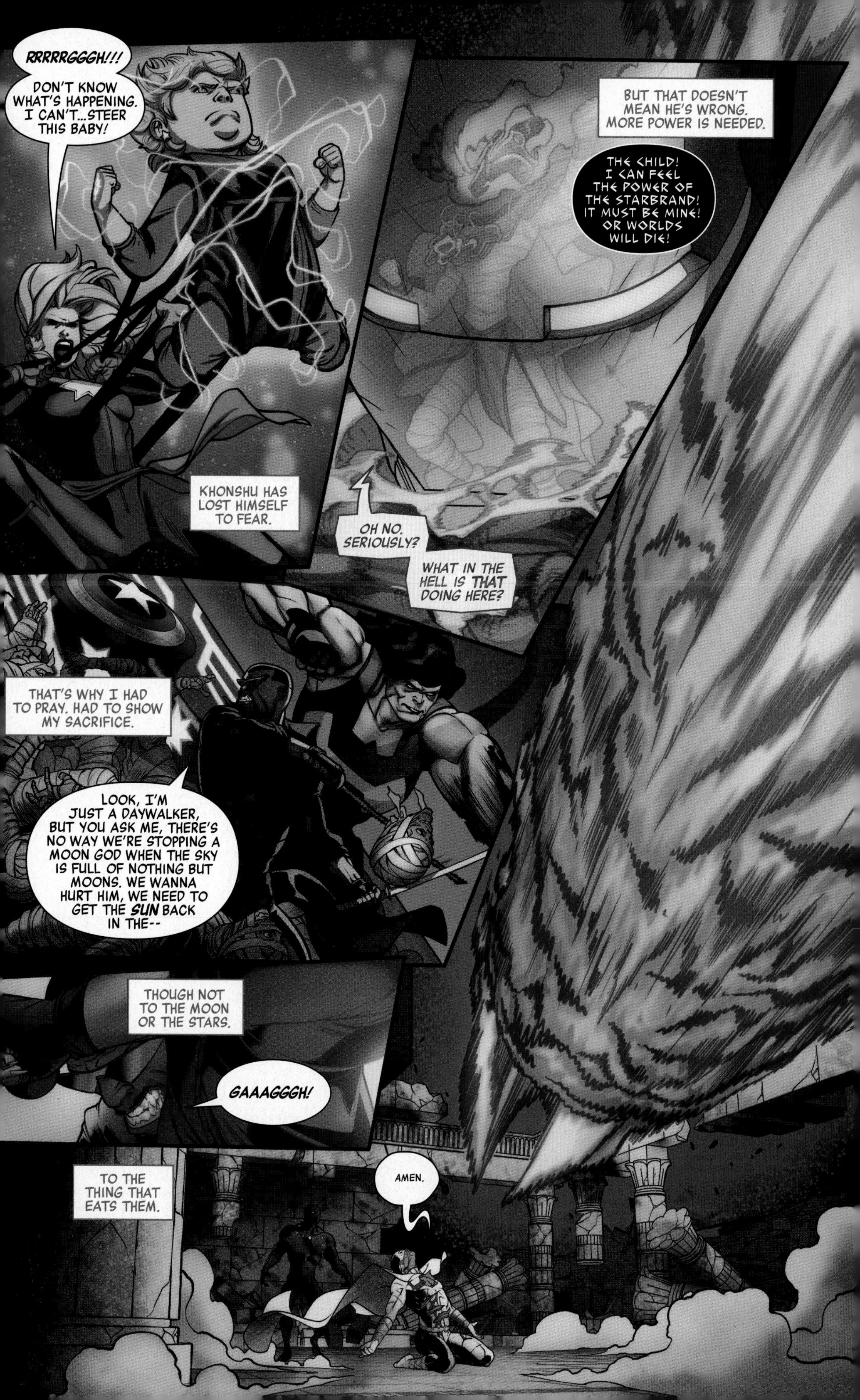
RRRRRGGGH!!!
DON'T KNOW WHAT'S HAPPENING. I CAN'T...STEER THIS BABY!
BUT THAT DOESN'T MEAN HE'S WRONG. MORE POWER IS NEEDED.
THE CHILD! I CAN FEEL THE POWER OF THE STARBRAND! IT MUST BE MINE! OR WORLDS WILL DIE!
KHONSHU HAS LOST HIMSELF TO FEAR.
OH NO. SERIOUSLY?
WHAT IN THE HELL IS THAT DOING HERE?
THAT'S WHY I HAD TO PRAY. HAD TO SHOW MY SACRIFICE.
LOOK, I'M JUST A DAYWALKER, BUT YOU ASK ME, THERE'S NO WAY WE'RE STOPPING A MOON GOD WHEN THE SKY IS FULL OF NOTHING BUT MOONS. WE WANNA HURT HIM, WE NEED TO GET THE SUN BACK IN THE--
THOUGH NOT TO THE MOON OR THE STARS.
GAAAGGGH!
TO THE THING THAT EATS THEM.
AMEN.

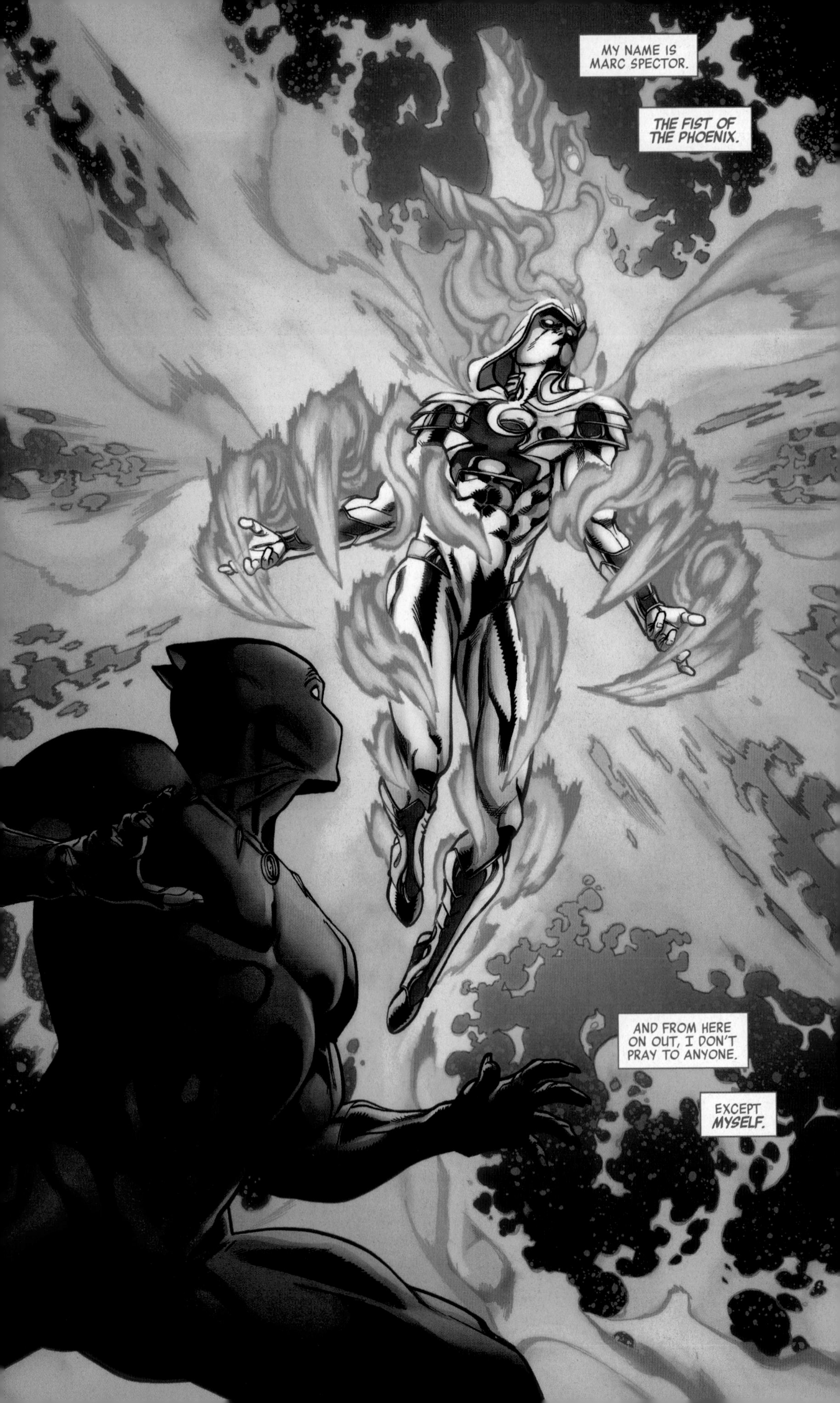
MY NAME IS MARC SPECTOR.
THE FIST OF THE PHOENIX.
AND FROM HERE ON OUT, I DON'T PRAY TO ANYONE.
EXCEPT *MYSELF*.

37 THE AGE OF KHONSHU CONCLUSION
PHOENIX: MOONSONG

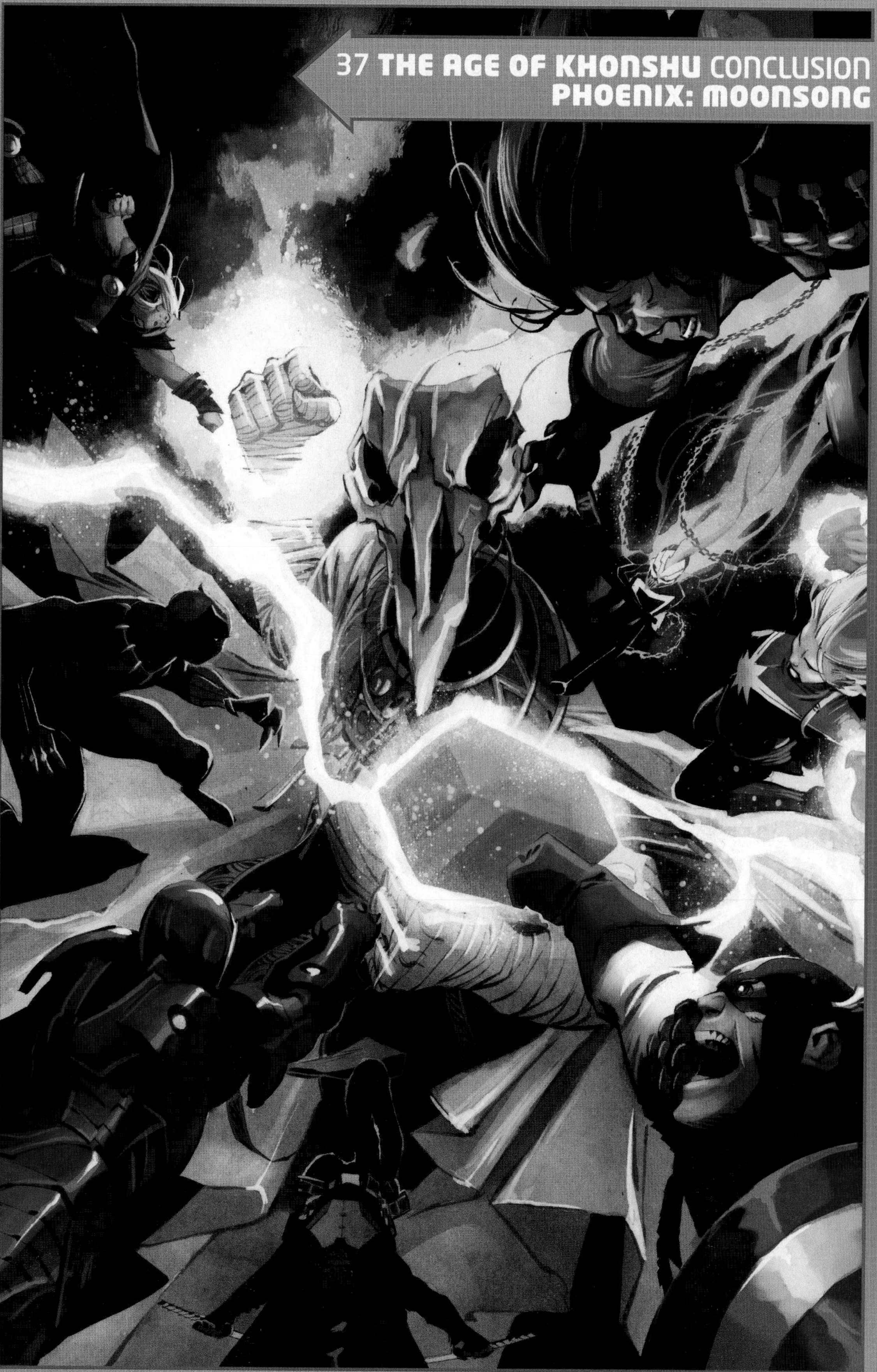

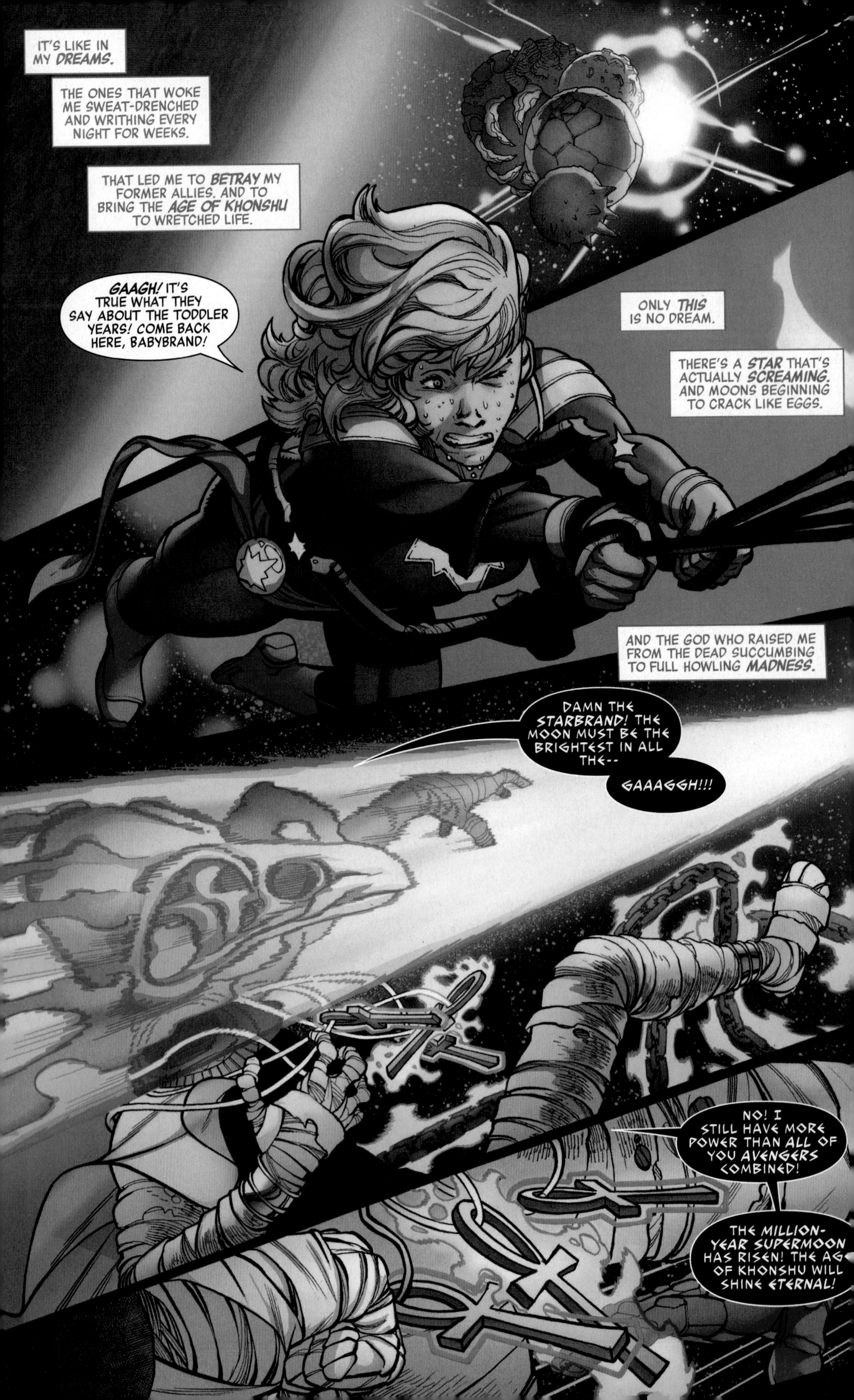
IT'S LIKE IN MY DREAMS.
THE ONES THAT WOKE ME SWEAT-DRENCHED AND WRITHING EVERY NIGHT FOR WEEKS.
THAT LED ME TO BETRAY MY FORMER ALLIES. AND TO BRING THE AGE OF KHONSHU TO WRETCHED LIFE.
GAAGH! IT'S TRUE WHAT THEY SAY ABOUT THE TODDLER YEARS! COME BACK HERE, BABYBRAND!
ONLY THIS IS NO DREAM.
THERE'S A STAR THAT'S ACTUALLY SCREAMING. AND MOONS BEGINNING TO CRACK LIKE EGGS.
AND THE GOD WHO RAISED ME FROM THE DEAD SUCCUMBING TO FULL HOWLING MADNESS.
DAMN THE STARBRAND! THE MOON MUST BE THE BRIGHTEST IN ALL THE--
GAAAGGH!!!
NO! I STILL HAVE MORE POWER THAN ALL OF YOU AVENGERS COMBINED!
THE MILLION-YEAR SUPERMOON HAS RISEN! THE AG OF KHONSHU WILL SHINE ETERNAL!

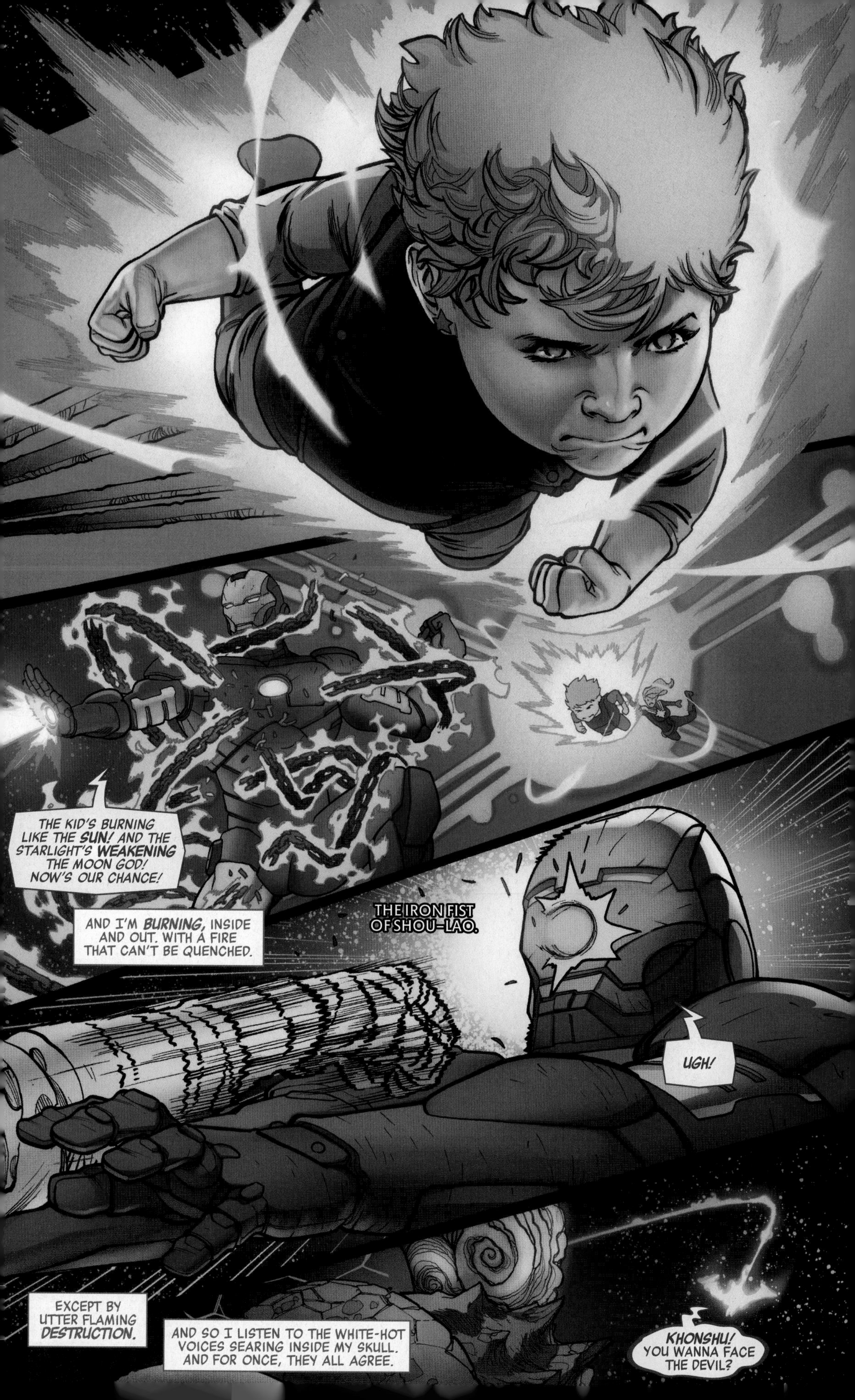

THE KID'S BURNING LIKE THE SUN! AND THE STARLIGHT'S WEAKENING THE MOON GOD! NOW'S OUR CHANCE!
AND I'M BURNING, INSIDE AND OUT. WITH A FIRE THAT CAN'T BE QUENCHED.
THE IRON FIST OF SHOU-LAO.
UGH!
EXCEPT BY UTTER FLAMING DESTRUCTION.
AND SO I LISTEN TO THE WHITE-HOT VOICES SEARING INSIDE MY SKULL. AND FOR ONCE, THEY ALL AGREE.
KHONSHU! YOU WANNA FACE THE DEVIL?

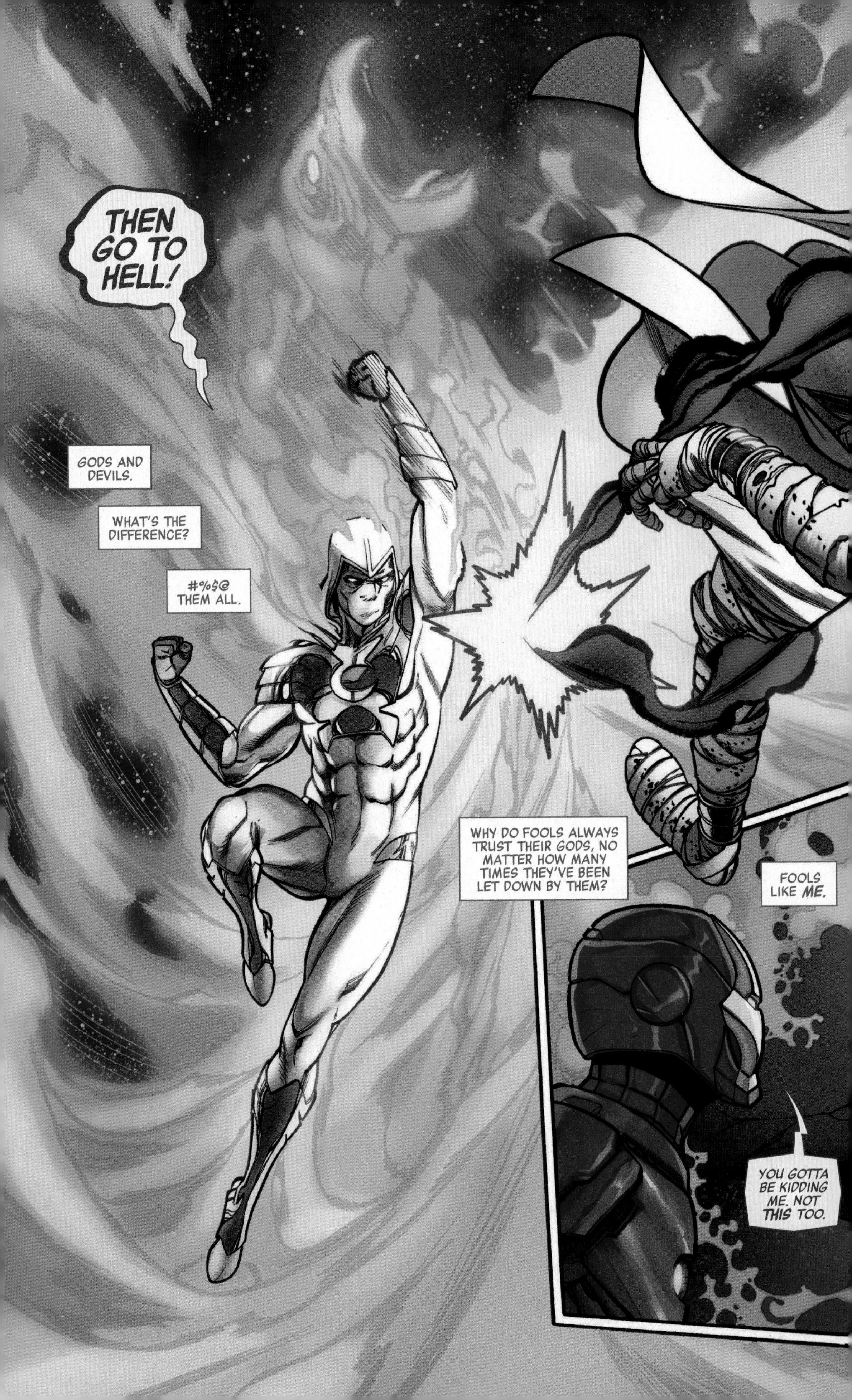
THEN GO TO HELL!
GODS AND DEVILS.
WHAT'S THE DIFFERENCE?
#%$@ THEM ALL.
WHY DO FOOLS ALWAYS TRUST THEIR GODS, NO MATTER HOW MANY TIMES THEY'VE BEEN LET DOWN BY THEM?
FOOLS LIKE *ME*.
YOU GOTTA BE KIDDING ME. NOT *THIS* TOO.

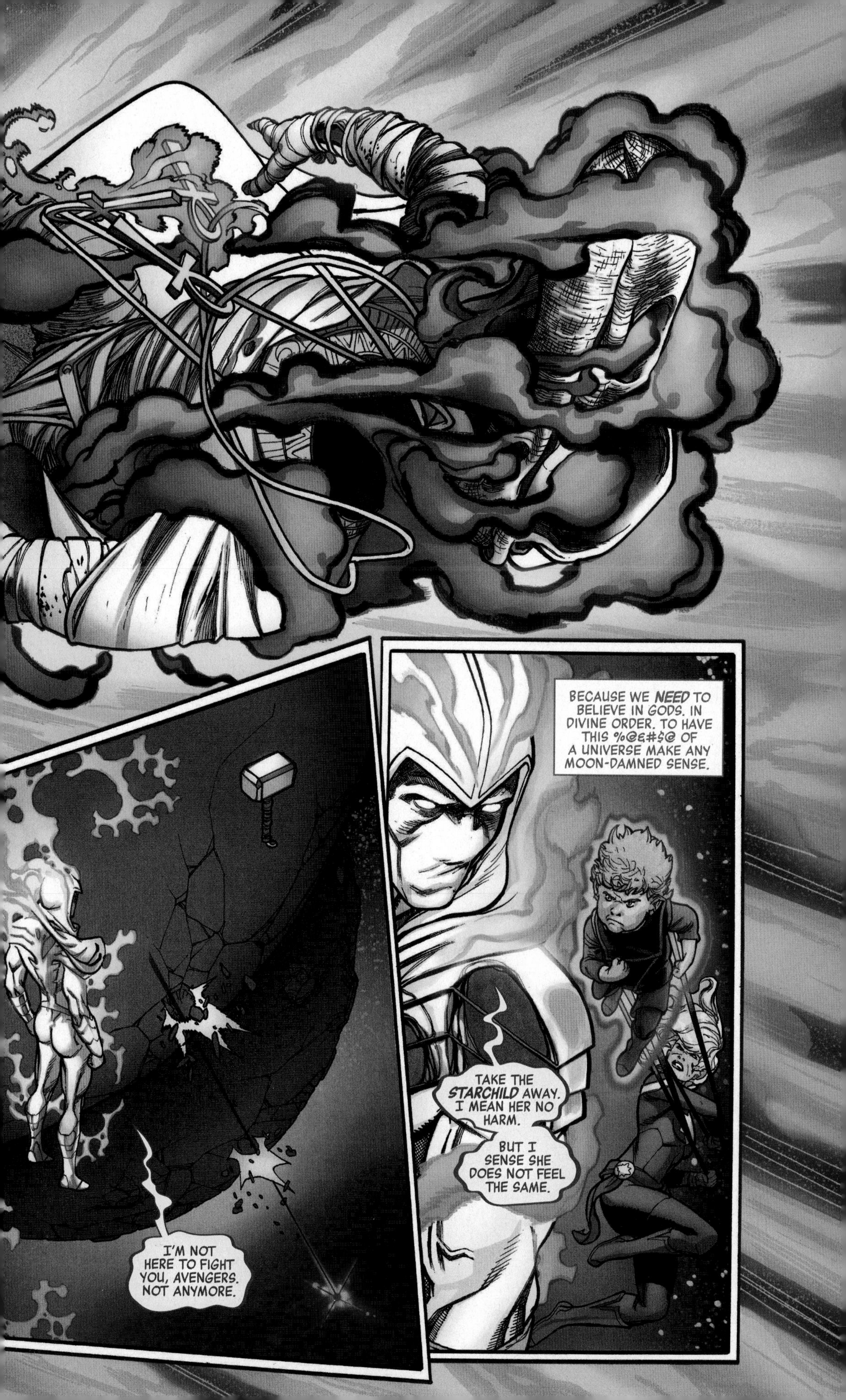
BECAUSE WE NEED TO BELIEVE IN GODS. IN DIVINE ORDER. TO HAVE THIS %@€#$@ OF A UNIVERSE MAKE ANY MOON-DAMNED SENSE.
I'M NOT HERE TO FIGHT YOU, AVENGERS. NOT ANYMORE.
TAKE THE STARCHILD AWAY. I MEAN HER NO HARM.
BUT I SENSE SHE DOES NOT FEEL THE SAME.

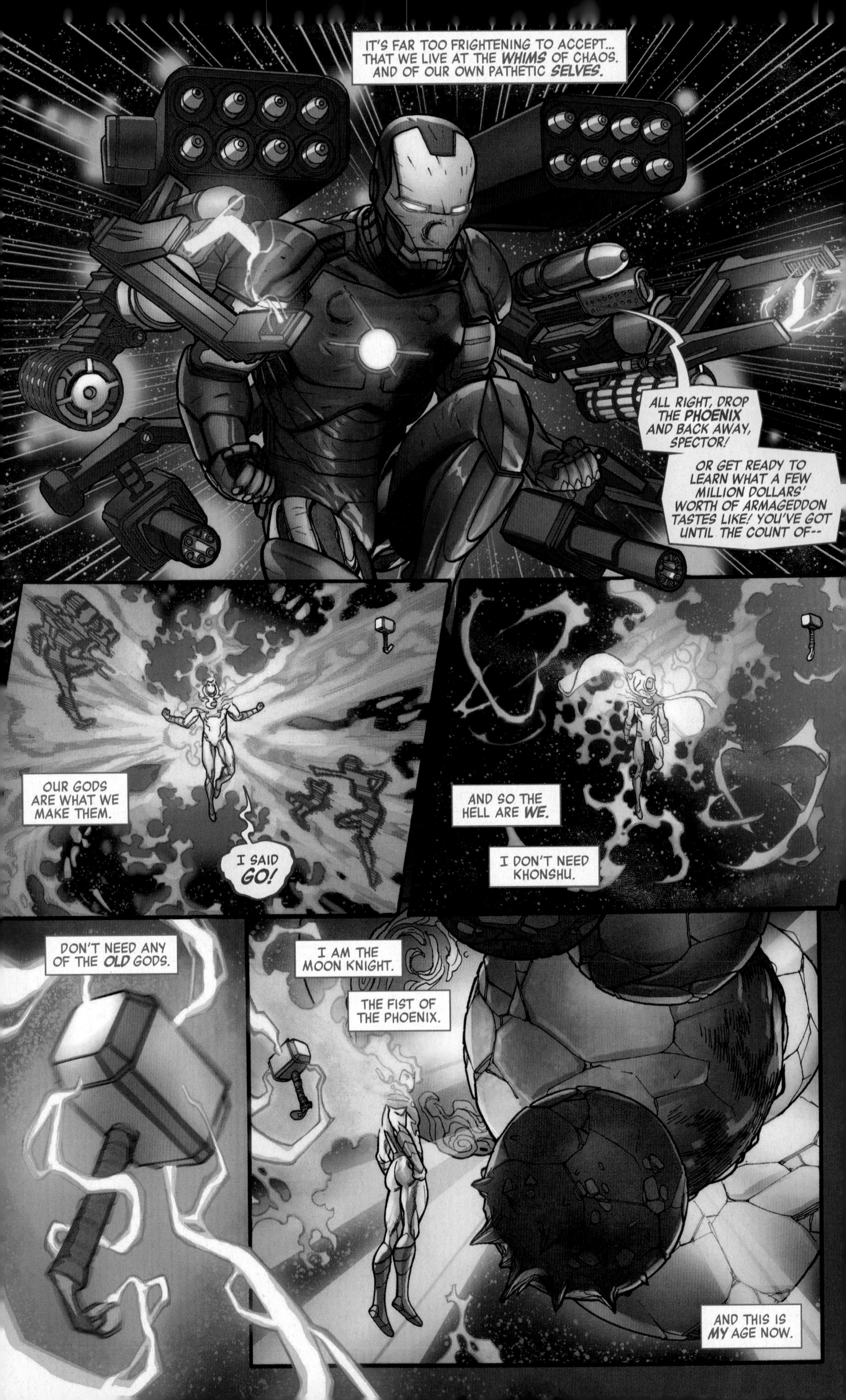
IT'S FAR TOO FRIGHTENING TO ACCEPT... THAT WE LIVE AT THE WHIMS OF CHAOS. AND OF OUR OWN PATHETIC SELVES.
ALL RIGHT, DROP THE PHOENIX AND BACK AWAY, SPECTOR!
OR GET READY TO LEARN WHAT A FEW MILLION DOLLARS' WORTH OF ARMAGEDDON TASTES LIKE! YOU'VE GOT UNTIL THE COUNT OF--
OUR GODS ARE WHAT WE MAKE THEM.
I SAID GO!
AND SO THE HELL ARE WE.
I DON'T NEED KHONSHU.
DON'T NEED ANY OF THE OLD GODS.
I AM THE MOON KNIGHT.
THE FIST OF THE PHOENIX.
AND THIS IS MY AGE NOW.

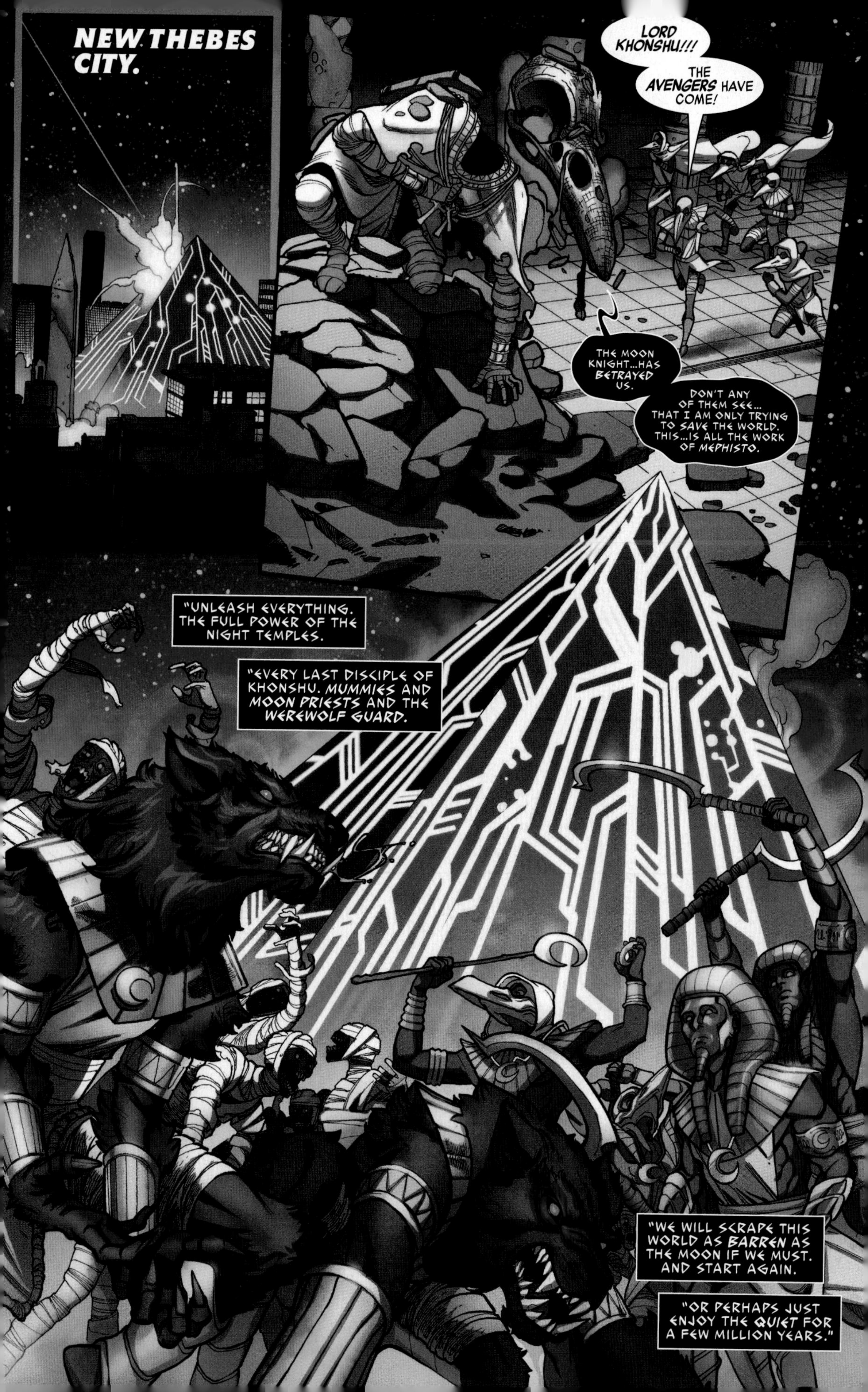
NEW THEBES CITY.
LORD KHONSHU!!!
THE AVENGERS HAVE COME!
THE MOON KNIGHT...HAS BETRAYED US.
DON'T ANY OF THEM SEE... THAT I AM ONLY TRYING TO SAVE THE WORLD. THIS...IS ALL THE WORK OF MEPHISTO.
"UNLEASH EVERYTHING. THE FULL POWER OF THE NIGHT TEMPLES.
"EVERY LAST DISCIPLE OF KHONSHU. MUMMIES AND MOON PRIESTS AND THE WEREWOLF GUARD.
"WE WILL SCRAPE THIS WORLD AS BARREN AS THE MOON IF WE MUST. AND START AGAIN.
"OR PERHAPS JUST ENJOY THE QUIET FOR A FEW MILLION YEARS."

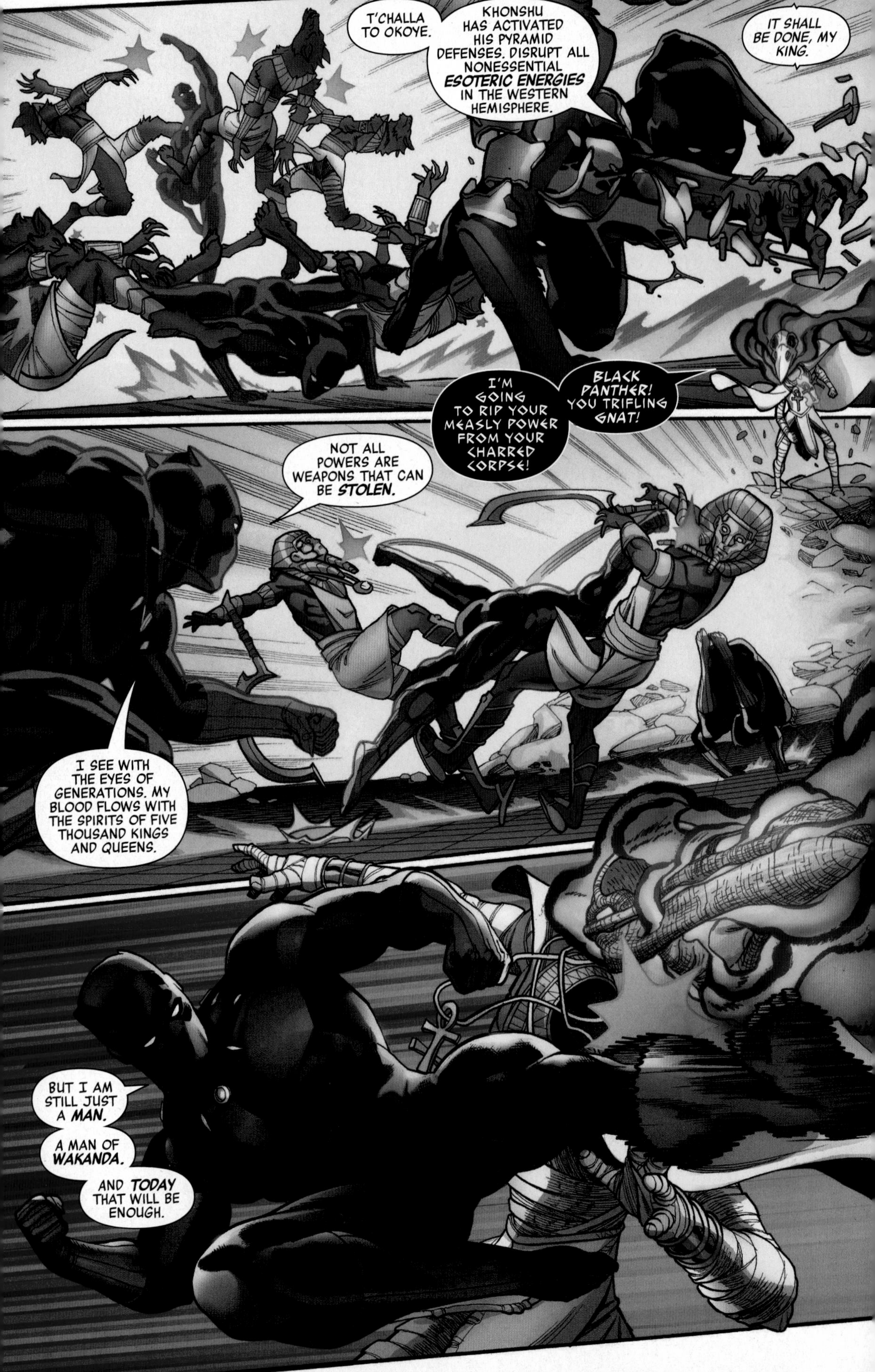
T'CHALLA TO OKOYE.
KHONSHU HAS ACTIVATED HIS PYRAMID DEFENSES. DISRUPT ALL NONESSENTIAL ESOTERIC ENERGIES IN THE WESTERN HEMISPHERE.
IT SHALL BE DONE, MY KING.
BLACK PANTHER! YOU TRIFLING GNAT!
I'M GOING TO RIP YOUR MEASLY POWER FROM YOUR CHARRED CORPSE!
NOT ALL POWERS ARE WEAPONS THAT CAN BE STOLEN.
I SEE WITH THE EYES OF GENERATIONS. MY BLOOD FLOWS WITH THE SPIRITS OF FIVE THOUSAND KINGS AND QUEENS.
BUT I AM STILL JUST A MAN.
A MAN OF WAKANDA.
AND TODAY THAT WILL BE ENOUGH.

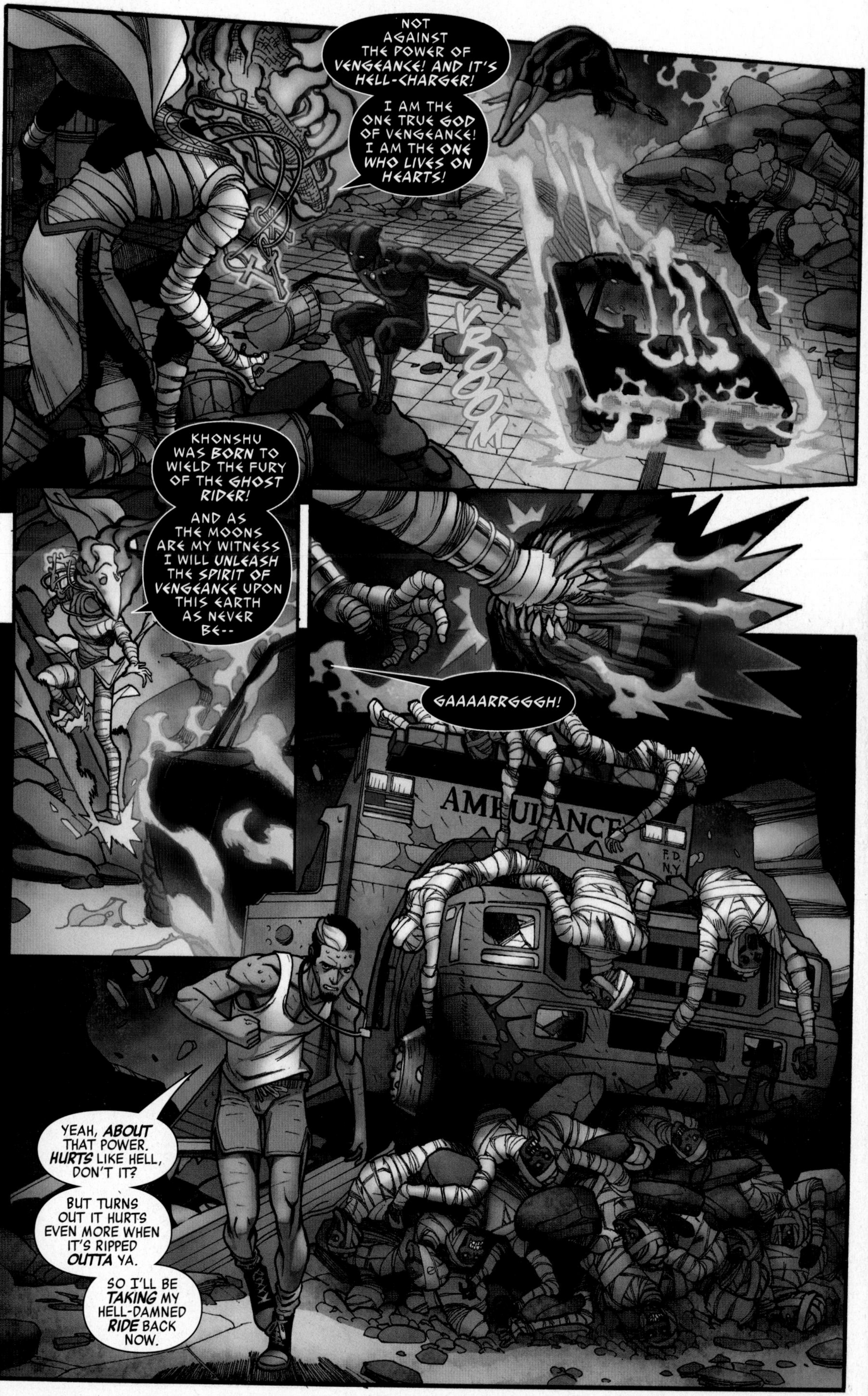

NOT AGAINST THE POWER OF VENGEANCE! AND IT'S HELL-CHARGER!
I AM THE ONE TRUE GOD OF VENGEANCE! I AM THE ONE WHO LIVES ON HEARTS!
VROOOM
KHONSHU WAS BORN TO WIELD THE FURY OF THE GHOST RIDER!
AND AS THE MOONS ARE MY WITNESS I WILL UNLEASH THE SPIRIT OF VENGEANCE UPON THIS EARTH AS NEVER BE--
GAAAARRGGGH!
AMBULANCE
F.D. N.Y.
YEAH, ABOUT THAT POWER. HURTS LIKE HELL, DON'T IT?
BUT TURNS OUT IT HURTS EVEN MORE WHEN IT'S RIPPED OUTTA YA.
SO I'LL BE TAKING MY HELL-DAMNED RIDE BACK NOW.

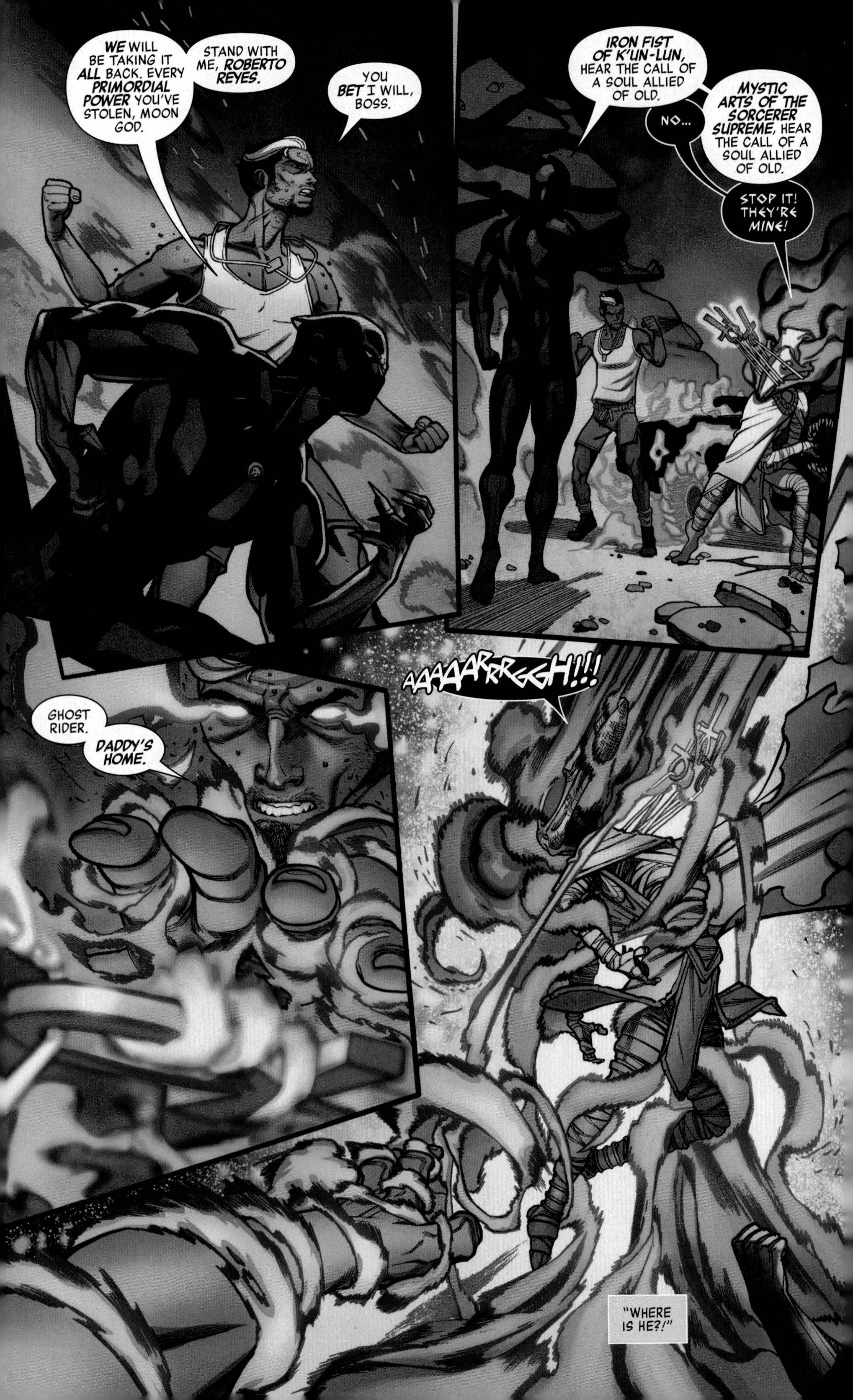
WE WILL BE TAKING IT ALL BACK. EVERY PRIMORDIAL POWER YOU'VE STOLEN, MOON GOD.
STAND WITH ME, ROBERTO REYES.
YOU BET I WILL, BOSS.
IRON FIST OF K'UN-LUN, HEAR THE CALL OF A SOUL ALLIED OF OLD.
NO...
MYSTIC ARTS OF THE SORCERER SUPREME, HEAR THE CALL OF A SOUL ALLIED OF OLD.
STOP IT! THEY'RE MINE!
GHOST RIDER.
DADDY'S HOME.
AAAAARRRGGH!!!
"WHERE IS HE?!"

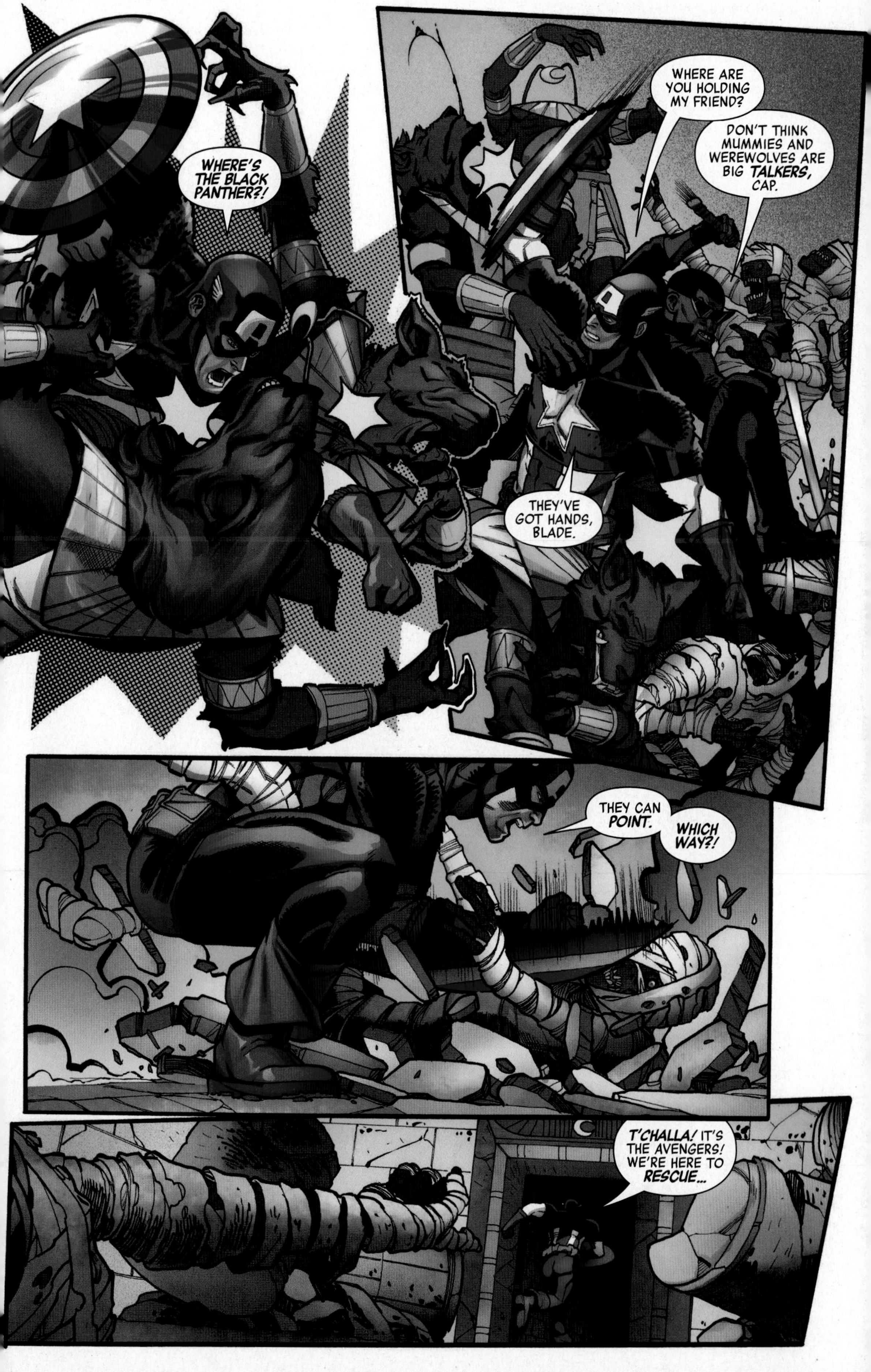
WHERE'S THE BLACK PANTHER?!
WHERE ARE YOU HOLDING MY FRIEND?
DON'T THINK MUMMIES AND WEREWOLVES ARE BIG TALKERS, CAP.
THEY'VE GOT HANDS, BLADE.
THEY CAN POINT.
WHICH WAY?!
T'CHALLA! IT'S THE AVENGERS! WE'RE HERE TO RESCUE...

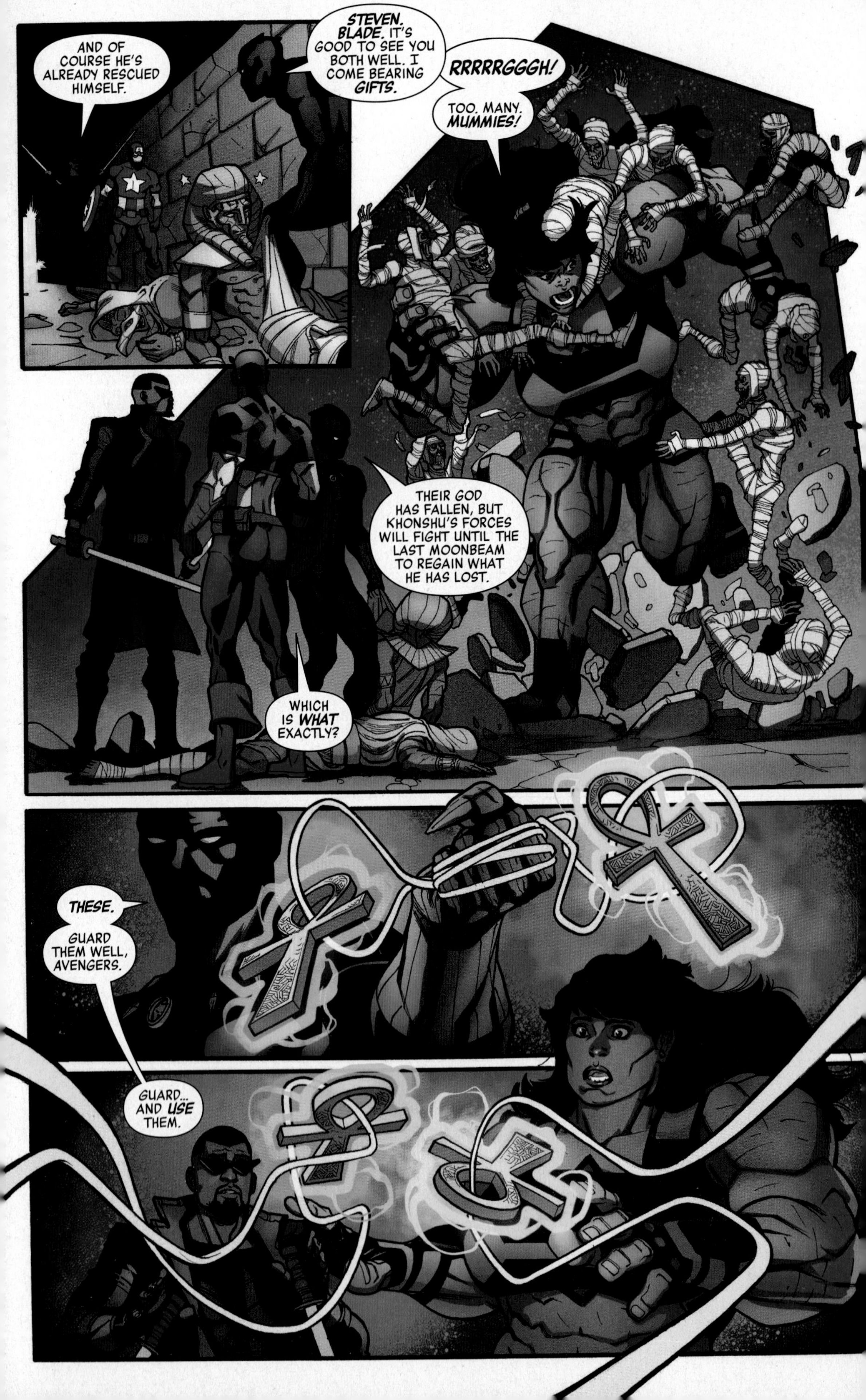
AND OF COURSE HE'S ALREADY RESCUED HIMSELF.
STEVEN. BLADE. IT'S GOOD TO SEE YOU BOTH WELL. I COME BEARING GIFTS.
RRRRRGGGH!
TOO. MANY. MUMMIES!
THEIR GOD HAS FALLEN, BUT KHONSHU'S FORCES WILL FIGHT UNTIL THE LAST MOONBEAM TO REGAIN WHAT HE HAS LOST.
WHICH IS WHAT EXACTLY?
THESE.
GUARD THEM WELL, AVENGERS.
GUARD... AND USE THEM.

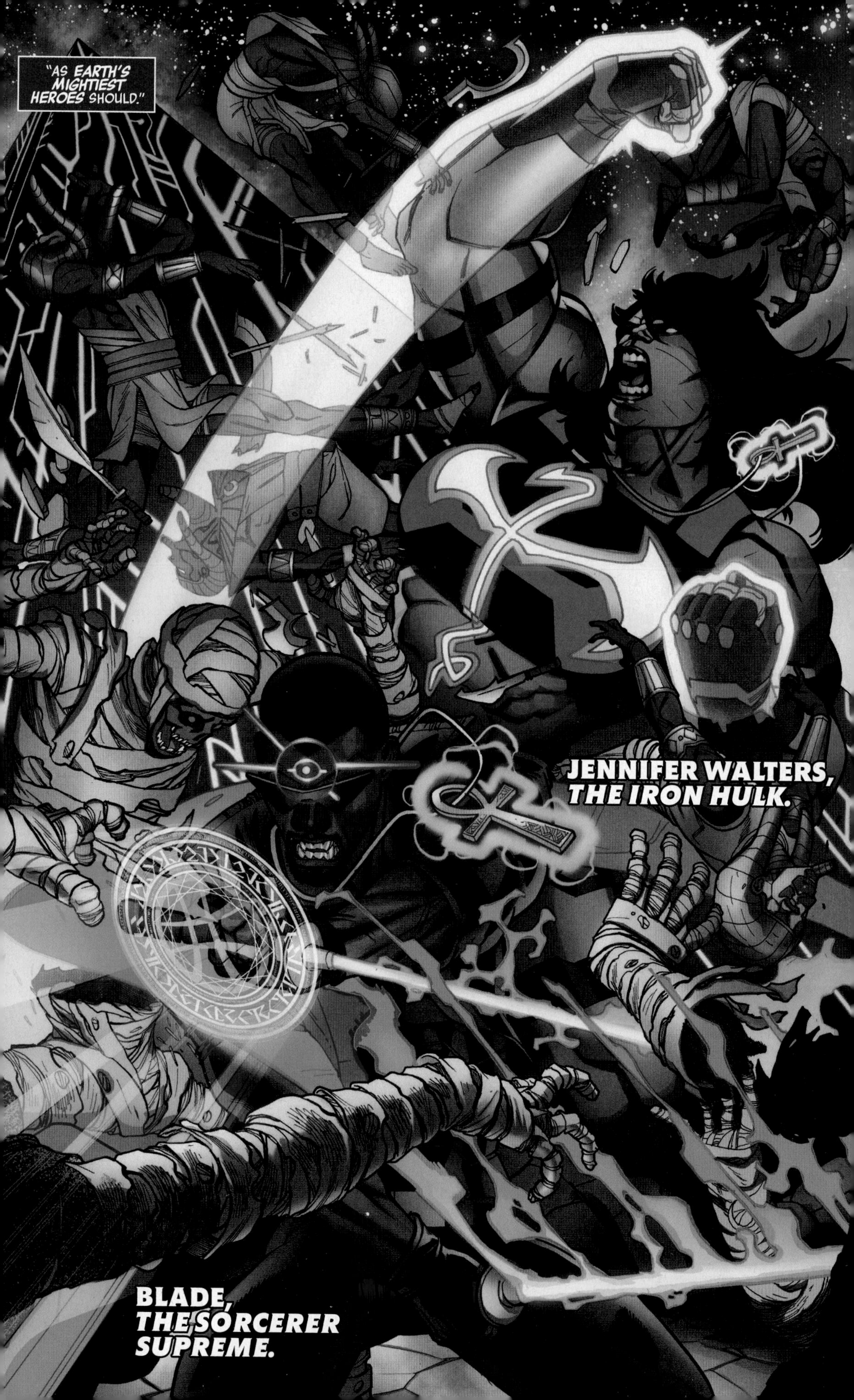
"AS EARTH'S MIGHTIEST HEROES SHOULD."
JENNIFER WALTERS, THE IRON HULK.
BLADE, THE SORCERER SUPREME.

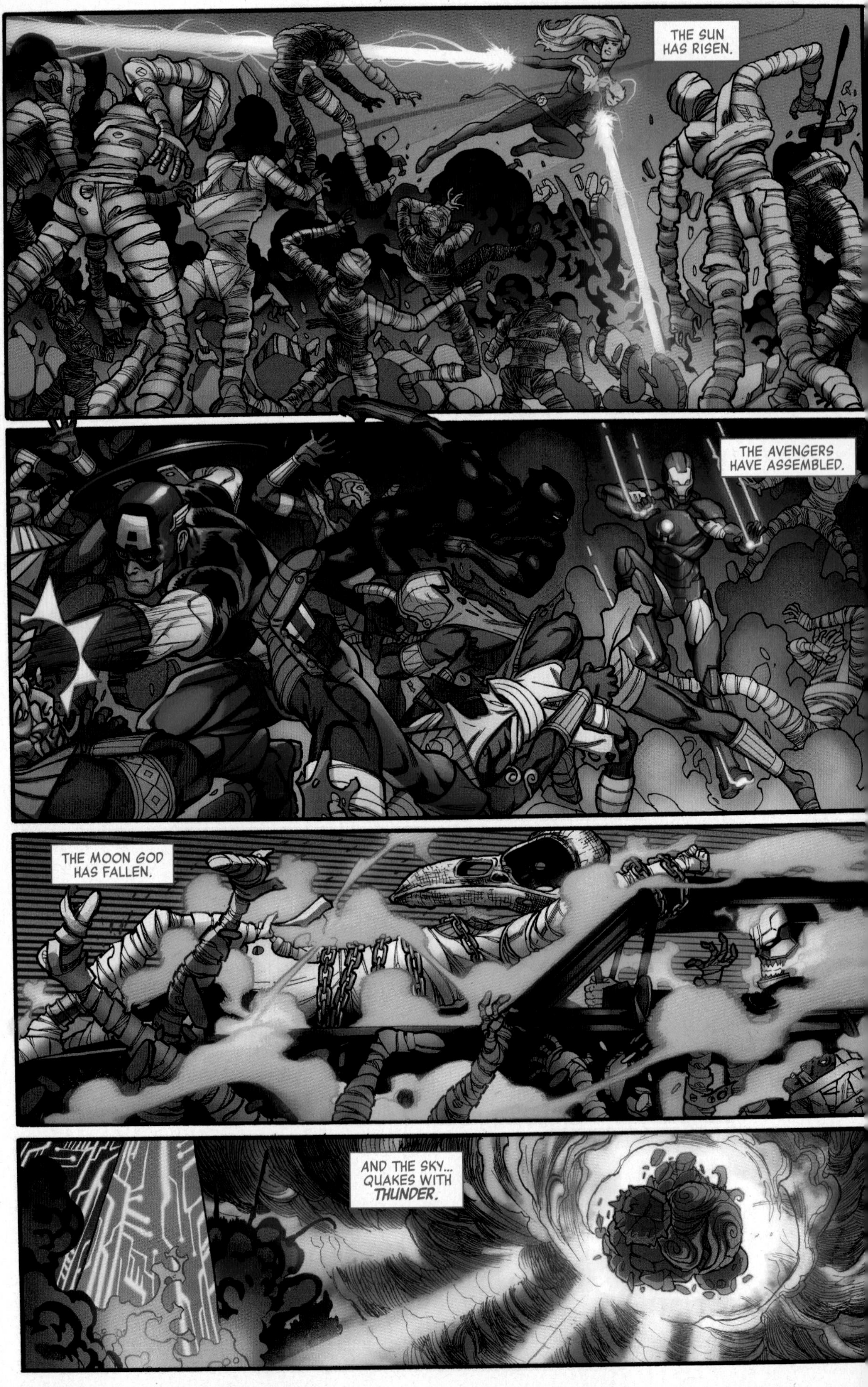
THE SUN HAS RISEN.
THE AVENGERS HAVE ASSEMBLED.
THE MOON GOD HAS FALLEN.
AND THE SKY... QUAKES WITH THUNDER.

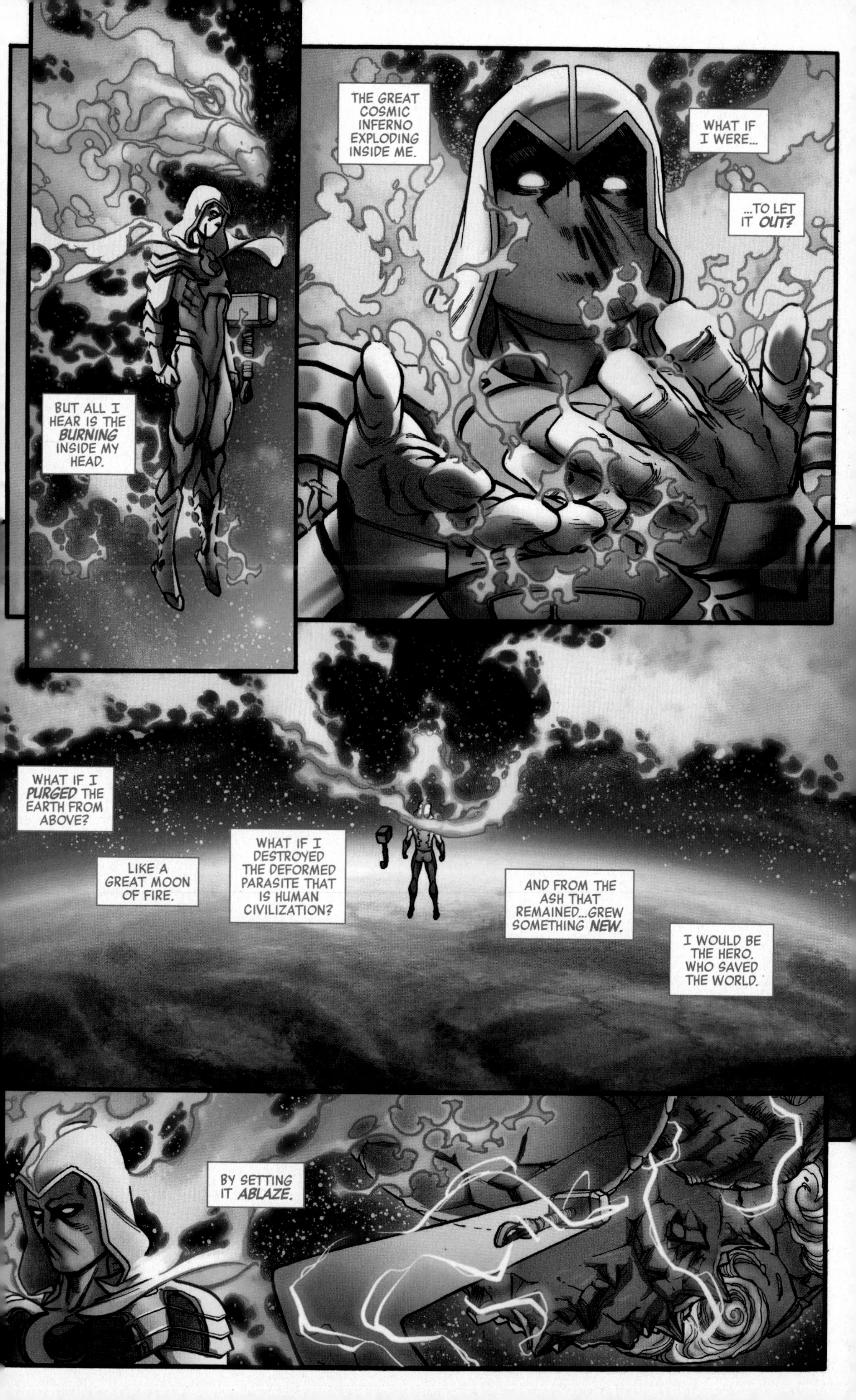
BUT ALL I HEAR IS THE BURNING INSIDE MY HEAD.
THE GREAT COSMIC INFERNO EXPLODING INSIDE ME.
WHAT IF I WERE...
...TO LET IT OUT?
WHAT IF I PURGED THE EARTH FROM ABOVE?
LIKE A GREAT MOON OF FIRE.
WHAT IF I DESTROYED THE DEFORMED PARASITE THAT IS HUMAN CIVILIZATION?
AND FROM THE ASH THAT REMAINED...GREW SOMETHING NEW.
I WOULD BE THE HERO. WHO SAVED THE WORLD.
BY SETTING IT ABLAZE.

"MAKE THE ENTIRE WORLD INTO THE *BURNT PLACE*"...

...SCREAMS THE VOICE OF FLAME FROM A GREAT WHITE ROOM.

I CONSIDER IT.

GOD HELP ME, I CONSIDER *GENOCIDE*.

NO.

WHICH IS WHEN I REALIZE... FOR THE VERY FIRST TIME...

...THAT I HAVE *TRULY* LOST MY MIND.

I NEEDED POWER TO HELP DEFEAT MY GOD. BUT I AM NOT THE PHOENIX.

AND THIS IS NOT THE SAGA OF *DARK MOON KNIGHT*.

I BREAK THE SPELL OF DARKNESS. I REIGNITE THE SUN. AND I REACH THROUGH THE FIRE FOR MY *USUAL* MADNESS.

MY NAME IS MARC SPECTOR.

I WEAR *WHITE*. SO THE BAD GUYS WILL SEE ME COMING.

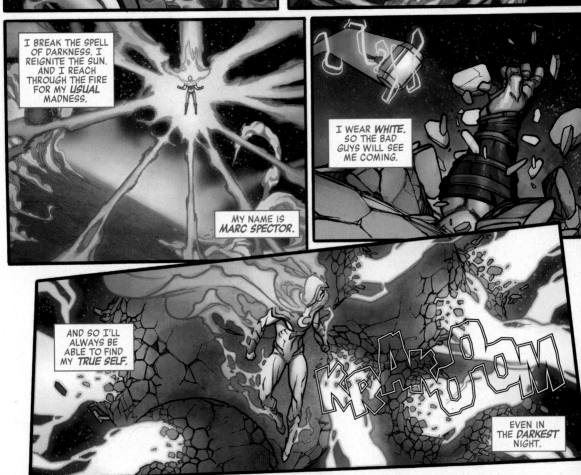

AND SO I'LL ALWAYS BE ABLE TO FIND MY *TRUE SELF*.

EVEN IN THE *DARKEST* NIGHT.

KRA-KOOM

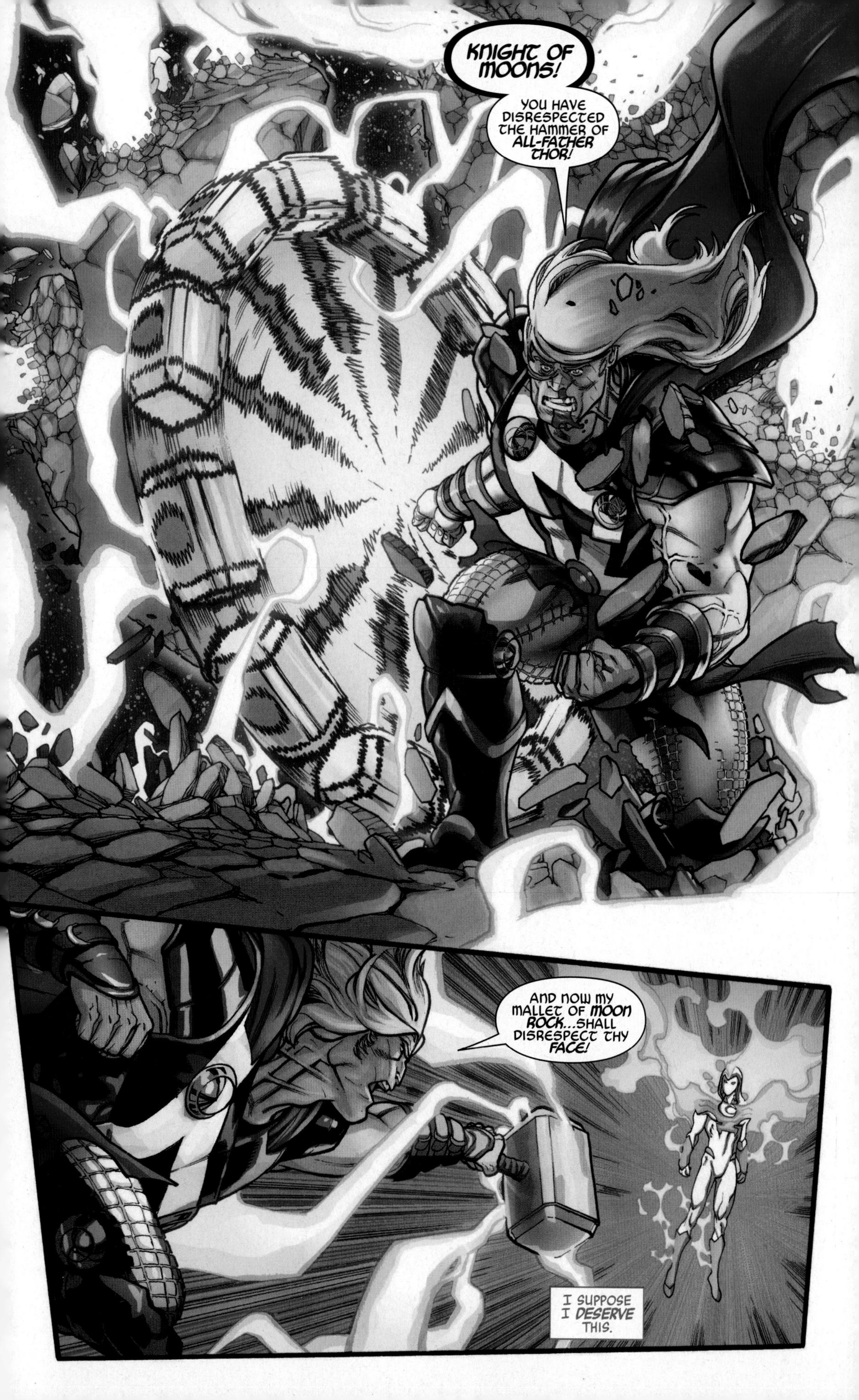
KNIGHT OF MOONS!
YOU HAVE DISRESPECTED THE HAMMER OF ALL-FATHER THOR!
AND NOW MY MALLET OF MOON ROCK...SHALL DISRESPECT THY FACE!
I SUPPOSE I DESERVE THIS.

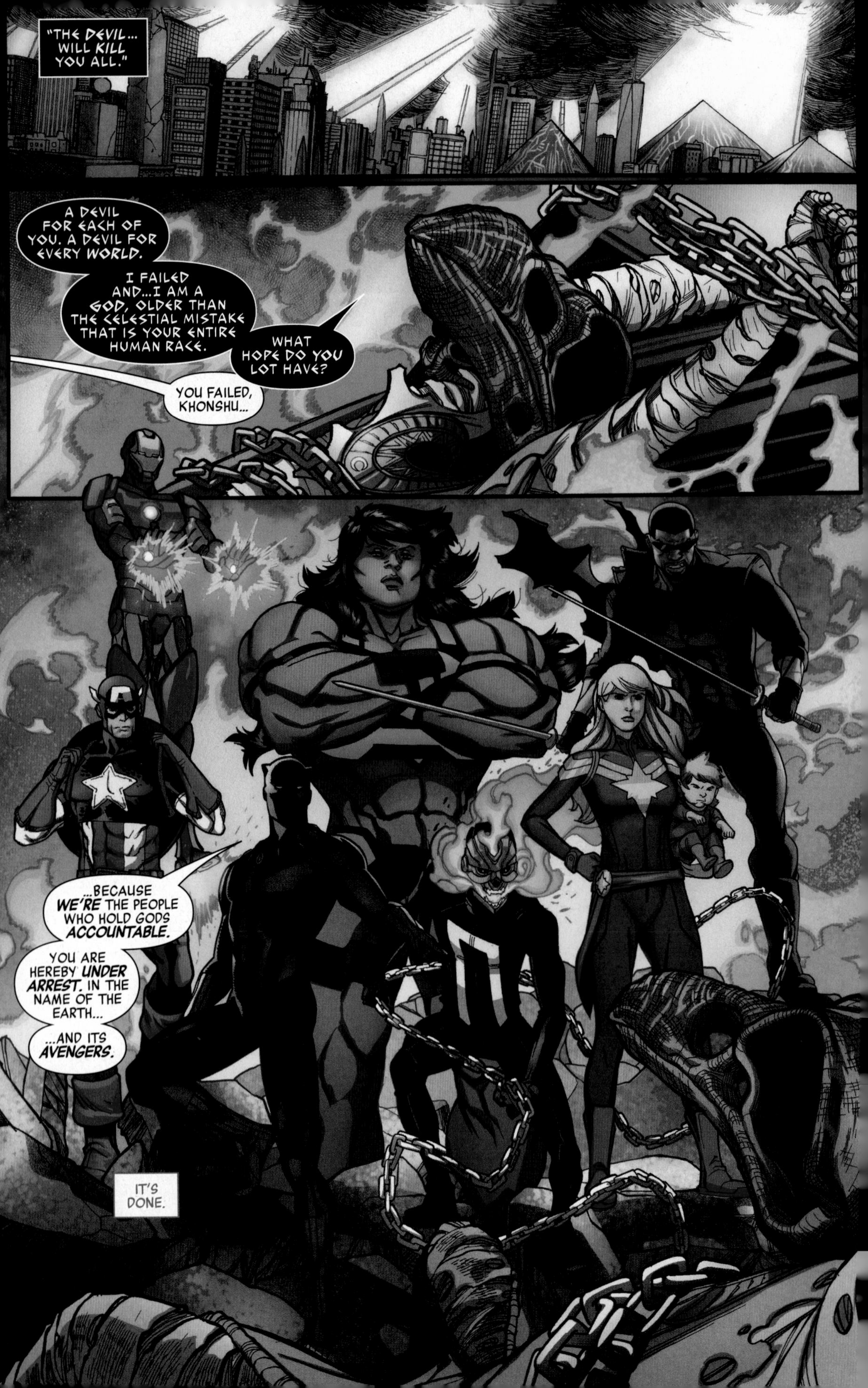
"THE DEVIL... WILL KILL YOU ALL."
A DEVIL FOR EACH OF YOU. A DEVIL FOR EVERY WORLD.
I FAILED AND...I AM A GOD, OLDER THAN THE CELESTIAL MISTAKE THAT IS YOUR ENTIRE HUMAN RACE.
WHAT HOPE DO YOU LOT HAVE?
YOU FAILED, KHONSHU...
...BECAUSE WE'RE THE PEOPLE WHO HOLD GODS ACCOUNTABLE.
YOU ARE HEREBY UNDER ARREST. IN THE NAME OF THE EARTH...
...AND ITS AVENGERS.
IT'S DONE.

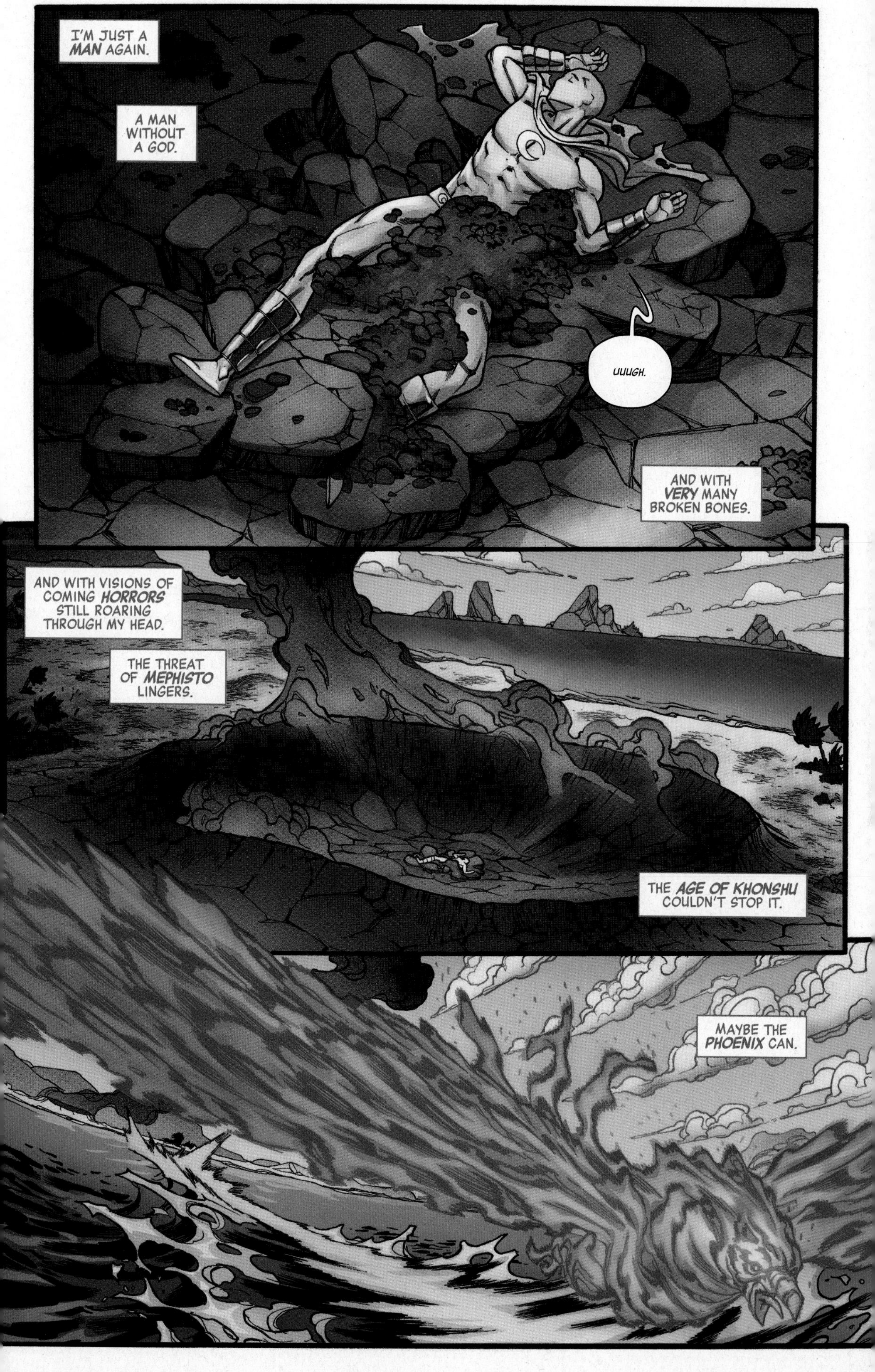
I'M JUST A MAN AGAIN.
A MAN WITHOUT A GOD.
UUUGH.
AND WITH VERY MANY BROKEN BONES.
AND WITH VISIONS OF COMING HORRORS STILL ROARING THROUGH MY HEAD.
THE THREAT OF MEPHISTO LINGERS.
THE AGE OF KHONSHU COULDN'T STOP IT.
MAYBE THE PHOENIX CAN.

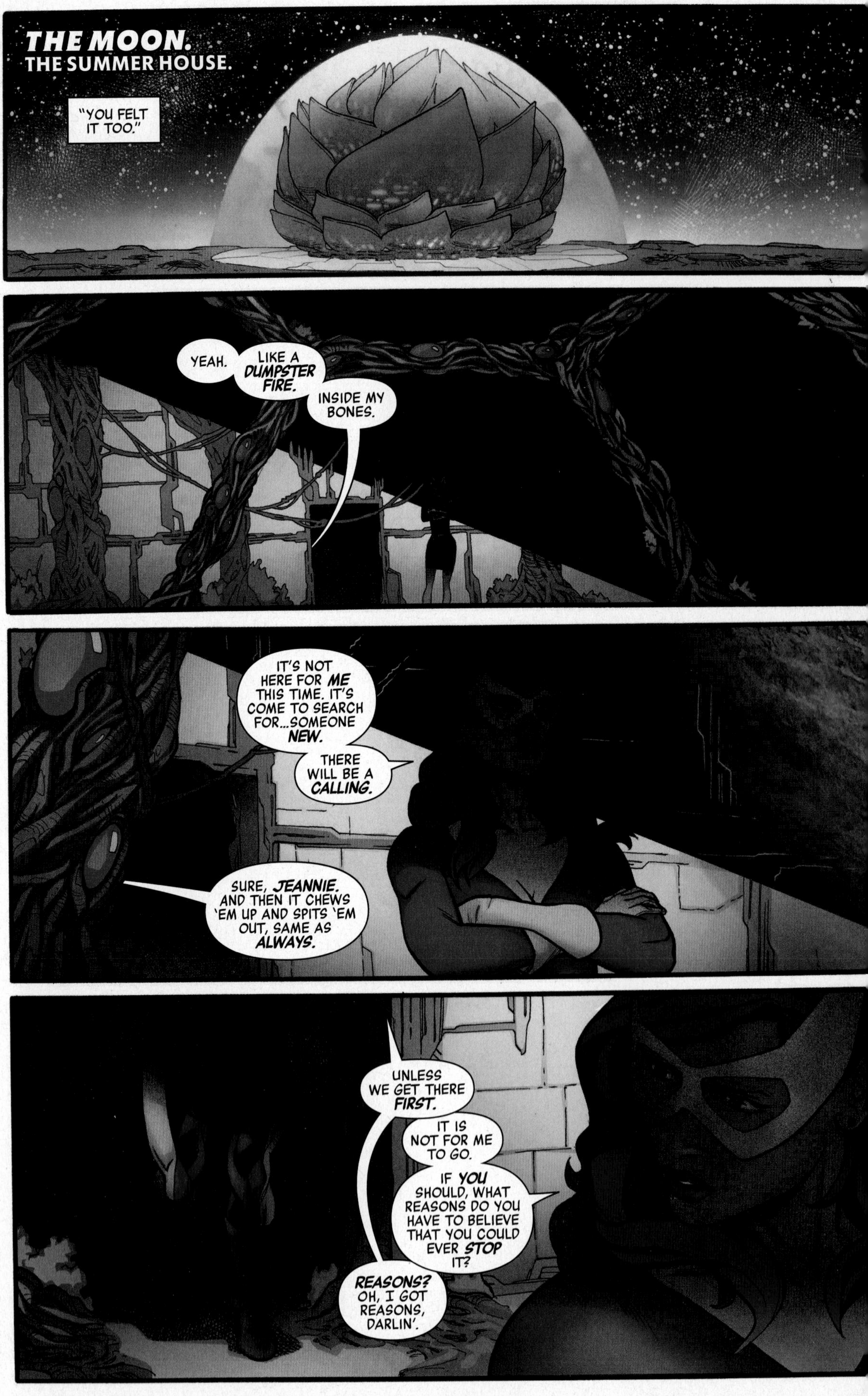
THE MOON.
THE SUMMER HOUSE.
"YOU FELT IT TOO."
YEAH.
LIKE A DUMPSTER FIRE.
INSIDE MY BONES.
IT'S NOT HERE FOR ME THIS TIME. IT'S COME TO SEARCH FOR...SOMEONE NEW.
THERE WILL BE A CALLING.
SURE, JEANNIE. AND THEN IT CHEWS 'EM UP AND SPITS 'EM OUT, SAME AS ALWAYS.
UNLESS WE GET THERE FIRST.
IT IS NOT FOR ME TO GO.
IF YOU SHOULD, WHAT REASONS DO YOU HAVE TO BELIEVE THAT YOU COULD EVER STOP IT?
REASONS? OH, I GOT REASONS, DARLIN'.

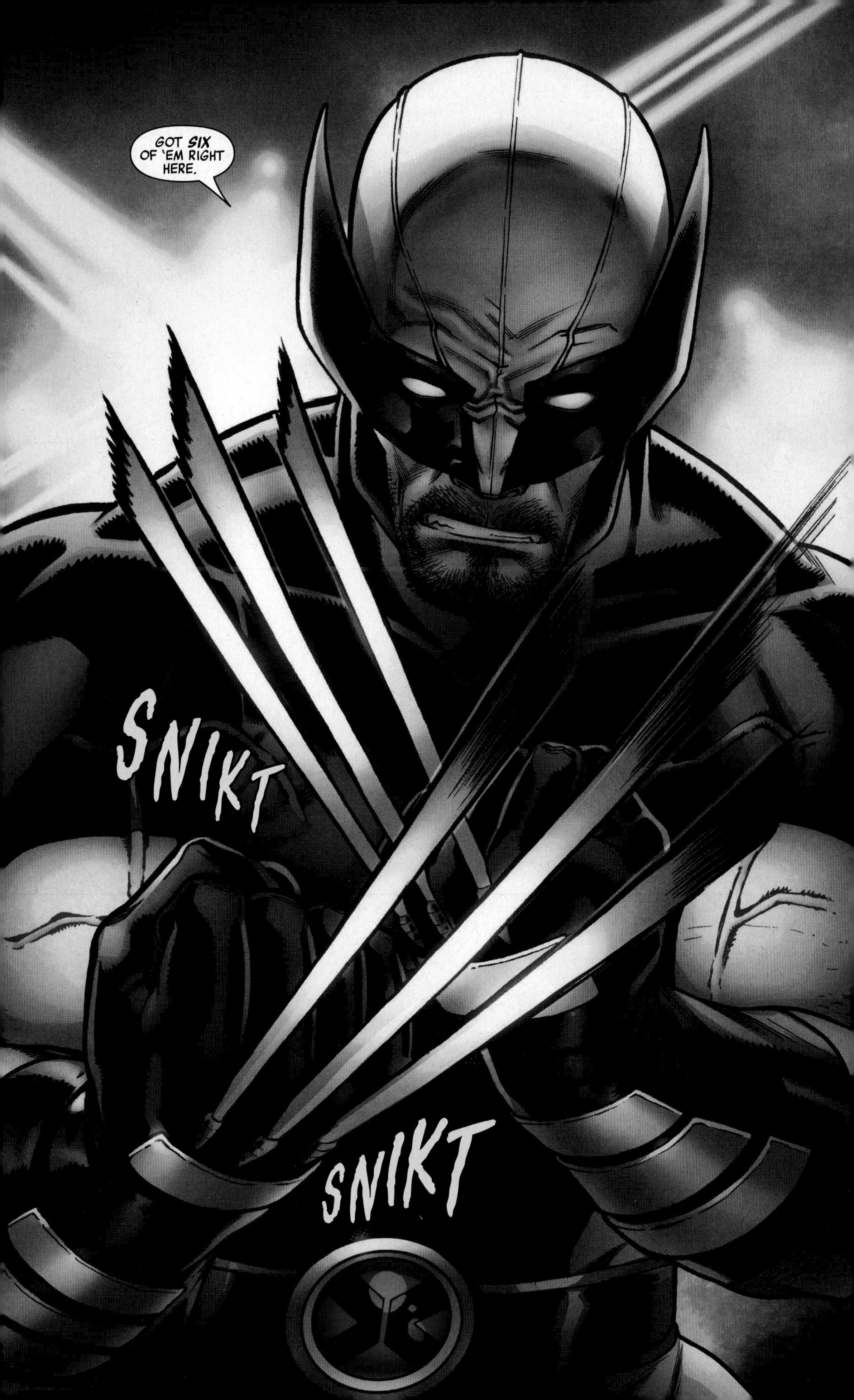
GOT **SIX** OF 'EM RIGHT HERE.
SNIKT
SNIKT

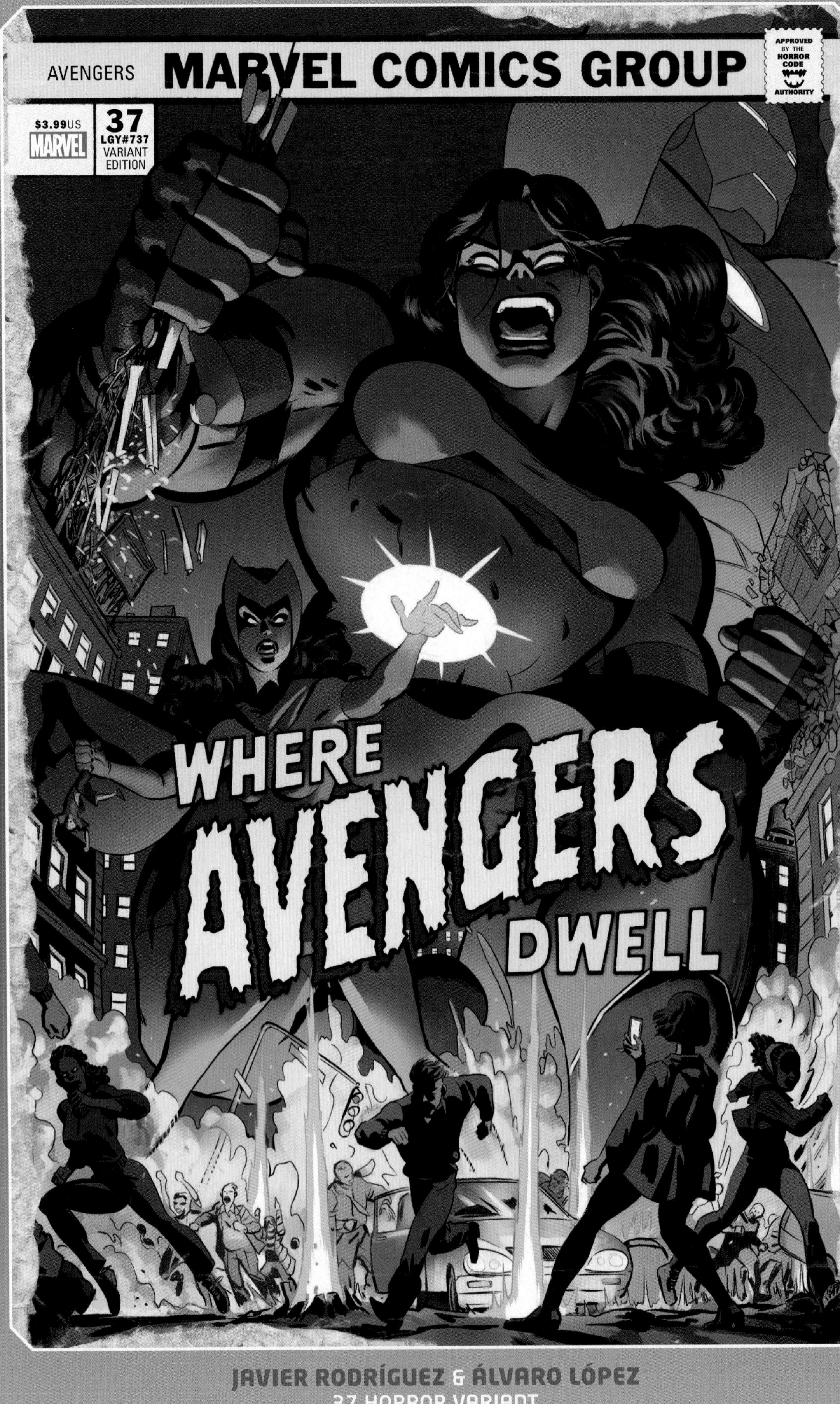

AVENGERS
MARVEL COMICS GROUP
APPROVED BY THE HORROR CODE AUTHORITY
$3.99US
MARVEL
37
LGY#737
VARIANT EDITION
WHERE AVENGERS DWELL

JAVIER RODRÍGUEZ & ÁLVARO LÓPEZ
37 HORROR VARIANT

38 THE FLY THAT LAID A BILLION MAGGOTS

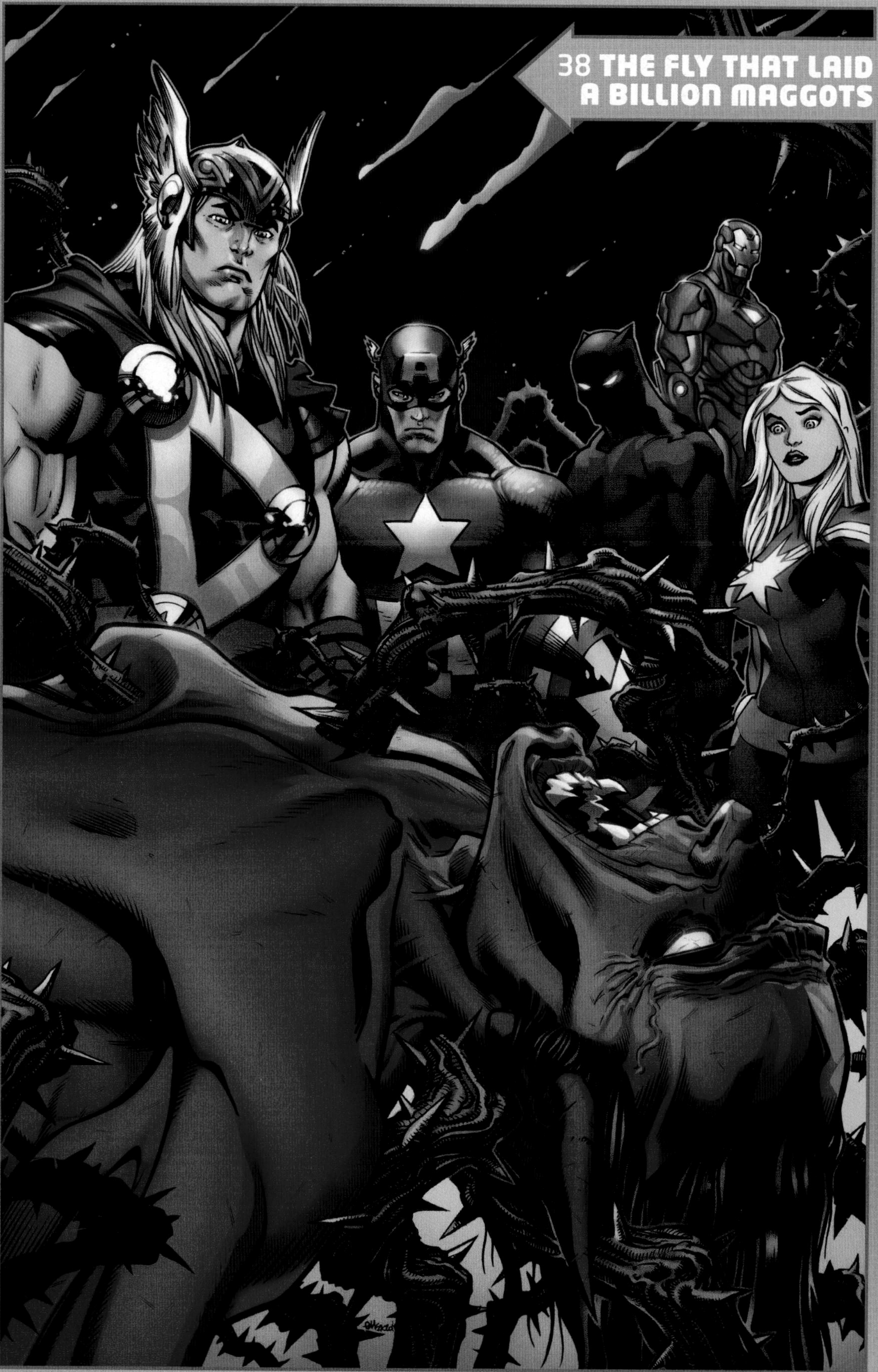

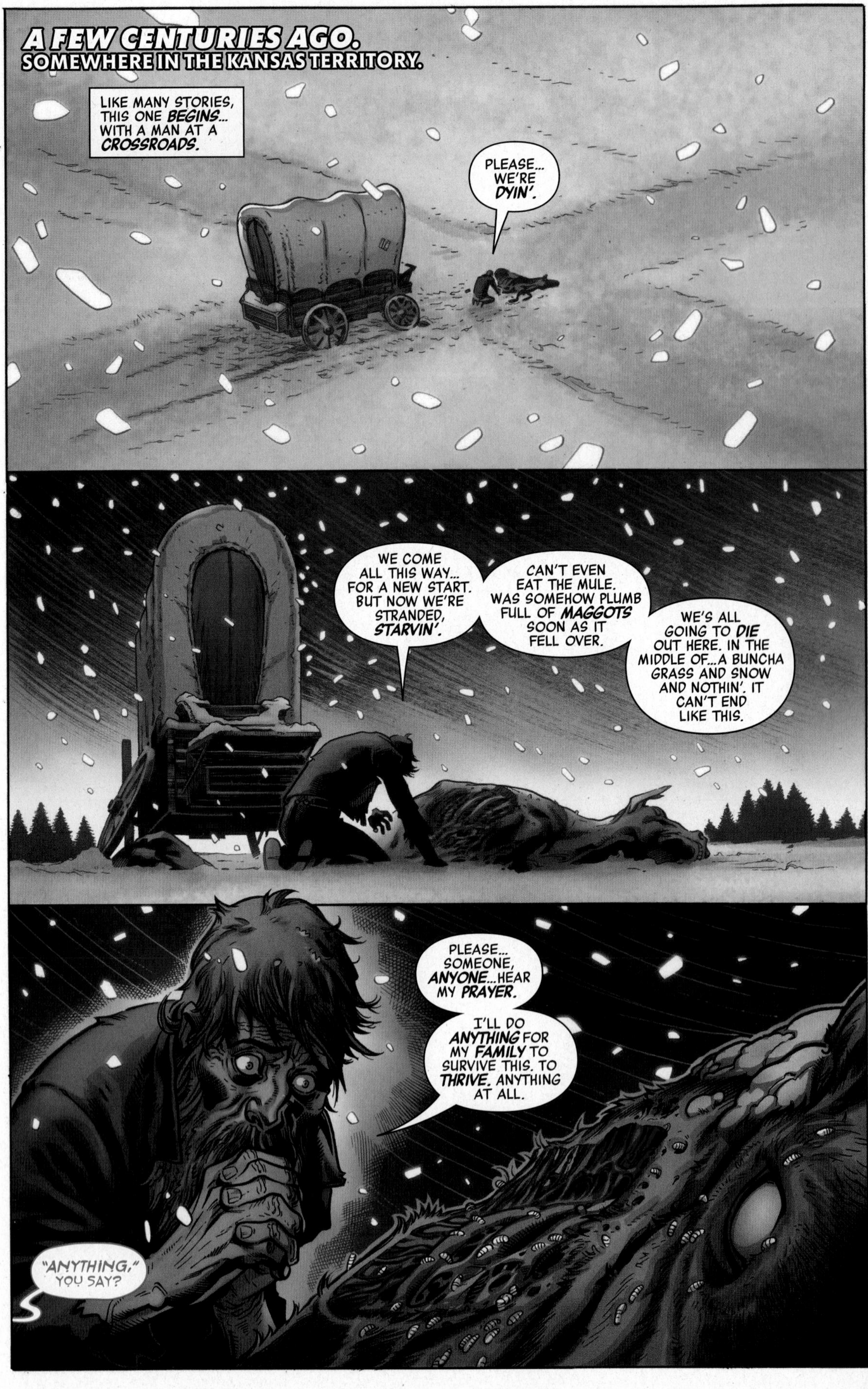
A FEW CENTURIES AGO.
SOMEWHERE IN THE KANSAS TERRITORY.
LIKE MANY STORIES, THIS ONE BEGINS... WITH A MAN AT A CROSSROADS.
PLEASE... WE'RE DYIN'.
WE COME ALL THIS WAY... FOR A NEW START. BUT NOW WE'RE STRANDED, STARVIN'.
CAN'T EVEN EAT THE MULE. WAS SOMEHOW PLUMB FULL OF MAGGOTS SOON AS IT FELL OVER.
WE'S ALL GOING TO DIE OUT HERE. IN THE MIDDLE OF...A BUNCHA GRASS AND SNOW AND NOTHIN'. IT CAN'T END LIKE THIS.
PLEASE... SOMEONE, ANYONE...HEAR MY PRAYER.
I'LL DO ANYTHING FOR MY FAMILY TO SURVIVE THIS. TO THRIVE. ANYTHING AT ALL.
"ANYTHING," YOU SAY?

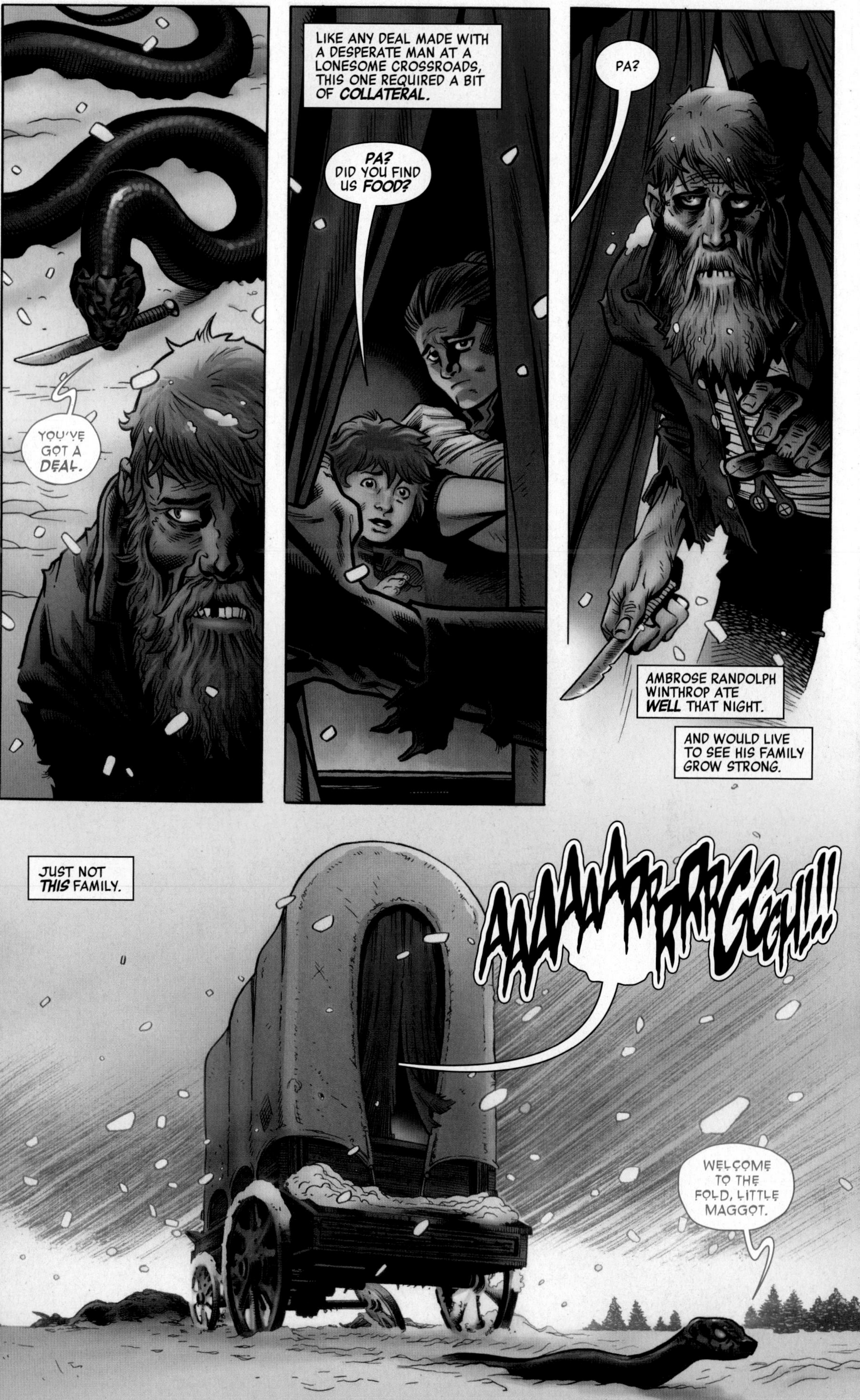
YOU'VE GOT A DEAL.
LIKE ANY DEAL MADE WITH A DESPERATE MAN AT A LONESOME CROSSROADS, THIS ONE REQUIRED A BIT OF COLLATERAL.
PA? DID YOU FIND US FOOD?
PA?
AMBROSE RANDOLPH WINTHROP ATE WELL THAT NIGHT.
AND WOULD LIVE TO SEE HIS FAMILY GROW STRONG.
JUST NOT THIS FAMILY.
AAAAARRRRRGGGH!!!!
WELCOME TO THE FOLD, LITTLE MAGGOT.

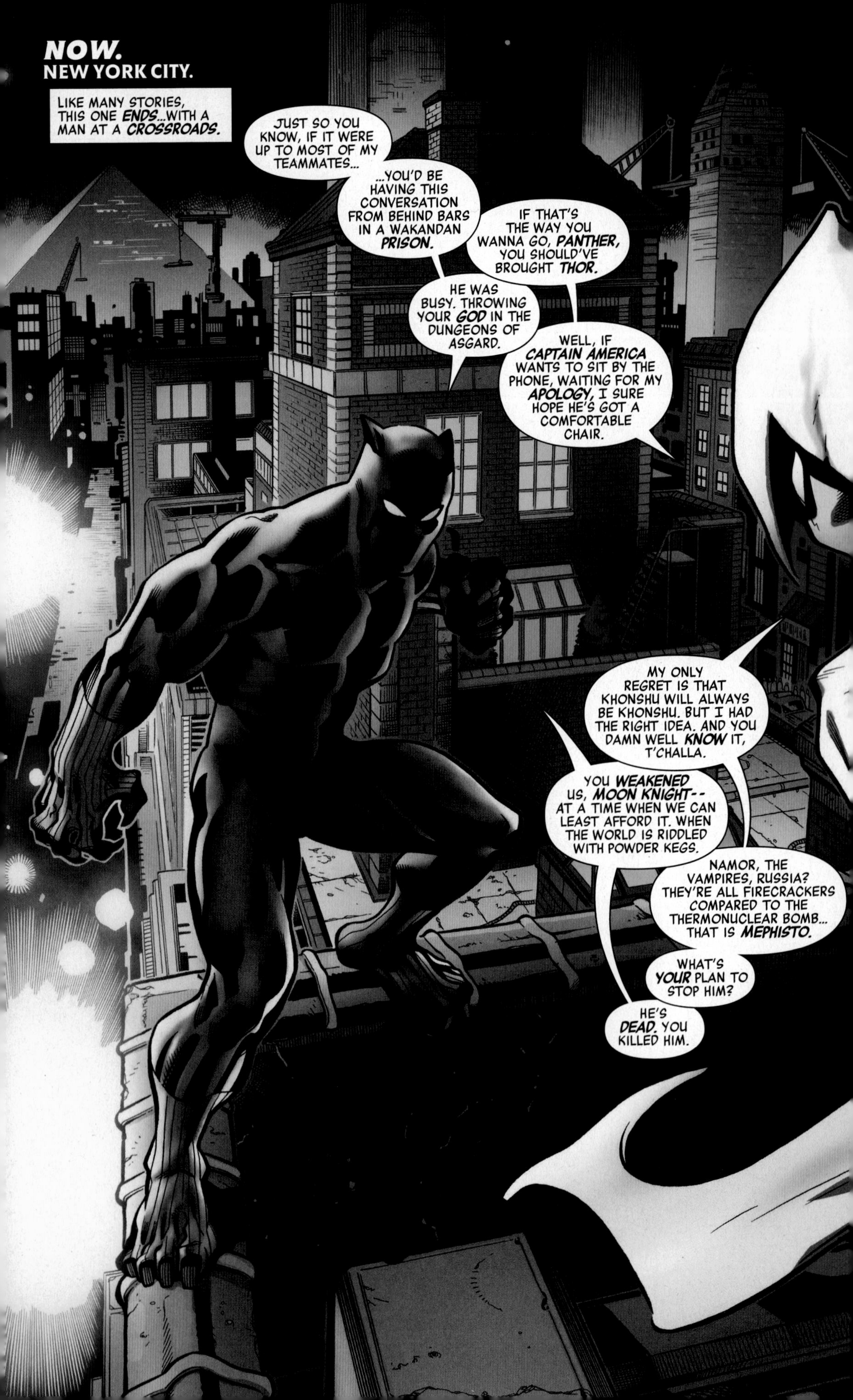
NOW.
NEW YORK CITY.
LIKE MANY STORIES, THIS ONE ENDS...WITH A MAN AT A CROSSROADS.
JUST SO YOU KNOW, IF IT WERE UP TO MOST OF MY TEAMMATES...
...YOU'D BE HAVING THIS CONVERSATION FROM BEHIND BARS IN A WAKANDAN PRISON.
IF THAT'S THE WAY YOU WANNA GO, PANTHER, YOU SHOULD'VE BROUGHT THOR.
HE WAS BUSY. THROWING YOUR GOD IN THE DUNGEONS OF ASGARD.
WELL, IF CAPTAIN AMERICA WANTS TO SIT BY THE PHONE, WAITING FOR MY APOLOGY, I SURE HOPE HE'S GOT A COMFORTABLE CHAIR.
MY ONLY REGRET IS THAT KHONSHU WILL ALWAYS BE KHONSHU. BUT I HAD THE RIGHT IDEA. AND YOU DAMN WELL KNOW IT, T'CHALLA.
YOU WEAKENED US, MOON KNIGHT-- AT A TIME WHEN WE CAN LEAST AFFORD IT. WHEN THE WORLD IS RIDDLED WITH POWDER KEGS.
NAMOR, THE VAMPIRES, RUSSIA? THEY'RE ALL FIRECRACKERS COMPARED TO THE THERMONUCLEAR BOMB... THAT IS MEPHISTO.
WHAT'S YOUR PLAN TO STOP HIM?
HE'S DEAD. YOU KILLED HIM.

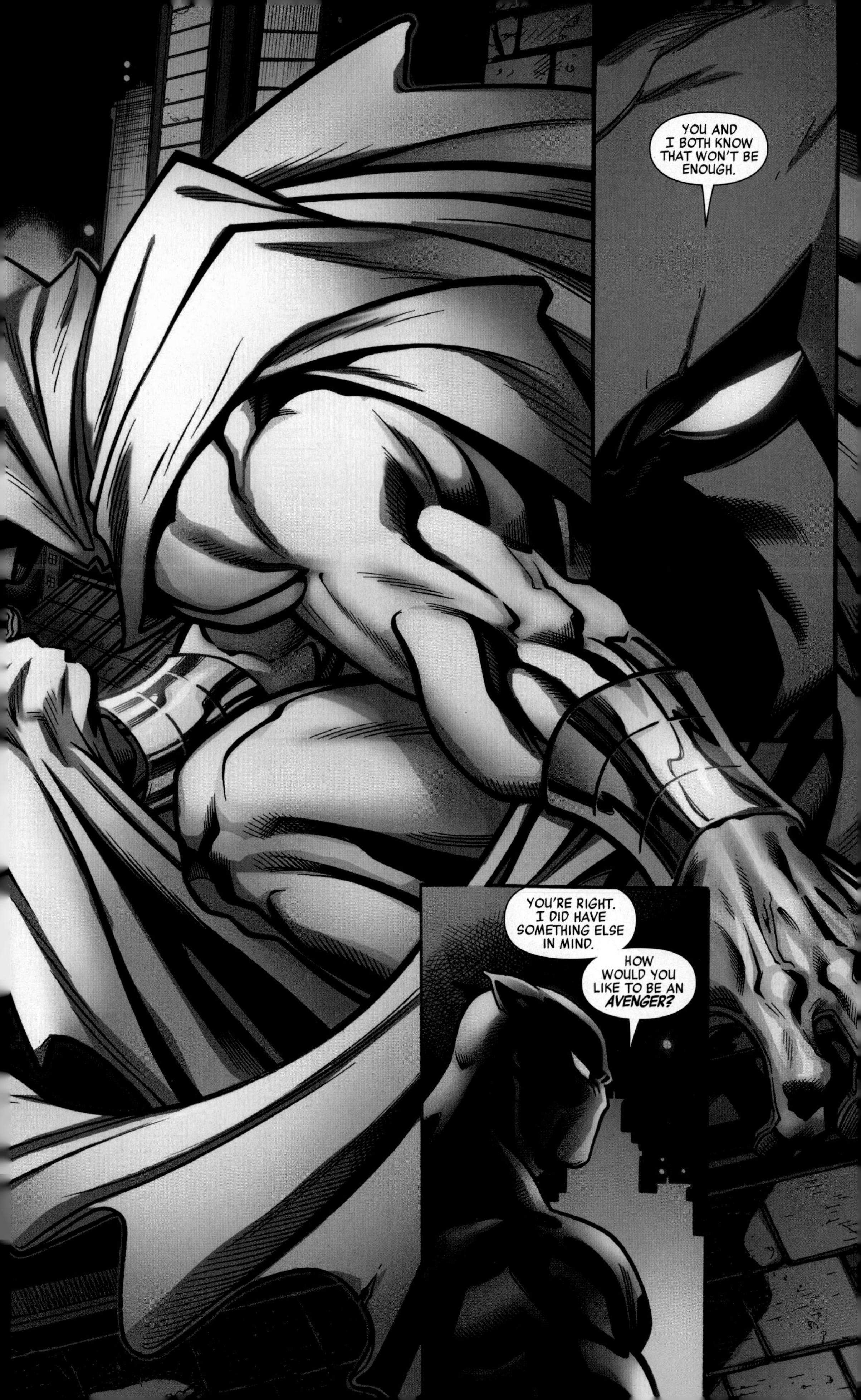

YOU AND I BOTH KNOW THAT WON'T BE ENOUGH.
YOU'RE RIGHT. I DID HAVE SOMETHING ELSE IN MIND.
HOW WOULD YOU LIKE TO BE AN *AVENGER?*

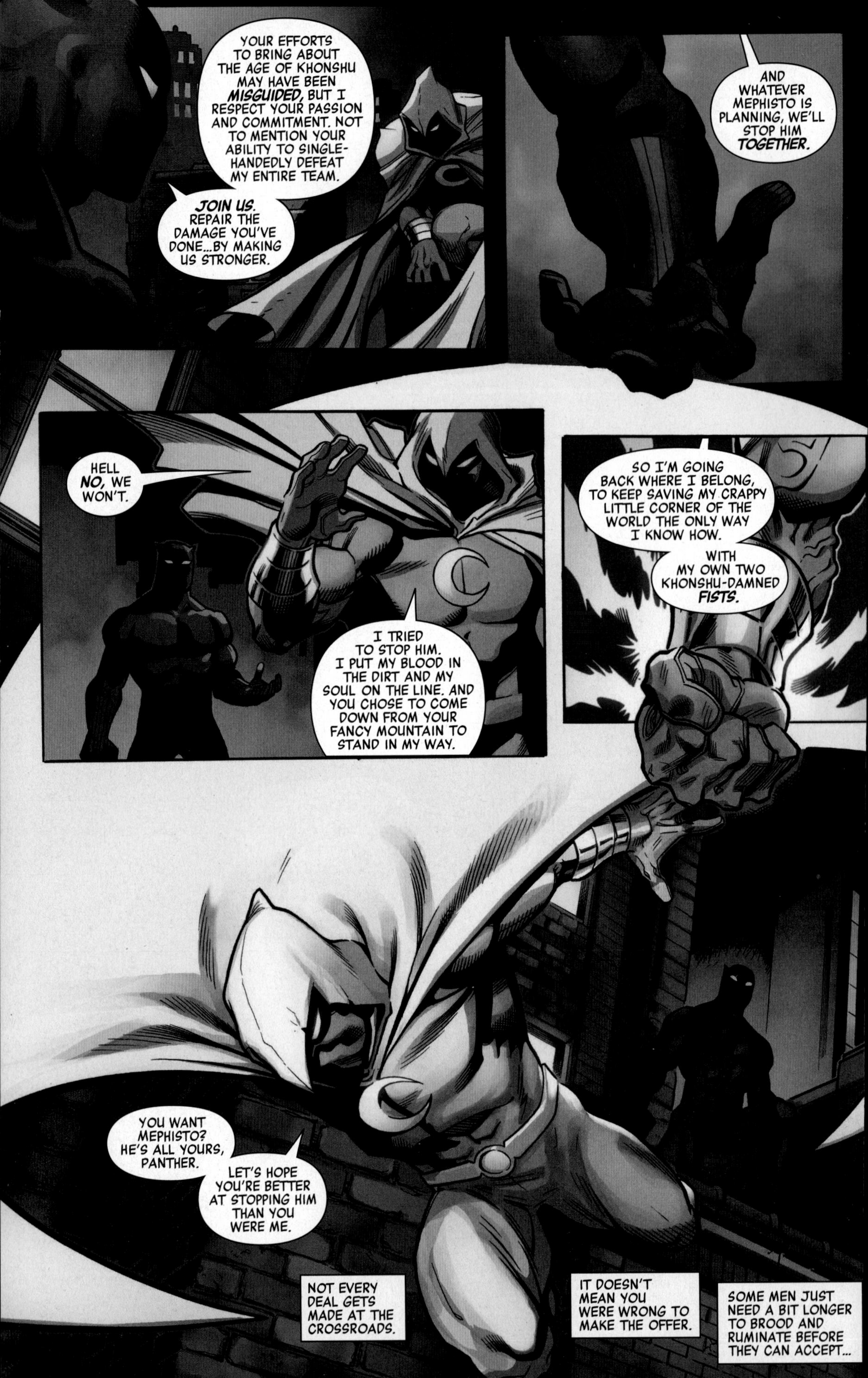
YOUR EFFORTS TO BRING ABOUT THE AGE OF KHONSHU MAY HAVE BEEN **MISGUIDED**, BUT I RESPECT YOUR PASSION AND COMMITMENT. NOT TO MENTION YOUR ABILITY TO SINGLE-HANDEDLY DEFEAT MY ENTIRE TEAM.
JOIN US. REPAIR THE DAMAGE YOU'VE DONE...BY MAKING US STRONGER.
AND WHATEVER MEPHISTO IS PLANNING, WE'LL STOP HIM **TOGETHER**.
HELL **NO**, WE WON'T.
I TRIED TO STOP HIM. I PUT MY BLOOD IN THE DIRT AND MY SOUL ON THE LINE. AND YOU CHOSE TO COME DOWN FROM YOUR FANCY MOUNTAIN TO STAND IN MY WAY.
SO I'M GOING BACK WHERE I BELONG, TO KEEP SAVING MY CRAPPY LITTLE CORNER OF THE WORLD THE ONLY WAY I KNOW HOW.
WITH MY OWN TWO KHONSHU-DAMNED **FISTS**.
YOU WANT MEPHISTO? HE'S ALL YOURS, PANTHER.
LET'S HOPE YOU'RE BETTER AT STOPPING HIM THAN YOU WERE ME.
NOT EVERY DEAL GETS MADE AT THE CROSSROADS.
IT DOESN'T MEAN YOU WERE WRONG TO MAKE THE OFFER.
SOME MEN JUST NEED A BIT LONGER TO BROOD AND RUMINATE BEFORE THEY CAN ACCEPT...

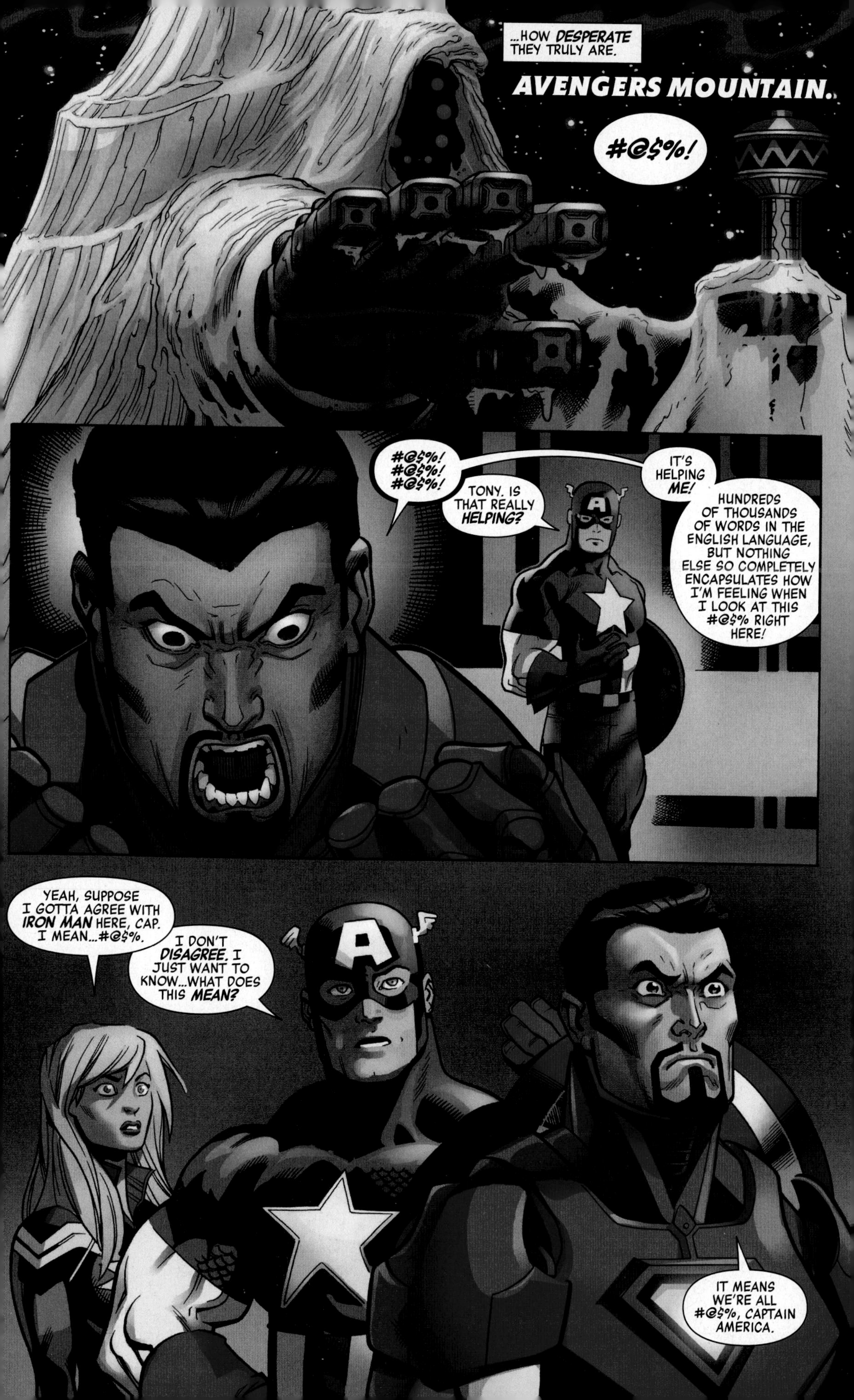
...HOW DESPERATE THEY TRULY ARE.
AVENGERS MOUNTAIN.
#@$%!
#@$%! #@$%! #@$%!
TONY. IS THAT REALLY HELPING?
IT'S HELPING ME!
HUNDREDS OF THOUSANDS OF WORDS IN THE ENGLISH LANGUAGE, BUT NOTHING ELSE SO COMPLETELY ENCAPSULATES HOW I'M FEELING WHEN I LOOK AT THIS #@$% RIGHT HERE!
YEAH, SUPPOSE I GOTTA AGREE WITH IRON MAN HERE, CAP. I MEAN...#@$%.
I DON'T DISAGREE. I JUST WANT TO KNOW...WHAT DOES THIS MEAN?
IT MEANS WE'RE ALL #@$%, CAPTAIN AMERICA.

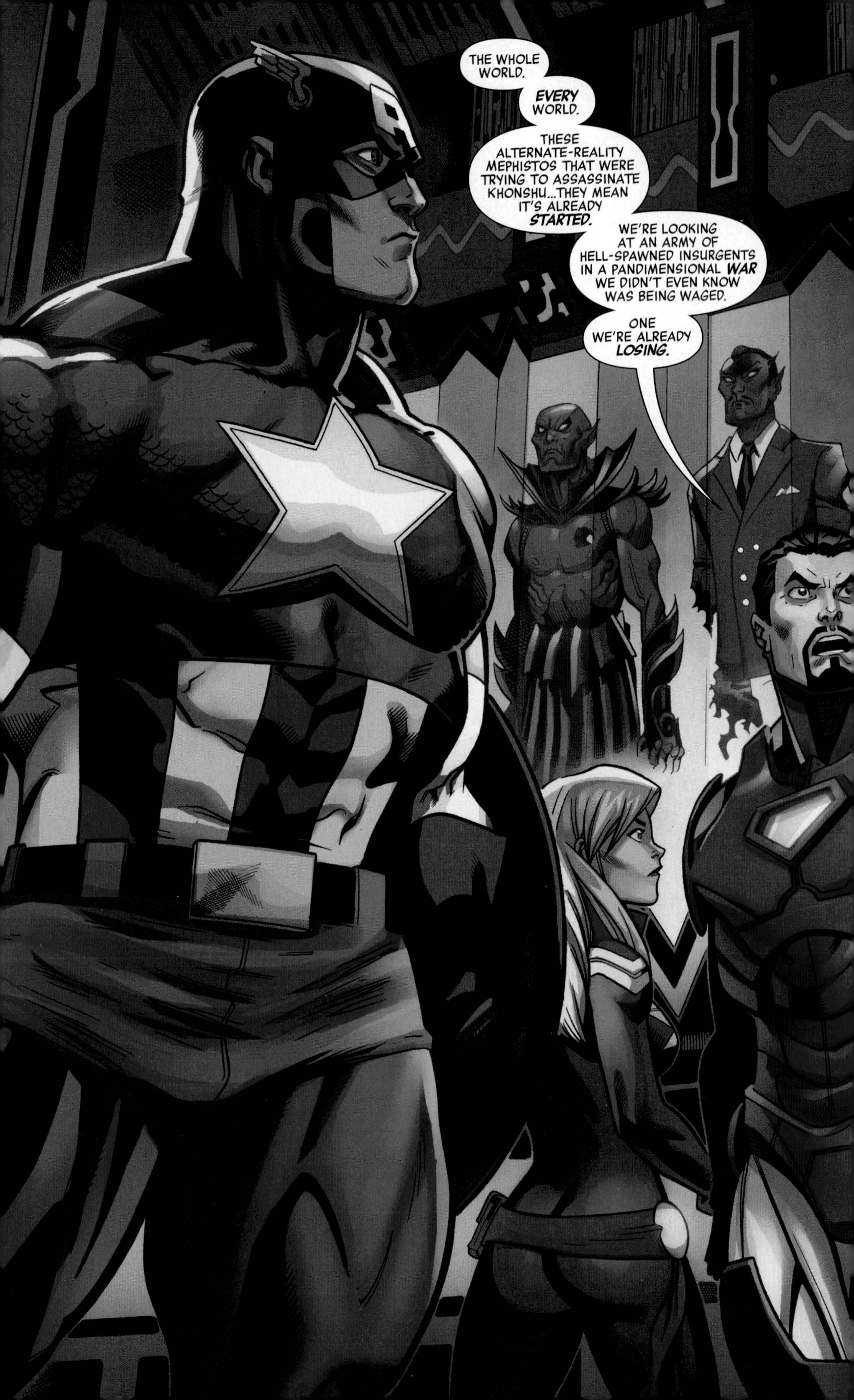
THE WHOLE WORLD.
EVERY WORLD.
THESE ALTERNATE-REALITY MEPHISTOS THAT WERE TRYING TO ASSASSINATE KHONSHU...THEY MEAN IT'S ALREADY STARTED.
WE'RE LOOKING AT AN ARMY OF HELL-SPAWNED INSURGENTS IN A PANDIMENSIONAL WAR WE DIDN'T EVEN KNOW WAS BEING WAGED.
ONE WE'RE ALREADY LOSING.

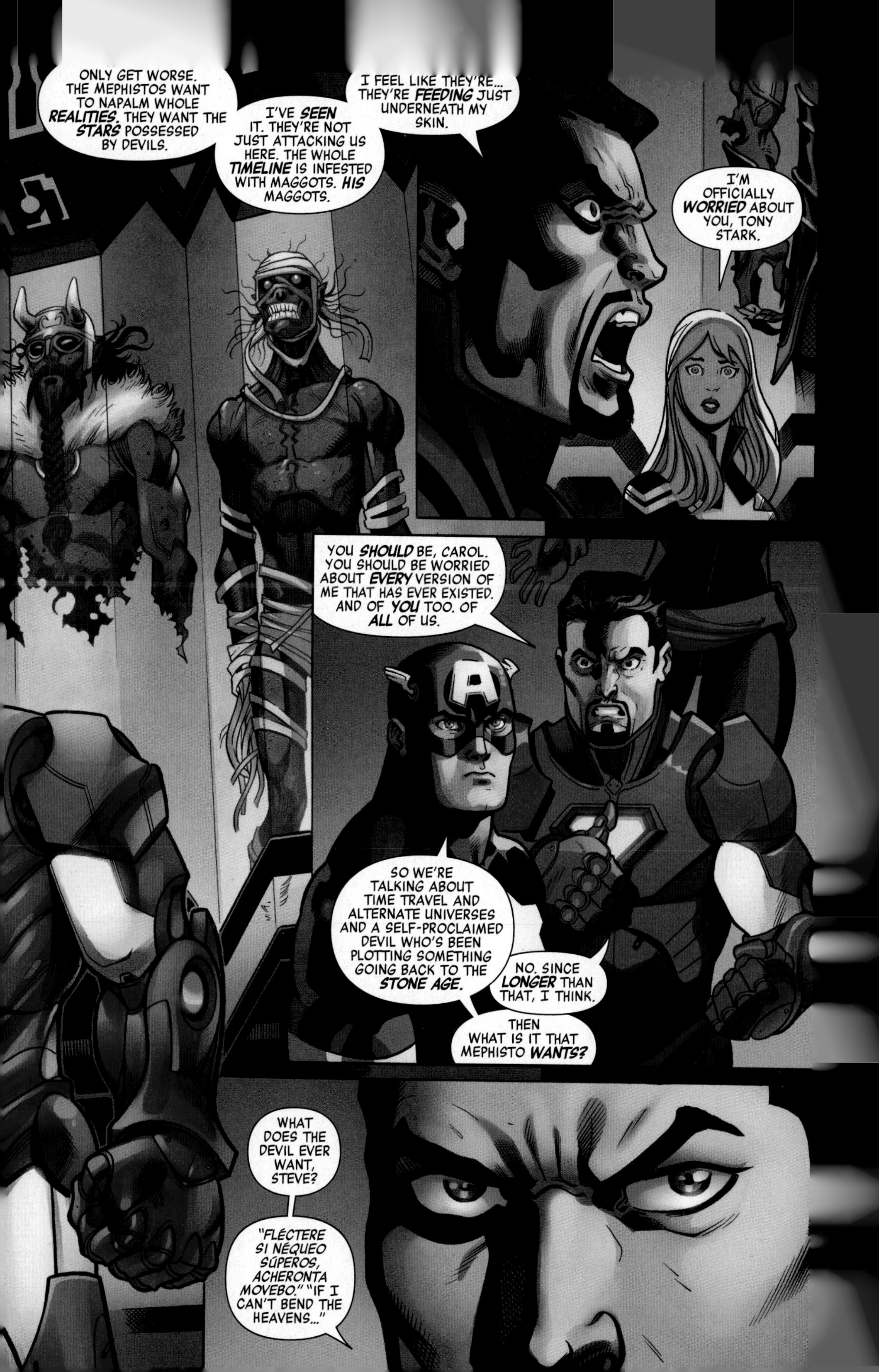
ONLY GET WORSE. THE MEPHISTOS WANT TO NAPALM WHOLE REALITIES. THEY WANT THE STARS POSSESSED BY DEVILS.
I'VE SEEN IT. THEY'RE NOT JUST ATTACKING US HERE. THE WHOLE TIMELINE IS INFESTED WITH MAGGOTS. HIS MAGGOTS.
I FEEL LIKE THEY'RE... THEY'RE FEEDING JUST UNDERNEATH MY SKIN.
I'M OFFICIALLY WORRIED ABOUT YOU, TONY STARK.
YOU SHOULD BE, CAROL. YOU SHOULD BE WORRIED ABOUT EVERY VERSION OF ME THAT HAS EVER EXISTED. AND OF YOU TOO. OF ALL OF US.
SO WE'RE TALKING ABOUT TIME TRAVEL AND ALTERNATE UNIVERSES AND A SELF-PROCLAIMED DEVIL WHO'S BEEN PLOTTING SOMETHING GOING BACK TO THE STONE AGE.
NO. SINCE LONGER THAN THAT, I THINK.
THEN WHAT IS IT THAT MEPHISTO WANTS?
WHAT DOES THE DEVIL EVER WANT, STEVE?
"FLÉCTERE SI NÉQUEO SÚPEROS, ACHERONTA MOVEBO." "IF I CAN'T BEND THE HEAVENS..."

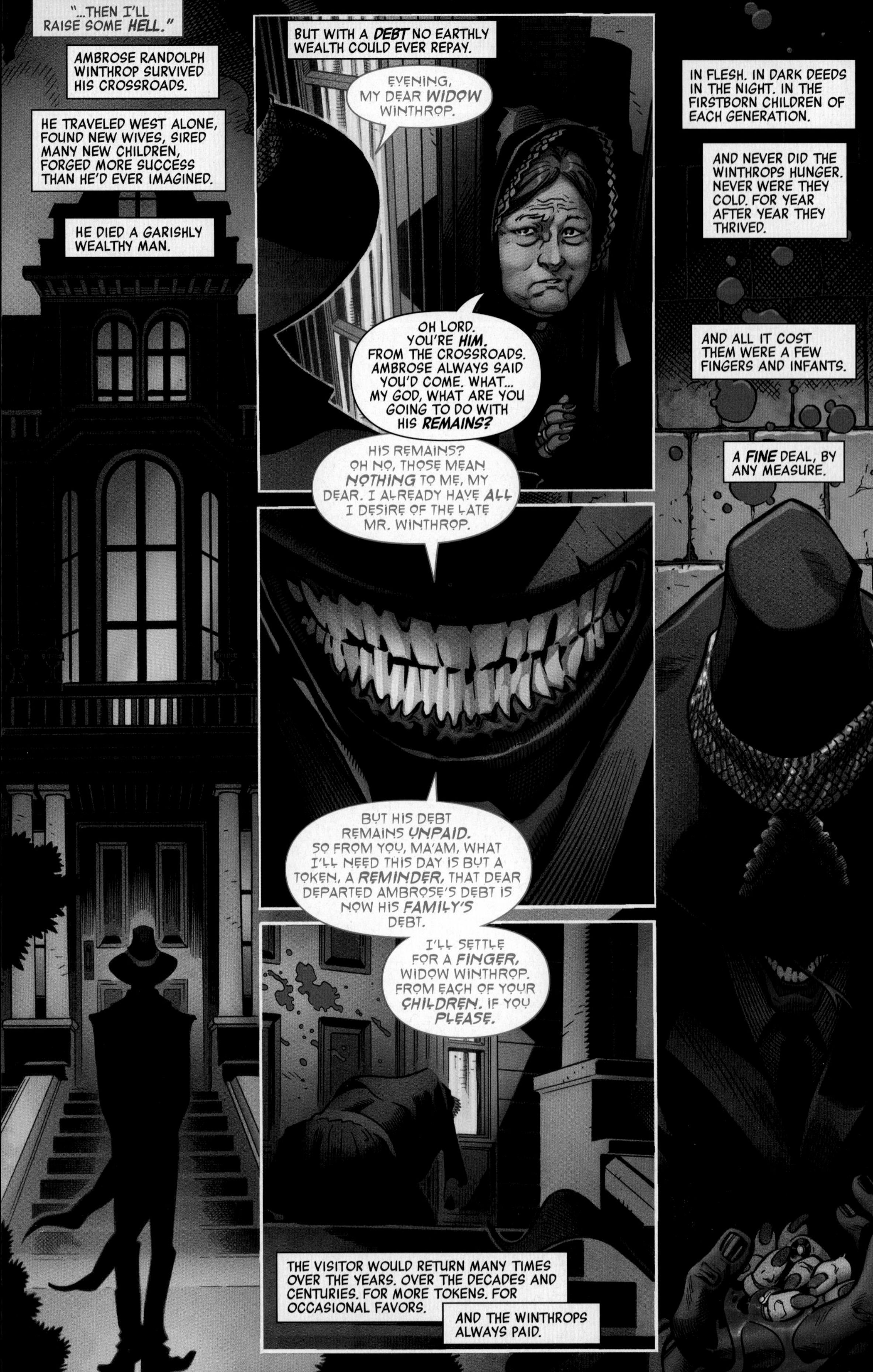
"...THEN I'LL RAISE SOME HELL."
AMBROSE RANDOLPH WINTHROP SURVIVED HIS CROSSROADS.
HE TRAVELED WEST ALONE, FOUND NEW WIVES, SIRED MANY NEW CHILDREN, FORGED MORE SUCCESS THAN HE'D EVER IMAGINED.
HE DIED A GARISHLY WEALTHY MAN.
BUT WITH A DEBT NO EARTHLY WEALTH COULD EVER REPAY.
EVENING, MY DEAR WIDOW WINTHROP.
OH LORD. YOU'RE HIM. FROM THE CROSSROADS. AMBROSE ALWAYS SAID YOU'D COME. WHAT... MY GOD, WHAT ARE YOU GOING TO DO WITH HIS REMAINS?
HIS REMAINS? OH NO, THOSE MEAN NOTHING TO ME, MY DEAR. I ALREADY HAVE ALL I DESIRE OF THE LATE MR. WINTHROP.
BUT HIS DEBT REMAINS UNPAID. SO FROM YOU, MA'AM, WHAT I'LL NEED THIS DAY IS BUT A TOKEN, A REMINDER, THAT DEAR DEPARTED AMBROSE'S DEBT IS NOW HIS FAMILY'S DEBT.
I'LL SETTLE FOR A FINGER, WIDOW WINTHROP. FROM EACH OF YOUR CHILDREN, IF YOU PLEASE.
THE VISITOR WOULD RETURN MANY TIMES OVER THE YEARS. OVER THE DECADES AND CENTURIES. FOR MORE TOKENS. FOR OCCASIONAL FAVORS.
AND THE WINTHROPS ALWAYS PAID.
IN FLESH. IN DARK DEEDS IN THE NIGHT. IN THE FIRSTBORN CHILDREN OF EACH GENERATION.
AND NEVER DID THE WINTHROPS HUNGER. NEVER WERE THEY COLD. FOR YEAR AFTER YEAR THEY THRIVED.
AND ALL IT COST THEM WERE A FEW FINGERS AND INFANTS.
A FINE DEAL, BY ANY MEASURE.

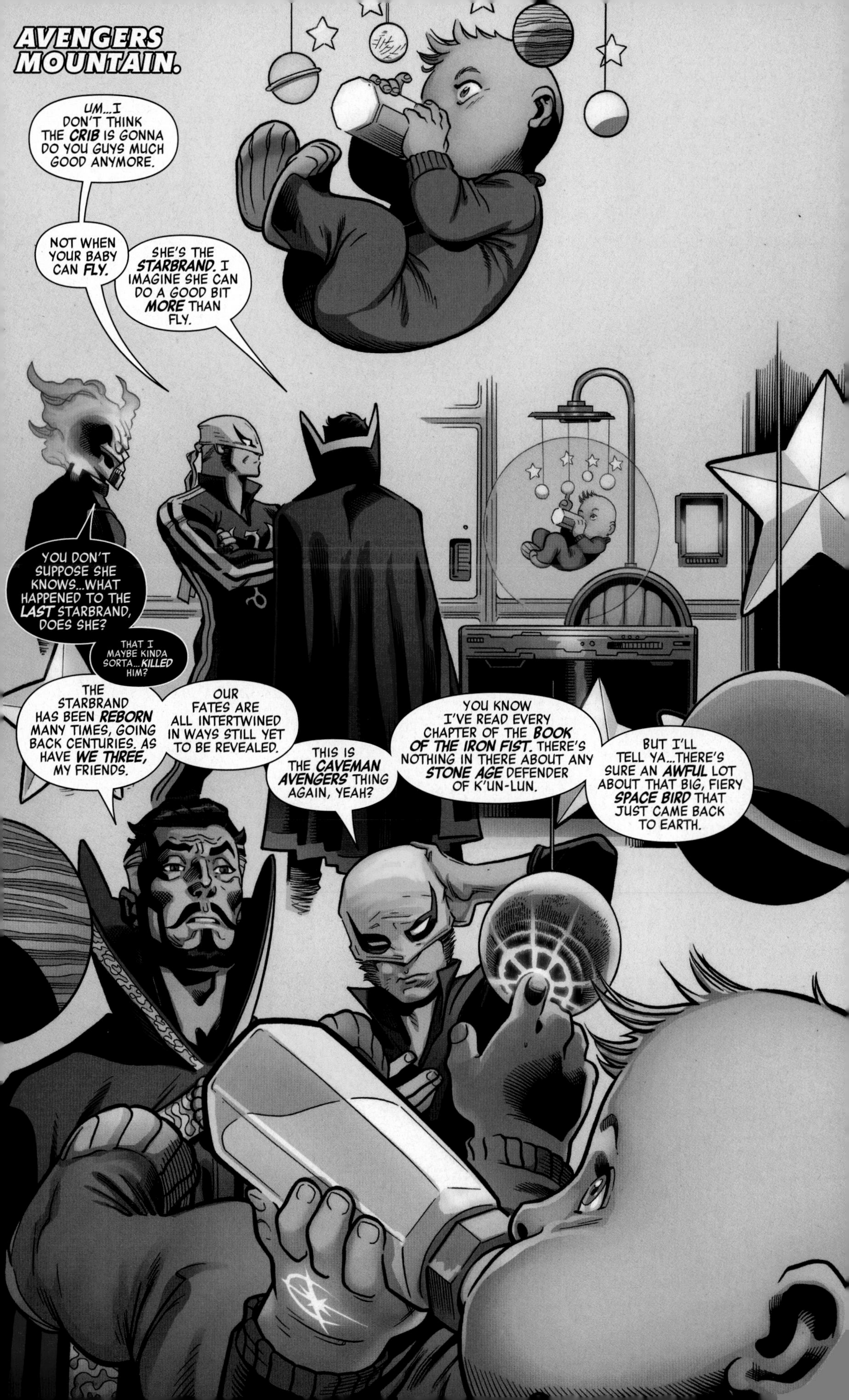
AVENGERS MOUNTAIN.
UM...I DON'T THINK THE CRIB IS GONNA DO YOU GUYS MUCH GOOD ANYMORE.
NOT WHEN YOUR BABY CAN FLY.
SHE'S THE STARBRAND. I IMAGINE SHE CAN DO A GOOD BIT MORE THAN FLY.
YOU DON'T SUPPOSE SHE KNOWS...WHAT HAPPENED TO THE LAST STARBRAND, DOES SHE?
THAT I MAYBE KINDA SORTA...KILLED HIM?
THE STARBRAND HAS BEEN REBORN MANY TIMES, GOING BACK CENTURIES. AS HAVE WE THREE, MY FRIENDS.
OUR FATES ARE ALL INTERTWINED IN WAYS STILL YET TO BE REVEALED.
THIS IS THE CAVEMAN AVENGERS THING AGAIN, YEAH?
YOU KNOW I'VE READ EVERY CHAPTER OF THE BOOK OF THE IRON FIST. THERE'S NOTHING IN THERE ABOUT ANY STONE AGE DEFENDER OF K'UN-LUN.
BUT I'LL TELL YA...THERE'S SURE AN AWFUL LOT ABOUT THAT BIG, FIERY SPACE BIRD THAT JUST CAME BACK TO EARTH.

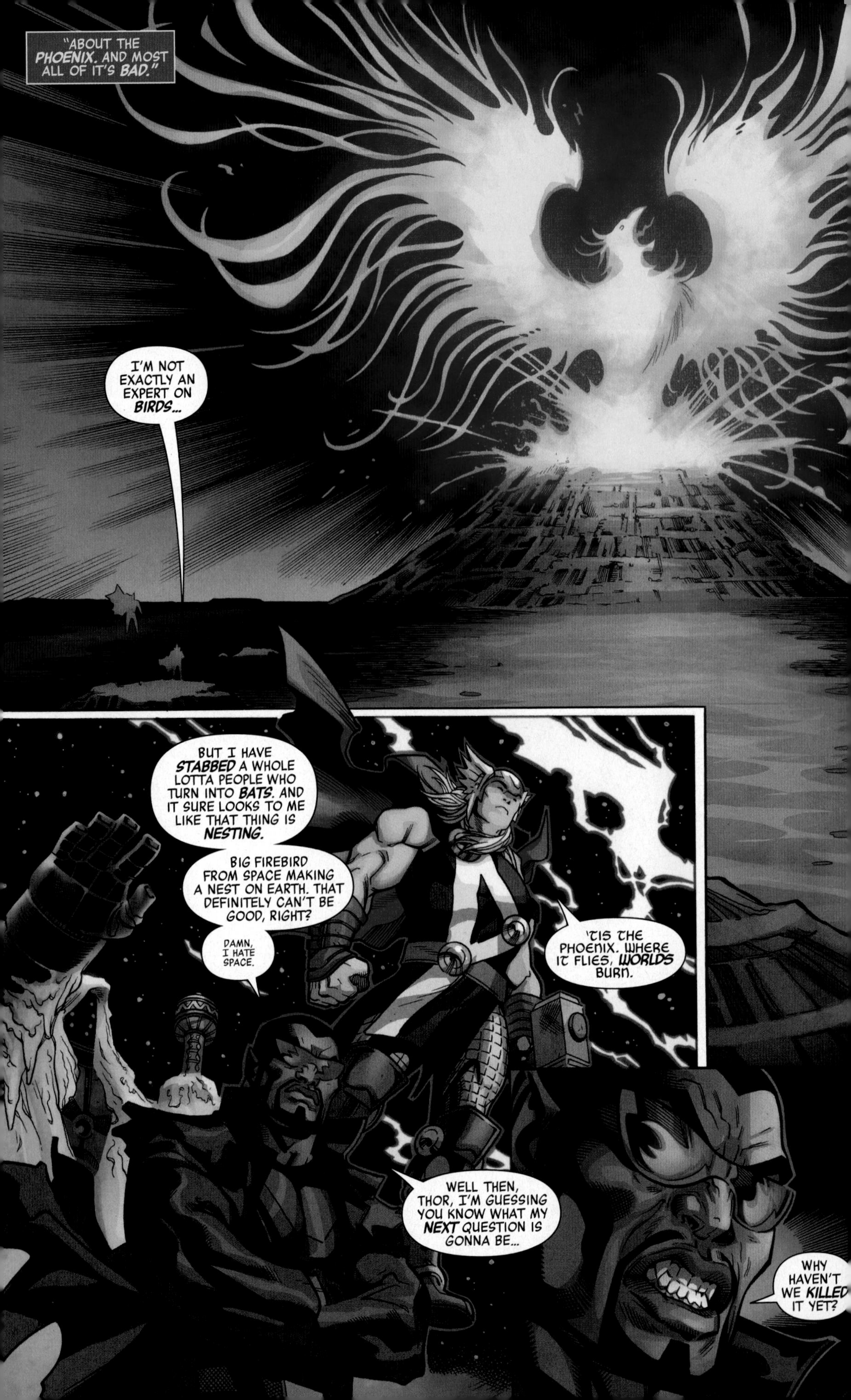
"ABOUT THE PHOENIX. AND MOST ALL OF IT'S BAD."
I'M NOT EXACTLY AN EXPERT ON BIRDS...
BUT I HAVE STABBED A WHOLE LOTTA PEOPLE WHO TURN INTO BATS. AND IT SURE LOOKS TO ME LIKE THAT THING IS NESTING.
BIG FIREBIRD FROM SPACE MAKING A NEST ON EARTH. THAT DEFINITELY CAN'T BE GOOD, RIGHT?
DAMN, I HATE SPACE.
'TIS THE PHOENIX. WHERE IT FLIES, WORLDS BURN.
WELL THEN, THOR, I'M GUESSING YOU KNOW WHAT MY NEXT QUESTION IS GONNA BE...
WHY HAVEN'T WE KILLED IT YET?

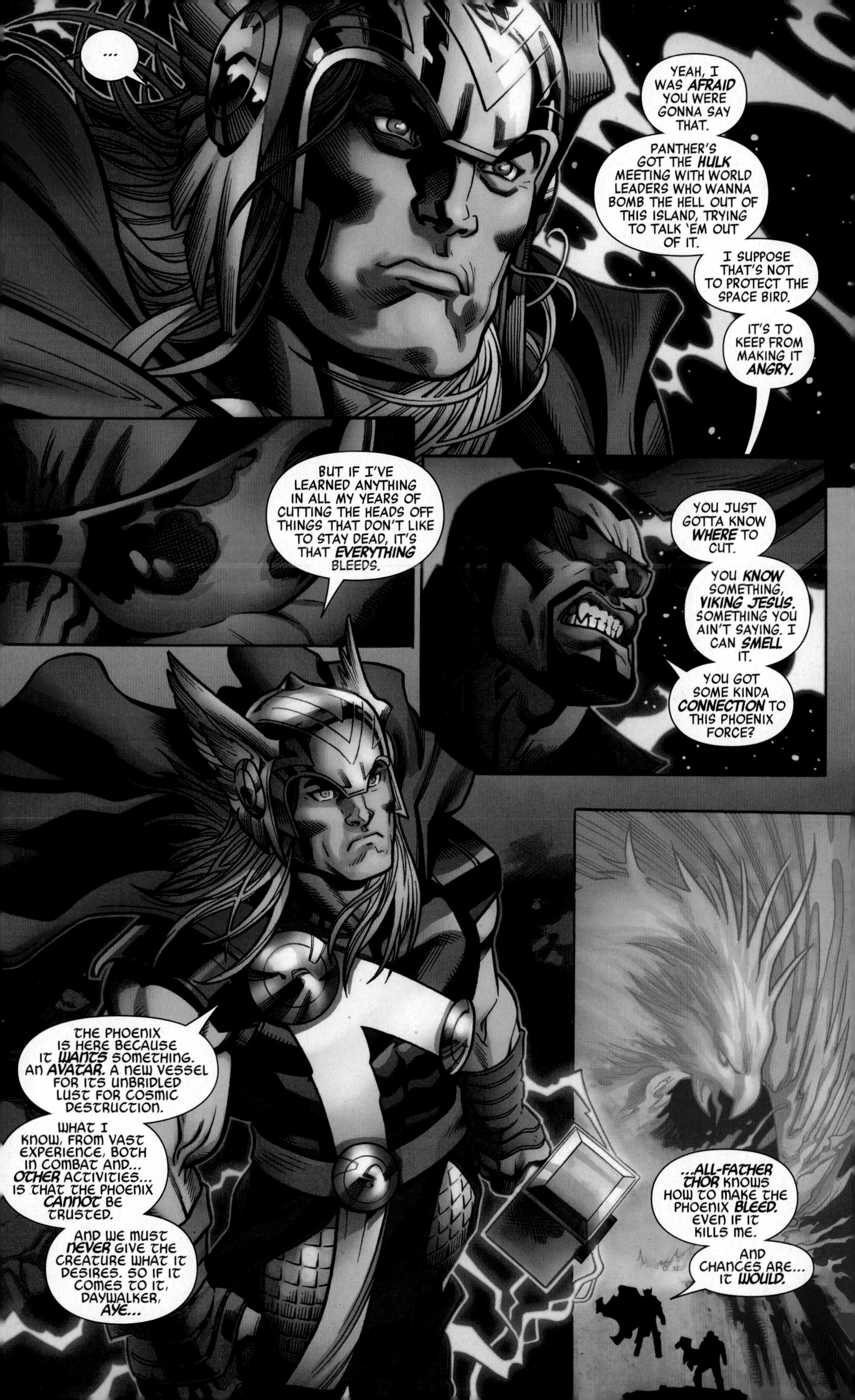
...
YEAH, I WAS AFRAID YOU WERE GONNA SAY THAT.
PANTHER'S GOT THE HULK MEETING WITH WORLD LEADERS WHO WANNA BOMB THE HELL OUT OF THIS ISLAND, TRYING TO TALK 'EM OUT OF IT.
I SUPPOSE THAT'S NOT TO PROTECT THE SPACE BIRD.
IT'S TO KEEP FROM MAKING IT ANGRY.
BUT IF I'VE LEARNED ANYTHING IN ALL MY YEARS OF CUTTING THE HEADS OFF THINGS THAT DON'T LIKE TO STAY DEAD, IT'S THAT EVERYTHING BLEEDS.
YOU JUST GOTTA KNOW WHERE TO CUT.
YOU KNOW SOMETHING, VIKING JESUS. SOMETHING YOU AIN'T SAYING. I CAN SMELL IT.
YOU GOT SOME KINDA CONNECTION TO THIS PHOENIX FORCE?
THE PHOENIX IS HERE BECAUSE IT WANTS SOMETHING. AN AVATAR. A NEW VESSEL FOR ITS UNBRIDLED LUST FOR COSMIC DESTRUCTION.
WHAT I KNOW, FROM VAST EXPERIENCE, BOTH IN COMBAT AND... OTHER ACTIVITIES... IS THAT THE PHOENIX CANNOT BE TRUSTED.
AND WE MUST NEVER GIVE THE CREATURE WHAT IT DESIRES. SO IF IT COMES TO IT, DAYWALKER, AYE...
...ALL-FATHER THOR KNOWS HOW TO MAKE THE PHOENIX BLEED. EVEN IF IT KILLS ME.
AND CHANCES ARE... IT WOULD.

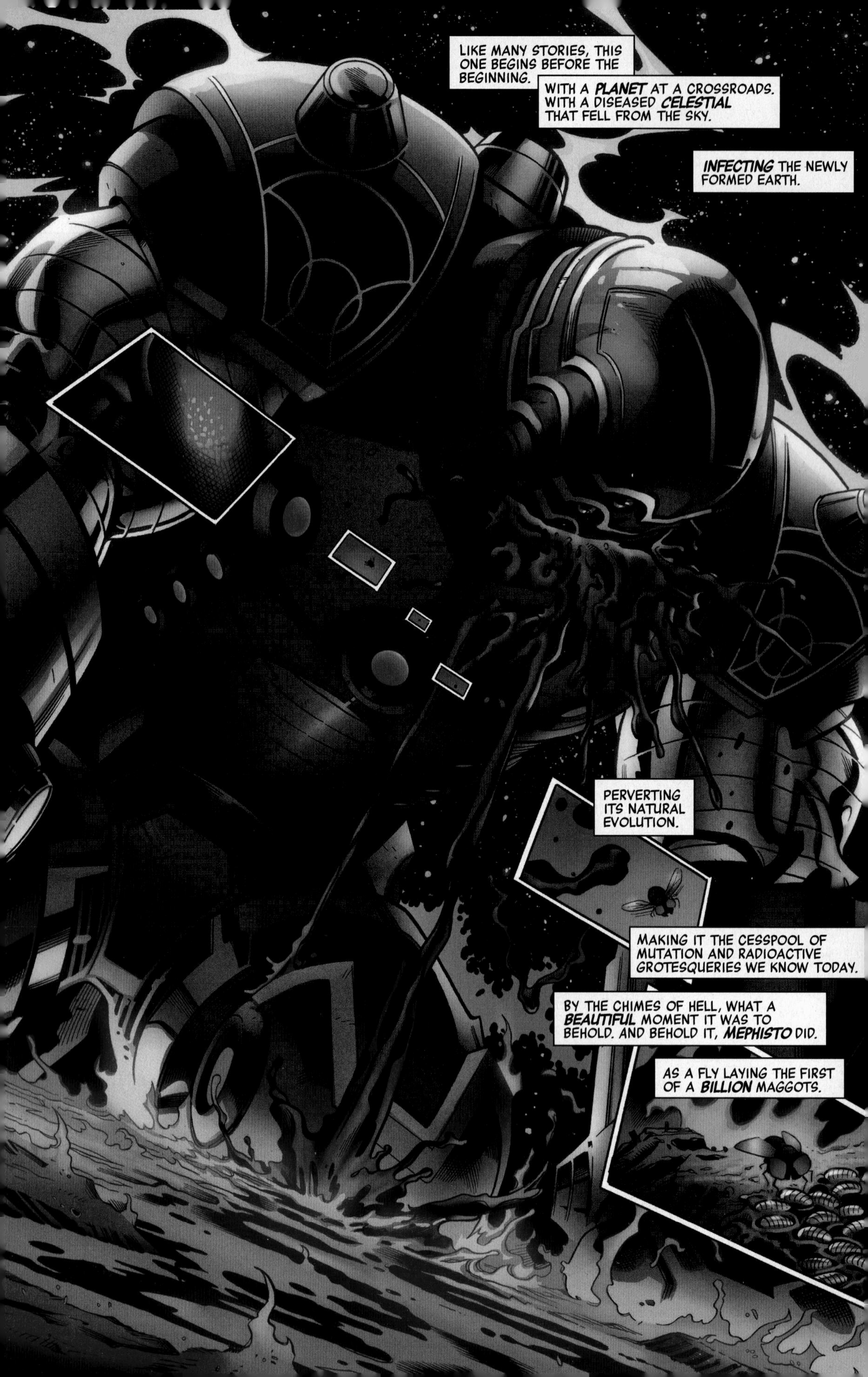
LIKE MANY STORIES, THIS ONE BEGINS BEFORE THE BEGINNING.
WITH A PLANET AT A CROSSROADS. WITH A DISEASED CELESTIAL THAT FELL FROM THE SKY.
INFECTING THE NEWLY FORMED EARTH.
PERVERTING ITS NATURAL EVOLUTION.
MAKING IT THE CESSPOOL OF MUTATION AND RADIOACTIVE GROTESQUERIES WE KNOW TODAY.
BY THE CHIMES OF HELL, WHAT A BEAUTIFUL MOMENT IT WAS TO BEHOLD. AND BEHOLD IT, MEPHISTO DID.
AS A FLY LAYING THE FIRST OF A BILLION MAGGOTS.

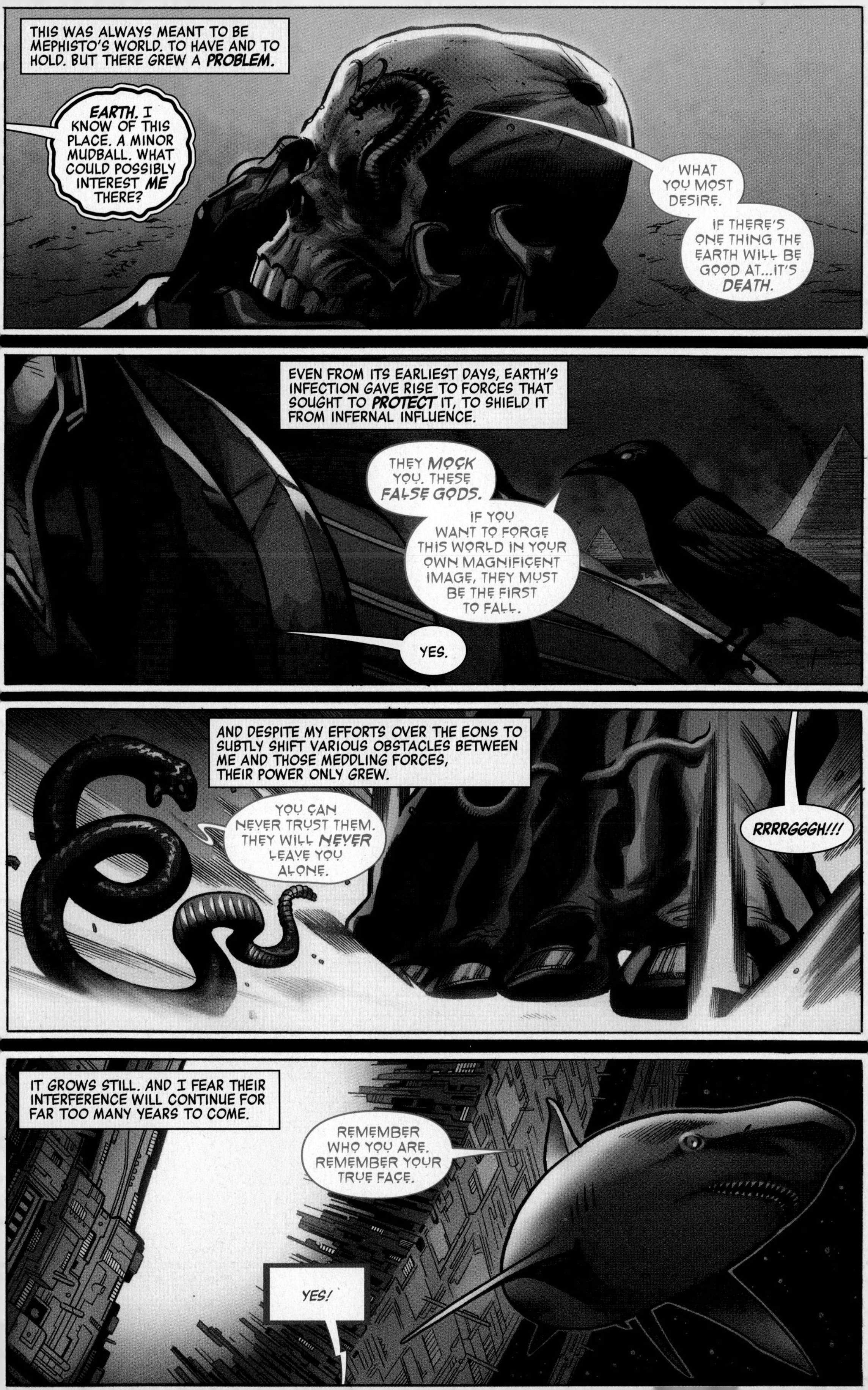
THIS WAS ALWAYS MEANT TO BE MEPHISTO'S WORLD. TO HAVE AND TO HOLD. BUT THERE GREW A *PROBLEM.*
EARTH. I KNOW OF THIS PLACE. A MINOR MUDBALL. WHAT COULD POSSIBLY INTEREST *ME* THERE?
WHAT YOU MOST DESIRE.
IF THERE'S ONE THING THE EARTH WILL BE GOOD AT...IT'S *DEATH.*
EVEN FROM ITS EARLIEST DAYS, EARTH'S INFECTION GAVE RISE TO FORCES THAT SOUGHT TO *PROTECT* IT, TO SHIELD IT FROM INFERNAL INFLUENCE.
THEY *MOCK* YOU. THESE *FALSE GODS.*
IF YOU WANT TO FORGE THIS WORLD IN YOUR OWN MAGNIFICENT IMAGE, THEY MUST BE THE FIRST TO FALL.
YES.
AND DESPITE MY EFFORTS OVER THE EONS TO SUBTLY SHIFT VARIOUS OBSTACLES BETWEEN ME AND THOSE MEDDLING FORCES, THEIR POWER ONLY GREW.
YOU CAN NEVER TRUST THEM. THEY WILL *NEVER* LEAVE YOU ALONE.
RRRRGGGH!!!
IT GROWS STILL. AND I FEAR THEIR INTERFERENCE WILL CONTINUE FOR FAR TOO MANY YEARS TO COME.
REMEMBER WHO YOU ARE. REMEMBER YOUR TRUE FACE.
YES!

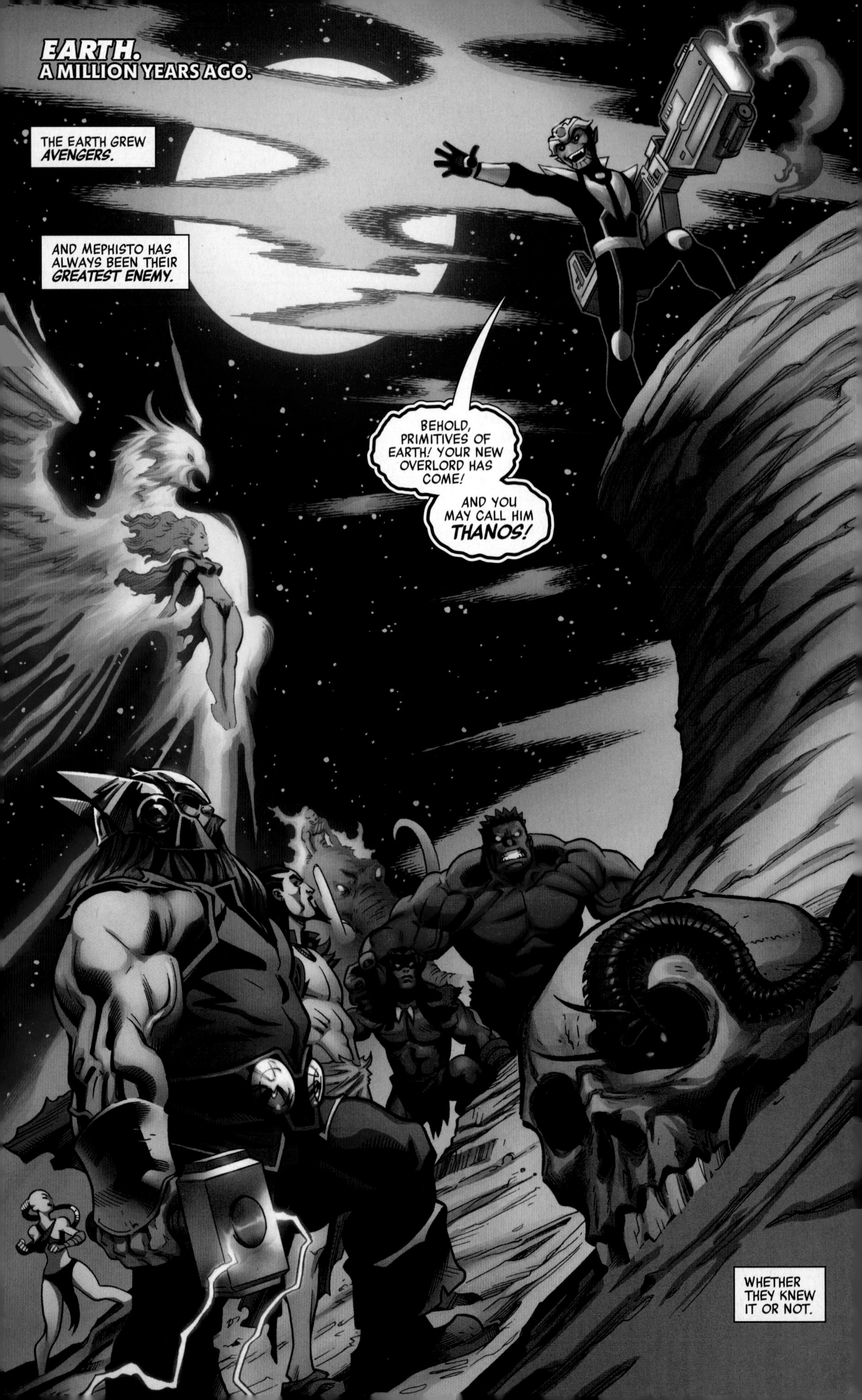
EARTH.
A MILLION YEARS AGO.
THE EARTH GREW AVENGERS.
AND MEPHISTO HAS ALWAYS BEEN THEIR GREATEST ENEMY.
BEHOLD, PRIMITIVES OF EARTH! YOUR NEW OVERLORD HAS COME!
AND YOU MAY CALL HIM THANOS!
WHETHER THEY KNEW IT OR NOT.

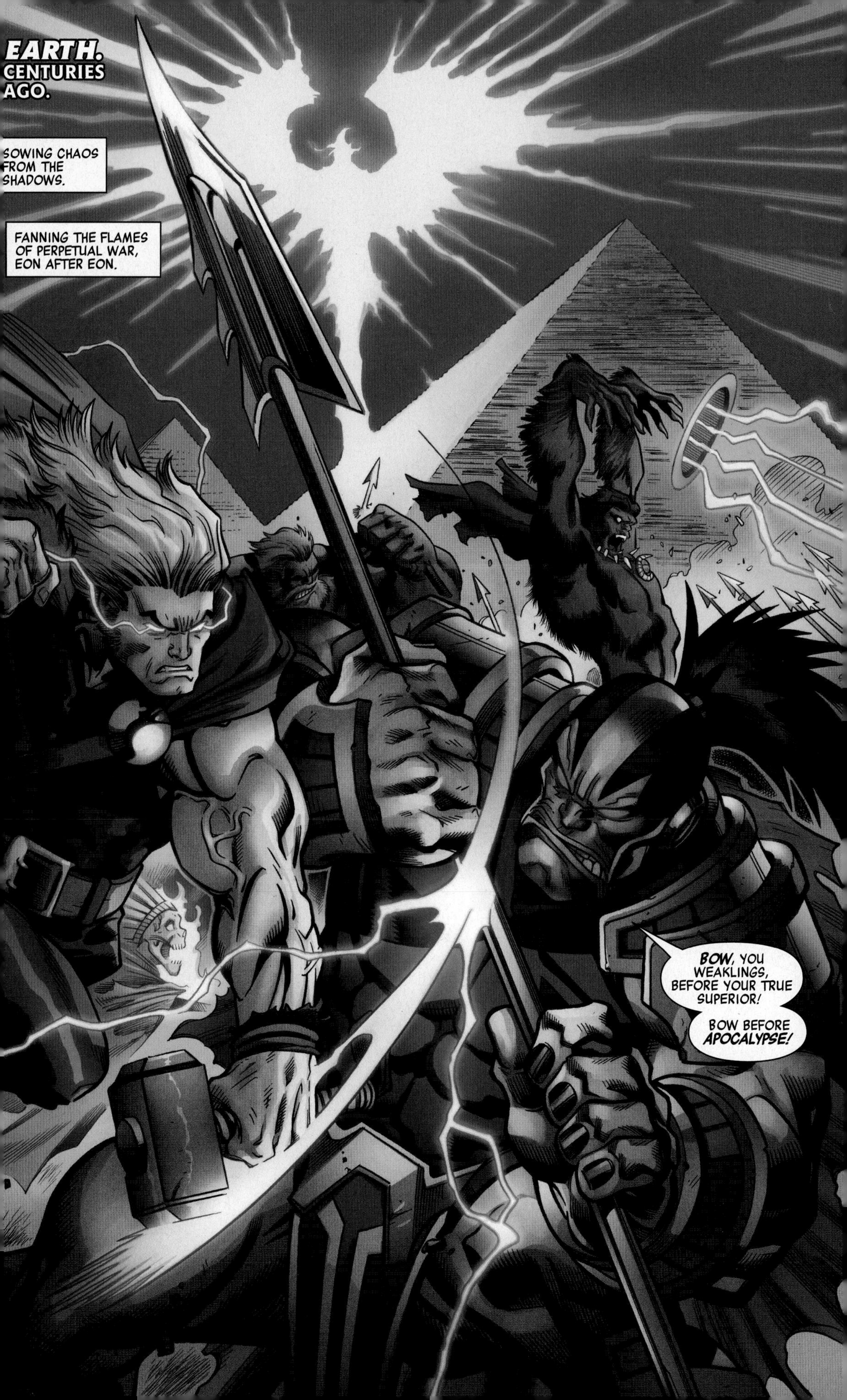
EARTH. CENTURIES AGO.
SOWING CHAOS FROM THE SHADOWS.
FANNING THE FLAMES OF PERPETUAL WAR, EON AFTER EON.
BOW, YOU WEAKLINGS, BEFORE YOUR TRUE SUPERIOR!
BOW BEFORE APOCALYPSE!

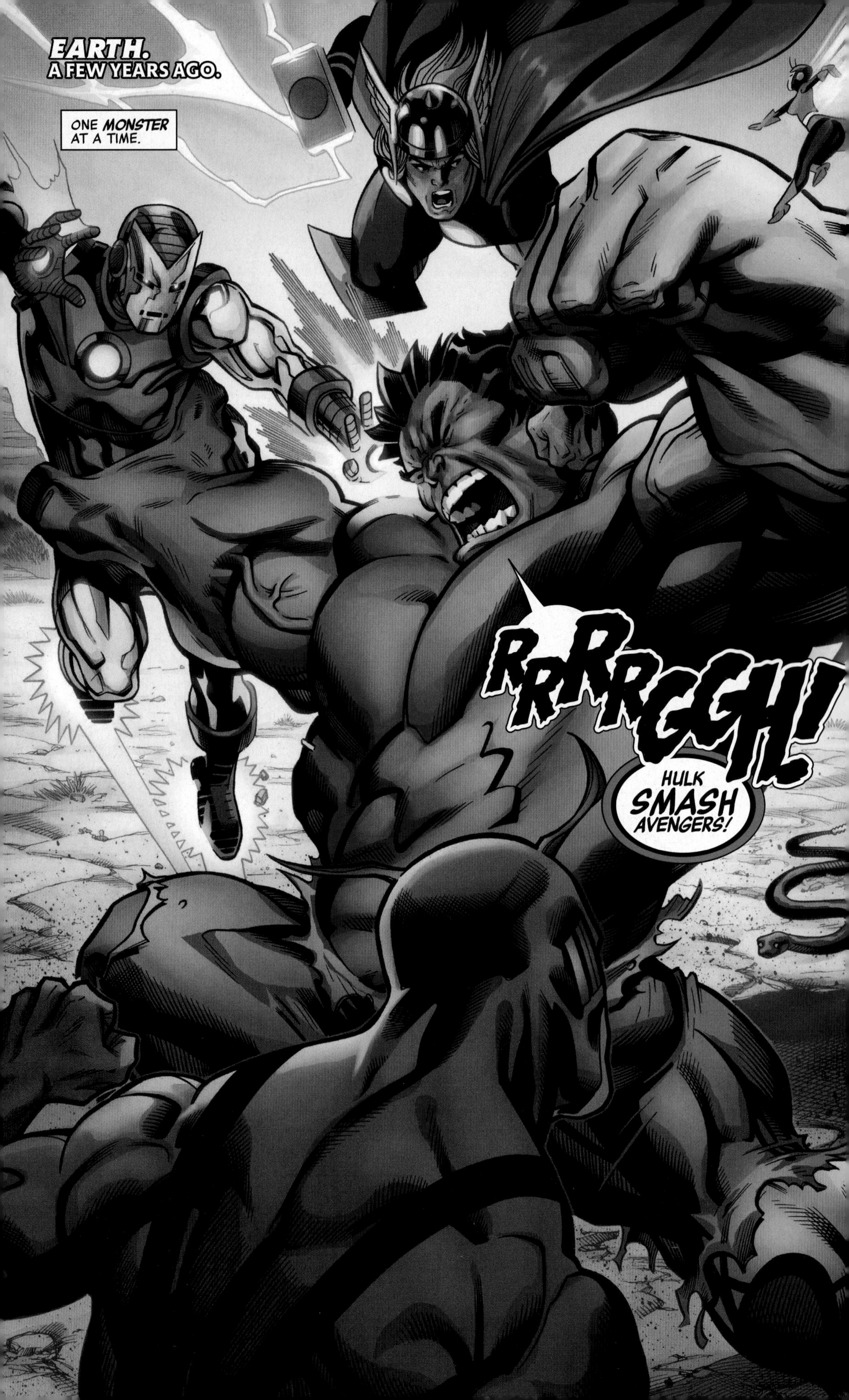
EARTH.
A FEW YEARS AGO.
ONE MONSTER AT A TIME.
RRRRGGH!
HULK SMASH AVENGERS!

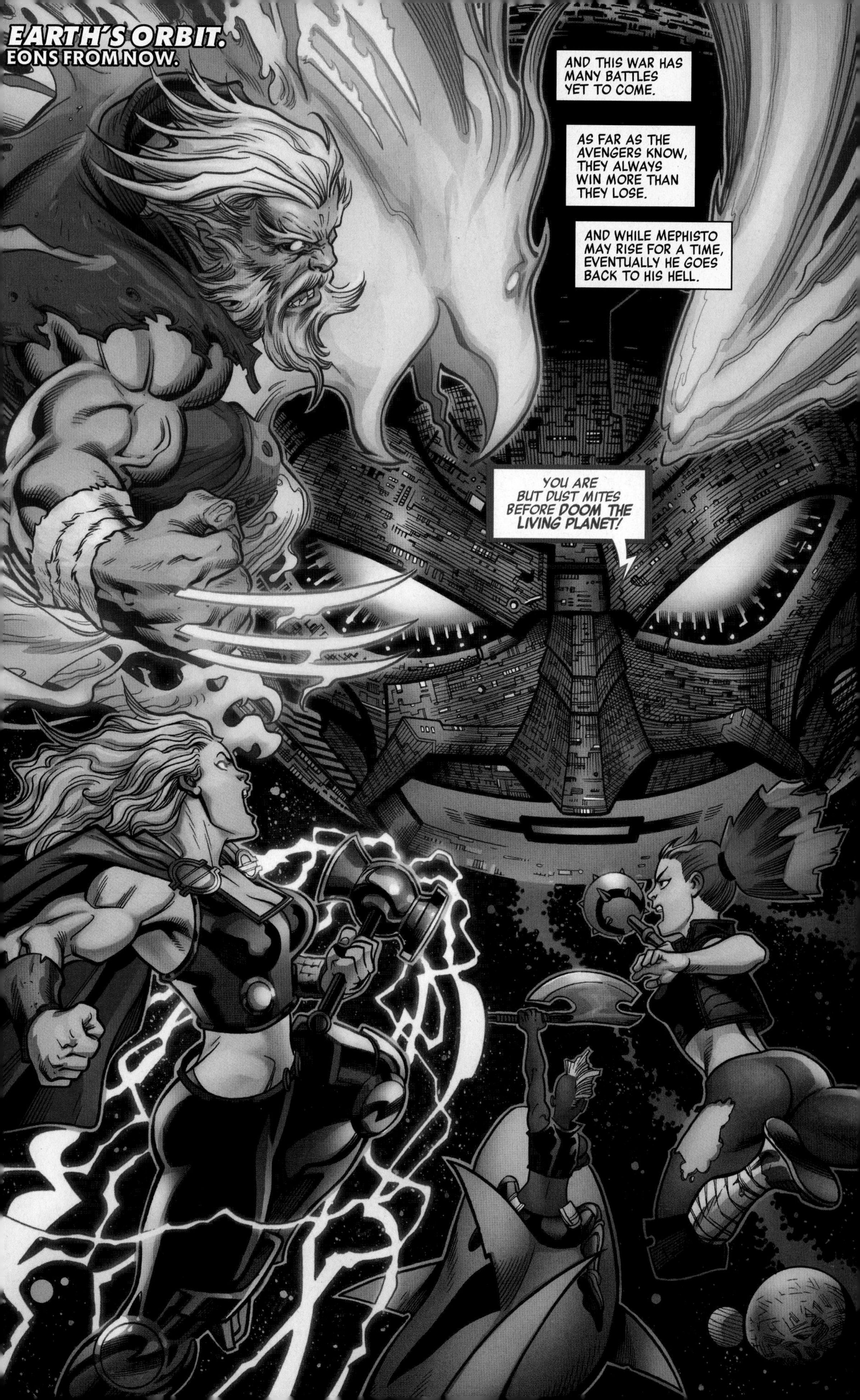
EARTH'S ORBIT.
EONS FROM NOW.
AND THIS WAR HAS MANY BATTLES YET TO COME.
AS FAR AS THE AVENGERS KNOW, THEY ALWAYS WIN MORE THAN THEY LOSE.
AND WHILE MEPHISTO MAY RISE FOR A TIME, EVENTUALLY HE GOES BACK TO HIS HELL.
YOU ARE BUT DUST MITES BEFORE DOOM THE LIVING PLANET!

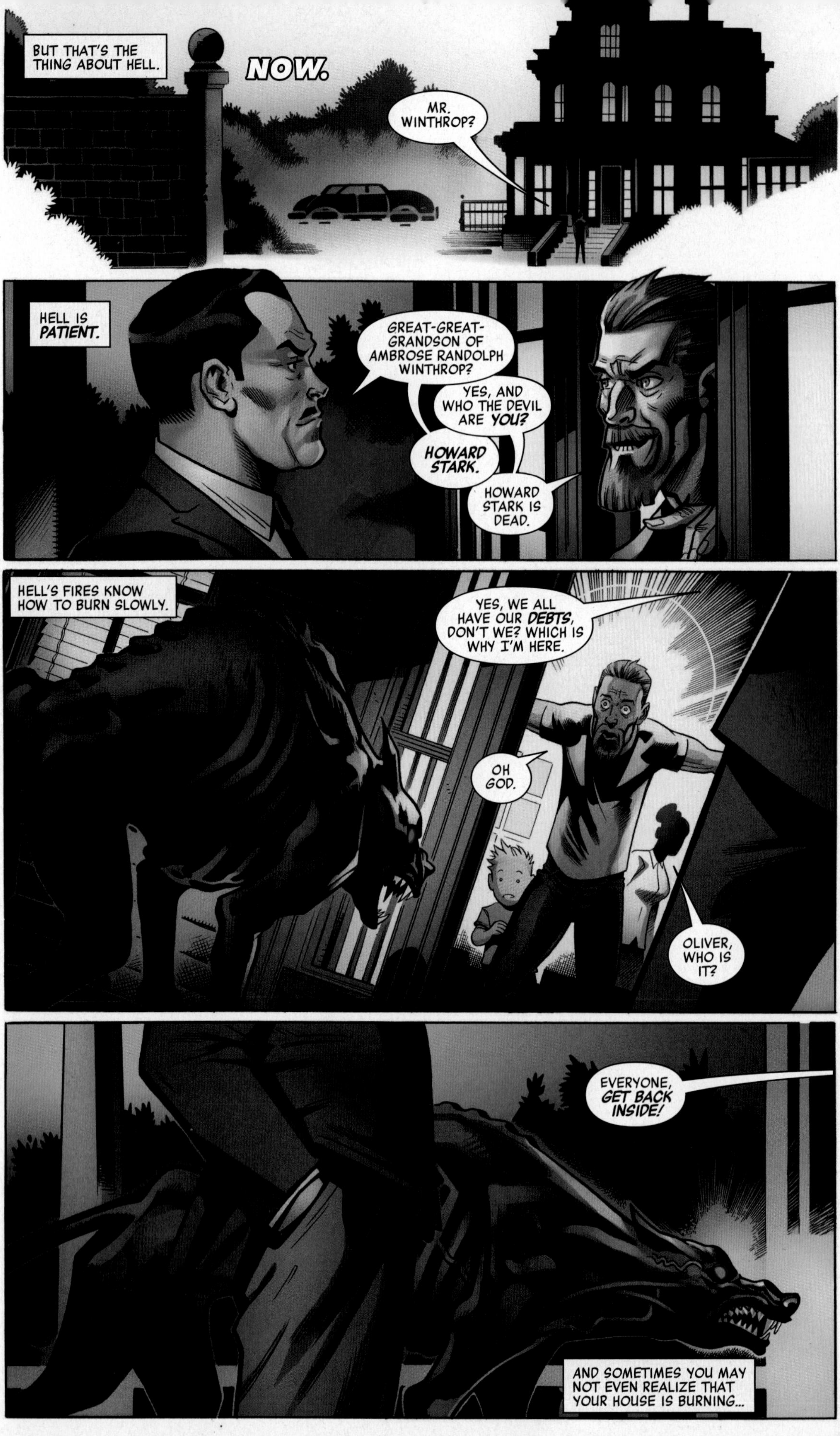
BUT THAT'S THE THING ABOUT HELL.
NOW.
MR. WINTHROP?
HELL IS PATIENT.
GREAT-GREAT-GRANDSON OF AMBROSE RANDOLPH WINTHROP?
YES, AND WHO THE DEVIL ARE YOU?
HOWARD STARK.
HOWARD STARK IS DEAD.
HELL'S FIRES KNOW HOW TO BURN SLOWLY.
YES, WE ALL HAVE OUR DEBTS, DON'T WE? WHICH IS WHY I'M HERE.
OH GOD.
OLIVER, WHO IS IT?
EVERYONE, GET BACK INSIDE!
AND SOMETIMES YOU MAY NOT EVEN REALIZE THAT YOUR HOUSE IS BURNING...

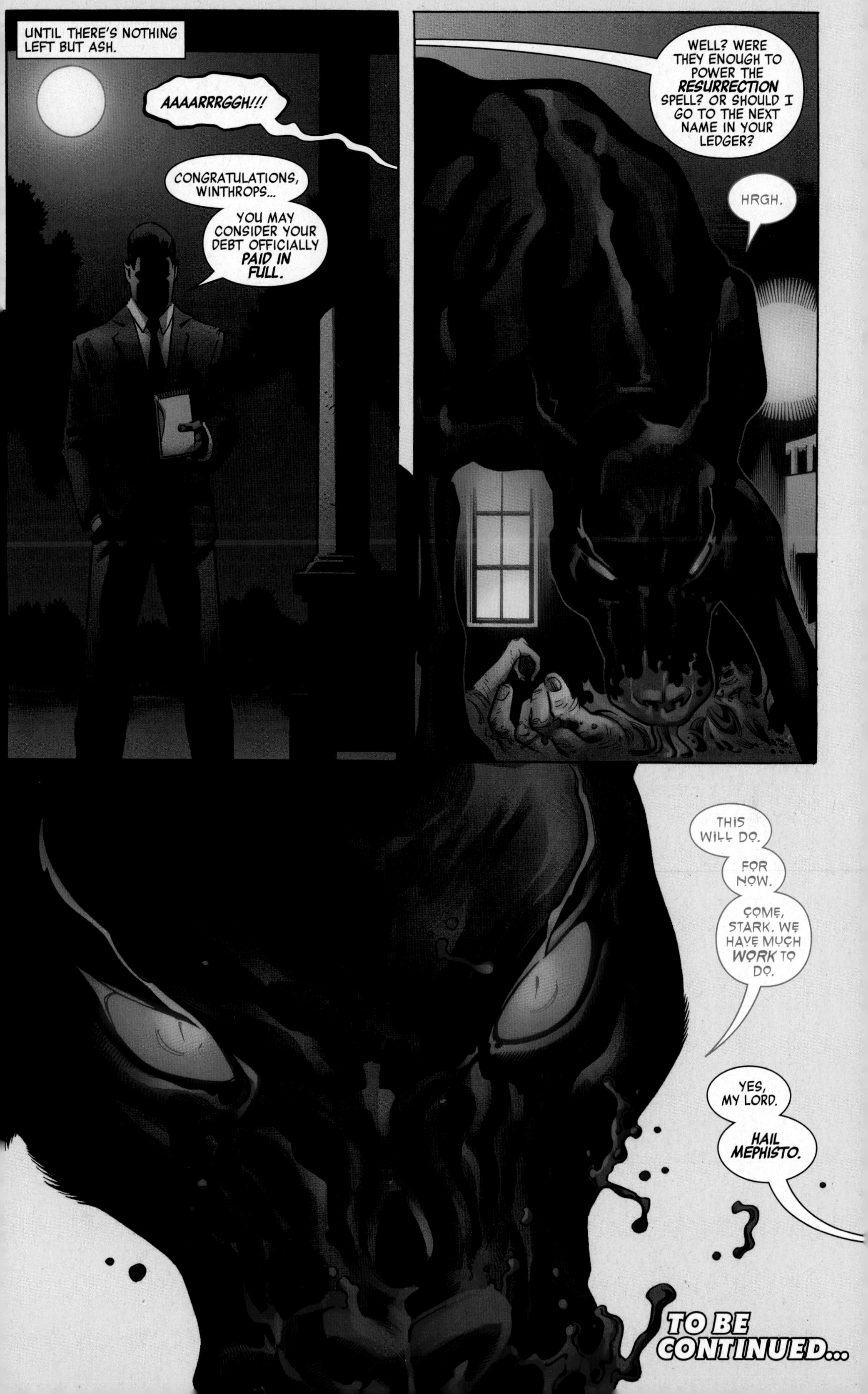

UNTIL THERE'S NOTHING LEFT BUT ASH.
AAAARRRGGH!!!
CONGRATULATIONS, WINTHROPS...
YOU MAY CONSIDER YOUR DEBT OFFICIALLY PAID IN FULL.
WELL? WERE THEY ENOUGH TO POWER THE RESURRECTION SPELL? OR SHOULD I GO TO THE NEXT NAME IN YOUR LEDGER?
HRGH.
THIS WILL DO.
FOR NOW.
COME, STARK. WE HAVE MUCH WORK TO DO.
YES, MY LORD.
HAIL MEPHISTO.
TO BE CONTINUED...

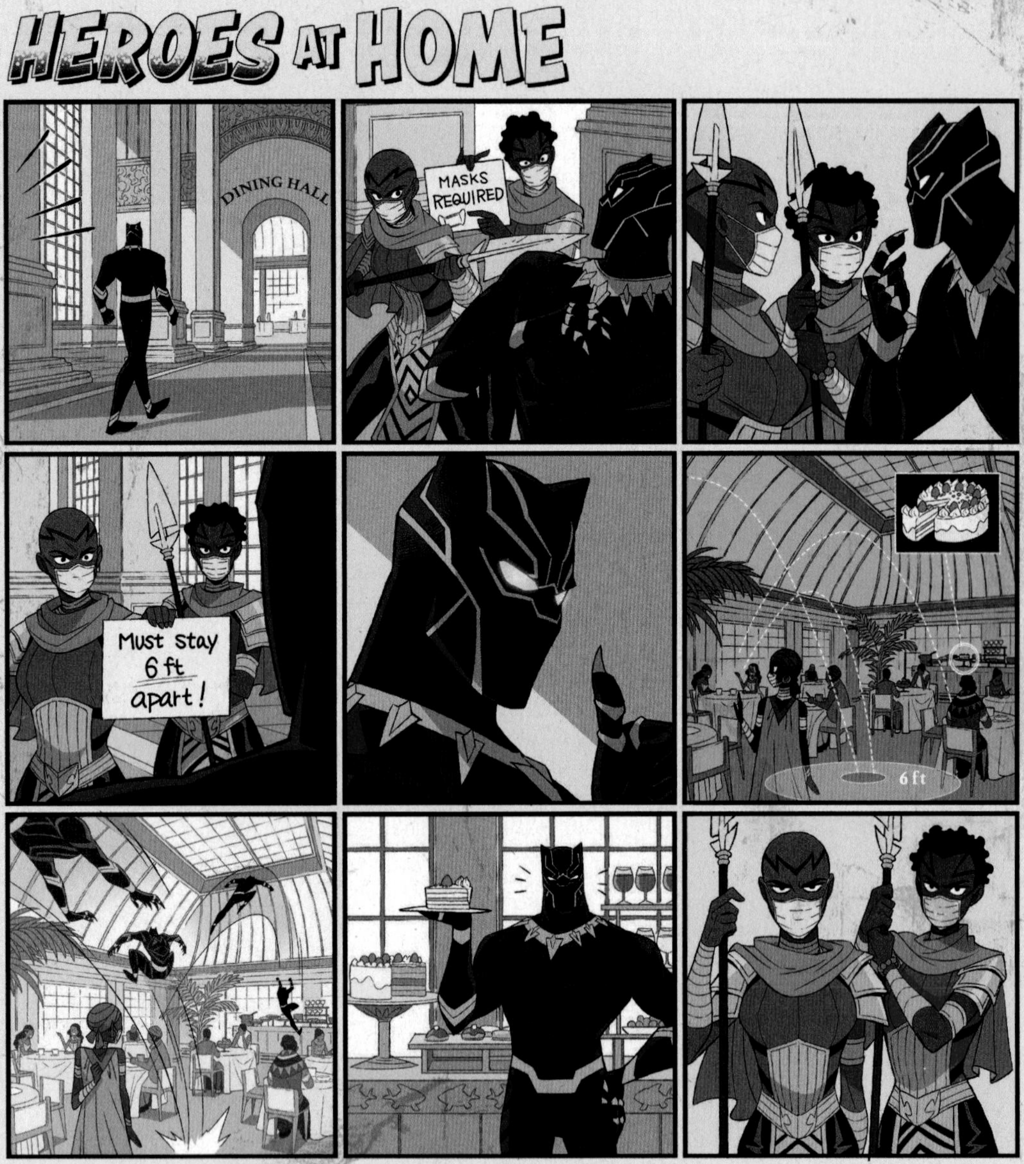
HEROES AT HOME
DINING HALL
MASKS REQUIRED
Must stay 6 ft apart!
6 ft

GURIHIRU & ZEB WELLS
36 HEROES AT HOME VARIANT